How Effective Are Your Community Services?

Procedures for Measuring Their Quality

Second Edition

Harry P. Hatry, Louis H. Blair,
Donald M. Fisk, John M. Greiner,
John R. Hall, Jr.,
and Philip S. Schaenman

THE URBAN INSTITUTE

ICMA

 THE URBAN INSTITUTE

The Urban Institute is a nonprofit policy research and educational organization established in Washington, D.C., in 1968. Its staff investigates the social and economic problems confronting the nation and government policies and programs designed to alleviate such problems.

ICMA is the professional and educational organization for chief appointed management executives in local government. The purposes of ICMA are to strengthen the quality of local government through professional management and to develop and disseminate new approaches to management through training programs, information services, and publications.

ICMA members, who have a wide range of titles, serve cities, towns, counties, and councils of governments in all parts of the United States, Canada, Australia, and other countries.

ICMA was founded in 1914.

For information about The Urban Institute and its programs and publications, call 202/857-8729 or write to The Urban Institute, 2100 M Street, N.W., Washington, D.C. 20037.

For information about the publications or subscription services for local governments offered by ICMA, call 800/745-8780 or write to Publications Department, ICMA, 777 North Capitol St., N.E., Suite 500, Washington, D.C. 20002-4201.

Originally published as *How Effective Are Your Community Services? Procedures for Monitoring the Effectiveness of Municipal Services*
© 1977 The Urban Institute

© 1992 The Urban Institute and ICMA, the International City/County Management Association
All rights reserved
Published 1977. Revised Edition 1992
Printed in the United States of America

ISBN: 0-87326-804-0

979695949392
54321

Cover design by Melissa Machulski and Jeanne Berger. Text design by Brian Derr. Design assistance and production by Lynne Hofman.

Table of Contents

List of Exhibits

F ifteen years after the publication of the first edition of *How Effective Are Your Community Services?* performance measurement is still a new frontier for local governments. The need for performance measurement is perhaps greater than ever, as local governments struggle to use shrinking resources more efficiently. This volume presents a comprehensive approach to documenting the quality of services, whether those services are provided by local government employees or by third-party contractors.

The first edition built on a foundation laid in 1943 when Clarence E. Ridley and Herbert A. Simon wrote *Measuring Municipal Activities.* By the 1970s, the rationale for effectiveness measurement was generally accepted, but managers needed practical techniques for collecting and analyzing data on performance. To meet this need, the International City Management Association, The Urban Institute, and the local governments of St. Petersburg, Florida, and Nashville/Davidson County, Tennessee, cooperated on a project extending over several years to develop and apply effectiveness measures. The project produced two reports. The first, *Measuring the Effectiveness of Basic Municipal Services: Initial Report* (1974), described the measurement system developed. The second was *How Effective Are Your Community Services?*, a thoroughgoing guide to specific measures, tools, and techniques for effectiveness measurement.

This completely revised edition revisits performance measurement at a time when local governments are learning to see their citizens as customers, when citizens' perceptions are given increased weight in measuring the quality of services. The report looks again at nine functional areas of local government activity and discusses tools of measurement, putting special emphasis on customer surveys.

Local governments will find in the present volume a precise guide to developing a local system for measuring service performance, based on decades of observation and experience.

— William H. Hansell, Executive Director
International City/County Management Association

— William Gorham, President
The Urban Institute

Acknowledgments

This report grew out of a cooperative effort of The Urban Institute, the International City/County Management Association (ICMA), and the governments of St. Petersburg, Florida, and Metropolitan Nashville-Davidson County. The work was initially supported by the National Science Foundation and the U.S. Department of Housing and Urban Development. The National Center for Productivity and the Quality of Working Life also contributed support through its project with ICMA on municipal productivity improvement.

For this second edition, the authors have also drawn on the experiences of a number of other cities and counties that have undertaken regular efforts to monitor the quality of their services. These include: Arlington County, Alexandria, and Charlottesville, Virginia; Charlotte, North Carolina; Dayton, Ohio; New York City, New York; Savannah, Georgia; Greenville, South Carolina; and Sunnyvale, California.

Harry P. Hatry, Director of State and Local Government Research Programs at The Urban Institute, directed the overall effort and was also the author of chapters 1, 13, 14, 15, 16, and 17 and coauthor of the chapters on parks and recreation, libraries, and crime control. The following people were authors or coauthors of chapters in this report: Louis H. Blair, Executive Secretary, Harry S. Truman Scholarship Foundation—Solid Waste Collection, Water Supply, Trained Observers Rating Procedures, and Surveying Customers; Donald M. Fisk, consultant—Park and Recreation Services, Library Services, and Solid Waste Collection; John M. Greiner, Office of Management and Budget, Prince George's County, Maryland—Handling Citizen Complaints and Requests, Park and Recreation Services, General Transportation Services, and Public Mass Transit; John R. Hall, Jr., Assistant Vice President

for Fire Analysis and Research, National Fire Protection Association—Fire Protection, Solid Waste Disposal, and Water Supply; and Philip S. Schaenman, TriData Corporation—Crime Control, Fire Protection, General Transportation Services, and Public Mass Transit.

ICMA provided guidance for the project and on-site personnel to work with St. Petersburg and Nashville-Davidson County in testing the measurement procedures. For ICMA, James L. Cavenaugh and John Pazour worked on the project efforts in St. Petersburg and Nashville, respectively. Donald Borut, Steve Carter, and George Barbour were coordinators of the work for ICMA. George Barbour was also a coauthor of Appendix 11.

For St. Petersburg, Paul Yingst was the overall project coordinator; he was assisted by William Owens. Mr. Yingst also provided extensive reviews of the draft material. For Nashville, Tom Finnie was the overall project coordinator, assisted by Martha Groomes, Richard Brant, and Jon Seaman.

The authors received considerable assistance in the development of procedures or review of manuscripts from the following persons, some of whom helped with the first or the second edition only:

Solid Waste Collection: Herman Mueller and Attileo Corbo, St. Petersburg; Vijay Alsii and Eugene Melgaard, District of Columbia; Michael Miller, Los Angeles; and Hilary Green, American Public Works Association.

Solid Waste Disposal: Dave Holihan and Herman Mueller, St. Petersburg; Fred L. Smith, Jr., Cindy McLaren, and Steve Levy, Environmental Protection Agency; Richard Sullivan, American Public Works Association; Edward Dexter, Solid Waste Enforcement Division, Department of the Environment, State of Maryland; David Lake, Montgomery County, Maryland; Lori Swain, Governmental Refuse Collection and Disposal Association; Janice Wall, Institute of Recycling Industries; and Michael Miller, Los Angeles.

Park and Recreation Services: Charles Spears, Ruth Allen, and Chris McLean, Nashville; Jack Puryear, Ruth Stenger, and Susan Warren, St. Petersburg; Robert Fiore, William Spitzer, and Merle J. Van Horne, U.S. Bureau of Outdoor Recreation; Peter Verhoven, National Recreation and Parks Association; Diana R. Dunn, Temple University; Joe McGee, Greenville; Tyra Liebman, New York City Board of Education; and John Clarke, Fund for the City of New York.

Library Services: DeLyle Runge and Patricia Broad, St. Petersburg; Sheila Douglass, Nashville; Ellen Altman, University of Toronto; Mary R. Power and Mary Jo Lynch, American Library Association; and Judy Fair and Carol Pyke, The Urban Institute.

Crime Control: A. Lee McGehee, Lt. John Schrive, and Richard Smith, St. Petersburg; Lt. R. Kirschner, Jr., Nashville; Joseph Lewis, Police Foundation; Ralph Anderson, Norman Darwick and John Quinn, International Association of Chiefs of Police; M.H. (Jim) Estepp, Prince George's County, Maryland; Peter B. Block, The Urban Institute; and Woodie Johnson, Federal Bureau of Investigation.

Fire Protection: Chief Jerry Knight, St. Petersburg; Joe Swartz, Michael Karter, and Dave Novak, National Fire Protection Association.

Transportation: Jim Anderson, St. Petersburg; Milton Tharp and Francis May, Nashville; William A. Hyman, The Urban Institute; and John Williams, Metropolitan Washington Council of Governments.

Water Supply: Elroy Spitzer, J.P. Waters, Rick Harmon, and John Brittan, American Water Works Association; Richard Sullivan, American Public Works Association; Ciro Farina, Cincinnati; and Edward G. Blundon, Phoenix.

Citizen Complaints and Requests: Milton Reese, Don Donley, and William Bateman, St. Petersburg; and Camille Cates, Sunnyvale.

Citizen Surveys: Sidney Hollander, Jr., Sidney Hollander Associates (Baltimore, Maryland); Jack Vernon, Suncoast Opinion Surveys, Inc. (St. Petersburg, Florida); Carol H. Weiss, Bureau of Applied Social Research, Columbia University; Robert Sadacca, The Urban Institute; and Nancy Belden, Belden and Russonello (Washington, D.C.).

Survey of Businesses: Ivan Elmer, U.S. Chamber of Commerce; and Steven C. Carter, Champaign, Illinois.

Efficiency: Milton Weiss, Charlotte; and W.E. Vickery, Research Triangle Institute.

The project team received considerable assistance in the early stages of the work from the project advisory group, which included David A. Burkhalter, Charlotte, North Carolina; James L. Caplinger, Kalamazoo, Michigan; Comer Coppie, Washington, D.C.; Stanley R. Cowle, Hennepin County, Minnesota; Corwin S. Elwell, Brattleboro, Vermont; Robert E. Goldman, National Science Foundation; Ray Harbaugh, St. Petersburg, Florida; Cole Hendrix, Charlottesville, Virginia; Whitney Shartzer, Dayton, Ohio; George A. Sipel, Palo Alto, California; Stanley Stern, Indianapolis, Indiana; John Thomas, National Association of Counties; Robert Thomas, Orange County, California; Joseph Torrence, Nashville-Davidson County, Tennessee; Richard Wall, Boston, Massachusetts; Robert Wilson, Fairfax County, Virginia; and Ward Wright, National League of Cities. In addition, Jerry Coffman and Milton Weiss of Charlotte, North Carolina, provided important advice.

Other staff members from The Urban Institute provided assistance: Alfred Schainblatt assisted in preparing the chapter on fire protection. Lynn Bell provided major input for the survey of businesses chapter. Richard Winnie contributed to the transportation chapters. Alfred I. Schwartz helped with the solid waste collection, trained observers, and crime control chapters. Jennifer Marth made a major contribution to the solid waste disposal chapter. Winstanley Luke, Harold Parker, and Meir Lakein provided assistance in a number of program areas.

The views expressed herein are those of the authors and not necessarily those of the sponsoring agencies.

A t the outset of the 1990s, local government agencies still only rarely do regular and systematic tracking of the quality of their services to the public. They know what they spend, and most know what they do, but very few know what effect they have. How can employees produce quality or managers supervise for quality if they lack solid information for tracking the quality of the work? If managers don't know the score, how can they play the game?

Finding better ways to keep score was the goal 14 years ago in 1977, when the Urban Institute and the International City Management Association produced the first edition of *How Effective Are Your Community Services?* Since then the principle of regularly measuring the quality of city and county services has become more and more popular, but the practice has lagged far behind. Because it is unfamiliar, because it is sometimes hard to do, because it costs money (even if it often saves more), routine quality measurement has remained a greatly underused tool. Agency managers have tried to make do with indicators of the amount of work performed, with their perceptions of the quality of their agencies' services, and with occasional feedback, perhaps through citizen complaints.

New Developments

Much has occurred over the past 14 years that calls for a new look at procedures for regularly measuring service quality.

Public officials, as never before, are being encouraged to examine the quality of their services. National and international events have greatly increased public sector attention to service quality.

- International economic competition, for example, from Japan, has pushed U.S. business to a much greater focus on quality. Though this concern began in the private sector, it has spread to the public sector as well.

- The work of a number of management consultants has captured the attention of public as well as private sector managers. Especially important has been the work of Thomas Peters and Robert Waterman in their enormously popular *In Search of Excellence* (and Peters's subsequent volumes and television programs) and that of W. Edwards Deming (as reported in *Out of the Crisis*). These authors repeatedly stress the importance of quality and customers' perception of quality. While these efforts have been oriented toward the private sector, they are receiving considerable attention from public sector officials.

- The federal government began in the late 1980s to push "total quality management," which dictates continuous attention to service quality, including its measurement on a regular basis, so that improvements can be made continuously.

- The Governmental Accounting Standards Board (GASB), whose usual focus is developing ground rules for public financial accounting and reporting, decided in the 1980s that government financial reports fell far short of providing elected officials and the public with adequate information on the condition of public services and the value citizens were getting for their tax dollars. GASB issued a series of reports examining the state-of-the-practice and the state-of-the-art in performance measurement and reporting. The GASB report titled *Service Efforts and Accomplishments Reporting: Its Time Has Come—An Overview* indicates the team's finding that the time has come for public reporting of information on service accomplishments for public services. GASB has called for extensive and widespread experimentation with measurement and reporting of service effectiveness.

Measurement technology has advanced. For example, customer survey procedures have become more streamlined since the 1970s. Telephone surveys, using random-digit dialing techniques to improve the randomness and thus the validity of samples, have become widely accepted as an appropriate substitute for the much more expensive in-person, at-home household surveys. (Personal interviews are still essential for some in-depth studies.)

Mail surveys—less expensive yet—are gaining credibility, especially for surveys of customers of particular services. Experiments have uncovered ways to increase response rates, the major problem reducing the validity of mail surveys. Refined mail techniques now include use of multiple mailings and improved questionnaire formats.

Data processing and analysis technology has changed radically. New technology enables agency personnel to obtain rapid and inexpensive feedback—and on a regular basis. Small, inexpensive microcomputers are widely available. The prospects are mind-boggling. Software is probably the most immediate problem, but software for processing service quality data is becoming more convenient, inexpensive, and user-friendly. Available software can, for example, provide multiple cross-tabulation data in reasonably attractive formats. Color, graphics, and even three-dimensional images are realistic prospects for the near future.

Managers can quickly obtain not only printed reports but also special cross-tabulations of information. They can even use a computer themselves to analyze data on the spot.

More exotic data processing technology is emerging at reasonable cost. With hand-held computers, interviewers or trained observers can enter data in the field, enabling tabulations and reports to be prepared very quickly. Computer-assisted telephone interviews, already in use by many professional survey organizations, guide interviewers through the questionnaire and enable direct data entry, making reports available almost immediately.

Local governments have been increasing their use of contracting. Contracting governments are concerned about the quality of the product they are getting and interested in tracking the quality of contractors' performance.

Some negative developments during the last 14 years have discouraged or limited the use of performance measurement. For example, the squeeze on local government funds and the shrinking of external funds have discouraged communities from applying resources to regular performance measurement. (On the other hand, tight budgets have also pressed public officials to weed out poor-performing programs and so have helped spur interest in performance measurement.)

Measurement technology is still by no means perfect. It probably never will be. Regular performance measurement is not appropriate for assessing service outcomes that occur long after the services have been provided. Nor do these procedures replace in-depth studies and program evaluations that dig into the actual causes for changes in service quality.

Finally, the proliferation of surveys by the private sector has had a negative impact on performance measurement by local governments. Many households feel barraged by surveys. Fortunately, most citizens still respond to surveys by local governments, particularly surveys asking about their experiences with public services.

Changes in This Second Edition

The authors were surprised to find that most performance measures and data collection procedures identified in the first edition of *How Effective Are Your Community Services?* are still applicable. This indicates that customers of basic municipal services are concerned about the same service characteristics they were concerned about in the 1970s. Nevertheless, this new edition contains several major revisions and new examples, and has been largely rewritten.

The second edition places considerably more emphasis on the importance of analyzing and reporting quality by major subgroups of the client population and by the service office. It emphasizes breaking out each performance indicator by major demographic and service characteristics likely to be helpful to operating managers. Over-aggregation of performance data means that operating managers and their personnel receive little specific information within their own scope of responsibility about what and where problems are.

For example, for each service, measurements should show the performance of each service delivery unit for each major location within the jurisdiction and for each major category of customer. Each manager should receive information tailored to his or her area of responsibility. More frequent reporting, at least quarterly, is recommended for most performance indicators. If performance data are provided to service managers only once a year, they will be better able to budget, but they will not receive timely or seasonal information that can help them improve their programs during the year.

This report encourages public agencies to collect information at least quarterly, so that each season is covered separately and managers can quickly identify the results of service changes made in previous quarters. To apply this suggestion to surveys of customers, agencies can split their annual samples into quarterly segments and report quarterly as well as yearly totals. If customers are surveyed quarterly, they can be asked about their experiences over the past three months only, rather than, say, twelve months. Problems with respondent memory are alleviated and responses are more accurate.

More space is devoted in the second edition, particularly in Chapter 16, to a discussion of how to use performance information. Managers need encouragement, technical assistance, and training to make full use of information on service quality. They need ways to translate results into actions to improve service quality, and they need ways to motivate staff to continually seek service quality improvements (for example, by using quarterly performance reports as a basis for staff planning meetings).

In making suggestions for implementing a performance measurement system (Chapter 17), the second edition emphasizes the need for input from program managers and personnel in selecting the information to be obtained by the measurement procedures and deciding how that information is to be presented. To alleviate service managers' fear that the performance information will be used more against them than for them, local governments are urged to give managers the opportunity to review and comment on performance data before the information is transmitted to higher levels and to outside audiences.

The second edition places more emphasis on obtaining feedback from *customers of each service* and less emphasis on surveys of random samples of households. Systematic surveys of customers of a particular service are usually quite feasible. Customers are likely to respond to mail or on-site requests to complete questionnaires because they have a built-in interest in the service. After all, they have been users of the service. And usually the agency will have the names and telephone numbers or addresses of its customers—if not the customers' actual physical presence—making it easier to administer surveys. Nevertheless, regular surveys of random samples of households in the community are still recommended particularly to obtain information about citizens who do not use the service and their reasons for nonuse.

The chapter on solid waste disposal reflects an increased concern for recycling, with more measurements of recycling success. Also, the trained observer procedures proposed for solid waste disposal sites include tests for indicators of *potential* health and safety problems for preventive maintenance, in addition to observations of actual problems such as contamination outside the site.

The title of the recreation chapter has been changed to "Park and Recreation Services," and the new chapter includes indicators of the effectiveness of park and recreation services and an extensive discussion of trained observers' procedures for rating various physical conditions of park and recreation facilities, procedures that have been tested in recent years. The household park and recreation survey questionnaire included in Appendix 4 has been simplified so that a recreation agency can administer it more easily on a regular basis.

The chapter on library services has been modified to include library performance measurement concepts developed in recent years by such organizations as the public library division of the American Library Association. The new measurements include more focus on the relative availability of library holdings (the "percentage of user searchers . . . that are successful," the "percentage of reference transactions successfully completed," and the "percentage of requests available within 7, 14, and 30 days or longer").

Although the crime control chapter places somewhat more focus on drug-related crimes, the authors (as well as others) feel that the drug-related performance measures are only tentative. In keeping with modern community policing concepts, the chapter also places more emphasis on citizen perceptions of police performance and helpfulness.

The fire protection chapter in the second edition puts considerably greater emphasis on fire prevention than did the first edition, including measurements of the success of inspections, the clearance of violations, public education outreach, and the use of smoke detectors and sprinklers.

The chapter on general transportation reflects increased concern about the nation's infrastructure, especially in the measurement of road surface characteristics such as rideability and basic structure, which can indicate problems before rideability has been affected. Performance measures have been added to reflect the time taken to repair conditions, such as potholes, reported by citizens.

In the field of public transit, the new chapter includes more explicit treatment of rail mass transit in the light of its increased use by local governments. It also puts more emphasis on indicators of level of service, such as time between runs and handicapped access.

The chapter on water supply reflects the greatly expanded requirements laid on local governments by the federal government.

For the most part, however, the performance indicators presented in the first edition remain valid as summary indicators of compliance with whatever requirements are in place.

In the area of handling citizens' complaints and requests for services and information, the second edition places more emphasis on the accessibility of the process to citizens, not only on what happens after customers have gained access to the system. It also stresses the greatly enhanced ability of complaint-handling agencies to use computers to process data in many useful ways—a point also applicable to performance measurement for other local government services.

Final Comments

Local governments regularly track their expenditures and work activity. It is no less important that local governments track the service quality they are getting for that effort.

The authors hope that the performance indicators and data procedures in this volume will encourage local governments to undertake performance measurement on a regular basis, both to achieve better accountability and to improve services to citizens.

Chapter 1

Introduction and Scope

P ublic officials, both managerial and elected, need regular feedback on the effectiveness of their operations to help them make improvements. Officials and citizens are frequently frustrated in their attempts to determine how well local government is serving the public. Complaints of poor service may be reported in the media or brought directly to the attention of local government offices. Success stories may come to light in a similar haphazard fashion. Typically, however, comprehensive information on the effectiveness of individual services is not available.

This report provides suggestions by which local governments and their individual agencies might regularly, preferably at least quarterly, obtain information on the effectiveness and quality of their services.

The suggestions constitute a "menu" of ideas from which local governments can select those that appear most applicable to their needs. As experience is gained by a local government, some of the procedures may need modification. This material is intended to encourage individual governments to develop effectiveness measurement procedures tailored to their own special needs.

Throughout this report, the words "effectiveness" and "quality" are used synonymously. Some governments may prefer using the word "effectiveness" to cover indicators that measure results and leave the word "quality" to apply to characteristics of the service delivery process, such as its timeliness, accessibility, and courteousness. Also, a good case can be made for substituting the word "outcome" for "effectiveness." The word "outcome" does not imply as strongly as the word "effectiveness" that the measured values were *caused* completely by the public agency. As discussed at the end of Chapter 16 ("Using Effectiveness Measurement Information"), the procedures described in this volume do not attempt to establish strong causal links between program activities and the measured results.

Background

The measures and data collection procedures described here have been developed from a number of efforts. The most extensive one was a 1973–1974 effort sponsored by the National Science Foundation and the Office of Policy Development and Research of the Department of Housing and Urban Development. Principal participants were St. Petersburg, Florida, and Metropolitan Nashville-Davidson County, Tennessee; the International City Management Association, which provided guidance on national measurement needs, as well as on-site project coordinators in both "test" cities; and The Urban Institute, which provided overall coordination and technical guidance. Results of that project were reported in the first edition of *How Effective Are Your Community Services?* published in 1977.

This new edition draws on recent efforts by local governments and their experiences in developing and implementing procedures that measure effectiveness. This report draws on experiences in Palo Alto, California; Savannah, Georgia; Randolph Township, New Jersey; Dallas, Texas; Charlotte, North Carolina; Dayton, Ohio; Aurora, Colorado; New York City; Alexandria, Virginia; Charlottesville, Virginia; and Sunnyvale, California. The report identifies specific measures and data collection procedures.

Measures and data collection procedures are presented for the following basic services:

- Solid waste collection
- Solid waste disposal
- Parks and recreation
- Libraries

- Crime control
- Fire protection
- Local transportation—public transit and other ground transportation activities
- Water supply
- Handling of citizen complaints and requests for services.

The procedures described here can also be adapted for services not discussed in this report or for aspects of services not covered here. Because of their potential applicability to many government services, three procedures—customer surveys, trained observer ratings, and business surveys—are subjects of separate chapters.

Measures of government efficiency, although important in any effort to measure government performance, are not a focus of this report. Chapter 15, however, discusses efficiency measures, especially as they relate to effectiveness measurement, and provides some suggested measures. Improvements in cost per unit of output, or, conversely, output per unit of input, achieved at the expense of quality of service can be said to represent an improvement in efficiency only by twisting the meaning of that term. The effectiveness measurements discussed in this report can help local governments develop efficiency measurement procedures that include checks on whether quality is at least being maintained.

Most, if not all, of the service characteristics covered by the suggested measures should be familiar and readily accepted as being of interest and concern to local officials and the public. Indeed, two major sources used to identify the service characteristics for which measures should be developed were citizen complaint files and interviews with citizens. Because some of the *procedures* for collecting data for the measures depart from current government procedures, however, they may seem unusual to many local governments.

Each chapter identifies objectives for the local government service and identifies relevant effectiveness measures. Next, procedures to obtain the data are suggested. The sources used to identify the objectives and measures presented in this report include (1) statements of goals, objectives, and lists of measures currently in use, such as those displayed in program budgets; (2) suggestions by professionals in each service area, obtained from discussions with agency personnel and representatives of national professional organizations; (3) citizen complaint files from several local governments; (4) citizen concerns as expressed in newspaper articles and open-ended interviews with project staff; (5) professional literature; and (6) suggestions by reviewers of draft reports. These same sources might also be used by lo-cal governments to identify additional measures for themselves.

The data collection methods described in this report are intended to enable public officials to undertake regular measurement to track problems, progress, and trends. These procedures were not developed to identify why conditions are as they are, nor what should be done about them. Accurate information about the outcomes of a service is, however, likely to be of significant help to local decision makers. Such information should aid in identifying priorities for further examination by program personnel.

This report focuses on services and the specific outcomes associated with them, rather than on individual government agencies. For most of the services examined, however, a single government agency is associated with the service, such as the fire department with fire services or a parks and recreation agency with parks and recreation services. This means that a specific agency can be assigned primary responsibility for the measures of outcome associated with each service.

Of course, in many if not all cases, other government agencies can also affect the outcomes of the service. Transportation services, for example, can affect outcomes in recreation accessibility. Recreation services can affect crime. Housing and code enforcement agencies can affect fire services outcomes. Also, external factors such as weather conditions and various social conditions can have substantial effects. No single agency is likely to have *complete control* over the effectiveness measures associated with the services it provides.

Some important effects of local services are not captured by the measures and data collection procedures described in this report. These include secondary but important effects such as the effect of government services on economic development, on property values, and on the jurisdiction's tax base. The estimation of such complex interrelationships seems more appropriate for in-depth studies than for the regular monitoring procedures discussed in this report.

Criteria for Selection of Measures and Data Collection Procedures

In selecting measures of effectiveness and data collection procedures, the following criteria were used:

- *Appropriateness and Validity*. Does the measure relate to the government objectives for that service and does it really measure the degree to which a customer need or desire is being met—

including minimization of detrimental effects?

- *Uniqueness*. Does it measure some effectiveness characteristic that no other measure encompasses?
- *Completeness*. Does the list of measures cover all or at least most objectives?
- *Comprehensibility*. Is the measure understandable?
- *Controllability*. Is the condition measured at least partially the government's responsibility? Does the government have some control over it?
- *Cost*. Are cost and staffing requirements for data collection reasonable? The answer to this will depend partly on the government's funding situation and its interest in a particular measure.
- *Timeliness of Feedback*. Can the data be obtained quickly enough so that managers and staff can act on it before the information becomes obsolete?
- *Accuracy and Reliability*. Can sufficiently accurate and reliable information be obtained?

Local governments and their individual agencies might use these same criteria as they select their own measures of effectiveness.

Keeping the Number of Measures Manageable

For each service area, approximately 15 to 25 measures are presented. Each measure addresses a service characteristic not covered by any other measure. The monitoring of multiple measures is desirable to avoid excessive focus on one aspect of a service at the expense of others. Yet the cost of data collection and analysis and the need to prevent information overload are reasons for keeping the number to a minimum.

In some instances, data for a number of the measures can be gathered as part of the same collection procedure. For example, if a customer survey is undertaken, additional questions that provide data for different effectiveness measures can be included at little extra cost.

To reduce the burden of a large number of measures, consider four basic alternative approaches:

- Include only the more "global" measures; delete those that focus on narrow service characteristics. For example, one can obtain information on customers' overall level of satisfaction with public transit services rather than asking customers for specific ratings of transit frequency, accessibility, and comfort. The global measures provide an important overview to upper-level lo-

cal officials such as municipal managers, major executive officers, and council members. However, this information is likely to be much less useful to operating personnel than measures that address specific attributes of the service.

- Include measures focused on specific service characteristics and eliminate the global measures. Individual operating agencies are likely to find measurements of specific service characteristics more useful in determining needed actions. However, because relatively few global measures are proposed, their deletion would not significantly reduce costs or managerial overload.

- Include global and specific measures but reduce their coverage. One way to do this is to exclude service characteristics judged to be of minor importance. Another possibility is to exclude measures of conditions that are deemed unlikely to change substantially from one period to another.

- Minimize the potential information overload, especially for upper level officials, by providing summaries that focus on key measures and on those measures that, for the period under review, show unusually high or low values. This approach is the recommended one.

Focus on Implications of Services to Customers, Not on Physical Outputs

This report emphasizes effectiveness as related to customer concerns. The measures in some instances may seem less directly useful to lower-level supervisors. For example, park maintenance supervisors may be more immediately concerned with whether the grass is cut on schedule than with citizens' ratings of park appearance. Citizens, however, are more likely to be concerned with overall park appearance. Sensitizing supervisors to customer concerns can lead to improved services.

Periodic Auditing of Effectiveness Data

It is desirable to review data collection procedures periodically to ensure that data continue to be of satisfactory quality. Government data collection procedures and the data collected should be checked for possible sources of error and bias. Customer survey questions should be checked for possible ambiguities, and biases and survey procedures should be reviewed with the survey firms that have been hired.

Application to Small Communities

The various service characteristics and the associated measures identified for each service (presented in Chapters 2–11) should apply to small as well as large governments if the government is responsible for the particular service. Small communities have fewer dollars and staff persons available for measurement procedures and analysis, but they will probably find their measurement needs correspondingly smaller. The volume of records, the number of streets, and the number of different population groups for which data are needed are smaller than those for larger jurisdictions. Many of the procedures can be scaled down to fit the needs of these smaller governments. For example, the customer survey procedures can be scaled down considerably, although required sample sizes depend less on the size of the population than on its homogeneity.[1] A customer survey similar to the one proposed here has been undertaken by a number of small communities with populations below 20,000, including Randolph Township, New Jersey; Falls Church, Virginia; Zealand, Michigan; and Washington, North Carolina.[2]

Differentiating Results for Customer Groups and Organizational Units

A major use of the collected data is to provide information on the effectiveness of services for various population groups in the community to obtain a perspective on the need for, and equitableness of, services. Thus measurement values for major population groups, as well as aggregate jurisdiction-wide totals, are needed. Populations are often grouped by age, sex, household composition, income level, and race. Grouping by geographic areas is also important for government services. Communities often have major neighborhood divisions. Effectiveness data can be displayed for each area. Residential neighborhoods are one way to divide a jurisdiction geographically. Geographic groupings might be made by city or county council districts. Groupings of census tracts or census enumeration districts could be used; often these groupings can be assembled in different ways to form various types of districts.

These demographic and geographic categories appear to be relevant to most government services. For measuring some individual services, other customer-group breakouts seem appropriate. For example, measures of the adequacy of transportation services should distinguish families with and without automobiles. Such special breakouts are suggested in the appropriate individual chapters.

Many data collection procedures discussed in this report permit the separation of measurement data for various customer groups. Customer surveys, for instance, can be used to collect information on age, sex, race or ethnic group, household composition, income, residence location, and automobile ownership. But some measures rely on collection procedures that do not obtain such data. For example, customer complaints about various services are likely to provide information on location of residence but not on the age, race or ethnic group, or income category of the complainant. Examples of summary formats displaying breakouts by various population groups within a jurisdiction are presented in Chapter 16.

Similarly, the performance information will be more useful to operating managers if the data are provided for each organizational unit, such as each facility (e.g., park or library) or each service district or office (e.g., park police, fire, or sanitation district).

Principal Data Collection Procedures

Four principal types of data collection procedures are recommended throughout this report:

- Data from existing government records, although often with suggested modifications as to data elements and ways to group the data.

- Ratings of conditions by "trained observers" using specific predesignated rating criteria to maximize the likelihood of obtaining reliable and consistent ratings.

- Surveys of samples of the general population and of businesses in the community to obtain ratings of specific aspects of individual services, as well as certain factual data such as extent of use of government facilities and programs.

- Surveys of samples of users of specific government facilities (such as parks or libraries) or services to obtain user ratings of specific aspects of these facilities or services. For most, if not all, public services, surveys of the service's customers can be an excellent way to track performance on many important service characteristics.

Separate chapters discuss trained observer ratings, customer surveys, and business surveys because they are suggested for use in measuring a number of government services.

Specific applications of these procedures are discussed in the individual service chapters.

Organization of the Report

The next ten chapters (2–11) discuss the specific measures and data collection procedures suggested for consideration for specific government services, including information on limitations, costs, and special validity problems. Chapters 12–14 deal with three special data collection procedures: trained observer ratings, customer surveys, and business surveys. Chapter 15 categorizes various types of efficiency measures, discusses their relationship to effectiveness measurement, and illustrates the various types of efficiency measures. Chapter 16 discusses some uses for service effectiveness data, briefly discusses basic analysis for making the most use of the data, and provides suggestions as to how the data might be summarized and reported to be of most use to government officials. The report concludes in Chapter 17 with a brief discussion of some key issues in the implementation of effectiveness measurement procedures.

This report is not intended to be read from cover to cover. Because each chapter discusses specific procedures in detail, perhaps it should be considered a handbook of local government effectiveness measurement procedures. The reader interested in only a particular service area should read the chapter on that service area plus Chapters 16 and 17, and those on special procedures that apply, such as Chapters 13, 14, and 15.

---

1 Because there are likely to be fewer (if any) service districts, fewer distinct neighborhoods, and possibly fewer population groups, only 100 to 300 interviews may be required in small communities. The number of questions and length of interviews probably also can be reduced.

2 These communities used sophisticated procedures but were able to obtain volunteer help to keep costs down.

How clean are streets, alleys, sidewalks, and vacant lots? Are they cleaner or dirtier than they were last year? To what extent? How do these conditions vary among areas of the community? What progress is being made to overcome undesirable conditions? How well are private collectors under contract to the government performing and how can they be held accountable? How often do solid waste collection crews miss collecting from households? To what extent are citizens and businesspersons satisfied with their solid waste collection services?

In most communities, answers to such questions are not readily available. Current measurement practices in most local governments focus on effort expended—households served, tons of refuse collected, number of special pick-ups, and miles of streets swept. These pieces of information are important for controlling operations, but they say little, if anything, about the quality of the service. Sometimes complaints are tallied, and the results used as an indicator of performance. But citizen complaints rarely indicate the views of the whole community— only of those who know how to complain and are sufficiently motivated or incensed to take the time to complain. Based on their personal observations, most sanitation officials have opinions of the cleanliness or dirtiness of streets and alleys in the various neighborhoods. But such opinions are difficult to quantify because they vary among observers. They can be based on observations of only a portion of the neighborhood—such as a main street—that may not be representative of the neighborhood. Officials relying solely on memory might have difficulty distinguishing levels of cleanliness and degrees of differences among various parts of the community and changes that occur over time.

This chapter presents suggested measures and data collection procedures for regularly obtaining more comprehensive and reliable information on the effectiveness or quality of solid waste collection services. A sanitation organization embarking on effectiveness measurement can review the objectives presented here and tailor them to its own needs. The bibliography at the end of this book lists a number of publications that provide additional details on the procedures discussed in this chapter.

Objectives and Related Effectiveness Measures

The following basic objectives for solid waste collection seem appropriate for most communities, whether the service is provided by the government or by private contractors under government regulation:

> **To promote the aesthetics of the community and the health and safety of the citizens by providing an environment free from the hazards and unpleasantness of uncollected refuse with the least possible citizen inconvenience.**

The suggested measures of effectiveness relating to these objectives, and the proposed sources of data on them, are summarized in Exhibit 2-1. The order of the measures does not indicate their importance. They are discussed in four groups:

- Pleasing aesthetics—clean streets (Measures 1–4)
- Health and safety (Measures 5–10)
- Minimum citizen inconvenience (Measures 11–14)
- General citizen satisfaction (Measure 15).

The measurements can be undertaken for the community as a whole and for individual areas of the community. These measures are appropriate for commercial and residential collection services and for monitoring services that are provided directly by the government or by private contractors under government regulation.

The measures apply primarily to household and commercial refuse collection and street- and alley-cleaning services. But some measures can be used,

or at least adapted, for specialized activities such as abandoned automobile removal and code enforcement. The findings from some measures—such as the trained observer ratings of street cleanliness and citizen ratings of neighborhood cleanliness—are affected jointly by street-cleaning and refuse-collection operations. A local government can use the procedures suggested here to identify specific responsibility and possible action for correcting undesirable conditions.

Exhibit 2-1

Objectives and Principal Effectiveness Measures for Solid Waste Collection

Overall objective: To promote the aesthetics of the community and the health and safety of the citizens by providing an environment free from the hazards and unpleasantness of uncollected refuse with the least possible citizen inconvenience.

Objective	Quality characteristic	Specific measure[1]	Data collection procedure
Pleasing aesthetics	Street, alley, and neighborhood cleanliness	1. Percentage of (a) streets, (b) alleys, the appearance of which is rated satisfactory (or unsatisfactory).	Trained observer ratings
		2. Percentage of (a) households, (b) businesses rating their neighborhood cleanliness as satisfactory (or unsatisfactory).	(a) Household survey (b) Business survey
	Offensive odors	3. Percentage of (a) households, (b) businesses reporting offensive odors from solid wastes.	(a) Household survey (b) Business survey
	Objectionable noise incidents	4. Percentage of (a) households, (b) businesses reporting objectionable noise from solid waste collection operations.	(a) Household survey (b) Business survey
Health and safety	Health	5. Number and percentage of blocks with one or more health hazards.	Trained observer ratings
	Fire hazards	6. Number and percentage of blocks with one or more fire hazards.	Trained observer ratings
	Fires involving uncollected waste	7. Number of fires involving uncollected solid waste.	Fire department records
	Health hazards and unsightly appearance	8. Number of abandoned automobiles.	Trained observer ratings
	Rodent hazard	9. Percentage of (a) households, (b) businesses reporting having seen rats on their blocks in the past three months.	(a) Household survey (b) Business survey
	Rodent bites	10. Number of rodent bites reported per 1,000 population.	City or county health records
Minimum citizen inconvenience	Missed or late collections	11. Number and percentage of collection routes not completed on schedule.	Sanitation department records
		12. Percentage of (a) households, (b) businesses reporting missed collections.	(a) Household survey (b) Business survey
	Spillage of trash and garbage during collections	13. Percentage of (a) households, (b) businesses reporting spillage by collection crews.	(a) Household survey (b) Business survey
	Damage to private property by collection crews	14. Percentage of (a) households, (b) businesses reporting property damage caused by collection crews.	(a) Household survey (b) Business survey
General citizen satisfaction	Citizen complaints	15. Number of verified citizen complaints, by type, per 1,000 households served.	Sanitation department records
	Perceived satisfaction	16. Percentage of (a) households, (b) businesses reporting overall satisfaction with the solid waste collection service they receive.	(a) Household survey (b) Business survey

[1]Officials who wish to focus on the amount of local *dissatisfaction* may substitute "unsatisfactory" for the term "satisfactory" in many of these measures.

Principal Measures and Measurement Procedures

Because solid waste collection is intended to remove unsightly and unsanitary wastes, the chief measurement issues are how to measure the resulting cleanliness and the extent of any health and safety hazards on streets and alleys in the community. Two complementary approaches are described here.

- The first procedure relies on trained observers using a photographic rating scale to rate regularly the cleanliness of streets and alleys in the community. Observers also identify the presence of health and fire hazards, abandoned automobiles, and miscellaneous bulk items. This procedure can provide the government with reliable information as to the nature and location of unsightly conditions in small or large areas of the community, depending on the scope of the measurement effort.

- The second procedure is that of periodic telephone or mail surveys with a sample of households and possibly businesses in the community. The interviews can obtain representative viewpoints on neighborhood cleanliness, as well as ratings on refuse collection service, including the frequency of missed collections, trash spillage during collections, incidents of objectionable noise during solid waste collection, odors from uncollected refuse, and rat sightings. Although citizen perceptions are subject to memory limitation and inaccurate observation, they are an important indicator of how the clients view their service. This interview procedure becomes especially practical if the survey covers a number of services in addition to solid waste collection, so that survey costs can be shared across agencies. Quarterly surveys are desirable to cover conditions for each of the four seasons.

The data obtained from these procedures should be broken out by area of the community and, for customer feedback data, by type of household. Such information will better enable sanitation officials to identify problem areas.

Individual Measures

Pleasing Aesthetics—Clean Streets (Measures 1–4)

Keeping streets and alleys clean—maintaining a satisfactory appearance—is a major aim of solid waste collection. In addition, keeping sidewalks, off-street parking areas, vacant lots, and yards free from accumulations of unsightly or hazardous wastes (such as abandoned automobiles, discarded furniture and appliances, garbage, or extensive amounts of combustible litter) is a government responsibility often shared by code enforcement, street-cleaning, and refuse collection personnel. However, sanitation data used by most local governments do not provide reliable, regular information on cleanliness and appearance. The occasional observations of collection personnel and other public officials are not systematically collected. Moreover, they provide little useful data for comparative assessments of improvement or degradation in appearance as, for example, from one year to the next.

Complaints from citizens often identify specific problems. But many people do not complain because they do not like to, do not know how to, or do not feel it would do any good. Often complaints are not valid—they misrepresent the condition. Complaint data cannot be depended on to represent either actual conditions or the views of all the jurisdiction's citizens.

But can more reliable, quantitatively based measurements of cleanliness be provided? Two complementary approaches to such measurement seem appropriate. The approach discussed in Measure 1 (see below) is based on a photographic rating scale used by trained observers to make objective ratings of actual conditions. The other approach presented in Measure 2 is based on subjective citizen perceptions of neighborhood cleanliness.

Measure 1: *Percentage of (a) streets, (b) alleys, the appearance of which is rated satisfactory (or unsatisfactory).*

Two different procedures have been developed for rating community cleanliness using visual ratings. Both use photographs. One requires taking and interpreting a set of photographs each time a rating is made; that is, a sample set of locations is identified, pictures are taken, and a count is made of the number of pieces of litter as shown in the pictures. This count is compared with counts from earlier periods to determine whether the cleanliness of the jurisdiction is changing.[1]

The other procedure uses photographs as a base from which specially trained observers make comparisons of litter. The cleanliness and appearance of a street or alley are graded in accordance with a set of photographs and written descriptions that cover a range of litter conditions generally found throughout the community. Trained observers driving along the streets (or through the alleys) assign to each block face a numerical rating that corresponds most

Exhibit 2-2

Examples of Street Litter Conditions

Condition 2, Moderately clean

Condition 4, Heavily littered

Condition 1, Clean

Condition 3, Moderately littered

closely to a grade described in the photographs and written descriptions. The observer does not have to leave the car to make the ratings. These ratings constitute a readily understood measure, especially when results are presented with examples of the photographs on which the rating scale is based. An example of a typical set of grades is shown in Exhibit 2-2. Under proper supervision, the trained observer program provides a reliable way to measure changes in community cleanliness over time.[2]

Cleanliness and appearance problems can arise from a number of sources: littering, inadequate household or commercial storage practices, slipshod collection services, spillover from private property, or construction debris. To distinguish the specific type of problem in the dirtier areas and to help identify corrective strategies, trained observers can identify the apparent nature or source of the refuse. Trained observers also can note problems such as refuse not in containers, construction or excavation debris, overflowing public trash containers, or discarded bulky items.

Cleanliness-rating information can be tabulated to indicate cleanliness by neighborhood, by sanitation service area, or for the entire community. This is illustrated in Exhibits 2-3 and 2-4 (New York City and Savannah have used trained observer procedures for many years). Exhibit 2-4 also shows changes over time in cleanliness by sanitation district, and this map format is effective for reporting cleanliness data.

Exhibit 2-3 shows the use of the cleanliness information to help establish priorities for corrective action. Savannah's sanitation bureau adjusts sweeping frequency based on the cleanliness condition. Savannah assigns a priority level to each of its 28 planning areas: first-priority areas are those with the most severe problems, and they receive first attention with available resources.

Exhibit 2-3

Street Cleanliness and Cleaning Priorities
Savannah, Georgia

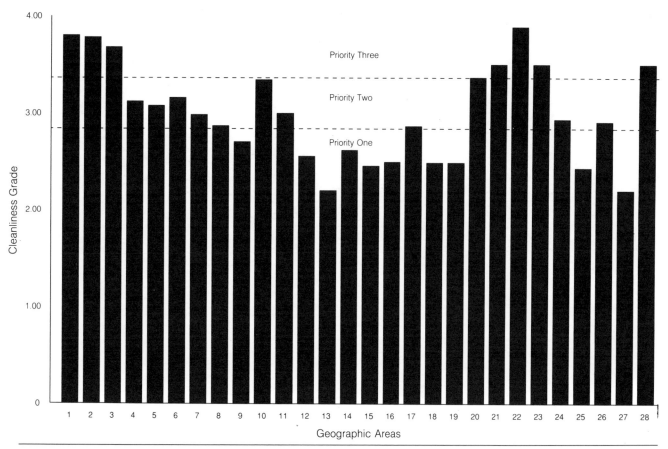

Note: Rating is based on a 5-point scale with grades 0, 1, 2, 3, 4. Grade 4 is "clean" (no litter, sand, dirt or leaves). Grade 0 is "dirty" (heavy accumulation of leaves, sand, dirt or litter).

Source: "Responsive Public Services Program: 1988," City of Savannah Community, Housing and Economic Development Department, Savannah, Georgia, October 1988.

Exhibit 2-4

Street Cleanliness Report: New York City

New York City FY 1991 Change in Levels of Cleanliness for the 59 Sanitation Districts

Number of districts△		Cleanliness level		Number of districts	Degree of change— FY 1990–1991
FY 1991	FY 1990				
0	0	■	Very dirty	10	Significant improvement ▲ in cleanliness of +5.0% or more
9	9	▨	Dirty		
22	27	▦	Marginal	2	Significant decline in ■ cleanliness of −5.0% or more
28	23	□	Acceptable		
July–Dec.△					

Source: City of New York, New York, "The Mayor's Management Report," January 30, 1991.

Special Validity Considerations for Measure 1. The visual rating procedure, despite its attractive features, can degenerate into an unreliable procedure unless proper care—particularly in supervising observers—is taken. Over time, observers may forget the definitions, become careless in applying them, or even make up ratings. Scale compression is common when observers do not adhere to photographic or written standards. Without retraining, disparities in ratings are to be expected. Several actions are needed to ensure that the data remain reasonably reliable. These include the following:

- The visual, photographic rating scale should be developed systematically (as described later in this chapter) to ensure that the different levels of cleanliness can be distinguished.

- Adequate training in the use of the rating procedure for new observers and periodic retraining for experienced observers to prevent deterioration in rating skill should be provided.

- Sample ratings should be checked regularly to determine whether observers maintain sufficient accuracy. Perhaps 10 percent of each inspector's ratings should be replicated by the supervisor. The local government should set reliability targets; for example, 75 percent of the inspector's ratings could be required to agree with those of the supervisors, and 90 percent to agree within one-half point on a four-point scale. If the checks do not indicate sufficient accuracy, raters should be retrained immediately and photographs and written standards for the ratings should be refined.

Measure 2:   *Percentage of (a) households, (b) businesses rating their neighborhood cleanliness as satisfactory (or unsatisfactory).*

Another important perspective on the cleanliness of the community and, by implication, on the community's satisfaction with solid waste collection services, is provided by the perceptions of households and businesses. This information can be obtained from a survey of a representative sample of the community. The same survey can be used to provide data for several other solid waste collection measures. Question 47 of Appendix 1 (for households) "...would you say that your neighborhood is usually very clean, fairly clean, fairly dirty, or very dirty?" and Question 26 of Appendix 2 (for businesses) can be used to obtain these data. Satisfaction with cleanliness in these examples is expressed in terms of how clean the respondents rate their neighborhoods rather than directly in terms of how "satisfied" they are.

Because the household survey procedure is covered in Chapter 13, it will not be discussed in detail here. A local government will find the survey to be most practical if it simultaneously obtains information on a number of other local government services. If a wide-ranging household survey is not undertaken, the sanitation department might conduct its own annual survey to monitor a number of aspects of collection operations. If a low-cost, five-minute telephone or mailed survey is a feasible option, Questions 47–52 of Appendix 1 can be used.

Special Validity Considerations for Measure 2. Although Chapter 13 discusses the potential validity factors applicable to any survey of households or businesses in a community, there is an additional concern here about the wording of the question used to collect data on this measure. The survey question on rating of neighborhood cleanliness is straightforward, but respondents' ratings may also include litter on private property and possibly even the condition of buildings and yards over which the department has little or no direct control. Buildings needing paint or repairs or unkept lawns can make an area look dirty. Citizens responding "somewhat dirty" or "very dirty" might be asked, "Why do you say that?" or "What contributes most to the neighborhood's being dirty?" The replies would help identify the specific nature of the problem.

Citizen Perceptions versus Trained Observer Ratings. Measures 1 and 2 are treated separately because they measure different aspects of service effectiveness (i.e., citizen perceptions of neighborhood cleanliness as opposed to an "objective" physical evaluation of street and alley cleanliness). However, if the results for these two measures are highly correlated and seem likely to remain so under most conditions, it would be adequate to use only one as a proxy for the other.

Past tests indicate that some correlation exists between trained observer ratings and household responses, but not enough to depend solely on one or the other measure. Measures 1 and 2 appear to measure different aspects of cleanliness; it is desirable to collect information for both. For places where the outcomes for the two measures are quite different, the data might provide clues to corrective action. They could indicate (1) whether physical conditions had actually changed or whether the problem appeared to be a perceptual change or (2) that conditions on streets and alleys had changed but not those on private property (or vice versa).

Measure 3:   Percentage of (a) households, (b) businesses reporting offensive odors from solid wastes.

Improperly stored organic solid wastes, particularly food wastes, can decompose and putrefy in a few days in warm weather, creating noxious odors and causing health hazards. Low-income housing areas or dense, inner-city residential areas frequently suffer from such odors in warm weather. The prevalence of odors can be estimated by surveying households and businesses concerning their perceptions and recollections of odors caused by solid wastes, as part of the household or business surveys mentioned previously. Question 50 of Appendix 1 (households) and Question 33 of Appendix 2 (businesses) can be used to obtain the data.

The measure's validity may be affected by certain factors. Citizens may not be able to identify the source of odors in their neighborhoods, especially in areas with polluted waterways or with extensive commercial operations that emit odors. Even if respondents are able to identify an odor as coming from solid wastes, much of the waste might be on private property or in buildings over which the sanitation department has no control. Furthermore, the season when the survey is conducted will affect the results. Odors are likely to be more pronounced in hot weather, but if the survey is conducted in cold or moderate weather, the respondents might not remember the problems experienced during extended warm periods.

Measure 4:   Percentage of (a) households, (b) businesses reporting objectionable noise from solid waste collection operations.

Household refuse collection and street cleaning can be noisy. Noise levels can be measured with appropriate equipment, but it is difficult to relate noise levels to effects on citizens and to measure citizen dissatisfaction. The extent to which noise is objectionable to citizens depends not only on the absolute noise level but on such factors as the following: whether the noise is sharp or dull, constant or intermittent; the proximity of the residence or business to the collection operation; the extent of other noises; the time of day the noise is made; and whether citizens have become conditioned to collection noises. Surveys should indicate the extent to which the noises are considered to be objectionable. If a household or business survey is being conducted by the local government, Question 49 of Appendix 1 (households) and Question 32 of Appendix 2 (businesses) can be used to obtain the data.

Health and Safety Measures (Measures 5–10)

Measure 5:   Number and percentage of blocks with one or more health hazards.

Avoidance of environmental health problems caused by uncollected, improperly stored refuse is perhaps the most important purpose of solid waste collection. Solid waste often contains organic wastes and food scraps that provide breeding areas for insects in hot weather. Piles of discarded food containers or furniture offer food and harborage for rats. Discarded refrigerators or extensive amounts of broken glass endanger children.

The extent of these hazards can be estimated by trained observers inspecting for block-face and alley cleanliness (Measure 1). Many of these hazards are found on private property—backyards, vacant lots, and other privately owned illicit dumping areas where the sanitation department may have limited power to correct conditions. The department will have to decide whether the inspection will cover these areas. Because the local government will probably want to immediately correct a situation posing serious danger to health—or have the health or zoning department issue a citation—the location of all health hazards detected should be recorded also.

There is as yet no generally accepted definition for how large an accumulation has to be to constitute a health hazard. The term "health hazard" might be defined as the presence of any of the following: abandoned bulk items (such as stuffed chairs, mattresses, and appliances), to be noted separately; dead animals; abandoned automobiles (also counted in Measure 8); piles of organic refuse exceeding some minimum size shown in a photograph; or piled rubbish (such as boards, boxes, or brush) that appear to harbor rats. Each local government should attempt to provide and adhere to a specific definition so that counts taken in different parts of the community by different inspectors and at different times will be at least roughly comparable.

The decision whether to note health hazards on private property will probably depend on the amount of responsibility the department has for removing such hazards. The inspection of private property can become time-consuming because of the need to drive slowly, examine a much larger area than just the street or alley, and to drive through alleys to note conditions in backyards (where fences may block the view).

Health hazards (and fire hazards—see Measure 6) are likely to be correlated with certain street or alley litter ratings. Hazards are almost never present when the litter ratings indicate small amounts of litter (e.g., 1 or 2 on a four-point scale). But because hazards do not always correlate with litter ratings and because of public concern about health hazards and their potential effects on the public, it seems desirable to include this measure.

Measure 6:   Number and percentage of blocks with one or more fire hazards.

A "fire hazard" is defined as an accumulation of combustible solid wastes that, if ignited, would cause substantial property damage or a blaze of such a size that a prudent citizen would call the fire department. Fire hazards on the public way can be detected by trained observers as part of the procedure used for Measure 1. If the information is to be used only for sanitation department purposes, the inspections probably can be confined to the public way and the information gathered with little additional effort. If the information is also to be used by the agency responsible for private property (such as the fire marshal), then more time-consuming inspections of private property will be required.

Probably few of the fire hazards on streets and alleys will lead to fires, even when not removed for weeks or months. Measure 7 is included to provide estimates of this "ultimate outcome." Still, because of the potentially serious nature of fire hazards, reporting the number and specific locations of fire hazards seems appropriate to encourage any needed correction actions. Fire hazards can be seasonal (piles of brush or leaves not collected promptly are an example), so special attention might be devoted to this measure during certain seasons.

Measure 7:   Number of fires involving uncollected solid waste.

One direct measure of solid waste problems is the number of fires that originate in refuse. In many localities the fire department investigates each fire to determine its cause. Some departments categorize the fires by cause and location. A review of fire incident records can be conducted to determine the number and geographical areas of fires from solid wastes on the public way. It might be hard to determine whether the accumulation was located in a place from which it should have been collected by sanitation personnel or whether it was on private property where it should have been detected and cited by sanitation inspectors. Data collection could be simplified if fire department personnel specify which fires involve solid wastes on the public way. Fires might be classified additionally according to size or severity of damage.

Measure 8:   Number of abandoned automobiles.

Abandoned automobiles are ugly, are sometimes fire hazards, often harbor rats, and are inviting nuisances for children. The same trained observer inspection procedure discussed earlier can be used to collect data on abandoned automobiles. If the sanitation agency wants to know the exact location of such vehicles—perhaps to direct automobile collection operations—trained observers will have to inspect all blocks: streets, alleys, and perhaps even private property. If the agency wants only an estimate of the number of abandoned vehicles to determine how much effort will be needed to collect them or how effective collection efforts have been, inspections of a sample of streets will be adequate. When the agency is responsible for removing automobiles from private as well as public property, inspections of private property may be needed.

Measure 9:   Percentage of (a) households, (b) businesses reporting having seen rats on their blocks in the past three months.

Solid wastes often provide refuge and food for rats. Estimates of the presence (or at least visible evidence) of rats over some interval of time can be obtained inexpensively with household or business surveys using Question 52 of Appendix 1 (households) and Question 28 of Appendix 2 (businesses). Although the responses are impossible to translate into *numbers* of rats, the responses can identify areas where rats are seen most often. Such data are adequate for tracking the rat problem.

It is not known how accurate citizens' memories will be of such sightings. The questions in Appendix 1 ask about rat sightings over the past three months. If the survey is scheduled less frequently, such as once a year, households can be asked to consider the past twelve months, but their memories will be less accurate. Respondents could still be asked only about the past three months, but then responses will reflect only their most recent experiences.

Rat infestations are not necessarily the result of improper solid waste collection practices of the sanitation agency. Poor food handling and food storage practices by citizens and commercial establishments, open sewers, and buildings with ground-level openings for unobstructed rat entry are examples of other practices that attract rats. Agencies other than sanitation departments, such as health departments, typically have responsibility for enforcing ordinances dealing with these matters. Therefore, this measure provides an estimate of the effectiveness of the sanitation department and of related health inspection activities.

Measure 10: Number of rodent bites reported per 1,000 residents.

This is a more dramatic measure of the rat problem for which data would be obtained from city or county health records. As with Measure 9, uncollected or improperly stored solid wastes appear to be only one facet of the rat problem. Other factors, such as poor housing conditions and poor food-handling practices, are probably more responsible. Thus, this measure reflects the combined effectiveness of many local activities including those of the departments of health, housing or zoning, and sanitation.

Measures of Citizen Inconvenience (Measures 11–14)

The measures presented here address citizen inconvenience. However, one area of growing concern, solid waste recycling, is excluded from the discussion. The effects of recycling on citizen convenience can be addressed through questions added to the household and business surveys. The effects of recycling on the environment are addressed in Chapter 3.

Measure 11: Number and percentage of collection routes not completed on schedule.

A missed collection is poor service. Refuse left on the streets or in alleys and awaiting collection is unsightly, and scattering produces dirty streets and alleys. Customers become irritated. There are four principal data collection sources for information on missed collections: information provided by crews and their foremen, tallies of citizen complaints on missed collections, citizen responses in sample surveys, and observations by trained observers who spot-check collection points shortly after scheduled collections. The last two sources are discussed under Measure 13.

Many agencies require each crew to report at the end of the day whether it completed its route. This information is the data source for this measure. Its value is questionable unless the government takes pains to ensure accurate reporting. Some crews might be reluctant to report a route as uncompleted if they feel it will be taken as a sign of poor crew performance. Another drawback for some jurisdictions is that the data may not be available when private firms make the collections.

Tallies of citizen complaints of missed collections can be used as an alternative data source. Because not all citizens will complain, the counts are likely to underrepresent the number of missed collections. Nevertheless, the ready availability of this information makes it an attractive measure. (A complaint-count gauge has been included as Measure 15, which considers complaints for all reasons, not just missed collections.)

Measure 12: Percentage of (a) households, (b) businesses reporting missed collections.

The measurement data here are likely to be more credible than data from the previous measure because they do not depend on self-appraisals by public or private collection personnel.

Question 48a of Appendix 1 (households) and Question 29 of Appendix 2 (businesses) can be used to obtain the data. These surveys can also inquire about the dependability of special pick-ups. To obtain feedback on tree limb and brush pick-up service, Question 51 of Appendix 1 can be used.

There are some special validity problems with the data for this measure:

- Some residents might not be aware of a missed collection. Residents of multifamily units with a central storage/disposal facility would probably not know if collections are missed occasionally; these responses should be separated from those of single-family households (for instance, by using the instructions to the interviewers for Question 48 in Appendix 1).

- Sometimes citizens will set out refuse late, after the refuse collection team has passed through, and then blame the collectors for missing them.

- Memories of respondents may be poor even for three-month periods, but especially if asked about periods as long as twelve months.

The specific number of missed collections reported should be considered as only rough estimates.

Measure 13: Percentage of (a) households, (b) businesses reporting spillage by collection crews.

Spillage of refuse leads to dirty streets, causes irritation and inconvenience to households and businesses, and attracts animals and insects. Scattering can be the fault of the collectors or of customers who do not use proper containers.

The prevalence of spillage can be estimated by asking Question 48b of Appendix 1 (households) and Question 30 of Appendix 2 (businesses). Responses should be considered rough estimates because of the problems of memory and knowledge described under Measure 12. Moreover, a person who shares a central collection point with other households may not know if spillage was caused by sloppy handling of refuse by the collectors, by other householders, or by animals.

If trained observer ratings indicate that spillage is a serious problem, a trained observer might conduct special inspections just before and just after collections at a random sample of perhaps 50 to 70 collection points to determine the following:

Just Before Collection
- Are proper solid waste containers being used?
- Are the refuse set-out areas clean, except for refuse in proper containers that is awaiting collection?

Just After Collection
- Has refuse been scattered or have spills occurred during the collection?

Measure 14: *Percentage of (a) households, (b) businesses reporting property damage caused by collection crews.*

Collection crews sometimes damage refuse containers, shrubbery, and parked vehicles while picking up refuse. Although rarely a major problem, this practice can irritate customers. This measure might be of particular interest if a major change is made in collection procedures or if collectors frequently go onto private property. Complaints would probably be made only for the more serious incidents of damage; thus, reported complaints would likely understate the frequency of incidents. When the service is provided by a private contractor, the government may receive few complaints, even if the government has regulatory authority.

Question 48c of Appendix 1 (households) and Question 31 of Appendix 2 (businesses) can be used to obtain the data. It will be hard to determine that the damage was caused by collection forces. Damage caused by vandals or irresponsible persons could be attributed by the respondent to collectors. However, if a survey of households or businesses is already being conducted, the cost of the added question on damage is minimal.

Measure of Overall Citizen Satisfaction

Measure 15: *Number of verified citizen complaints, by type, per 1,000 households served.*

Measure 16: *Percentage of (a) households, (b) businesses reporting overall satisfaction with the solid waste collection service they receive.*

Although citizen complaints are sometimes inaccu-

rate evaluation measures, some governments use them to evaluate the quality of service for a number of the problems covered by Measures 1–16. Complaints, when tabulated by type and compared with those in previous time periods, can indicate important trends and emerging problems. The data tallied could exclude complaints found to be invalid after investigation by the government, perhaps by having an inspector examine the complaint to determine if the condition really exists and if it is the responsibility of the sanitation department.

Citizen complaint data should be summarized regularly, perhaps monthly or quarterly by type of complaint, by neighborhood, and by sanitation district. Data should be compared with data from previous periods to help identify problems and trends.

An alternative to the specific questions on solid waste collection is a question asking respondents to rate their overall satisfaction with solid waste collection. ("How do you rate the solid waste collection services you received over the past three months? Excellent, Good, Fair, or Poor?")

If the survey covers a properly drawn sample of households and businesses, the findings should be representative of the community.

The Photographic Litter-Rating Procedure

This section discusses various aspects in the development and implementation of a photographic litter-rating procedure—used particularly for Measure 1 but also for Measures 5, 6, and 8.

How to Develop a Photographic Rating Scale

A local government can use one of the scales already developed, for instance, by Charlotte, North Carolina; Washington, D.C.; New York City; or Savannah, Georgia, because conditions in many cities or counties are similar. However, each of these four cities developed its own rating scales because local officials felt more comfortable with scales that used photographs of actual local conditions. (Savannah used the set of photos developed for the Washington, D.C., system but with a different rating scale.) If a community prefers its own rating scale, the scale has to be developed carefully to ensure that the photographs used to represent the various levels of cleanliness represent significantly different cleanliness levels that observers can reliably distinguish. Each city that developed its own photographic rating scale also wrote its own definitions to accompany its photographs.

The procedure used for developing the rating scales is as follows:

1. Photograph many scenes that are representative of the range of existing litter conditions on streets and alleys, and of the variety of backgrounds, structures, and land uses in which the conditions occur. A number of photographs should be taken to represent the various litter conditions encountered. Following a review, additional photographs should be taken if necessary to give complete coverage.

2. Have a number of "judges" separate the photographs into four groups corresponding to four different levels of litter conditions, from the cleanest to the most-littered categories. The judges should be persons who have varied backgrounds and who are not associated with the measurement activities. Photographs on which there is complete or nearly complete agreement concerning the category labels should be included in the set to be used as the visual inspection standard.

3. Use trained observers to field-test the set of photographs and the written definitions to determine if the set provides sufficient guidance for making ratings and for obtaining close agreement among ratings in a trial test.

Washington, D.C., took about 400 photographs; a panel of nineteen "judges" then classified them. Nashville took about 200 photographs, and a panel of six classified them. In St. Petersburg, a photographer spent two days taking 150 pictures, and an analyst spent ten days constructing the final photographic rating scale. In Washington and Nashville, additional photographs and guidelines were needed to help observers differentiate between Condition 2 and Condition 3 situations. (See Exhibit 2-2.)

Several scales have been used in the photographic rating system. One city started with a four-point scale but went to a nine-point scale because of the inability of the inspectors to agree. The scale uses five major points (1.0, 2.0, 3.0, 4.0, and 5.0) that are tied to photographs, and four midpoints (1.5, 2.5, 3.5, 4.5) that are used when an observer cannot decide between the major points. Two cities used a seven-point scale, with the four major points tied to photographs and three midpoints used to resolve cases in which the inspector was unable to decide on the main points. Another city used a four-point scale (1.0, 1.5, 2.0, and 3.0) that was tied to photographs. Intermediate ratings (1.2, 1.8, and 2.5) were assigned to conditions that did not conform to the photograph standards. Ratings of 1.5 or lower were considered acceptable according to a public survey and to the agency's own standards.

How Often Should Inspections Be Made?

The answers depend on local conditions and the expected uses of the information. Litter conditions in large areas normally change little from day to day and from week to week. But there can be strong seasonal effects on cleanliness, such as leaves in the fall, brush and other vegetation in the summer, and more street litter in tourist seasons. If the local government wants to know about cleanliness during differ-

Exhibit 2-5

Activities and Cost for Measuring Solid Waste Collection

Activity	Staff requirements and cost
Trained observer ratings	
Design procedures Select measures; establish neighborhood boundaries; prepare procedures manual, photographs for trained observer ratings, and maps; establish data collection and reporting procedures; train and retrain inspectors	3–4 employee-months
Collect ratings	
Inspect	1 week per inspector
	If only a sample is to be inspected, 1 day of inspector time for every 30 to 60 block faces, or 20 to 40 alleys inspected
	If continuous inspection of all block faces or alleys is wanted, 1 day of inspector time for every 200 to 250 block faces or every 60 to 90 alleys inspected
Replicate a sample of ratings	1 day of supervisory time for each 4 to 6 person-days of inspection time
Provide clerical support (set up and prepare routes, transcribe ratings)	1 day of clerical time for each 2 to 3 person-days of inspection time
Citizen surveys	
Set up telephone or mail survey of households and businesses Decide on questions and make arrangements with other government agency or with private survey firm to carry out	1 staff-week
Conduct survey (25–50 responses per neighborhood or sanitation service area)	$2.00 (mail) to $5.00 (phone) per response
Reporting	
Prepare report Prepare tables, charts, and appropriate narrative descriptions of conditions, changes over time, variations among neighborhoods	1 employee-month of time for each report

ent seasons—perhaps to help direct cleaning efforts—quarterly inspection may be appropriate.

If the litter information is used in the day-to-day direction of cleaning forces, more frequent inspection is necessary. Weekly inspections have been used in New York's most littered areas, but the cleaner areas are inspected only one to three times a month, depending on their level of cleanliness.

How Many Block Faces or Alleys Should Be Inspected?
The decision as to how many streets or alleys should be inspected depends largely on what use is to be made of the information and how much statistical confidence is required. If the information is to be used to direct crews to specific locations or to evaluate the performance of individual crews, it will be necessary to inspect most streets and alleys, at least in those areas of the community generally known to have problems. If the information is only to detect changes in conditions over time or differences among areas, inspection of a sample of 50 to 70 block faces or alleys in each area, randomly selected before the inspection, should be sufficient in most cases.

Who Should Make the Ratings?
Persons with a variety of educational backgrounds and experience have been used as trained observers. City sanitation inspectors, sanitation supervisors, summer interns from a local university, and ex-addicts and ex-offenders have made the ratings. Any of these groups seems appropriate, as long as employees are properly trained and ratings are periodically checked (as discussed later). This activity might be an excellent use of employees obtained on a short-term basis.

Can Cleanliness Ratings Be Made for Private Property?
Some governments may want to measure the cleanliness of private property, perhaps as a check on health and litter code enforcement activities. As has been noted, making ratings on private property slows the inspection process. It is doubtful that many communities will find a combined cleanliness rating of public and private property useful because the agency responsible for maintaining the cleanliness of public property will probably be different from the one responsible for private property.

What Rating Should Be Set as a Criterion for an "Unsatisfactory" Condition?
As with all measures of effectiveness, the criterion for what constitutes an "unsatisfactory" condition probably should be set by each community itself. Some cities have used a rating of "worse than 2.0." (Each had photographs and written guidelines defining a rating of "2.0.")

Summary data can be presented as average ratings (such as for each area of the community) or as the percentage of ratings exceeding the determined satisfactory level. The latter is likely to be a more meaningful form than the average litter rating. A community might report both forms.

Costs and Staffing Requirements for the Data Collection Procedures

Many factors will affect measurement costs (see Exhibit 2-5). These include the size of the community, the number of measures for which data are being collected, the frequency of inspections, the num-

---

Exhibit 2-6

Estimated Annual Costs for Solid Waste Collection Measurement Procedures

Option	Approximate number of blocks in locality		
	1,500	5,000	9,000
Trained observers			
Quarterly inspection of a sample of streets (person-years of effort)[1]	0.25	0.75	1.0
Quarterly inspections of all streets (person-years of effort)[1]	0.5	1.5	2.5–3.0
Household survey			
Sample size (each quarter/annually)[2]	100/400	150/600	250/1,000
Annual cost[3]	$800/$2,000	$1,200/$3,000	$2,000/$5,000

[1]Time includes inspection, clerical, and supervisory effort. See Chapter 12 for more information.
[2]The sample size depends more on variability within the community than on its size. The annual cost of the survey is related to the sample size, not to the size of the community.

[3]The lower figure is the estimated cost if the questionnaire is mailed (with 1–2 follow-ups to nonrespondents). The higher figure is the estimated cost of a short, approximately five-minute, telephone survey, possibly the sanitation agency's share of a multiservice household survey such as that shown in Appendix 1.

ber of service districts from which sample blocks or sample households are selected, the intensity of inspection (all blocks or only a sample), the extent to which the costs of surveys and trained observer operations can be shared among other government agencies, local pay rates, the use of existing staff rather than out-of-pocket expenses for additional staff or consultants, and the extent of analysis of the data collected.

Exhibit 2-6 presents estimates of measurement activity requirements for several city sizes and for two basic types of inspections: one involving inspection of a randomly selected sample of streets and alleys and one involving an inspection of virtually all streets and alleys. The time requirements include training inspectors; photographing conditions; and preparing inspection forms, maps, and procedure manuals. Requirements in succeeding years would be lower. If more than two sets of inspections are conducted or if a number of conditions in addition to street and alley cleanliness are rated (for example, cleanliness of private property, road surface conditions, or street signs), or if traffic congestion impedes inspection operations, the time requirements could be higher. Out-of-pocket expenses would be reduced to the extent that existing personnel or volunteers can be used.

---

1 Fleming, *Street Cleaning Practice*; Sullivan, "Measurement of Relative Amounts of Litter."

2 Blair and Schwartz, *How Clean Is Our City?*; Fund for the City of New York, "Project Scorecard: Purpose, Function, Method, and Structure."

T he effectiveness measures for municipal solid waste disposal presented in this chapter cover the environmental and aesthetic effects of solid waste disposal processes at landfills, incinerators, recycling facilities, or other solid waste facilities. Only people living, working, or traveling near disposal facilities are exposed to the aesthetic effects of disposal operations. However, certain outcomes that result from the disposal of municipal waste can have environmental effects that concern the entire community.

Performance measurement in local government solid waste disposal has tended to follow the usual approach for engineered systems. It focuses on resources, physical features, and procedures and evaluates them against lists of specification standards and a consensus on best practices.

Such measurement is appropriate for management but does not by itself indicate the environmental and other effects of municipal solid waste disposal on the community. For example, a standard-oriented measurement might call for noting the presence or absence of screens to reduce problems with paper that blows off-site, but that would not indicate whether visible blown paper was present at or near the site. Similarly, another standard-oriented measurement might call for noting the presence of specific fire control equipment but not the number or size of fires that have occurred during the year.

Regular, direct measurement of these effects of municipal solid waste disposal facilities does not occur in most communities. This chapter describes measurement procedures to fill this gap.

Objectives of Solid Waste Disposal

The following is the statement of solid waste disposal objectives used to identify appropriate effectiveness measures in this report:

To provide for solid waste disposal in a safe, environmentally sound, and aesthetically acceptable manner.

The next section summarizes the major recommendations, followed by more detailed discussion of the individual measures.

Principal Recommendations for Measuring Solid Waste Disposal Effectiveness

Full specification of effectiveness measurement requires specification of what data are to be collected and how, how often the data are to be collected, what measures should be developed from the data, and how and when the values of the measures should be reported. The following data collection and analysis activities are recommended:

- *Regular technical tests* for air and water quality that emphasize the particular dangers of the site. Tests for leachate in groundwater and runoff into surface water are needed at any landfill site. Tests for air hazards are needed primarily for sites where burning is conducted, particularly at incinerators. The range and frequency of tests may need to exceed legal requirements to provide for safe and environmentally sound solid waste disposal.

- *Regular observations by trained observers* of conditions that sight, smell, or hearing can detect. This should be done by trained observers using a systematic rating procedure. Ratings of air quality conditions (such as the presence of smoke, dust, and ash); aesthetic conditions (unsightly appearance, odor, and noise); and some health and safety problems (the presence of flies, rats, or mosquitoes; uncontrolled gas emissions; or other hazards) will give public officials a clearer picture of the current condition of each solid waste disposal site.

- *Summarized results* of the disposal site inspec-

tions, both for each site and collectively, should be compiled and reported.

The list of suggested measures is shown in Exhibit 3-1. Exhibit 3-2 illustrates how data for those measures can be displayed. Summary reports using a format such as that of Exhibit 3-2

Exhibit 3-1

Effectiveness Measures for Solid Waste Disposal Services

Overall objective: To provide for solid waste disposal in a safe, environmentally sound, and aesthetically acceptable manner.

Objective	Quality characteristic		Specific measure	Data collection procedure
Environmental soundness	Effects on groundwater (for operations involving land disposal)	1.	Number of days that tests for leaching indicated imminent danger to nearby water users.	Chemical testing of water quality characteristics affected by leaching
	Effects on surface water (for operations involving land disposal)	2a.	If landfill runoff is captured and treated before release: Number of days that landfill runoff released to nearby bodies of water failed to meet standards on quality.	Chemical tests of landfill runoff
			or	
		2b.	If landfill runoff is not captured and treated before relase: Number of days that any body of water in the community failed to satisfy quality standards for its class because of landfill runoff contamination.	
	Effects on groundwater and surface water (for operations involving land disposal)	3.	Number of water sites rendered unusable as a result of contamination from landfill sites.	Department or local government records
	Effects on air (for operations involving controlled burning)	4.	Number of presumed days that stack emissions from incinerators exceeded federal or state standards.	Automated monitoring or periodic inspections
		5.	Number of major smoke, dust, or ash problems at each disposal site, and number of sites with at least one major problem.	Trained observer ratings
		6.	Number of valid complaints per year about smoke, dust, ash, or other airborne emissions from solid waste disposal sites.	Agency records
	Extent of recycling	7a.	Number of pounds and percentage of all material diverted from the waste stream to be recycled.	(7a). Agency records
			and/or	
		7b.	Percentage of households participating in local recycling program.	(7b). Agency records or customer surveys
Aesthetics	Appearance, odors, and noise around disposal sites	8.	Number of major odor, noise, or appearance problems at each disposal site and the number of sites with one or more major problems.	Trained observer ratings.
		9.	Number of valid citizen complaints per year concerning odor, noise, or appearance problems arising from a local disposal site.	Agency records
Health and safety	Health and safety hazards	10.	Number of major problems with pests, gas, fires, or other health or safety hazards found at each site and the number of sites with one or more major problems.	Trained observer ratings
	Safety incidents	11.	Number of incidents of injury and damage requiring repair or replacement of citizen property.	Agency records
Overall site conditions		12.	Total number of major problems found at each disposal site and the number of sites with one or more major problems.	Trained observer ratings

Exhibit 3-2

Illustrative Summary Report: Solid Waste Disposal

Effectiveness measure	This period	Previous period	Same period last year
1. Number of days of leaching danger evidence (a) Site A (b) Site B (c) Overall			
2. Number of days of contamination evidence at test points (a) Site A (b) Site B (c) Overall			
3. Number of water sites where previous use was curtailed by contamination evidence (a) Site A (b) Site B (c) Overall			
4. Number of days of stack emission violations (incinerator) (Measure 4)			
5. Number of major smoke, dust, or ash problems at each disposal site (a) Site A (b) Site B (c) Number of sites with at least one major problem			
6. Number of valid complaints— smoke, dust, ash, etc. (a) Site A (b) Site B (c) Overall			
7. (a) Number of pounds of material to be recycled (b) Percentage of pounds of material to be recycled (c) Percentage of households participating in local recycling program			
8. Number of major odor, noise, or appearance problems (a) Site A (b) Site B (c) Number of sites with one or more major problems			
9. Number of valid complaints—odor, noise, appearance, etc. (a) Site A (b) Site B (c) Overall			
10. Number of major problems with pests, gas, fires, or other health or safety hazards (a) Site A (b) Site B (c) Number of sites with one or more major problems			
11. Number of incidents of injury or damage to citizen property (a) Site A (b) Site B			
12. Total number of major problems found (a) Site A (b) Site B (c) Number of sites with one or more major problems			

should provide summary performance data for each site and overall.

The measures are grouped for discussion into four categories as follows:

- Environmental soundness (Measures 1–7)
- Aesthetics (Measures 8–9)
- Health and safety (Measures 10–11)
- Overall site conditions (Measure 12).

Measures of Environmental Soundness

Effects of Land Disposal Facilities on Groundwater and Surface Water

Measure 1: *Number of days that tests for leaching[1] indicated imminent danger to nearby water users.*

Measure 2a: *If landfill runoff is captured and treated before release: Number of days that landfill runoff released to nearby bodies of water failed to meet standards on quality.*

Measure 2b: *If landfill runoff is not captured and treated before release: Number of days that any body of water in the community failed to satisfy quality standards for its class because of landfill runoff contamination.*

Measure 3: *Number of water sites rendered unusable as a result of contamination from landfill sites.*

Measures 1–3 apply to land disposal techniques. Landfill permits issued by most states specify site-specific water quality standards developed from the pre-permit testing of water samples. Monitoring of groundwater and surface water is required by the federal government under regulations from the Environmental Protection Agency (EPA). These regulations require groundwater monitoring and forbid the discharge of pollutants from landfills into the surface waters of the United States.

Some local governments test water in monitoring wells and surrounding streams or lakes as frequently as weekly. Tests should probably be done on at least a quarterly basis to provide public officials with a current check on the conditions of the water sources surrounding the disposal facility. However, the appropriate frequency will depend on local conditions, such as soil permeability and so forth.

Measures 1 and 2 call for an annual sum of "violation days"—the number of days between the first test that shows a problem and the first subsequent test that shows no evidence of a problem. (Note that "number of days" does not imply daily testing. Periods of up to a week or more will be required to complete some tests, and daily testing is not needed for most characteristics.) Measures in this form are conservative estimates of the duration of the problem, because there will be no way to know exactly

---

Exhibit 3-3

An Example of How to Calculate "Number of Days Outside Acceptable Conditions"

| | January | | | | | | | Test for lead contamination of runoff | | | | | | | | | | |
Date	1	2	3	4	5	6	7	8	9	10	11	12	13	14	15	16	17	18
Reading	.01							.06	.06	.04	.03				.07	.06	.05	.03
Did test show satisfactory conditions?	Yes							No	No	Yes	Yes				No	No	Yes	Yes
Cumulative number of violation-days during the year								1	2						3	4		

Scenario: Normally, testing is performed weekly with a standard for lead contamination of 0.05 mg/liter. The test on January 8 showed a violation. Steps were taken to cure the problem; at the same time, the testing schedule was accelerated to monitor the success of corrective actions. The January 9 test still showed violation, but the test on the following day indicated that the standard was again being met. The days on which the last test showed a violation are January 8 and 9, leading to a value of "two days." Subsequent tests on January 15 and 16 revealed contamination and two more violation-days.

how long the contamination was present before the "unacceptable" test result appeared. The criteria for an unacceptable test result for Measure 1 should consider contaminant levels at the test point, speed and direction in which groundwater is moving at that point, and distance to the nearest point of groundwater use. (Generally, only the contaminants' level and the speed of movement will change from one test to the next.)

The criteria for an unacceptable test result for Measure 2 can be based on set standards for the same contamination-related water quality characteristics as in Measure 1 plus, in the case of Measure 2b, a procedure for identifying the source of contamination. Exhibit 3-3 shows how a calculation of violation-days might be made.

The "number of days" measure represents a departure from current practice in local government. This change is recommended because for these kinds of effects the *duration* of undesirable conditions is as important as the *degree* of contamination.

In addition, the "number of days unacceptable" measure is recommended instead of "percentage of tests failed" because the former gives more comparable results across different testing frequencies. Nevertheless, one drawback of any measure is that its values can be unstable if the frequency of measurement is low. This raises a validity problem: Community managers could improve their ratings by reducing the frequency of measurement (and increasing the frequency if problems occur—to receive the earliest possible credit for removal of the problems). This method produces invalid results and also endangers the community.

This definition of violation-days creates an incentive for infrequent testing because the period of time (of unknown length) that unacceptable conditions existed before they were discovered is not charged against the agency's performance. An option is to count the period before the test that shows a problem (back to the time of the last test that showed no problem) as a violation. However, this would be an incentive to make measurements *more* frequently than is necessary or desirable. (This would increase the number of violation-days in Exhibit 3-3 from four to thirteen.) A third option is to assign each test's readings to all days for which that is the closest test, whether the days occurred before or after the test. (The number of violation-days in Exhibit 3-3 would then be eight days.)

The normal interval between tests should reflect a clear, explicit judgment on the speed with which serious problems could develop and the length of time they can go undetected without serious health consequences. Also, if a pattern develops in which regularly scheduled tests often show violations, even if they are quickly corrected as shown by an accelerated frequency of testing, then the normal frequency of testing should be increased.

Most states now have standards for the quality of their bodies of water, which could be used for Measure 2b. Some states have added the requirement that all runoff into those bodies of water meet the standards of the receiving body of water; this could be used for Measure 2a.[2] The standards generally specify the water quality required for certain uses (for example, fishing compared with no fishing).

Measure 2b provides a better measure of actual effect, but it involves a much greater problem of interpretation, including the issue of deciding whether, or to what extent, solid waste site runoff is to blame for existing conditions. This measure involves checking the effluent streams of all sources that might have contributed to the problem, so that particular pollutants found in source effluents and at the point of use can be assessed. Even then, a positive determination of the cause of the problems may not be possible, in which case a community may need to press for improvements in effluents from all possible sources of the problem. Measure 2a (condition of runoff water from landfills) gives a poorer picture of direct effects on citizens because the runoff is not directly reused. This measure greatly simplifies the problem of attributing responsibility for the existing conditions.

Measures 1 and 2 can use the same battery of tests on water samples; they differ only as to the points at which those samples are taken. However, the analyses performed at testing laboratories on water samples from different disposal sites may not be the same. Preliminary water testing done when disposal site permits are issued often determines what later monitoring tests should be done. Differences in the geological surroundings and environmental history of sample source sites will determine the extent of pre-existing dissolved solids, level of hardness, level of sulfates and metals, and so forth, found in water samples. These conditions will influence the relative acceptable levels of water quality for the site and therefore the lab test analysis.

Each landfill is a dynamic environment, constantly changing as new wastes are disposed. These changes affect the leachate produced within the landfill and therefore the types of contaminants that can be found in the groundwater and surface water. As a result, the types of analyses performed on each site's water samples to identify specific contaminants may change over time.

The actual cost to a particular local government for water monitoring will depend on how its lab tests are done (for example, in its own lab or on-site or through contracts with local private labs). Costs include labor, test equipment, and lab expenses. Gathering and analyzing samples can require 4 to 8 hours depending on the ease with which the samples are collected from the wells. The National Water Well Association estimates that the current cost for lab analysis ranges from $2,000 to $10,000, depending on what contaminants are being tested for, the quantity of samples tested, and the frequency of testing. Tests for inorganic material in samples cost about $500, and tests for pesticides and specific solvents could cost considerably more. EPA has identified 127 pollutants (as of this report) to watch for in water testing, but it would be very costly to test for each impurity every time the wells were monitored. To use resources wisely, local governments should test for contaminant *indicators* in maintenance monitoring and test for specific contaminants only when indicators show reason to do so.

If monitoring wells are not already in place, start-up costs will be needed for Measure 1 in placing the test well (an estimated $10,000 to $25,000, depending on the depth required to reach the water table and the nature of the material that must be drilled through) and for Measures 1 and 2 in acquiring chemical testing equipment (which may cost up to $500,000). However, most local governments will already have contracted with private labs to perform other tests (those needed by the water, sewer, health, or environmental protection services). Although these costs may seem high, water monitoring is essential to the safe operation of a disposal site, and much of it is, or will soon be, required by law. The added cost of converting the information to the form of these measures for easy managerial review is small. If standards for surface water do not exist or are judged to be too loose, they will have to be set (or possibly borrowed from a neighboring state) before test results can be interpreted.

Measure 3 is a rudimentary gauge of the ultimate effects of failure to control water pollution at solid waste disposal sites. The measure calls for a tally of the number of sites where contamination from a disposal site has helped render unusable either groundwater (for example, wells on a nearby farmer's property that are used for water supply) or surface water (for example, a creek running through a landfill and into nearby farm property, or a lake located near the site). The judgment as to "unusability" may be made by applying specified water quality criteria for the use involved. Because the measure does not indicate the significance of the water site, data collected should be supplemented by relative magnitudes of the use and purpose of the site.

Testing of nearby water near disposal sites could be either a regular part of the local government's performance measurement activities or a special act triggered by certain findings at the solid waste disposal site test wells and test runoff-sampling points. If readings at those points indicate danger, the endangered water use site would be tested. Otherwise it would not. This would prevent the problem of trying to conduct regular testing on private property.

Waste Disposal Effects on Air

Measure 4: *Number of presumed days that stack emissions from incinerators exceeded federal or state standards.*

Measure 5: *Number of major smoke, dust, or ash problems at each disposal site and number of sites with at least one major problem.*

Measure 6: *Number of valid complaints per year about smoke, dust, ash, or other airborne emissions from solid waste disposal sites.*

Each of these measures covers a somewhat different aspect of air quality. Measure 4 applies to incinerator facilities, and Measures 5 and 6 apply to incinerator and landfill sites.

The development of procedures for Measure 4 has been hampered by the lack of an inexpensive, reliable way of measuring stack emissions. Generally, monitoring equipment is physically attached to the incinerator stacks; this process involves several days and several thousand dollars.[3]

Federal performance standards and numerical emission limits for incinerators have been fairly broad in the past as a result of limited monitoring technology.[4] At this writing, new regulations have been proposed by EPA that would require initial compliance tests for particulate matter and opacity of stack emissions. In addition, combustor owners and operators may be required to operate a continuous monitoring system for measuring opacity and to conduct annual tests for particulate matter in emissions. New emission guidelines for metals, organics, and acid gases may also be added to existing standards for stack emissions of particulates.

The cost of collecting data for Measure 4 will depend on the changes that must be made at the combustion facility as a result of these upcoming regulations and on the frequency and extent of monitoring that is performed. Measure 5 is included to provide a reliable indicator of major smoke, dust, or ash problems at disposal sites. This measure has two forms: the number of major problems found at each disposal site (to enable the agency to determine the extent of major problems at each site) and the number of sites with at least one major problem (to enable agencies in communities with more than one solid waste disposal site to determine how many of sites have major problems). This measurement could also be analyzed looking at data in the "number of violation-days" format described in detail for Measure 1. The agency may also want to break out this information by type of problem (smoke, dust, or ash). Data can be collected by the trained observer inspection procedure described later in this chapter and in Appendix 3.

The form of Measure 5 presented here omits two factors: the duration of the problem (which might be captured by converting to a measure such as "number of days after trained observers detected problems until inspections showed these problems were corrected") and the size of the population affected by the problems (which would be hard to capture unless figures for affected populations could be attached to each of the site's observation points).[5] Also, the trained observer inspections for smoke, dust, and ash examine only the visible aspects of these airborne pollutants. Such inspections, when used at incinerator sites, do not adequately substitute for direct tests of stack emissions for particulates (see Measure 4).

Measure 6 requires that valid complaints on smoke, dust, or ash problems be routed to a central location for annual tabulation. This measure is not expressed in terms of complaint rates per 1,000 population (as is done with complaint measures in other services) because there are likely to be few complaints in a year. Also, the geographic isolation of some disposal sites makes it less likely that the number of complaints will grow with the population. At any rate, the cost of this procedure should be inexpensive.

To validate citizen complaints, agency personnel should determine, usually by direct inspection, whether the facts are as stated by the complainant and whether the problems result from a solid waste disposal site. Many local governments have a validation procedure for this type of data, and some provide regular tallies on such complaints.

Some citizens are reluctant to use the complaint process, others are chronic complainers, and many are confused about how to use the complaint process. Some potentially dangerous airborne pollutants are not detectable by the citizens' unaided senses. These problems render complaint tallies unreliable as sole indicators of pollution-related issues. At the same time, substantial changes in the number of valid complaints generally are associated with changes in underlying conditions, making a regular complaint tally appropriate as a general indicator. See Chapter 11 for suggestions on the use of complaint measures.

Extent of Recycling

Measure 7a: Number of pounds and percentage of all material diverted from the waste stream to be recycled.

Measure 7b: Percentage of households participating in local recycling program.

Recycling has become a major activity for many local governments and will continue to grow in importance. Its long-run objectives are to extend landfill life, reduce energy use, and reduce pressure on natural resources. The effects of recycling on these objectives over a long period of time involve so many controversies over true costs and benefits that no regular local measurement procedure is likely to be adequate. We suggest the short-term measurements of Measures 7a and 7b. The larger question of the relative value of various levels of recycling is left for in-depth special analyses.

Measure 7a focuses on the *amount and percentage of waste* that is recycled, and Measure 7b focuses on the *percentage of households* that participate in recycling.

The ease of obtaining data for Measure 7a depends on factors such as the place (or places) in the solid waste disposal process that the recyclable waste is separated from the waste stream. Household separation of recyclables can be measured by the collection agencies, whether the household receives curbside collection or takes its separated waste to community collection sites. The separated and unseparated waste can be weighed (on a sample basis) by the collection agency to find the percentage of waste diverted from landfill or incineration disposal.

Data resulting from source separation at transfer stations or at the actual disposal site is often less thorough and therefore less reliable as a measure of recycling levels in the community. Estimates of the percentages of waste recycled by material type are seldom recorded, although figures on the total weights of waste recycled and disposed of by other means are often available in the records for the site involved. If percentages of waste recycled by each material type are wanted, local governments will need breakdowns on nonrecycled waste by weight and type of material.[6]

Measure 7b provides an indicator of the success of a local government's progress in getting citizens to separate and put out their waste for recycling. (Measure 7b could have been included under solid waste collection in Chapter 2. It has been included here because of its importance in diverting solid waste from disposal facilities.) The collection of data for this measure depends on the type of recyclable waste collection involved. For communities that voluntarily take their separated wastes to central collection locations, the number of households (and businesses) that bring in their separated materials can be recorded and compared with the total number in the community. An alternative is to use customer surveys that ask random samples of households whether they are recycling materials. Chapter 13 provides additional information on customer surveys.

Local governments that collect recyclable waste, such as newspapers and clear and colored glass, from households and businesses can directly identify those who are recycling. For example, every year waste collectors in Montgomery County, Maryland, record the addresses of recycling households to calculate citizen participation in its mandatory newspaper recycling program. Problems with household recycling counts, such as accounting for infrequent household participation or determining whether a household has recycled all the material it was supposed to, can make estimates of this measure inaccurate. Also, although continuous tracking of participation would provide more accurate information, it is also burdensome and expensive. Less frequent tallies, such as monthly or quarterly tallies, will reduce the time and effort needed to make the measurement.

A measure of the profitability of recycling has not been included as an indicator of recycling progress, although it is likely to be of interest to the local government. Such monetary measures are outside the scope of this report.

Measures of Aesthetic Conditions around Disposal Sites

Measure 8:   *Number of major odor, noise, or appearance problems at each disposal site and the number of sites with one or more major problems.*

Measure 9:   *Number of valid citizen complaints per year concerning odor, noise, or appearance problems arising from a local disposal site.*

The information for Measure 8 can be obtained by trained observer procedures that produce reliable data on the presence or absence of disagreeable odors, noises, and unsightly appearances such as blowing litter. The same basic inspection procedure used to obtain data in Measure 5 would be applied here; the details of the procedures are discussed at the end of this chapter and in Appendix 3. As described for Measure 1, collection of data concerning

the number of violation-days could be used for Measure 8.

As with Measure 5, Measure 8 has two forms to permit the agency to track the extent of major problems at each site and the existence of the problems in the community as a whole. The agency also might want to break out the information by type of problem (odors, noise, or appearance). Also as with Measure 5, neither the duration nor the size of the population affected is captured by this form of the measurement.

Measure 9 requires that complaints be handled and validated, as in Measure 6. As with Measure 6, the cost of this process should be low. The number of complaints alone is not sufficient to measure the aesthetic effects of a site because citizens differ widely in their sensitivity to particular odors, noises, and sights. They also differ tremendously in their willingness to register a formal complaint when they find some condition unacceptable. People passing in moving vehicles may be affected by odors, noise, or appearance but are less inclined to complain about these momentary annoyances.

Measures of Safety and Health Conditions

Measure 10:   *Number of major problems with pests, gas, fires, or other health or safety hazards found at each site and the number of sites with one or more major problems.*

Measure 11:   *Number of incidents of injury and damage requiring repair or replacement of citizen property.*

Measures 10 and 11 reflect the presence of real and potential hazards that could or do lead to injuries or damage. These measures can be used to indicate to local government officials the need for preventive action.

Data for Measure 10 can be collected using the same trained observer procedures required for Measures 5 and 8; these procedures are discussed at the end of this chapter and in Appendix 3. As with Measures 5 and 8, Measure 10 does not indicate the duration of problems nor the size of the population affected. However, as noted previously, variations can be constructed in the measure to reflect these aspects if experience indicates this is desirable.

As with Measures 5 and 8, Measure 10 has two forms: the extent of major problems at each site and how many of the sites in the community have major problems. The agency also may want to break out the information by type of major problem (pests, gas, fire, or other safety hazards).

High concentrations of combustible gases, such as methane, within a landfill or collected in basement areas of nearby buildings can cause explosions and underground fires that could endanger the community. Although at this writing there are no specific federal requirements for monitoring gas, there are EPA performance standards and a requirement to control decomposition gases generated at landfill sites.[7] Regulations proposed by the EPA may require a routine methane monitoring program to be implemented by the owner or operator of a municipal solid waste landfill. Monitoring is most often achieved through examination of gas meters. Gas monitoring as frequently as weekly has been noted at some closed sites, although the frequency will depend on factors such as the age of the site. Tests to monitor methane gas are technical in nature and require special training.

The incidents of injury or property damage noted in Measure 11 include incidents of children injured by hazardous objects on the site, cars damaged by the roughness of access roads to public dumping areas, and off-site incidents such as: rat infestations of private property that are traceable to the site, traffic accidents at or near the site entrance that are caused by sanitation vehicle drivers, collection of methane in the basements of nearby buildings, waterborne infections contracted from water polluted by site leaching or runoff, and airplane encounters with birds drawn to the site. A special problem here is that, as with complaints, citizens may choose not to report such instances for a variety of reasons.

The collection of data for Measure 11 requires tabulation and, where necessary, validation of reported conditions. Because the number of incidents is likely to be very small in any given year, the cost of collecting data should be low.[8] Communities that permit the use of disposal sites by private citizens are likely to have more such incidents and to be concerned with tracking the values for this measure. Limiting access to disposal sites can keep on-site nonemployee injuries negligible.

Overall Disposal Site Conditions

Measure 12: Total number of major problems found at each disposal site and the number of sites with one or more major problems.

This summary measure covers all site problems that trained observers check—smoke, dust, ash, odors, noise, unsightly appearance, pests, gas emissions, and other health and safety hazards. Measure 12 also should cover major leachate or air quality problems found in Measures 1–6. This measure can be used to pinpoint problem sites.

The data for this measure would be obtained from the findings of previous measures. As with Measures 5, 8, and 10, Measure 12 does not reflect the duration of the problem or the population affected, but it may be modified to do so using such methods as the number of violation-days (as described for Measure 1).

Most current state or local agency inspections look at process elements, such as operation maintenance, equipment, and procedures, rather than outcomes. Process elements indicate a *potential* for problems, and outcome measures indicate the *current existence* of an environmental or health hazard. Inspections should examine both. Except for Measure 12, the measures suggested throughout this chapter are primarily outcome indicators. For Measure 12 we suggest also including those problems rated in process inspections as "major." As noted later in this chapter, few inspection forms call for designating problems as "major" or "minor." Thus, in most cases, the inspection process needs to be altered to define major process problems and include the categories on the inspection form so that major process problems can be noted.

Measure 12 summarizes the results of past inspections and helps public officials formulate solid waste disposal policy in their community.

Other Measures

The following measures have not been included in the suggested set of measures because of special difficulties in problem definition, data collection, or interpretation. Local governments, however, may want to add these measures.

Number of fires and number of fire-days per year at landfills. Because fires at landfills are generally evidence of poor management and because uncontrolled fires can cause pollution, the number of fires per year and the number of days when fires occur (or fire-days) per year are of potential importance. However, fires vary greatly in their spread and their effects on citizens. For example, some fires may be ignited by hot or smoldering refuse just brought in. A small, quickly extinguished fire of this type is inconsequential to citizens. Some fires may constitute controlled burning to reduce the risk of vast, uncontrolled fires. As sanctioned by local health officials, and with proper controls to keep smoke and other airborne pollutants from escaping, these fires need not be hazards and should not be counted as such.

There is also the problem of collecting the data. Unless an independent observer is stationed at the site to check for fires, the records would have to be kept by landfill personnel, who might be inclined to minimize the number of fires reported. Hence, it is suggested that fire detection be handled through trained observer procedures and citizen complaints (see Measures 5 and 10). Some local governments may also want to track the number of fire citations made by local health authorities. These health inspections would provide another source of data on fires at landfills.

Number of years of expected lifetime remaining at currently owned solid waste disposal sites. This provides an indication of the adequacy of current facilities. It is important to public officials and can indicate major future problems. If tracked by a community, the measure can project a figure such as the tons per week expected over time (possibly assuming a fixed percentage of growth in population and waste per person), convert that figure to cubic yards by using the compression ratios being achieved, and compare the result with the amount of space available.

The Trained Observer Rating Procedures at Disposal Sites

Trained observer ratings are called for in Measures 5, 8, 10, and 12. This section presents suggestions

---

Exhibit 3-4

Trained Observer Rating Scales at Solid Waste Disposal Sites

Characteristic	Rating scale
1. Cleanliness of areas near site	1.0 to 4.0, based on photographic standards (see Chapter 2 for details).
2. Appearance of site from areas nearby	1.0 View from the perimeter point has no unattractive features of the disposal site in foreground; any unattractive features are visible only in the distant background. ("Unattractive features" are any of the items listed in the definitions of ratings 2, 3, and 4 as unattractive.)
	2.0 The only unattractive features in view are raw earth or sanitation trucks.
	3.0 Sanitation equipment (excluding trucks) can be seen either parked or in motion, or queues of sanitation equipment trucks delivering refuse to the site can be seen extending outside the site perimeters into areas of substantial general traffic.
	4.0 Uncovered refuse (loose or in bags or containers) or blowing paper can be seen.
3. Odors	1.0 No odor detectable.
	2.0 Odor detected could be from site but cannot be confirmed; or is part of pattern of similar odors and is not principal component.
	3.0 Odor detected, confirmed as principally coming from site, but not offensive enough to cause an individual to take steps to avoid it.
	4.0 Odor detected, confirmed as principally coming from site, and is offensive enough to cause an individual to seek to avoid it.
4. Noise	1.0 No noise detectable.
	2.0 Noise detected could be from site but cannot be confirmed; or site noise is part of pattern of similar noise and is not principal component.
	3.0 Noise detected, confirmed as principally coming from site, but is not offensive enough to cause an individual to take steps to avoid it.
	4.0 Noise detected, confirmed as principally coming from site, and is offensive enough to cause an individual to seek to avoid it.
5. Smoke, dust, and ash	1.0 No blowing dust, no burning; for incinerator sites, no ashes stored in exposed places or in open containers where they can be blown by winds.
	2.0 No blowing dust, no visible smoke escaping from area of burning operation (defined as five feet from burning material); for incinerators, some ashes stored in exposed places or open containers where they could be blown by winds but no ashes currently being blown.
	3.0 Considerable blowing dust, or some visible smoke does escape area of burning operation; or for incinerators, intermittent blowing dust, ash, or visible smoke.
	4.0 Visible smoke is escaping from burning area continuously or almost continuously; for incinerators, blowing dust or ash or visible smoke is in evidence continuously or whenever wind blows.

for local governments to use in trained observer rating systems for solid waste disposal services. Each government adopts its own procedures and standards to be compatible with state and federal regulations, and to reflect local conditions. The general requirements for trained observer operations are discussed in more detail in Chapter 12. Appendix 3 details procedures for solid waste disposal sites.

The trained observer inspections are aimed at obtaining ratings on the following characteristics: the presence of airborne emissions such as smoke, dust, and ash (Measure 5); the presence of odors, noise, or unsightly appearance (Measure 8); and the presence of pests and other safety hazards (Measure 10). The inspection procedure consists of two parts: (1) an external inspection of the entrance and selected perimeter points around the disposal or incineration area (to obtain ratings on appearance, odors, and noise) and (2) an internal inspection of the landfill or incineration area (to obtain ratings on other characteristics).

Exhibit 3-4 provides illustrative rating scales for inspections. The scales shown use four rating categories. For Measures 5, 8, 10, and 12 the agency will need to determine which categories, represent a "major" problem. For example, any rating of 3.5 or 4.0 probably should be considered a major problem. Exhibit 3-5 illustrates how the trained observer ratings might be summarized in a report for local government.

In addition to outcomes, Measure 12 includes major problems in the procedures (process) of site operation. To include these, the agency needs to use an inspection rating form that distinguishes major

---

Exhibit 3-4, continued

Trained Observer Rating Scales at Solid Waste Disposal Sites

Characteristic	Rating scale
6. Pests	1.0 No evidence of rats or insects.
	2.0 Evidence of insects but no evidence of rats.
	3.0 Evidence of rats but no rats seen.
	4.0 Rats seen.
7. Health and safety hazards	1.0 No uncovered wastes.
	2.0 A few scattered items, but no uncovered food wastes, toxic wastes, dead animals, or bulky goods providing potential shelter for pests.
	3.0 A few scattered items or uncovered, unprocessed[1] waste including food waste, toxic wastes, dead animals, or some bulky goods providing potential shelter for pests.
	3.5 For landfill: widespread uncovered waste, but no piles of wastes and most of the ground is visible; for incineration: widespread, uncovered, unprocessed[1] waste, but no piles of waste and most of the ground is visible.
	4.0 Uncovered or (for incineration) unprocessed[1] wastes either cover large areas of the ground or are in piles.
8. Other hazards	1.0 Restricted area.
	2.0 Unrestricted area but no hazards.
	3.0 Unrestricted area with some hazards but none likely to lead to serious injury. Hazards included are small amounts of broken glass, metal furniture, and other structures; and improper or inadequate directions on access roads used by citizens, but no hazards likely to lead to damage, even if citizens inadvertently ride over or walk on them.
	4.0 Unrestricted area with some hazards capable of leading to serious injury. Hazards included are refrigerators with doors still attached, places where steep falls to the sludge bed are possible for citizens disposing of refuse on their own, uncontrolled fires, large amounts of broken glass, and rusty nails.

[1]Unprocessed wastes require same-day covering with earth to prevent insect and rodent problems. Wastes processed through incineration or milling, by contrast, may often be disposed of without the need for daily earth covering.

from minor deficiencies. Exhibit 3-6 is a typical form used for rating solid waste facilities. Such a form will need to be modified to include and define thoroughly what constitutes a "major" deficiency to provide the information for Measure 12. Inspection forms might provide three options for each element examined: "major deficiency," "minor deficiency," and "no deficiency."

These options enable officials to gauge the extent of the problems discovered through the inspection. Many local governments do not use a standard inspection form to record inspection observations; local inspectors tend to report their findings only if a problem is discovered. An inspection form or checklist, however, helps to ensure a thorough inspection and records the results so that others can judge whether disposal facilities are working well or are in violation of inspection standards or have major problems.

Frequency of Trained Observer Inspections

The principal considerations in determining frequency are the variable effects of weather, the cost per inspection, and the likely variability in ratings from one inspection to another. High temperature, high humidity, and high wind all tend to aggravate the problems associated with disposal operations, such as odors or blowing dust and paper. If inspections are made once every two weeks or more frequently, there will probably be sufficient variety in weather conditions to provide an overall picture of site conditions. However, if inspections are made monthly, quarterly, or only annually, weather conditions should be considered in setting the times of inspections. (A procedure for accounting for weather is given in Appendix 3.)

If conditions vary considerably over time, more frequent inspections will be required to adequately track site performance than will be required if conditions vary only slightly from inspection to inspection. To consider this factor, the initial inspections might be done on a weekly basis, followed by a shift to less frequent inspections if the range of ratings over the initial period is narrow. In general, inspections and reporting should be done at least quarterly.

Trained Observer Procedure Testing

Local governments using trained observer procedures should test the procedures to determine if the terms used in the rating definitions are adequately

---

Exhibit 3-5

Illustrative Format: Results of Trained Observer Ratings for Solid Waste Disposal Sites A and B

| Characteristic | Check column if a major problem exists[1] | | | | | |
| | Site A | | | Site B | | |
	This period	Previous period	Same period last year	This period	Previous period	Same period last year
Cleanliness of areas near site						
Appearance of site from areas nearby						
Presence of odors near site						
Presence of noise near site						
Presence of at least one of the above aesthetic problems (Measure 8)						
Smoke, dust, or ash (Measure 5)						
Pests						
Gas level						
Fires						
Other hazards						
The presence of at least one of the above hazards (Measure 10)						
The presence of at least one of the above conditions (Measure 12)						

[1]Only a check mark representing the latest condition for the period need be shown.
Adding the check marks will give the number of major problems for measures in
Exhibit 3-1. A "major" problem might be defined as one with a trained observer rating
of "3.5" or "4.0" on a rating scale such as contained in Exhibit 3-4.

Exhibit 3-6

Sample Form for Solid Waste Disposal Site "Process" Inspections: State of Maryland

The following is an official Waste Management Administration inspection report of the below-named solid waste management facility Failure to correct any violations within the time and manner specified by the Administration may result in a suspension or cessation of operations at this facility. Any violations observed during this inspection are described in the attached report of observations

I. GENERAL INFORMATION

Permit Number [ ][ ][ ][ ][ ][ ][ ][ ]   YR ___ MO ___ DY ___   TIME ___   TELEPHONE _____

Facility Name _____   Owner's Name _____

Address _____ Zip _____

Description of Work Activity _____

_____

Weather Conditions _____

Facility is in compliance with site specific conditions of the permit, _____ Yes _____ No

II. SUPERVISOR'S EVALUATION (S = SATISFACTORY, U = UNSATISFACTORY, N/A = NOT APPLICABLE)

General Waste Management Practices _____ Records and Reports_____ Compliance Schedule_____

Operation and Maintenance _____ Compliance Action Required _____ Yes _____ No   Date of Evaluation _____ / _____ / _____

Comments _____

_____

Supervisor's Name _____ Supervisor's Signature _____

III. SANITARY LANDFILL

	IN COMPLIANCE	
	YES	NO
A. Unloading of solid waste is restricted to the working face of the landfill.	☐	☐
B. Cover Material		
1) Daily Cover	☐	☐
2) Cover in intermediate areas	☐	☐
3) Cover in completed areas	☐	☐
C. Grading and surface water drainage of working face is adequate.	☐	☐
D. Access roads are adequate and controlled.	☐	☐
E. Available equipment is adequate to handle present waste load.	☐	☐
F. Nuisances and vectors are controlled.	☐	☐
G. Erosion and sediment control measures are in accordance with approved operating plans.	☐	☐
H. Litter is controlled.	☐	☐
I. Fire protection is adequate.	☐	☐
J. Site is properly supervised.	☐	☐
	YES	NO
K. Operating information (days, hours) is posted at entrance.	☐	☐
L. Monitoring wells are operational.	☐	☐
M. Landfill gas control devices are operational.	☐	☐
N. Leachate is observed?	☐	☐
If Yes, is leachate controlled?	☐	☐
O. Unacceptable waste types are observed?	☐	☐
P. Sewage sludge is acceptable at facility?	☐	☐
If Yes, is it permitted?	☐	☐
Q. Tires are accepted at facility?	☐	☐
If Yes, are tires handled adequately?	☐	☐

IV. COMPOSTING FACILITIES

	IN COMPLIANCE	
	YES	NO
A. Facility is free of odors and/or nuisances.	☐	☐
B. Facility, including equipment, access roads, and composting pad is maintained in a clean and sanitary manner.	☐	☐
C. All sediment and erosion control measures including ponds, are properly maintained.	☐	☐
D. All trucks are leak-proof and cleaned before leaving the facility.	☐	☐
E. All measures to insure complete pathogen kill are properly carried out.	☐	☐
F. Air, water, sludge, and compost samples are analyzed and reported on schedule as per facility's Operation and Maintenance Manual.	☐	☐
G. All observed finished compost (ready for distribution) meets State requirements.	☐	☐

V. SEWAGE SLUDGE LANDSPREADING

	IN COMPLIANCE	
	YES	NO
A. Site is properly prepared (including sediment and erosion control, if necessary) for application of sewage sludge.	☐	☐
B. Sludge is applied only to permitted area.	☐	☐
C. Digested sewage sludge is properly applied to land.	☐	☐
D. Odors and/or nuisances are controlled.	☐	☐
E. Transport vehicles are leak-proof and are cleaned after disposing of sewage sludge.	☐	☐

VI. TRANSFER STATIONS

	IN COMPLIANCE	
	YES	NO
A. Operating information (days, hours) is posted at entrance.	☐	☐
B. Facility access roads are of sufficient construction to withstand anticipated loads.	☐	☐
C. Dust is controlled.	☐	☐
D. Litter is controlled.	☐	☐
E. The transfer of solid waste is confined to loading area.	☐	☐
F. Facility is maintained in a clean and sanitary condition.	☐	☐
G. Adequate fire-control equipment is available.	☐	☐
H. Truck wheel curbs and tie-downs are provided.	☐	☐
I. Tipping, loading, and unloading areas are constructed of impervious material.	☐	☐
J. A written emergency operational plan is provided for an alternative waste handling system.	☐	☐

VII. INCINERATORS

	IN COMPLIANCE	
	YES	NO
A. Access roads are adequate and controlled.	☐	☐
B. Tipping, unloading and loading areas are constructed of impervious materials.	☐	☐
C. Disease vectors are controlled.	☐	☐
D. Nuisances (dust and odors) and vermin are controlled.	☐	☐
E. Ash storage area is properly maintained.	☐	☐
F. Wash-down water is properly managed.	☐	☐
G. Surface runoff is adequately controlled	☐	☐

Inspector's

Name: _____ Sign: _____

Title: _____

Agency: _____ Office Location: _____

Date of Inspection: _____ / _____ / _____

I acknowledge receipt of this inspection report however, my signature should not be construed as indicating agreement with the conditions described therein.

Facility Rep: _____ Sign: _____

Title: _____

Telephone Number: _____

Source: State of Maryland, Department of the Environment, Solid Waste Management Facility Inspection Report

defined to ensure that a reasonable level of reliability can be maintained among trained observers. This testing should be done before full implementation of the procedure. A sample of observation points initially rated at each site should be rerated independently by a second person, so that the ratings can be compared. A high percentage—at least 75 percent—of the ratings should be identical for the procedure to be considered operational.

A period of approximately three months should be allowed for initial preparations, such as setting up the rating forms and identifying the observation points at the sites where ratings will be taken. An additional period of three months is advisable to train the observers, check their reliability, and note the reasonableness and meaningfulness of the range of ratings obtained. After that, if rater reliability is satisfactory, regular operations can be undertaken.

Once trained observer inspecting is implemented, local governments should continue to provide training in the use of the procedures for trained observers and periodically check each inspector's ratings by another "judge" to assure the continued reliability of the observers.

Trained Observer Costs

Landfill inspections require about two hours, depending on the size of the site, with some of that time taken up in transit to perimeter points. Inspection of incineration sites should also take about two hours. The time required to perform and record the observations at each of the perimeter points and at the operation within the facilities will generally take only a few minutes. The process inspections, used for Measure 12 (as well as for other regulatory purposes), will likely require one-half of a day.

The estimated time per site for performing trained observer inspections once every two weeks for a year is about 13 employee-days, assuming that the disposal sites are not widely scattered. Analytical and clerical time will probably double the total to close to 30 employee-days per site. The cost will depend on the size and remoteness of a disposal site and the dispersion of its activities.

1 Leaching is the process by which moisture in the waste, or rainwater infiltrating through the soil cover and the waste, may carry contaminants through the underlying soil into groundwater below and around a landfill. Water contamination characteristics attributed to leaching include changes in five-day biological oxygen demand (BOD_5), coliform count, dissolved solids, conductance, and alkalinity.

2 The particular quality characteristics of concern include coliform, BOD_5, and suspended solids. Because contaminated runoff may be well mixed into receiving bodies of water before any contact or use occurs, mixing should be considered in determining whether the pollutants have been caused by the runoff. In contrast, leaching into groundwater involves the percolation of contaminants into the water across a broad front without substantial opportunity for mixing. State codes vary considerably as to how much mixing is permitted before the water quality criteria must be met.

3 An alternative procedure is to measure the ambient air quality in the vicinity of the incinerator, using the concentration of particulates per cubic meter as the measure and the EPA ambient air quality standards for reference.

4 Currently, the EPA requires performance testing at start-up and then afterward by a trained tester only when the agency desires to inspect.

5 See Appendix 3 for a discussion of the procedure for selecting observation points.

6 Such estimates would require some periodic (probably quarterly at most) sampling of refuse composition, but this sampling should not require more than a few employee-days per sample, given the relatively broad categories used. For example, the city of Los Angeles has performed weekly analyses of a sample of all refuse collected at cost of about two employee-days per analysis. A sample consists of a truckload from a specified area.

7 EPA, "Guidelines for the Land Disposal of Solid Waste." Code of Federal Regulation, Number 40, Part 241.206.1, July, 1989.

8 Local governments should consider continuing to report measures that consistently indicate no problem, particularly if the data-collecting costs are small. Such measures help assure a more balanced picture of service performance than will occur if only measures showing problems are reported.

Chapter 4

Park and Recreation Services

Most local governments measure the effectiveness of park and recreation services, but their current procedures have major deficiencies. Past evaluations of local government park and recreation activities have focused more on inputs, such as the number of acres of land, the number of facilities, and the number of arts-and-crafts programs provided, rather than on outputs, such as the number of persons served and their satisfaction with those services. The park and recreation agencies of most local governments lack systematic information on even the most fundamental facts: What percentage of the population is being served? How satisfied are citizens with their park and recreation services? Who does not use the services and why not? To what extent do accessibility, dislike of the facility, or lack of knowledge about recreation opportunities affect the use of facilities and programs? How many park and recreation areas have unusable—or even unsafe—facilities that can mar the enjoyment of users?

The objectives, measures, and data collection procedures in this chapter focus on park and recreation opportunities for individual citizens and households. For this report, park and recreation services are considered an end product, not a means to another end such as reducing juvenile delinquency, alleviating drug dependency, or improving mental and physical health.

Objectives and Related Effectiveness Measures

A basic objective for park and recreation services that seems common to most communities is

> **To provide for all citizens a variety of enjoyable leisure opportunities that are accessible, safe, uncrowded, physically attractive, and well maintained.**

A set of measures to help indicate progress toward meeting the various parts of this objective is presented in Exhibit 4-1.

The objectives and measures identified in this chapter can assist in evaluating the total park and recreation system. Most of the procedures can assess effectiveness in each major geographic area of the community. These procedures also can be used to assess specific agency functions (such as park maintenance or public information about recreation opportunities), or specific activities (such as swimming or arts and crafts). Some of the data collection procedures, such as the on-site surveys of users and trained observer ratings, permit conclusions about specific facilities.

Although these measures focus on public facilities and activities, private and quasi-public efforts (such as voluntary youth-serving agencies) indirectly influence some of the measured values. For example, data on the accessibility of swimming opportunities can include the availability of private but non-restricted facilities. The measure of "households rating neighborhood's park and recreational opportunities as satisfactory" (or unsatisfactory) reflects private and public opportunities. As such, the measure can be used to indicate the adequacy of and the need for more or different facilities.

Group Measurement Data by Population and Client Characteristics

The different perspectives of various population or client groups are very important, and the performance relative to each group should be distinguished whenever data collection procedures permit. Eight factors are important to recreation decisions: area of residence, age, sex, income, race or ethnic group, education, existence of handicap, and access to an automobile or public transportation. The last characteristic is important because differences exist in the character, variety, and level of satisfaction with recreation experiences between those with and those without access to automobiles or public transportation.

The data collection procedures suggested in this chapter generally permit performance data to be grouped by these eight characteristics if there are not too many categories for any one characteristic. For example, the household survey sampling procedures probably can permit a government to distinguish four to six different geographic areas or income groups within a jurisdiction.

The particular clientele groupings used should be related to the specific characteristics of those groups for which programs and activities are planned and operated by the park and recreation agency. For example, an agency might use the following six age groupings: less than 6 years old, 6 to 13, 14 to 19, 20 to 34, 35 to 64, and 65 and over.

Principal Recommended Measurement Procedures

Five data sources are presented here for collecting the data for the measures listed in Exhibit 4-1.

Exhibit 4-1

Effectiveness Measures for Park and Recreation Services

Overall objective: To provide for all citizens a variety of enjoyable leisure opportunities that are accessible, safe, uncrowded, physically attractive, and well-maintained.

Objective	Quality characteristic	Specific measure[1]	Data collection procedure
Enjoyableness	Citizen satisfaction	1. Percentage of households rating neighborhood park and recreation opportunities as satisfactory.	Household survey
	User satisfaction	2. Percentage of those households using community park or recreation facilities and programs who rate them as satisfactory.	Household or user survey
	Use—participation rates	3. Percentage of community households using (or not using) community park or recreation facilities at least once over a specific past period, such as three months.	Household survey
	Use—attendance	4. Number of visits at park and recreation sites.	Attendance statistics
Fewer crowds	User satisfaction	5. Percentage of user households rating community facilities as too crowded.	Household or user survey
	Nonuser satisfaction	6. Percentage of nonuser households giving crowded conditions as a reason for nonuse of facilities.	Household survey
	Crowding factor	7. Average peak-hour attendance divided by capacity.	Attendance statistics and estimates of carrying capacity
Physical attractiveness	User satisfaction	8. Percentage of user households rating physical attractiveness as satisfactory.	Household or user survey
	Nonuser satisfaction	9. Percentage of nonuser households giving lack of physical attractiveness as reason for nonuse.	Household survey
	Facility cleanliness	10. Percentage of user households rating cleanliness as satisfactory.	Household or user survey
		11. Percentage of facilities whose cleanliness is rated satisfactory by a trained observer.	Trained observer ratings
Well-maintained facilities	Facility/equipment condition	12. Percentage of user households rating the condition of facility/equipment as satisfactory.	Household or user survey
		13. Percentage of parks and other recreation facilities whose physical condition is rated as satisfactory (by a trained observer). Ratings should also be presented for specific features—lawns, playing areas, restrooms, benches and picnic tables, and so forth.	Trained observer ratings
Safety	Hazardous facilities/ equipment	14. Number of serious injuries (say, per 10,000 visits).	Accident and attendance statistics
		15. Percentage of facilities with one or more safety hazards.	Trained observer ratings

Household Surveys

A periodic survey of a random sample of a jurisdiction's households is a very useful tool for collecting effectiveness data. Data for 19 of the 27 measures of effectiveness proposed in Exhibit 4-1 can be collected with such a survey.

The household survey can obtain information on overall satisfaction with park and recreational opportunities and ratings of accessibility, cleanliness, safety, helpfulness of personnel, and condition of the facilities. In addition, the same survey can obtain figures on the percentages of the community that use park and recreation facilities. For those who do not use local government recreation services, the survey can also provide the percentage of citizens and give reasons for nonuse. This will enable park and recreation planners to distinguish reasons that can be affected by the local government from those that cannot.

An example of this type of questionnaire is provided in Appendix 4.

To undertake this type of survey, a park and recreation agency will likely need outside assistance. Preferably, the sample of households should be split into four quarterly samples, so public managers can obtain seasonal and more timely information.

Exhibit 4-1, continued

Effectiveness Measures for Park and Recreation Services

Objective	Quality characteristic	Specific measure[1]	Data collection procedure
	Criminal incidents	16. Number of criminal incidents (say, per 10,000 visits).	Criminal incident statistics of some park and recreation agencies and most municipal police forces; attendance statistics
	User satisfaction	17. Percentage of user households rating safety of facilities as satisfactory.	Household or user survey
	Nonuser satisfaction	18. Percentage of nonuser households giving lack of safety as a reason for nonuse of facilities.	Household survey
Accessibility	Physical accessibility	19. Percentage of citizens living within (or not within) 15 to 30 minutes of travel time of a community park or recreation facility, distinguished by type of facility and principal relevant mode of transportation.	Counts from mapping latest census tract population figures against location of facilities, with appropriate travel-time radius drawn around each facility
	Physical accessibility— user satisfaction	20. Percentage of user households rating physical accessibility as satisfactory.	Household or user survey
	Physical accessibility— nonuser satisfaction	21. Percentage of nonuser households giving poor physical accessibility as a reason for nonuse.	Household survey
	Hours/days of operation— user satisfaction	22. Percentage of user households rating hours of operation as satisfactory.	Household or user survey
	Hours/days of operation— nonuser satisfaction	23. Percentage of nonuser households giving unsatisfactory operating hours as a reason for nonuse.	Household survey
Variety of interesting activities	User satisfaction	24. Percentage of user households rating the variety of program activities as satisfactory.	Household or user survey
	Nonuser satisfaction	25. Percentage of nonuser households giving lack of program variety as a reason for nonuse.	Household survey
Helpfulness of staff	Staff helpfulness— user satisfaction	26. Percentage of user households rating helpfulness or attitude of staff as satisfactory.	Household or user survey
	Staff helpfulness— nonuser satisfaction	27. Percentage of nonuser households giving poor staff attitude as a reason for nonuse.	Household survey

[1]Officials who wish to focus on amount of local dissatisfaction may substitute "unsatisfactory" for the term "satisfactory" in many of these measures.

The multiservice household survey, as discussed in other chapters of this book, can be used for this purpose. However, the number and scope of the questions will probably have to be pared down. The advantage of the multiservice household survey is that the agency can obtain information on park and recreation operations at less cost.

User Surveys

Surveys of park and recreation users are an excellent source of information. Such surveys can provide customer feedback on satisfaction with specific programs and facilities. They are within the capability of most park and recreation agencies to conduct. Because they are administered at park and recreation sites, user surveys are easier to administer than household surveys. To avoid poorly worded questions and sloppy surveying techniques, some outside assistance is recommended.

User surveys can produce data on 10 of the 27 measures of effectiveness. An example of a park and recreation user questionnaire is included as Appendix 5.

Trained Observer Ratings

Trained observers can collect information on the condition of park and recreation facilities. Their ratings provide data for measures of physical conditions such as cleanliness, the usability/maintenance of equipment and facilities, and the presence of physical safety hazards. Trained observer procedures involve visual ratings of conditions based on pre-specified checklists and rating scales. The latter incorporate written definitions and/or benchmark photographs to help ensure consistent ratings across facilities and through time. The observers can be government staff, citizen volunteers, or interns. The data collected by the trained observers complements user and household perceptions. Appendix 6 gives an example of trained observer procedures that can be used to collect these ratings.

Mapping

To gauge physical accessibility to facilities—a crucial factor contributing to facility use—a mapping technique is suggested. This technique plots a community's population distribution against the location of existing recreation facilities, providing a calculation of the percentages of the population within or beyond a convenient time or distance (such as fifteen minutes) of a neighborhood recreation facility.

Community Records

Basic community records can also be used to track attendance (where obtainable), overcrowding (measured as estimates of average daily attendance divided by carrying capacity), and rates of injuries and criminal incidents. Thus comparisons can be made over time, among various areas, and for particular facilities in the community.

Individual Measures

This section discusses the measures shown in Exhibit 4-1 and describes procedures for collecting data for each measure. The measures are arranged in eight groups:

- Enjoyableness (Measures 1–4)
- Crowdedness (Measures 5–7)
- Physical attractiveness (Measures 8–11)
- Facility maintenance quality (Measures 12–13)
- Safety (Measures 14–18)
- Accessibility (Measures 19–23)
- Variety of interesting activities (Measures 24–25)
- Helpfulness of staff (Measures 26 and 27).

Measures of Enjoyableness

Measure 1:   *Percentage of households rating neighborhood park and recreation opportunities as satisfactory.*

Measure 2:   *Percentage of those households using community park or recreation facilities and programs who rate them as satisfactory.*

Measures 1 and 2 are direct indices of satisfaction; they call for obtaining citizens' ratings of the level of satisfaction with their recreation opportunities.

Measure 1 is the more comprehensive of the direct satisfaction measures. Using the household survey (discussed in detail later), it produces a rating from a representative cross section of all households in the community. Measure 2 focuses only on those citizens who have used at least one local- government-operated facility during a recent time period. If the data are obtained from a household survey, the findings should represent a cross section of the whole population of users in the community. If feedback is obtained from a sample of users of specific facilities, those individuals will represent users of all local government facilities only to the extent that the user surveys cover all programs and facilities or at least represent them.

All measures that inquire into "satisfactory" ratings by citizens or users may be changed to focus on "unsatisfactory" ratings if the jurisdiction believes this focus is more useful.

Data for Measure 1 can be obtained by surveying a representative sample of households in the community. Question 27 in Appendix 1 or Question 3 in Appendix 4 can be used to obtain the data.

For ratings by users (Measure 2), either a household or user survey can be used. If a household survey is used, Question 6j in Appendix 4 could obtain the data. If a user survey is undertaken, Question 19 of Appendix 5 can be used.

One problem is how to define a "user." The questionnaire in Appendix 4 somewhat arbitrarily defines a user as any household that has used a facility at least once in the past three months (see Question 4, Appendix 4). A local government may prefer to alter the definition to consider a different time period or to require more uses during the given time before considering the household a "user." Another possibility is to tally the responses separately for households with varying amounts of use.

The longer the time period asked about, the more difficult it will be for respondents to remember accurately experiences and impressions. The period asked about should be no longer than the length of time between surveys.

In obtaining citizen ratings on overall satisfaction, it is desirable for the local government to also obtain ratings on particular aspects of the facilities. These include hours of operation, cleanliness, condition of equipment, helpfulness and attitude of personnel, crowdedness, safety, and accessibility. Questions 6a–i of Appendix 4 and Questions 3–15 of Appendix 5 illustrate how such data can be obtained. Most of these ratings are used in subsequent measures and are discussed later in the chapter.

Measure 3:   *Percentage of community households using (or not using) community park or recreation facilities at least once over a specific past period, such as three months.*

Measure 4:   *Number of visits at park and recreation sites.*

For Measures 3 and 4, the assumption is that people "vote with their feet." That is, citizens indicate their satisfaction with programs or facilities by using them. Others may argue that citizens, particularly the less affluent, have few choices and are a "captive audience." To the extent this is true, attendance and participation rates will not indicate the degree of enjoyableness of the facilities. Then, too, users of facilities will have different degrees of satisfaction. But use represents an important indicator of the value of the recreation activities offered.

The traditional method for estimating use is by attendance figures, as in Measure 4. Most agencies keep some statistics, for instance, the numbers of persons attending classes and using facilities with controlled access, such as community centers. Generally lacking are attendance counts at open facilities such as parks and playgrounds. In the latter cases, attendance estimates are obtained using various formulas, often based on counts at peak periods. For example, the National Park and Recreation Association has offered a "peak count" formula to determine summer playground attendance. This procedure calls for multiplying a factor of 1.8 by the morning peak attendance count, 2.5 by the afternoon peak count, and 1.8 by the evening peak count. These figures are added to produce the estimated daily attendance.[1]

However, attendance counts do not indicate how many different persons or families use the facilities because those attending may be repeat users. The household survey is possibly the only way to obtain participation rates. Measure 3 provides an estimate of the percentage of households that have (or have not) used community facilities. Questions 4 and 5 in Appendix 4 can be used to obtain this information.

Determining reasons for nonuse is critical in assessing the objective of reaching all citizens who desire to be served. Thus the nonuse rates should be broken down by reason for nonuse. Questions 7 and 8 in Appendix 4 can be used to obtain this information. The latter question includes a checklist of reasons for nonuse.

Many governments have found it helpful to group the reasons for nonuse into those that are potentially within local government control (facility unknown, too far away, activities not interesting, too dangerous, poor condition, too crowded, inconvenient hours) and those that are probably beyond local government control (too busy, poor health, do not like other users). Most of the reasons for nonuse that are categorized as potentially within government control are also used as the basis for other indicators of effectiveness—Measures 6 (crowded conditions), 9 (lack of physical attractiveness), 12 and 13 (poor condition), 18 (safety problems), 21 (inaccessibility), 23 (inconvenient hours), 25 (lack of interesting programs), and 27 (poor staff). Two other reasons for nonuse also could be added: lack of information or knowledge about the facility or programs, and the cost of using facilities or programs. Data for these latter characteristics can be obtained through Questions 8a and 8f of Appendix 4.

A note of caution is in order when basing action on reasons for nonuse. Experiences in other service areas, particularly in the use of public transportation, suggest that actions based primarily on reported reasons for nonuse do not always stimulate greater use. Thus, local government officials using these data should be careful to treat them as approximate and tentative, more indicative than definitive. Such information is useful for guiding local government action, but confirming information also should be sought.

Measure 3 is expressed as household participation rates. The questions in Appendix 4 ask about the household's participation. The accuracy of respondents' reports on use by other household members is not clear. This issue is discussed further in the section on the household survey and in Chapter 13.

Measures of Crowded Conditions

Measure 5:   *Percentage of user households rating community facilities as too crowded.*

Measure 6:   *Percentage of nonuser households giving crowded conditions as a reason for nonuse of facilities.*

Measure 7:   *Average peak-hour attendance divided by capacity.*

These three measures cover three complementary perspectives. Measure 5 obtains ratings of crowdedness directly from persons who have used community facilities, based on either the household survey (for example, see Question 6h of Appendix 4) or a user survey (see Question 7 of Appendix 5). Measure 6 provides the percentage of nonuser households that give crowded conditions as a reason for nonuse, as obtained from a question such as 8d in Appendix 4.

Citizen perception gives a different perspective from that obtained using attendance counts. The citizen ratings obtained from Measures 5 and 6 are important in assessing crowding because less crowding is not always preferred.[2]

Measure 7 provides a statistic based on actual attendance records. It attempts to relate attendance counts to an estimate of the "capacity" for various recreation sites. For some facilities, such as tennis courts and swimming pools, the capacity can be defined with some precision. However, defining capacity is more difficult for playgrounds, open space, and multiple-use facilities.

To consider all facilities rather than each one individually, Measure 7 can be changed to the "number of recreational facilities in which average daily attendances exceeded the capacity." However, the average figures may hide the specific frequency of occasions when capacity was exceeded. Preferably, the number of occasions when capacity was exceeded should be estimated, perhaps in number of hours. The feasibility of gathering such information comprehensively, given the current state of the art of atten-

dance measurements, seems questionable. The data collection does seem feasible for activities such as swimming, golf, tennis, and various recreation classes, in which it is possible to monitor attendance counts, waiting times, and perhaps the number of turnaways, especially during periods of peak use.

Measures of Physical Attractiveness

Measure 8:   *Percentage of user households rating physical attractiveness as satisfactory.*

Measure 9:   *Percentage of nonuser households giving lack of physical attractiveness as reason for nonuse.*

Measure 10:   *Percentage of user households rating cleanliness as satisfactory.*

Measure 11:   *Percentage of facilities whose cleanliness is rated satisfactory by a trained observer.*

Measures 8 and 10 rely on assessments from households that have used park and recreation facilities for ratings of overall physical attractiveness and facility cleanliness. The household or user survey can be used to obtain this information. Examples of appropriate questions are 6c and 6d in Appendix 4 and Questions 4 and 9 in Appendix 5.

Measure 9 provides the percentage of nonuser households that give lack of physical attractiveness as the reason for nonuse (based on a question such as 8e, Appendix 4). The same qualifications on reasons for nonuse mentioned in the discussion of Measure 3 also apply here. The data need to be obtained from the household survey.

To complement these subjective, survey-based assessments, objective measures of facility cleanliness can be obtained using trained observers (Measure 11). Trained observers are individuals (or teams) trained to make accurate visual ratings of cleanliness and other conditions using pre-specified rating scales. The ratings are based on photographic standards and/or precise written definitions that the observers assign to various cleanliness (or other) conditions.

The trained observer procedures are described later in this chapter and are illustrated in Appendix 6. The technique focuses on individual facilities and can identify specific problems in specific facilities as well as provide an overall measure for all facilities. Thus, the agency can use the findings from these ratings for allocating its resources, especially if the ratings are made frequently.

A local government will need to decide what constitutes an unsatisfactory level of cleanliness to translate the trained observer ratings into Measure 11.

Measures of Facility Maintenance Quality

Measure 12: *Percentage of user households rating the condition of facility/equipment as satisfactory.*

Measure 13: *Percentage of parks and other recreation facilities whose physical condition is rated as satisfactory by a trained observer. Ratings should also be presented for specific features—lawns, playing areas, restrooms, benches and picnic tables, and so forth.*

The condition of park and recreation facilities and equipment is closely associated with the facility's physical attractiveness, but it involves more than just attractiveness. How well does the equipment work? To what extent can it be used for its intended purposes? Are the ballfields and basketball courts ready for scheduled or unscheduled games? Are playground swings missing, tangled, or broken? Are paths and parking lots rutted or obstructed?

Measure 12 collects user perceptions concerning equipment and facility condition. See Question 5 in the user survey (Appendix 5) and Question 6e in the household survey (Appendix 4).

Measure 13 provides a more objective perspective on equipment and facility condition through actual ratings of the facilities by trained observers. Although an overall rating of the condition of facilities (parks, playgrounds, recreation centers, etc.) is probably of greatest interest to top management, the data can be broken down further by types of features and equipment that can be used by agency personnel to help them determine what actions need to be taken. The trained observer procedures discussed later in this chapter and in Appendix 6 allow an agency to prepare ratings at various levels of detail. Thus, in addition to overall facility ratings, the condition of the following elements of park and playground maintenance can be rated separately: playgrounds and playing fields, landscaping, restrooms, and other facilities such as paths, parking areas, picnic tables, and buildings. Ratings of more specific features and problems within these general categories (e.g., "the percentage of parks with widespread weed problems," "the percentage of restrooms with broken, leaking, or inoperable fixtures") can also be prepared. Such information can be valuable to park maintenance personnel in managing and planning maintenance operations. The ratings are based on a checklist of key potential maintenance problems similar to the lists used by supervisors and inspectors in

many park departments (see Appendix 6).

To use the trained observer results to prepare Measure 13, the ratings for individual facilities must be classified as "satisfactory" or "unsatisfactory." Each jurisdiction can define what is a satisfactory or unsatisfactory rating, depending on the trained observer scale used. For instance, using the park rating scales described in Appendix 6, an agency can define a park or playground as being in "unsatisfactory" condition if (1) it contains one or more "widespread" maintenance problems (involving more than one-third of the area, equipment, or facilities in question), or (2) if more than one-third of all the key features examined (grass and lawns; shrubs, trees, and plantings; play areas; etc.) have at least *some* problems, or (3) if the average overall rating for the four basic park maintenance responsibilities examined—landscaping, playgrounds and playing fields, restrooms, and other facilities—is 2.5 or greater (indicating numerous maintenance problems).

Measures of Safety

Measure 14: *Number of serious injuries (say, per 10,000 visits).*

Measure 15: *Percentage of facilities with one or more safety hazards.*

Measure 16: *Number of criminal incidents (say, per 10,000 visits).*

Measure 17: *Percentage of user households rating safety of facilities as satisfactory.*

Measure 18: *Percentage of nonuser households giving lack of safety as a reason for nonuse of facilities.*

Park safety—especially the safe design of playgrounds and playground equipment—has been of increasing concern in recent years.[3] Much of that attention has been stimulated by growing concerns over local government liability and a study of the safety of playground equipment conducted by the Consumer Product Safety Commission in the mid-1970s.[4] Five measures provide varying perspectives on park and recreation safety: Measures 14 and 16 draw on basic local government statistics, Measure 15 uses trained observer ratings, and Measures 17 and 18 use results from household or user surveys.

For legal and administrative reasons, most park and recreation agencies keep detailed statistics on reported injuries (Measure 14), and local police departments keep statistics on criminal incidents (Measure 16). Some park and recreation agencies also have their own police forces, which maintain crime statistics. However, what is lacking in many of these agencies is any attempt to track statistics through time to see if the situation is changing.

When comparing the number of injuries or criminal incidents (over various time periods, among recreation districts, or by facility), it is desirable to relate the number of incidents to some indicator of the population at risk. (After all, the playground or swimming pool with the fewest number of injuries would be the one that is not used at all.) One approach is to divide the number of injuries or incidents in a given time period by the attendance or number of attendance hours during that period, if such information is available or can be estimated.

Trained observer ratings can provide information on physical hazards existing at park and recreation facilities (Measure 15). Using a pre-specified checklist with precise definitions of the more likely types of hazards (perhaps including photographs that illustrate the conditions described), a local government employee or other trained observer can systematically rate park and recreation facilities for the presence of unsafe conditions. The procedure is similar to that proposed by the Consumer Product Safety Commission, although not as extensive.[5]

Data for Measure 15 can be collected along with trained observer ratings that assess the cleanliness (Measure 11) and maintenance (Measure 13) of park and recreation facilities (see Appendix 6). A "hazard" is defined as a problem that poses an immediate danger to health or safety. Consequently, hazardous conditions should be rated and tallied separately from cleanliness and maintenance/quality ratings.

Broken glass is one hazard in parks and at recreation centers, and it is considered as a potential problem in connection with each type of feature rated with the procedure given in Appendix 6. Other hazards include exposed electrical wiring, holes in ballfields, and faulty playground equipment. The observers should be instructed to report any additional hazards.

Measure 17 estimates the percentage of households that use recreation facilities who rate their safety as satisfactory (or unsatisfactory), using questions such as 6i in Appendix 4 (household survey) and 8 in Appendix 5 (user survey).

Measure 18 provides the percentage of nonuser households that give lack of safety as a reason for nonuse of local government facilities, by asking a question such as 8g of Appendix 4 in the household survey.

A concern for Measures 14 and 16 is that not all injuries that result from accidents or criminal incidents are reported. The household survey could be used to ask citizens whether they were involved in any recreation accidents or criminal incidents and whether they were reported. Estimates of the frequency of unreported incidents could then be tallied to obtain an estimate of the reported and unreported events. However, the small samples involved would provide only a crude indication of the extent of injuries or crime at those facilities.

Measures of Accessibility

Measure 19: *Percentage of citizens living within (or not within) 15 to 30 minutes of travel time of a community park or recreation facility, distinguished by type of facility and principal relevant mode of transportation.*

Measure 20: *Percentage of user households rating physical accessibility as satisfactory.*

Measure 21: *Percentage of nonuser households giving poor physical accessibility as a reason for nonuse.*

Measure 22: *Percentage of user households rating hours of operation as satisfactory.*

Measure 23: *Percentage of nonuser households giving unsatisfactory operating hours as a reason for nonuse.*

The concept of accessibility is complicated. It includes factors such as physical accessibility (Measures 19–21), problems caused by various forms of explicit or implicit discrimination, lack of transportation, inconvenient hours of operation (Measures 22 and 23), excessive waiting, or inadequate parking space. No specific measures of the extent of parking problems are included, but such elements can be included in questionnaires such as those shown in Appendices 4 and 5. Question 12 in Appendix 5 illustrates how the issue of parking might be included in the ratings sought in user surveys.

These illustrations do not explicitly address physical accessibility of facilities by the disabled, an important client group. Special variations of these procedures can be used to assess the extent of park and recreation facility accessibility to the handicapped.

Measure 19 focuses on the proximity of the population to park and recreation facilities and can be obtained by a mapping technique. Measure 20 focuses on ratings by user households in either the household or user survey. A user survey question such as Question 14 of Appendix 5 or Question 6b of the household survey of Appendix 4 captures this information. Measure 21 provides the percentage of nonuser households that give poor physical accessibility as a reason for nonuse (see Question 8c in Appendix 4).

Measure 19 involves two important considerations: How close are the individual citizens to facilities, and what is the extent of the individuals' mobility? For many potential users of recreation facilities, such as youths and others without access to automobiles, mobility is a problem, and the geographic distribution of facilities in a community is important. Therefore, the measurement of accessibility will vary with the mobility characteristics of the intended user groups.

One way to measure accessibility is to calculate the percentage of the total population (or of a particular potential user group) residing within a given distance of a facility.

The following steps, illustrated in Exhibit 4-2, are needed:

1. Obtain community maps, such as those prepared locally or by the U.S. Census Bureau. Census population statistics are keyed to census tracts, with block group and block numbers printed on the maps. Several census map sheets will probably be needed to cover each jurisdiction, plus a "fringe area" of at least three-fourths of a mile around its political boundary. Calibration marks, such as four "+"s, should be placed on the base map. These marks will align the map overlays described in succeeding steps.

2. Identify on the maps any physical barriers that would affect accessibility to recreation areas. These barriers, including freeways, railroads, industrial zones, and rivers, should be marked on the base maps. An examination of the local transportation planning agency highway map, or even a common street map, along with local government personnel's knowledge of the city, can help determine locations of barriers. On-site checks may be desirable in some instances.

3. Plot the population distribution on an overlay. Use the basic population data tabulations (from census statistics or more recent planning information) to prepare population overlays on tracing paper or acetate. Place the population overlay on the base map. Write population data on the overlay for the appropriate census tracts, block groups, or blocks.

4. Plot the location of recreation facilities on another overlay to the base map.

5. Draw an accessibility circle around each plotted facility on the facility location overlay. The radii used for these circles should reflect the mode of transportation persons are assumed to use and the estimated maximum travel time. We suggest 15- and 30-minute travel times. (For neighborhood facilities where walking is the usual mode of transportation, this would represent about ¾ and 1½ miles.) To account for physical barriers to access, the areas blocked from access should be eliminated from the circles.

6. Assemble overlays on the base map and use the calibration marks to align the maps and overlays.

7. Estimate the number and percentage of people living within the physical accessibility circles (or, if easier, the number and proportion of people not living within the circles). The proportion of the population in tracts or in blocks that are split by the accessibility circles should be estimated by visually estimating the percentage of the census tract or block group area lying within each physical accessibility circle and then splitting the population proportionately. This method assumes that the population is evenly distributed throughout the area.

Separate sets of overlays will be necessary to distinguish different population segments—for example, to consider accessibility for various age groups. In addition, car-oriented facilities, such as golf courses or major city or county parks, will require riding-time accessibility circles, whereas neighborhood facilities will require walking-time circles. (For client groups without access to automobiles, transit-time accessibility might be needed to estimate accessibility to major local recreation facilities, with such access plotted around transit stops. See Chapter 9 on public mass transit.)

Those park and recreation agencies with access to a computer-based geographic information system (GIS) will be able to make these calculations rapidly, easily, and probably more accurately than if they calculated the measure manually. Once the GIS database is established, it can be used to rapidly calculate accessibility for different types of park and recreation facilities and programs.[6]

For Measure 22, user ratings of the hours of operation can be obtained either from a household survey question such as 6a in Appendix 4 or from a user survey question such as 3 in Appendix 5.

For Measure 23, the proportion of nonusers giving hours of operation as a reason for nonuse, data can be obtained from the household survey by asking questions such as 8b in Appendix 4.

Exhibit 4-2

Mapping Technique for Measuring Physical Accessibility

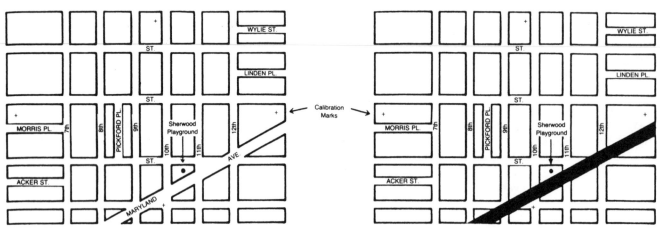

Step 1. Obtain base map.

Step 2. Identify and mark physical barriers on base map.

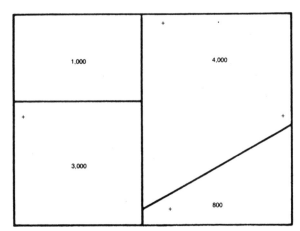

Step 3. Tabulate population; plot on map overlay.

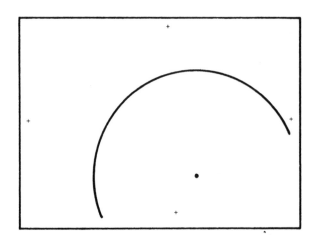

Step 4. Plot facility and activity locations on map overlay.
Step 5. Draw physical accessibility circles around each location.

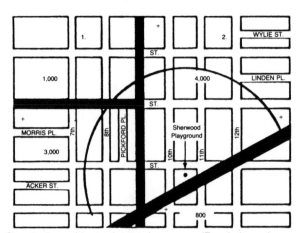

Step 6. Assemble overlays on base map. (For clarity, only overlays for population by block groups and facility are shown.)

Source: U.S. Department of the Interior, Bureau of Outdoor Recreation, *How Effective Are Your Community Recreation Services?*, p. 59.

Measures of Variety

Measure 24: *Percentage of user households rating the variety of program activities as satisfactory.*

Measure 25: *Percentage of nonuser households giving lack of program variety as a reason for nonuse.*

Two perspectives are provided on variety. Measure 24 obtains a rating from households that used the facilities, based on a question in the user survey such as 10 in Appendix 5. For Measure 25, the percentage of nonuser households giving lack of program variety as a reason for nonuse, data can be obtained from the household survey using a question such as 8k ("activities not interesting") in Appendix 4. At the same time, information can be obtained on the particular activities of interest to the nonuser households by asking respondents which activities they would like, such as shown under Question 8k.

A measure such as "the average number of different program activities per facility" is an easy way to gauge program variety. However, this measures inputs more than results, so it has not been included in the suggested effectiveness measures.

Measures of Helpfulness of Staff

Measure 26: *Percentage of user households rating helpfulness or attitude of staff as satisfactory.*

Measure 27: *Percentage of nonuser households giving poor staff attitude as a reason for nonuse.*

In providing recreational services, local government employees and the clients of recreational activities often interact. Some feedback seems appropriate on the degree to which the government employees are helpful and courteous to clients. Measure 26 provides a perspective on user households through questions such as Question 6f in Appendix 4 (household survey) and Question 11 in Appendix 5 (user survey). Measure 27 provides estimates of the percentage of nonuser households that give poor staff attitudes as a reason for nonuse. This information needs to be obtained from a household survey using a question such as Question 8i of Appendix 4.

The Household Survey

A household survey, if properly carried out, can produce knowledge that is difficult to obtain in any other way. First, the survey can obtain a representative citizen evaluation of local-government-operated facilities and programs. Second, it is probably the most efficient way to gather data on participation rates. Even when an agency collects attendance data, these data do not indicate how many different households participated. Finally, the household survey is about the only way to obtain information on the reasons for nonuse of facilities.

Data for 19 of the 27 effectiveness measures listed in Exhibit 4-1 can be obtained through a household survey. Exhibit 4-3 lists the measures and the survey questionnaire number, and Appendix 4 presents the questionnaire. The survey also obtains demographic and supplementary diagnostic information to help agency personnel interpret the data.

Household surveys require significant resources to conduct, and most park and recreation agencies will need outside expertise to help set up and conduct their own survey. Another less costly option is for the park and recreation agency to participate in multiservice surveys undertaken by the local government. Survey costs will be low, but the agency may have to include fewer questions (giving up, for example, questions about individual facilities).

Exhibit 4-3

Measures of Effectiveness Data Collected by a Household Survey

Service quality	Measure[1]	Survey question[2]
Overall citizen satisfaction	1	3
User satisfaction	2	6j
Use—participation rates	3	4, 5
Crowdedness—user rating	5	6h
Crowdedness—nonuser rating	6	8d
Physical attractiveness—user rating	8	6c
Physical attractiveness—nonuser rating	9	8e
Facility cleanliness—user rating	10	6d
Facility/equipment condition—user rating	12	6e
Facility safety—user rating	17	6i
Facility safety—nonuser rating	18	8g
Physical accessibility—user rating	20	6b
Physical accessibility—nonuser rating	21	8c
Hours/days of operation—user rating	22	6a
Hours/days of operation—nonuser rating	23	8b
Variety of activities—user rating	24	6g
Variety of activities—nonuser rating	25	8k
Helpfulness/courtesy of staff—user rating	26	6f
Helpfulness/courtesy of staff—nonuser rating	27	8i

[1]See Exhibit 4-1.
[2]See questionnaire in Appendix 4.

The household survey procedures (and costs) are discussed in Chapter 13. Some special elements unique to parks and recreation activities are discussed below.[7]

Interviewing Method
A complication is that many citizens will not be aware of the park and recreation facilities in their neighborhoods. Even if they are aware of the facilities and programs, most will not know which are operated by the state, city, county, school, special district, a nonprofit organization such as a boy's club or little league, or in some instances a private for-profit organization. If a park and recreation agency wants to learn how a community feels about its operations and about specific facilities and programs, it is necessary to be specific about the programs and facilities used and rated—perhaps by identifying the facilities and programs at the beginning of the interview.

The questionnaire can ask respondents to report on specific neighborhood park and recreation facilities and programs, as shown in Appendix 4. Each can be identified by name and by address. The questionnaire cannot ask respondents about every facility and program it administers; instead, respondents might be asked about a few major ones, about the closest park, pool and community center, or about the two closest facilities regardless of type. The questionnaire should also ask whether respondents have used any other park and recreation facility and if so which ones. It is important to identify the facility used to make sure it is operated by the agency.

In addition to the effectiveness measures noted in Exhibits 4-1 and 4-3, the questionnaire can collect information on issues of special interest to the jurisdiction such as interest in new or special programs or the willingness to pay user fees. Adding a few questions to the survey adds little additional time and cost.

Frequency and Timing of the Survey
For park and recreation services, the survey should encompass all seasons, or at least those seasons in which the local government sponsors activities and those in which activities are likely to differ.

If interviews are conducted at intervals throughout the year (such as 100 interviews every three months rather than 400 at one time during the year), timing would be of less concern because respondents would need to be asked only about the period involved. The full sample for the year would cover all seasons and all recreational activities during that year. This procedure would also provide more timely feedback to agency personnel.

If the household survey is undertaken only on an annual basis, the survey should be conducted at approximately the same time each year so that seasonal change does not affect the year-to-year comparisons.

Who Should Undertake the Survey?
Household park and recreation surveys have been conducted by several municipal park and recreation agencies. In at least one city the entire operation was conducted by local government employees and volunteers. However, primary reliance on local government employees and volunteers is not generally recommended. Even in the best of circumstances, a survey such as the one described here is a substantial undertaking.

Contracting may be the most desirable option but requires funds that most park and recreation agencies find hard to obtain. A professional survey firm will likely charge about $10–$15 per telephone interview (excluding costs for developing the questionnaire). Thus, a sample of 400 interviews would cost about $4,000–$6,000.

Even if an outside firm conducts the survey, the park and recreation department should take a major role in formulating the questionnaire and analyzing the data.

Options for Reducing Survey Costs
The questionnaire in Appendix 4 can be simplified, either for use in a park and recreation survey or for use as one section of a community's multiservice household survey. To simplify the questionnaire, respondents would not be asked to identify facilities but to indicate whether they had used any local government park and recreation facility during the period of interest. The respondents could be asked to rate all the facilities together or to identify the facilities and rate each type they had used. This approach is more likely to capture information on facilities operated by other suppliers.

The On-Site User Survey

A number of park and recreation agencies in the United States, particularly at the state and federal level, have conducted on-site surveys of users of park and recreation facilities. Although less common at the local government level, such surveys have been used by a number of city and county park and recreation agencies. Generally, these surveys have been one-time efforts that focused on the overall satisfaction of users and what additional recreational activities they would like. User surveys rarely have been used to collect information regularly on the effectiveness of current services.

The surveys described in this section focus on service effectiveness. They ask about users' recent experiences and attitudes toward existing facilities and activities. When administered regularly, these surveys can provide trend information on program and individual facility effectiveness.

On-site user surveys offer the following advantages over household surveys:

- They efficiently collect data that are related directly to users' experiences. Questionnaire administration is easier.
- They produce, at low cost, sample sizes large enough to determine the effectiveness of specific facilities or programs. This is in contrast with household surveys, which, because of cost, do not have samples large enough to determine the effectiveness of many individual facilities and programs.
- They are within the capability of most park and recreation departments to conduct.
- They are likely to be interesting to the user and as a result, users may give more accurate answers.

User surveys have three principal disadvantages:

- They do not permit a department to collect data on nonusers and their reasons for nonuse.
- They do not provide estimates of the percentage of different users in the community.
- They are difficult to conduct for large sites without controlled access, such as a large park.

The user surveys discussed here can produce data for 10 of the 27 measures shown in Exhibit 4-1. Those 10 measures are listed in Exhibit 4-4.

In addition to client ratings, questions should also be included that allow respondents to explain poor ratings and to provide suggestions for improvements. Demographic data, such as age, sex, race or ethnic group, and income of the respondents should be captured (see Questions 20–24 in Appendix 5).

User surveys are discussed at greater length in Chapter 13. Here we focus on special concerns when surveying parks and recreation users.

Method and Length of Interview

There are two surveying methods: face-to-face interviews and self-administered survey forms. The former requires an interviewer to read each question and record answers. With self-administered surveys, users complete the questionnaire themselves. Most park and recreation agencies will prefer the self-administered questionnaire, which requires less staff time and staff training than does the interviewing method. However, the self-administered survey may be impractical in some instances, such as for small children and the elderly who have trouble reading because of poor eyesight.

The self-administered questionnaire should require only five to ten minutes to complete.

Who Should Undertake the Survey Operations?

With only limited outside assistance, local government personnel should be able to design their own survey questionnaires, pretest the forms, conduct the surveys, and tabulate the results. Most local governments should have seek some professional advice, particularly for the initial survey design.

Can recreation personnel handle interviews without producing a bias in the results? Recreation personnel may unintentionally encourage responses that correspond to their own perceptions. Also, if the persons being interviewed believe park and recreation personnel are being rated on the basis of their responses, the interviewees might rate facility conditions more favorably than they otherwise would. To reduce this problem, an agency can assign its personnel to conduct surveys at facilities other than those where they normally work, or use interviewers from outside the park and recreation agency. Possibilities for interviewers include other local government personnel; volunteers from groups such as the League of Women Voters, park and recreation board, or health and welfare council; or paid outside help. When outside personnel are used, close supervision is important.

Frequency and Timing of the Survey

Because seasonal differences are important in recreation, surveys should be conducted at the end of each major recreational season. Local governments interested in evaluating a particular program, such as summer

---

Exhibit 4-4

Measures of Effectiveness Data Collected by a User Survey

Service quality	Measure[1]	Survey question[2]
User satisfaction	2	19
Crowded conditions	5	7
Physical attractiveness	8	9
Facility cleanliness	10	4
Equipment condition	12	5
Safety	17	8
Physical accessibility/convenience	20	14
Hours/days of operation	22	3
Variety of interesting activities	24	10
Staff helpfulness	26	11

[1]See Exhibit 4-1.
[2]See questionnaire in Appendix 5.

activities, may want to conduct the survey at the end of that season.

The survey should cover a representative cross section of users. The kind of user is likely to vary by time of the day, the day of the week, and week of the year. A survey should cover segments from each major period. For example, questionnaires might be given to users that come in during a one-hour period during the morning, afternoon, and evening and during one low-attendance day, one medium-attendance day, and one high-attendance day. This might be done during the last week of each season.

Sample Size and Selection

Sampling is less of a problem for a user survey than it is for a household survey because the users come to the site and to the interviewer. It is easy to select those to be sampled. The factor that determines the cost of the user survey is not the absolute sample size but the number of different facilities covered and the number of survey hours and days spent at each facility.

The sample size at each site should be large enough to permit grouping the user responses into desired categories, such as age, sex, race or ethnic group, and location of residence. At places where the expected attendance is small, everyone might be interviewed. At other sites and times, every other person or every third person might be interviewed; at even busier facilities, every fifteenth or twenty-fifth person might be interviewed. The added costs of increasing the sample size for a user survey are likely to be small, particularly if questionnaires are self-administered and if computer processing is used to tabulate the data.

Different sample strategies may be needed for different facilities, programs, and client groups. Where park and recreation access is controlled (e.g., swimming pools, recreation centers, and special events or programs), surveying is straightforward. Each person (or a sample of persons) is stopped and requested to complete the survey form. To minimize biases, strict rules should be applied in selecting persons for an interview or for receipt of a survey questionnaire (e.g., take the first person through the door after a given time, take every twenty-fifth person to enter or exit through a given portal). When users cannot complete the form by themselves, for instance, because they are too young to read and write, a member of the survey team will need to read the questions and help them complete the form. All respondents should be asked to put their completed forms into a ballot box (to keep their responses anonymous).

Surveys of users where access cannot be controlled (e.g., parks, nature centers, and playing fields) pose a more difficult sampling problem. One approach is to have interviewers (or questionnaire distributors) periodically travel through the facility, tracing a specified pattern or route and following specified selection rules (e.g., every tenth person encountered).

In those cases where lists of users are available (e.g., program registers, membership lists, mailing lists, and emergency care forms) and are reasonably complete and up-to-date, they can serve as a basis for selecting persons to be surveyed. If not available or if the necessary information is not provided (e.g., an address or phone number), operating procedures might be modified to develop suitable lists of users (for instance, by requiring the phone number of all participants or asking persons to sign in or formally register). Where addresses are available, questionnaires can be mailed to participants. The park and recreation agency should encourage persons given questionnaires to complete them. This can be done by: reminding persons about the questionnaire as they are leaving the facility, by having the person giving out the questionnaire wait for its completion (if so, fewer questionnaires can be given out), and, if a mailed questionnaire is used, by sending reminders and a second questionnaire.

Tabulating and Analyzing the Results

If the survey is larger than several hundred interviews, it is advisable to code the survey questionnaire and enter the results directly from the survey forms into the computer. There are several personal computer programs that can be used to tabulate and analyze the results. For small surveys the results can always be tabulated by hand, but this can be an onerous task and increases the possibility of error.[8]

Use of survey results requires complex tabulations. Examination of the data and consideration of their meaning by recreation personnel is necessary if the data are to be useful. Reports should be prepared for each park and recreation site, and these should be provided to site supervisors. Reports also should be prepared for agency management so that they can compare different sites.

User Survey Staffing and Timing Requirements

Exhibit 4-5 shows the estimated staff time required for a user survey. Designing the questionnaire and survey procedures will likely take about 2½ staff-weeks. Conducting the survey and tabulating results will take about 17–29 person-weeks per year (assuming data are collected quarterly from each of ten facilities). The amount of staffing and time will vary, depending mainly on the number of different sites and the number of hours over which the survey is conducted. Less important for user surveys is the number of questionnaires completed at any one facility.

Trained Observer Procedures

Trained observers can collect objective information on the conditions of park and recreation sites. This information provides accurate, reliable measures that objectively track park and recreation facility conditions over time. Measures 11, 13, and 15 are based on trained observer data (Exhibit 4-1). Appendix 6 presents a discussion of detailed procedures that can be used to collect the data.

As with other effectiveness measures, the park and recreation trained observer ratings should reflect the concerns of citizens and they should be understandable to the public as well as park and recreation administrators.

The trained observer provides information on maintenance of individual park and recreation sites. The ratings can pinpoint hazards that need immediate attention, identify routine maintenance that is needed, make estimates of the amount of labor needed to correct the deficiencies, and identify capital additions and renovations needed.

Determining the Characteristics to Be Rated
The first step in developing the trained observer ratings is to determine which characteristics will be rated. For Measures 11, 13, and 15, characteristics are cleanliness, usability, and safety.

For instance, the following basic aspects of park and recreation facility maintenance are addressed by the trained observer procedure described in Appendix 6.

- Landscaping
- Playgrounds, playing fields, and courts
- Restrooms
- Other facilities—paths, walks, parking areas, benches, tables, buildings, and other structures
- Overall cleanliness.

Each of these basic aspects of park maintenance should be subdivided into more specific "elements." For instance, landscaping can be split into two elements: grass and lawns, and shrubs, trees, and plantings. Maintenance problems can be identified for each element. For example, four common problems in connection with shrubs, trees, and plantings are "needs trimming"; "weeds present in planted areas"; "dead shrubs, trees, or foliage"; and "broken

glass." A category labeled "other" should be provided also to allow raters to record and assess any additional problems that they might encounter with shrubs, trees, and plantings. Appendix 6 illustrates how this approach can be expanded to cover each aspect of park maintenance.

The procedure described in Appendix 6 explicitly addresses 39 types of problems. New York City's condition assessment procedure focuses on 17 general features (but uses more complex rating scales). An "other" category can catch any problems not listed. Problems and hazards frequently encountered (such as broken glass) or that are of special interest to management (e.g., water fountain operability or the presence of graffiti) should be explicitly included on the rating form.

Rating Scales and Procedures
The rating scales should cover the range of conditions likely to be encountered. Each level of the scale should correspond to a meaningful distinction in the relevant condition. It is often useful to characterize each level in qualitative terms such as "excellent," "good," "fair," or "poor," or "no problems," "limited problems," or "widespread (or major) problems." However, each level needs to be defined as specifically as possible so that different raters, and the same raters in different years, will give similar ratings to similar conditions.

The ratings are made in two phases. First, the rater assesses the presence and extent of each type of "problem" using a simple three-level scale: (1) no problems, (2) limited problems, or (3) widespread (or

---

Exhibit 4-5

Estimated Time Requirements for a Parks and Recreation User Survey

For 100 interviews at each of 10 facilities

Task	Person-weeks
Initial design	
Select topics, specify accuracy, and design management plan	½
Design and pretest questionnaire	1
Design sampling plan and prepare material	1
Total	2½
Annual implementation	
Recruit and train interviewers	1
Conduct survey	10–20
Edit, code, keypunch, and tabulate	2–4
Analyze and prepare written findings	4
Total	17–29

Note: Figures assume that questionnaires are administered over a one- or two-hour period, three different times per day, three days during one week each season, at ten facilities.

major) problems. (See Appendix 6 for definitions of these rating levels.) If any problem also constitutes a safety hazard, that is noted.

The second phase of this rating process combines the problem-by-problem ratings into overall ratings. One approach is to tally the number of "limited," "widespread," "no problem," and "hazard" ratings corresponding to each element, each aspect, and the facility as a whole. Alternatively, the ratings for the potential problems corresponding to a given element or aspect can be combined using a numerical rating scale (see Appendix 6).

Photographic Scales. The consistency of trained observer ratings can be improved by providing the observers with photographs that illustrate the distinctions between rating levels. Exhibit 4-6 provides examples of reference photographs used in conjunction with three-level trained observer ratings similar to those described in Appendix 6.

In some cases, one can use (or adapt) existing reference photographs. In some instances, however, a jurisdiction may need to develop its own set of reference photographs. The procedures described in Chapter 2 can be used for this purpose.

Rating Forms. An easy-to-use form should be provided for recording the trained observer ratings—one form per park or other recreation facility. The facility should be identified on the form as to its location, neighborhood, service district, and any other characteristics that will be helpful in analyzing the data. The form should have space for entering the names of the raters, the date, the time, and the weather. Such information can sometimes be helpful in explaining certain ratings—for example, if a park was rated before the usual arrival of the clean-up crew, or if one team is especially severe in its ratings.

If the rating process is based on identifying and rating specific problems, the most common types of anticipated problems (and those whose importance merits a special search effort) should be listed explicitly on the rating form. Broken glass is such a ubiquitous problem in parks that it is usually appropriate to list it as a separate item with *each* maintenance element rated. The form should also provide places for the raters to record and assess any other problems and for summarizing the ratings for the given facility.

Appendix 6 provides an example of a form for recording problem-based trained observer ratings. It is designed to lead the rater through each step of the rating process, from problem identification to the preparation of overall ratings for each aspect of park maintenance examined. The basic definitions of the rating levels are repeated on the form as a convenience to raters.

Frequency and Timing of the Ratings

If the ratings are to be used by the agency to help it make regular operational decisions, such as to help allocate scarce maintenance resources, the ratings should be done frequently, perhaps monthly or even weekly during peak use periods. If not, quarterly ratings may be sufficient.

Some items such as safety hazards, cleanliness, and landscaping can vary considerably during a short period. The condition of other park and recreation features usually changes only slowly. Low-use facilities probably need to be rated less frequently than high-use ones. Also, because use is likely to vary from season to season and for holiday/tourist/vacation periods, frequencies can be altered to match these time periods.

In parts of the nation where many park features are likely to be obscured by leaves or snow in late autumn or winter, these seasons should be avoided. The best seasons in northern areas of the United States for conducting trained observer ratings are probably the late spring (when preparations for the summer have been completed) and early fall (when the effects of summer wear and tear versus the ongoing maintenance efforts can be observed).

The day of the week and the time of day selected for the ratings can be important. For example, a department may want to rate each park after the clean-up crew has completed its work. Ratings of recreation centers may be easiest after hours, when the observers will not disturb center users or staff.

Selecting the Sites to Be Rated

Each park and recreation facility should be rated if there is a limited number of sites or if the data are to be used for maintenance decisions as well as effectiveness measurement. An experienced park rating team will usually require 20 to 30 minutes to rate a facility, excluding travel time. Small neighborhood parks and recreation areas will require less time. a local government has a large number of facilities (say, more than 50) and only wishes to assess overall effectiveness levels, then the facilities should be sampled (in a way that selects representative samples of the facilities).

Selecting and Training the Raters

Nearly anyone can be a trained observer for park and recreation facilities. However, the best raters will have good eyesight and concentration and will be conscientious about detail. They can be municipal employees, summer interns, or even volunteers from the general public.

Although trained observer ratings can be conducted by individuals, the use of teams is preferable. Two pairs of eyes to identify problems and two opinions on ambigu-

Exhibit 4-6

Example of a Photographic Scale for Rating Playing Fields

Aspect: Playgrounds and playing fields

Element: Playing fields and courts

Potential problem: Playing fields infested with weeds

No problem

Limited problem

Widespread problem — more than one-third of field is weed infested

Source: Office of Management and Budget, City of Greenville, South Carolina (photos used by the city for 1990 ratings of playing field conditions).

ous rating decisions are better than one. If the number of facilities to be rated is small or if there is plenty of time, all ratings should be conducted by a *single* team to minimize inter-rater consistency problems. For speedier ratings or for handling a large number of facilities, several rating teams can be used.

Providing proper training (coupled with adequate quality controls) is critical to the effectiveness of trained observers. The quality of the training will,

to a great extent, determine rater accuracy and inter-rater consistency.

Although the time needed to train raters of park and recreation facilities depends on the number and complexity of the characteristics rated by each team (and the scales used), no more than one or two days of training should be needed. One day will probably be sufficient for a refresher course if the raters have participated in previous trained observer exercises.

Exhibit 4-7

Illustrative Display of Park Rating Results, by Maintenance Element and Geographic Area

(Percentage of parks and playgrounds with one or more widespread problems)

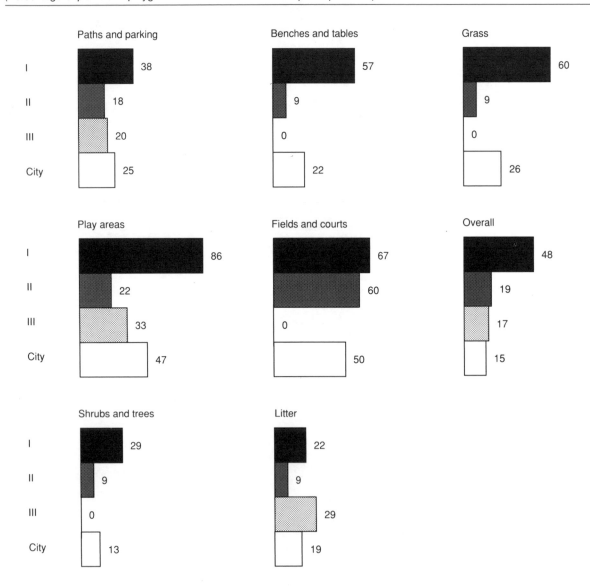

Source: Alexandria, Virginia, "What Is the Condition of Our Capital Plant?" TriData Corporation and the Alexandria Office of Management and Budget (Alexandria, Virginia, October 1982), p. 27. Percentages are shown for each of the city's three districts as well as the city as a whole; shading or coloring can be used to help readers quickly distinguish the findings for each district.

Conducting the Ratings

The trained observer team should systematically walk around and through the facility, taking extensive notes on the problems (if any) encountered. These notes should pinpoint the location of hazards and widespread problems so that work orders can be written to correct them at a later time. After covering the entire facility, the team should complete the rating form, referring to the notes made. Where there is a question or disagreement over a specific rating, the team should reobserve the relevant items. Hazards and other conditions requiring immediate attention should be flagged for quick follow-up. The raters should refer frequently to the photographs and written definitions of the various scales.

Strict quality controls are critical to maintaining accuracy and inter-rater consistency. A "judge" or supervisor of the trained observers should periodically check each team's ratings for accuracy. A random sample of 5 to 10 percent of the facilities rated (at least two per team) should be adequate. Any discrepancies identified in the ratings should be discussed and addressed through remedial training. Special emphasis should be given to items rated as hazards or as widespread problems because these determine many key effectiveness measures as well as the need for urgent remedial efforts. Verification of some of the "worst" ratings will also indicate whether the observers are rating problems too harshly. (There can be a tendency to become too severe in rating moderate problems, especially when most facilities are in very good condition.)

Tabulating and Analyzing the Results

Most trained observer ratings of park and recreation facilities have relied on manual tallies of the results, supported in some instances by computer spreadsheets. Already available are hand-held devices to record the data. New York City is using these devices in collecting data on school maintenance quality.

In addition to performance measures that address the overall condition of individual facilities and groups of facilities (Measures 11, 13, and 15), performance measures can be prepared that focus on the effectiveness of specific aspects and elements of a jurisdiction's park maintenance efforts, or on the incidence of specific types of problems.

In addition, each measure can be expressed in several alternate ways (e.g., as an "average" rating; as a percentage of the parks, facilities, elements, or problems rated; as a percentage of all the individual observations made; or as the number or percentage of ratings that exceed a certain critical level). Appropriate displays of the data, emphasizing park-by-park and district-by-district results, can further enhance the accessibility and utility of the information.

Exhibit 4-7 illustrates how the results might be displayed by type and district.

Cost and Staffing

The cost for trained observers is usually modest, especially if existing personnel or volunteers are used. Total expenditures will depend also on the number and type of facilities rated, whether the jurisdiction develops its own rating scales or adapts materials used by other local governments, and the frequency with which the ratings are repeated.

Exhibit 4-8 indicates the estimated personnel time associated with conducting trained observer ratings of 25 park and recreation facilities, using two-person teams. It is assumed that the local government initially develops its own rating scales and reference photographs with help from park and recreation department staff, and that raters are given two days of training. Each team is assigned 12 to 13 facilities. The average time for rating, write-up, and travel is assumed to be 60 minutes per facility. Quality control follow-ups are conducted for two facilities per team. Ratings (and quality control checks) are conducted four times a year.

About 25 person-days would be needed for designing the procedures. About 56 person-days would be needed to undertake the quarterly ratings. If the agency can use current staff or volunteers, the out-of-pocket or hard cost could be small.

Exhibit 4-8

Estimated Time Requirements for Trained Observer Ratings of Park and Recreation Facilities

Task	Person-weeks
Initial design	
Determine potential problems to be examined	0.8
Develop rating scales and criteria	1.0
Prepare and select reference photographs	1.0
Prepare forms, manuals, and photographic guides	2.0
Identify sample of facilities to be rated	0.2
Total	5.0
Conduct trained observer ratings	
Train raters	1.6
Conduct ratings	5.0
Follow up a sample of ratings	0.4
Total	7.0
Tabulate and analyze results	
Check, tally, and analyze data	2.6
Prepare reports	1.6
Total	4.2
Total, annual operations	11.2

Note: These times assume that a sample of 25 park and recreation facilities will be rated, using two two-person teams (12 to 13 facilities per team) four times a year. In addition to staff time there will be out-of-pocket expenditures for printing and reproduction of the photographs, reproduction of forms and training manuals, vehicle mileage/motor pool fees, and computer costs.

Overall Costs and Staffing Requirements for Measurement Procedures

The overall effort needed to collect the data on the measurements outlined in Exhibit 4-1 is likely to be about 40 person-weeks and $5,000 annually for a medium-size city (see Exhibit 4-9). This estimate assumes that the household survey is split into four quarterly segments of 100 households, user surveys are undertaken at the close of each season, and trained observer ratings are conducted four times each year. Other data collection efforts, such as accessibility ratings and attendance counts, are undertaken as discussed earlier.

The added expenditures required to support these effectiveness measurement procedures in any jurisdiction will depend on such factors as the availability of existing staff (and volunteers) and the local government's interest in particular measures of effectiveness. Most jurisdictions already collect some of the data. The frequency of reporting will also have an important impact on cost.

A problem in implementing park and recreation measures of effectiveness in local government is the lack of analytical personnel. Few park and recreation agencies have the staff needed to develop the measurement procedures and analysis.

Out-of-pocket expenditures can be reduced significantly if existing local government personnel undertake certain tasks such as interviewing and trained observer ratings. Citizen volunteers can also help with the ratings. Moreover, it is not necessary for a jurisdiction to adopt all the measurement procedures. Managers may need certain elements more than others. The measures selected will play a major role in the overall resource requirement.

Using the Park and Recreation Effectiveness Information

The use of effectiveness measurement information is the subject of Chapter 16. Presented here, however, are some findings related particularly to the park and recreation field. Park and recreation officials who discussed the measures of effectiveness generally demonstrated a lively interest in information that can be collected through trained observer ratings and surveys of citizens (the household survey and the on-site survey). These managers particularly desire data on individual programs or facilities and on each of their major park and recreation districts.

Recreation managers sometimes find survey information difficult to interpret and insufficiently relevant to their needs, especially when it is not clearly

and concisely presented or is not presented by facility and district. The user surveys and trained observer procedures lend themselves to collection by facility and district. These surveys can provide feedback to individual facility managers as well as to higher level officials on the effectiveness of their operations. The feedback provides a way to establish accountability in the park and recreation field.

Several jurisdictions that have conducted user surveys have summarized the results in a series of short (one-page) reports for each facility manager. These reports have provided park and recreation supervisors with systematic feedback on citizen viewpoints about operations in their individual geographic areas. These reports also have been used in meetings to discuss operations with center directors and area supervisors. Such meetings can be used to discuss issues that have escaped the notice of department managers and analysts, and they can provide a forum for outlining corrective steps where needed.

Although the user survey is helpful in providing feedback on the use of individual facilities, it tells nothing about the nonuser and reasons for nonuse. The household survey is the source for this information. It has been used to justify new facilities, speed up construction of planned facilities, identify facilities that needed rehabilitation and cleaning, and spark informational campaigns. One of the most surprising pieces of information taken from park and recreation household surveys is the large number of

---

Exhibit 4-9

Estimated Annual Time and Cost for a Park and Recreation Effectiveness Measurement System

Data collection procedure	Annual cost/person-weeks
Household survey (contract for 400 households in four 100-household segments)	$4,000–$6,000
User survey (two times each at 10–15 recreation sites)	17–29 person-weeks
Trained observer ratings (25 sites, four times per year)	11 person-weeks
Other procedures	
Physical accessibility	4
Attendance	1
Safety	0.5
Crowding	0.5
Total	$4,000–$6,000 34–46 person-weeks

Note: See the text for more details on the basis for these time and cost estimates. These resource requirements should be less for smaller jurisdictions, and more for larger ones—that is, they will vary with the number of households, users, and sites surveyed, and with the frequency of observation or surveying. These estimates do not include the resources required to design the various procedures and data collection instruments. See text for estimates of design costs.

citizens who are unaware of park and recreation facilities and programs in their immediate neighborhoods.

Trained observer ratings that can be translated into immediate or near-term operational decisions and actions have been of considerable interest to park and recreation managers. Some managers want hazards to be brought to their attention the day they are identified; they do not want to wait for a summary of the raw data. One manager identified a pattern of broken playground equipment from the trained observer statistics and was able to get the equipment's manufacturer to take remedial action. Another department found that it was not properly maintaining its shelters and small structures.

Effectiveness information is but one class of data—albeit a very important one—needed before major local government actions are taken. The information generated by the procedures discussed in this chapter and throughout this report does not indicate why conditions are bad or good nor what should be done about them. Effectiveness information indicates only the results of government services. It is necessary to compare results obtained from effectiveness data with other available information and with managers' experience.

1 Developed in 1938, this formula was retested nationally in 1960 and supported by the test findings. (See Butler, "Summer Playground Attendance Formula." So far as we know, the formula has not been retested since then.

2 Westover, "Urban Parks as Social Settings: Visitors' Perceptions of Anti-Social Behavior and Crowding."

3 See, for instance, Kozlowski, "Are You Familiar with the Public Playground Safety Guidelines?" and Wallach, "Playground Safety Update."

4 U.S. Consumer Product Safety Commission, *A Handbook for Public Playground Safety*, vol. I and vol. II.

5 U.S. Consumer Product Safety Commission, *A Handbook for Public Playground Safety*, vol. I, p. 12.

6 Chatfield, Deans, and Freshwater, "Computerizing Parks and Recreation."

7 An earlier report contained a detailed discussion of the survey procedures discussed here. See U.S. Department of the Interior, Bureau of Outdoor Recreation, *How Effective Are Your Community Recreation Services?*, especially Chapter 3 and Appendices A and B, and *How to Conduct a Recreation Effectiveness Telephone Survey*. More recent work has automated some of the procedures needed to conduct a park and recreation survey. See Dean, Wellman, and Charles, "PASSing the Computer Test," and Dean, *Public Assessment Survey System, Technical Assistance Manual*, and *User's Guide to the PASS Computer Program*.

8 Dean, *Public Assessment Survey System, User's Guide to the PASS Computer Program*.

Most public libraries report on various aspects of their operations, but few do so systematically from the perspective of users and potential users. Most library systems lack information on citizen satisfaction with library operations, including the comfort of facilities, hours of operation, speed of service, and helpfulness of the library staff; the availability of materials sought by the users; and the percentage of households that use the system, with estimates of reasons for nonuse by those that do not use the system. While many libraries have collected such information through special studies, few have regularly collected such information and systematically tracked it over time.

Considerable research and writing exists in library service measurements (see the Bibliography for selected citations). The American Library Association (ALA) and one of its divisions, the Public Library Association, have sponsored several major developmental efforts during the past 15 years. Much of this work is used and cited here. In addition, consultants, citizen groups, academic groups, and library staffs have made a number of studies of individual libraries.

Objectives and Related Effectiveness Measures

An objective for library services that seems applicable to most communities is

> **To present library services that provide the greatest satisfaction possible to citizens and are comprehensive, timely, helpful, and readily available in facilities that are attractive, accessible, and convenient.**

A set of measures to assess progress toward meeting this objective is presented in Exhibit 5-1. The data collection procedures for these measures have been used by a variety of library systems.

A public library system embarking on effectiveness measurement will want to review the objectives and measures presented here and tailor them to its own needs. Community needs and constituent group views differ from jurisdiction to jurisdiction. Effectiveness measurement is multidimensional and libraries should consider this when establishing their measurement systems.

The objectives and measures listed not only apply to the evaluation of the overall library system, but they can also provide information on specific units such as individual branches, or on individual activities such as reference, circulation, or special collections. Except for measures that use data from a survey of the general population and the measures on physical accessibility (which are concerned with accessibility of the public to the *set* of library facilities), most of the measures and associated data collection procedures can be tallied by individual facility.

To evaluate special programs, such as mobile or outreach programs or libraries for lawyers or schools, some measures should be modified. But many measures, such as those for "overall citizen satisfaction" and "helpfulness and courtesy of the staff," can be applied to special operations as well as to the overall system.

Principal Measures and Measurement Procedures

Exhibit 5-1 lists 19 effectiveness measures that can help assess library services. When data on these measures are collected regularly—at least annually and preferably more frequently to provide quicker, more seasonal feedback to library staff—progress can be tracked over time and emerging problems can be identified. The principal suggestions can be summarized as follows:

- A prime indicator of the quality of public library services is the overall satisfaction of the citizens of the community with those services. Both an annual survey of a random sample of citizens in the community and a periodic survey of a random sample of library users are suggested. Data from a survey of a representative sample of households throughout the community can obtain a reasonable estimate of the satisfaction level in the community. The practicality of a library system undertaking an annual survey of a representative sample of the community is enhanced if the survey covers a number of local services (not just one service such as the library). A multiservice household survey is suggested throughout this report. Information on user sat-

isfaction with the library can be obtained from a sample of library users.

- The household survey can also obtain information on the percentage of households in the community that have used a public library during a specific period, such as within the previous twelve months. The survey also can obtain reasons for nonuse, which can help public officials improve the attractiveness and effectiveness of library services.

- A number of specific qualities of library service that are important to library management and other public officials should be measured, including speed of service, helpfulness and courtesy of staff, comfort of the facilities, and physical accessibility and convenience (including hours of operation). Data to measure these qualities can be obtained from the same surveys of users and the general population used to obtain overall

---

Exhibit 5-1

Measures of Effectiveness for Library Services

Overall objective: To present library services that provide the greatest possible satisfaction to citizens and are comprehensive, timely, helpful, and readily available in facilities that are attractive, accessible, and convenient.

Objective	Quality characteristic	Specific measure[1]	Data collection procedure
Overall citizen satisfaction	Citizen satisfaction	1. Percentage of citizens who rate library service as satisfactory.	Household survey
	User satisfaction	2. Percentage of users who rate library service as satisfactory.	Library user survey or household survey
	Use—household	3. Percentage of households using (or not using) a public library a minimum number of times, such as four times over past twelve months—with reasons for nonuse.	Household survey
	Registration—household	4. Percentage of households with (or without) a valid registration card.	Library tabulations or household survey
	Use—visitation	5. Number of visits to library facilities per capita (or per household).	Library tabulations of number of users with population estimates from city planning department
	Use—circulation	6. Circulation per capita by type of material—e.g., fiction, nonfiction, records, film—divided between internal and external use.	External circulation figures, kept by most public libraries. Internal figures, estimated from periodic sampling
Comprehensiveness/ timeliness/availability of holdings and service	Diversity and availability of holdings	7a. Percentage of user searches—title, subject/author, browser—that are successful.	Library tabulations from special user survey
		7b. Percentage of users who rate materials as satisfactory.	Library user survey or household survey
		7c. Percentage of nonusers who cite poor materials as a reason for nonuse.	Household survey
	Speed of service	8. Percentage of requests available within 7, 14, and 30 days or longer.	Library tabulations of delivery dates
		9. Percentage of users who rate speed of service (e.g., book retrieval and checkout) as satisfactory.	Library user survey or household survey

satisfaction and use information. Such ratings by citizens seem to be the most direct way to obtain feedback on the quality of services.

- The availability of materials such as books, periodicals, videotapes, and so forth are important aspects of library service. The ALA has developed and tested a number of measures that use physical counts to determine availability. These provide a useful adjunct to customer survey results.

The individual measures and procedures for collecting data are discussed in the following sections.

Individual Measures

This section describes the measures for collecting data. Because data for many of the measures can be collected by a survey of a sample of library users, and many others by a survey of a sample of citizens throughout the community, these procedures are discussed in more detail in a later section.

The measures are grouped into five categories:

- Overall citizen or client satisfaction (Measures 1–6)
- Comprehensiveness, timeliness, and availability (Measures 7–9)
- Helpfulness of staff (Measures 10–12)
- Physical attractiveness, accessibility, and convenience (Measures 13–19).

Measures of Overall Citizen or Client Satisfaction (Measures 1–6)

Two types of measures seem appropriate for obtaining information on citizen and user satisfaction with public library services: ratings by citizens and library users as to their overall satisfaction (Measures 1 and 2) and estimates of library use (Measures 3–6).

Library use measures (Measures 3–6) assume

Exhibit 5-1, continued

Measures of Effectiveness for Library Services

Objective	Quality characteristic	Specific measure[1]	Data collection procedure
Helpfulness of staff	Helpfulness—courtesy of staff	10. Percentage of library users who rate helpfulness and general attitude of library staff as satisfactory.	Library user survey or household survey
	Helpfulness—quality of reference service	11. Percentage of users of library reference services who rate them as satisfactory.	Library user survey
		12. Percentage of reference transactions successfully completed.	Library tabulations of reference responses
Attractiveness, accessibility, and convenience of facility	User satisfaction with comfort, crowdedness, noise, etc.	13. Percentage of library users who rate the comfort, crowdedness, noise, cleanliness, and temperature/ventilation as satisfactory.	Library user survey or household survey
	Nonuser satisfaction	14. Percentage of nonusers who cite lack of comfort, crowdedness, noise, cleanliness, or temperature/ventilation as reasons for nonuse.	Household survey
	Physical accessibility, convenience	15. Percentage of users who rate convenience as satisfactory.	Library user survey or household survey
		16. Percentage of nonuser households who give poor physical accessibility as a reason for nonuse.	Household survey
		17. Percentage of citizens who live within a specific travel time (such as 15 minutes) of a public library.	Counts from mapping latest census tract population figures against location of facilities with appropriate travel time radius drawn around each facility
	Hours of operation	18. Percentage of users who rate hours of operation as satisfactory.	Library user survey or household survey
		19. Percentage of nonuser households who give poor hours as a reason for nonuse.	Household survey

[1]Officials who wish to focus on amount of local *dissatisfaction* may substitute "unsatisfactory" for the term "satisfactory" in many of these measures.

that because library use is voluntary, the amount of use is an indication of citizen satisfaction with the library services. Citizens in effect "vote with their feet." Moreover, because the alternatives to using libraries are to buy the materials or to forgo them, those persons interested in library services are partially a "captive audience." Thus Measures 1 and 2 also seem to be important.

The two types of measures—satisfaction and use—are complementary; using one without the other would cause a gap in information on the quality of library services. Together, the measures provide a more comprehensive picture of library quality.

Measure 1:   *Percentage of citizens who rate library service as satisfactory.*

Measure 2:   *Percentage of users who rate library service as satisfactory.*

Measure 1 can provide an estimate of the overall satisfaction level of a representative sample of the population of the community. This is done through a survey of a random sample of households in the community. Measure 2 can provide estimates of the overall satisfaction level of only library users. The data for Measure 2 can be obtained by special surveys of library users (generally conducted at the library facilities) or by questions included in the random household survey. User surveys are more efficient for reaching those who have used the services; furthermore, the surveys can obtain satisfaction levels for users of individual branches for library systems that have more than one facility.

The household survey, however, can obtain ratings of library services from those who did not use the libraries (or used them only a few times). If reasons for nonuse can be obtained (as discussed below), they should provide important information for program and policy decisions.

Question 21 of Appendix 1 (the multiservice household survey) provides data for Measure 1. Question 21 of Appendix 1 and Question 17 of Appendix 7 (the library user survey) can be used to obtain the data for Measure 2.

To obtain data on library user satisfaction from the household survey for Measure 2, it is necessary to distinguish the ratings provided by persons who have used the library system from those who have not. This could be done by making a cross-tabulation of Question 21 (satisfaction) in Appendix 1 against Question 23 (frequency of use). Both types of surveys can provide simultaneously not only an overall rating of library service, but also ratings on aspects of the service. These opportunities are discussed later in this chapter.

Measure 3:   *Percentage of households using (or not using) a public library a minimum number of times, such as four times over past twelve months—with reasons for nonuse.*

Measure 4:   *Percentage of households with (or without) a valid registration card.*

Measure 5:   *Number of visits to library facilities per capita (or per household).*

Measure 6:   *Circulation per capita by type of material—e.g., fiction, nonfiction, records, film—divided between internal and external use.*

Measures 4-6 use library tallies of the number of persons with registration cards, the number of visits, or the number of items circulated. None of these measures, however, indicates how many different households use the library. Visitation and circulation figures will be affected by repeated use by a small group of citizens. In every jurisdiction there will be a group of users—about 20 percent—who use the library more than once a month. Registration figures do not reflect actual use, may be out of date, and may contain many multiple-card households.

Measure 3 provides estimates of the number and percentage of different households who use the library services. A question such as Question 23 of Appendix 1 can be used to obtain the data in a household survey.

Measure 3 also obtains information on reasons for nonuse of the library facilities as part of the household survey procedure. One particular concern is to identify the percentage of persons whose reasons for nonuse can be affected by the local government (lack materials of interest, too much noise, too little parking, or inaccessibility), as distinguished from reasons that are outside the local government's control (such as the citizen's poor health, general lack of interest, or preference for purchasing needed materials). More detailed questions can pinpoint further the specific reasons for nonuse.

Library officials may find it useful to separate reasons for nonuse by certain demographic data collected by the survey. Examples of specific questions that could be used are shown in the various parts of Question 25 of Appendix 1.

Procedures for collecting data on Measures 4 and 5 (registration and visitation) are straightforward. However, some libraries will want to break down Measure 5, visitation, by purpose of visit. The ALA, for example, suggests a separate measure to tabulate attendance for library programs: "program attendance per capita."

Measure 6, circulation per capita, is divided between external and internal. Calculation of external circulation is quite common. Less common is calculation of internal circulation (where the library visitor uses materials but does not check them out), which requires special counts by library staff. Procedures for both measures are presented by the ALA.[1] A library system may also make calculations by type of material—fiction, nonfiction, periodicals, videotapes, and so forth.

Special Validity Considerations for Measures 3–6. Data from household surveys of library users may have the accuracy problems discussed later in this chapter and in Chapter 13. Some validity issues related specifically to these measures are discussed here.

- The validity of respondent information on reasons for nonuse is uncertain. Do respondents give accurate reasons? Can they give accurate reasons? Studies of nonuse of another local government service, public transit, have indicated service changes designed to remedy the reasons for nonuse have not always resulted in increased use. Currently, no information is available on the validity of reasons given for nonuse of libraries.

  Local governments may want to ask more in-depth questions about nonuse, at least during the initial testing of their survey. The checklist of possibilities for nonuse illustrated in Question 25 of Appendix 1 was developed from a number of interviews, which included "open-ended" questions on reasons for nonuse, as well as from examination of checklists used by other researchers and the judgments of local officials.

- The accuracy of data obtained for Measures 4–6 by various library tallies varies with the care taken in their collection. Because the procedures themselves are routine and are discussed by the ALA publication, they receive no special attention here. However, several problems exist with library registration figures (Measure 4) as a measure of current satisfaction. First, some library systems do not register patrons, whereas others automatically register all residents. Clearly Measure 4 is inappropriate in these cases. Second, in every jurisdiction some library users will not register. And third, many libraries do not keep registration figures up-to-date. This problem worsens if the interval between registration renewals is long or if renewal is not required. Also, as noted earlier, the total number of households with library cards cannot be accurately deduced from totaling the number of cards issued, because many households contain more than one cardholder.

This problem can be alleviated by devising a sampling procedure to estimate the number of households with more than one library card. This figure can be divided by the total number of households in the community to derive the percentage of households with cards.

Measures of Comprehensiveness, Timeliness, and Availability (Measures 7–9)

Measures 1–6 obtain information on overall library quality as reflected by citizen satisfaction. The remaining measures consider specific aspects of library performance.

Measures 7–9 assess the comprehensiveness, timeliness, and availability of library materials and services. Measure 7, which addresses availability, has three submeasures: user experiences, user perceptions, and nonuser perceptions.

Measure 7a: Percentage of user searches—title, subject/author, and browser—that are successful.

This measure reflects the likelihood that library users will find the documents they need. The measure is also known as the "fill rate," "find rate," or "materials availability rate." It captures several library system activities, including library material ownership, cataloging, shelving, and how successful users are in locating items. The ALA, which developed and tested the procedures for this measure, divides the measure into three forms—title, subject-author, and browser.

Title search is the number of titles found divided by the number of titles sought. It has an in-library and a telephone component. In the in-library procedure, persons in the library complete a questionnaire that lists the titles sought and whether they were found. The completed questionnaire is left in a response box or with the library attendant when the user leaves the library. In the telephone component, the library staff tallies titles requested by phone and determines if the materials are available.

The subject-author fill rate procedures are similar. Library users complete a questionnaire that lists the subjects and authors sought and the number found. The count is the number of "fills," that is, whether the user found anything about the subject or anything by the particular author. For this measure, telephone counts are not tallied.

The browser fill rate captures data on whether the browser found an item that was helpful. The measure is the number of people who found something helpful while browsing divided by the number of browsers. As with the title and subject-author measures, the data necessary to calculate this measure are taken from the questionnaire given to library users and collected when they leave the library. Survey and computational techniques for this measure are enumerated in the ALA publication on measuring library outputs.[2] The three types of fill rates must be tabulated and analyzed separately because the fill rate for browsers is likely to be much higher than that for specific book titles.

These measures can be broken down further by type of collection (such as adult and juvenile), whether assistance was requested in locating the materials, and what other things the user did while in the library.

Some controversy exists concerning the validity of fill rates as a measure of library effectiveness. Fill rates seem to be valid because they capture user success; however, tests in a number of libraries suggest that the measure captures a variety of considerations. Some statistical tests have found that fill rates were not explained by either library or user characteristics.[3] Although the ALA continues to recommend the measures, it also recommends that local government officials be aware of the questions surrounding the measures when using them for decision making.

Measure 7b: *Percentage of users who rate materials as satisfactory.*

Measure 7c: *Percentage of nonusers who cite poor materials as a reason for nonuse.*

Measures 7b and 7c provide another dimension on the availability or nonavailability of library materials. These measures can help answer the validity questions of Measure 7a.

Measure 7b, the rating of the user, can be collected by a library user survey or by a general household survey. For Measure 7b, data can be obtained by use of a question such as 24b in Appendix 1 or 9 in Appendix 7. In the household survey, only user ratings should be sought. In either survey a question could be added as to the type of additional materials desired.

Measure 7c asks nonusers whether the lack of desired materials is the reason for nonuse. To obtain data for Measure 7c, Question 25a in Appendix 1 can be used. The question could be extended to ask the respondent the type of material desired; such information could be useful given the diversity of media material stocked by public libraries today.

Measure 8: *Percentage of requests available within 7, 14, and 30 days or longer.*

This measure reflects the timeliness of obtaining materials that are not readily available to the user. The library may own the material, but it may be checked out or in use elsewhere. Or the library may not own it and must obtain it elsewhere, either by borrowing it from other branches or other library systems or by purchasing it. The computational procedure is a count in days, from the day of the request until the day that the material is available for borrowing.

The procedure developed by the ALA to calculate this measure calls for a log to be kept by the library showing the date of the request and the date when the item is available for the user.[4]

There are several variations of this measure, including separation by different type of materials (such as books, periodicals, videotapes, and compact disks) and separation by source (such as branches and interlibrary loans).

Measure 9: *Percentage of users who rate speed of service (e.g., book retrieval and checkout) as satisfactory.*

Even though books and materials are available on the shelves, library patrons may still encounter delays in finding them and in checking them out. This measure estimates the degree to which users are satisfied with the speed of service.

If a periodic survey of library users is undertaken, patrons can be queried to obtain ratings of the speed of service they have experienced during the period under review. The household survey can obtain similar information. (See Questions 13 and 14 of the library user survey in Appendix 7 and Question 24f of Appendix 1 for the household survey.)

An alternative, or additional, procedure is to estimate delay times. Measure 8 involves such a procedure. Another procedure is to sample lines at the checkout counter at randomly selected times during the library year. Either length of lines or length of waiting time or checkout times can be sampled. Note that the measurements of delay times provide only an indirect measure of client satisfaction because it is not known to what extent satisfaction correlates with waiting times.

Measures of Staff Helpfulness (Measures 10, 11, and 12)

Each of the following three measures provides ratings of specific aspects of staff helpfulness. Two rely on user ratings and one on librarian ratings.

Measure 10: *Percentage of library users who rate helpfulness and general attitude of library staff as satisfactory.*

Measure 11:   Percentage of users of library reference services who rate them as satisfactory.

Measure 12:   Percentage of reference transactions successfully completed.

Measure 10 obtains information from the library user survey or the household survey; in the latter, only those persons indicating that they have used the library should be counted. Data on Measure 10 can be obtained by using survey questions such as Question 12 in Appendix 7 and Question 24e in Appendix 1.

Measures 11 and 12 focus on library reference services. Measure 11 draws on user feedback using the special library user survey. Measure 12 relies on librarian judgment to assess whether customer queries are answered successfully. The two measures complement each other.

Measure 11 requires a question such as 16 of Appendix 7. The household survey is not appropriate for Measure 11 because there are likely to be too few citizens in a household survey who have used the reference service. Even a library user survey may need large sample sizes to capture enough users of reference services.

Measure 12 can be tabulated from logs maintained by reference librarians using procedures developed by the ALA. These procedures suggest that the answers be categorized in several ways to reflect accurately public requests and interests. For example, reference questions can be (1) completed, (2) redirected, or (3) not completed. Redirected questions can go to (1) another department in the library, (2) another library, or (3) to an agency outside the library. Not completed reference questions remain unanswered because (1) the material is owned but not available, (2) material is not owned, (3) staff time is not available, or (4) other reasons such as patron's time constraints.[5]

Much has been written about the difficulty of determining the accuracy of answers to reference questions.[6] Simulation, follow-up studies, and retests have been used to assess how well reference questions are answered. Most of these tests are difficult to administer, and there are questions surrounding the validity of each. These problems are another reason for seeking the perspectives of citizens (Measure 11) and librarians (Measure 12).

Measures of Facility Attractiveness, Accessibility, and Convenience (Measures 13–19).

The following seven measures address library facility attractiveness, accessibility, and convenience. Six of the seven require the household survey or library user survey to collect the necessary information. Measure 17 uses a physical count.

Measure 13:   Percentage of library users who rate the comfort, crowdedness, noise, cleanliness, and temperature/ventilation as satisfactory.

Measure 14:   Percentage of nonusers who cite lack of comfort, crowdedness, noise, cleanliness, or temperature/ventilation as reasons for nonuse.

Measures 13 and 14 obtain information either by querying a sample of library users with the library user survey or by querying nonusers with the household survey. In the latter case, ratings on these issues should be sought only from those who indicate that they have used the library. In general, the user survey is the more efficient way to obtain feedback on Measure 13.

For specific question wording to obtain data on Measure 13, see Question 10 in Appendix 7 and 24c in Appendix 1. These questions about comfort and cleanliness could be split into separate questions. The term "comfort" is ambiguous and could encompass considerations such as ventilation, lighting, and seating. Attributes of particular concern could be addressed in specific questions.

Measure 14, the nonusers' ratings, can be obtained from the household survey. A question such as 25i of Appendix 1 can be used to collect this type of information, even though it asks only about noise and crowding.

Measure 15:   Percentage of users who rate convenience as satisfactory.

This measure provides information on library users' perception of convenience. Data can be obtained from either the library user or household survey. Questions 24d (convenience to home) and 24g (ease of parking) of Appendix 1, and Questions 11 and 15 of Appendix 7 could be used to obtain the data.

Parking is a problem for many library systems. To reflect the extent to which inadequate parking space relates to nonuse, an additional question about parking can be included (see Question 25k of Appendix 1).

Measure 16:   Percentage of nonuser households who give poor physical accessibility as a reason for nonuse.

Whereas Measure 15 measures library user ratings of convenience, this measure considers nonuser views. Data needs to be drawn from the household survey. A question such as 25h of Appendix 1 can be used.

Measure 17:   Percentage of citizens who live within a specific travel time (such as 15 minutes) of a public library.

This measure provides a more "objective" measure of physical accessibility, but it is not necessarily a "better" measure because citizen perceptions of accessibility may be more meaningful than physical proximity. This measure looks at the percentage of household residents within a given distance or travel time of a public library. This measure can be calculated by plotting population locations from the latest census data on a city or county map. Contours representing perhaps fifteen minutes of travel time can then be drawn from the map around each of the branch libraries. The population within the contours can be used to calculate the percentage of the total city population within this travel time or distance. These procedures are discussed in Chapter 4.

Travel times for walking, biking, busing, or driving could be used. The population distribution might be separated by age group. For example, in measuring convenience for children, a 15-minute walking distance might be used, whereas in measuring convenience for adults, driving time might be used.

In analyzing the results of Measure 17, library personnel should compare the data with Measures 15 and 16, because many people will not be interested in using these library services regardless of geographic convenience.

Measure 18: *Percentage of users who rate hours of operation as satisfactory.*

Measure 19: *Percentage of nonuser households who give poor hours as a reason for nonuse.*

Because of the increase in the number of working spouses, library hours of operation have become more

of an issue. Concerns include the total number of hours of operation, the hours of operation each day, and the days of the week of operation. A library system that finds the overall hours of operation rating unsatisfactory, or deteriorating through successive surveys, can add questions to determine the reason behind the change in the ratings.

Data for Measure 18 can be obtained from either the library user survey or the household survey. Such questions as 7 and 8 of Appendix 7 and Question 24a of Appendix 1 can be used.

Data on Measure 19 should be obtained from the household survey with a question such as 25g of Appendix 1.

The Library User Survey

An annual survey of a sample of library users has been mentioned as a source of data for eight of the measures (see Exhibit 5-2).

A number of public libraries have conducted user surveys. Generally, these have been one-time efforts that focus on overall user satisfaction and on opinions as to desirable modifications in library services. Surveys seldom have been used to collect information regularly and systematically on the effectiveness of current services.

The library user survey focuses on service effectiveness. It obtains information on users' recent experiences and attitudes toward existing services. When administered annually, a library user survey can provide time-trend information on library services, including the effectiveness of branch operations.

A library user survey questionnaire is included as Appendix 7. It includes questions on the measures and on demographic matters. The demographic questions permit library staffs to cross-tabulate the measures for client groups, such as those categorized by age, sex, or race. Modifications, some of which have been noted in previous sections, will help meet the needs of each library system.

User surveys offer some advantages over household surveys:

- User surveys are efficient if a local government is interested primarily in the interests and actions of users. For example, more than 50 percent of the respondents in many past household surveys did not use the library during the previous twelve months and therefore could not be asked for user ratings.

- User surveys are within the capability of the average-size or even small library system to conduct.

Exhibit 5-2

Measures of Effectiveness Data Collected by Library User Survey

Service quality	Measure[1]	Survey question[2]
Overall user satisfaction	2	17
Availability of materials	7b	9
Speed of service	9	13, 14
Helpfulness or courtesy of staff	10	12
Quality of reference service	11	16
Comfort of facilities	13	10
Convenience to home	15	11
Hours of operation	18	7, 8
Ease in parking	15	15

[1]See Exhibit 5-1.
[2]See Appendix 7.

- User surveys are inexpensive and can obtain responses at each branch to obtain sample sizes that are large enough to determine the effectiveness of individual branch operations. In contrast, household surveys may become expensive if large samples must be obtained to permit precise ratings about operations of individual libraries.

The user survey has two disadvantages compared with the household surveys. First, it does not permit a library system to collect data on nonusers. Second, it provides inadequate information to estimate Measure 3, the number and percentage of different users within a community. The same persons may use different library branches, and users will have varying frequencies of library use.

Exhibit 5-3 illustrates some of the types of data that can be obtained from a library user survey. It illustrates how the findings can be summarized to compare branches. Such summaries can highlight problem areas and areas of high performance. Tables that compare ratings for different groups by age, sex, and race can be prepared also. After data are obtained for more than one time period, performance for different time periods can be compared.

The questionnaire presented in Appendix 7 contains a number of other questions, such as frequency of use, length of stay, mode of transportation to the library, distance between home and library, and open-ended questions on respondent likes, dislikes, and suggestions for changes. These are peripheral to the effectiveness measurement data but provide additional interpretative information to library and other officials. Questions also could be added to the questionnaire to obtain feedback on issues of special concern to library officials at the time of the survey.

Survey Procedures

Administration of Questionnaire. The questionnaire in Appendix 7 requires about four minutes to complete. In the cities where it has been administered, users were canvassed at library facilities. Both children and adults should be included in the survey. However, very young children, say below the age of 8, will not be able to complete the survey form even if it is read to them. Different survey techniques are needed for this group.[7]

There are two variations for administering the questionnaire: interviews and self-administered surveys. In the interview, an interviewer reads each question and records the answer. In self-administered surveys, users complete the questionnaire themselves. A combination of the two procedures can be useful. Most users are willing to complete the questionnaire themselves, but some patrons, such as those with poor eyesight, will need the questions read to them and the forms completed by a member of the survey team. Completed forms can be placed in a "ballot" box. Names should not be requested.

Sample Size and Selection. The sample size at each site should be large enough to permit grouping of user ratings by age, sex, race, and library branch. One sample design is to conduct interviews each day for two days in each library. Different sampling rates can be used in different libraries. At branches where the expected attendance is small, everyone can be requested to complete the survey form. At

---

Exhibit 5-3

Illustrative Performance Report Comparing Library Branches

(Percentage rating the characteristics as either "fair" or "poor" rather than "excellent," "good," or "no comment" for each branch)

| Measure (number) | Branch | | | | | | | | | | | | |
	1	2	3	4	5	6	7	8	9	10	11	12	Overall
Overall rating (2)	4	3	4	4	3	10	2	3	10	0	3	2	3
Availability of material (7b)	14	13	9	15	22	㉝	20	16	18	11	24	16	18
Ease in finding material (9)	6	5	14	8	14	4	3	7	0	2	7	7	8
Ease in checking out material (9)	4	1	6	5	1	0	1	2	6	0	3	3	2
Staff helpfulness and courtesy (10)	4	3	4	4	3	7	1	2	6	1	2	3	3
Reference help (11)	9	6	5	2	10	15	4	7	4	3	8	8	9
Comfort and cleanliness (13)	13	11	10	14	15	㊴	4	11	20	㊲	23	17	15
Convenience to home (15)	14	7	17	20	21	9	12	㊺	21	12	13	16	㉘
Ease in parking (15)	20	10	11	5	14	㉖	2	㉒	8	17	6	4	㉗

Note: To illustrate how selected findings might be emphasized, all entries that reveal "dissatisfaction" levels of 25 percent or more were circled. Clearly, inconvenience to home and ease in parking were the major problem areas.

larger libraries, every other, every fifth, or every tenth person can be given a survey form, depending on the expected attendance. The goal should be to obtain at least 100 completed interviews at each library facility.

With equal samples at each library, the number of completed questionnaires at each library will not correspond to each library's proportion of total system activity. To arrive at systemwide results, the survey analyst can multiply responses at each library facility by their approximate proportion of the total library system's customers. The resulting weighted percentages can be totaled to obtain the percentage of the entire system's users giving that response.

Large numbers of repeat patrons can bias the results. Such users will have a larger probability of being in the sample than others, and thus the findings will tend to be weighted toward the perceptions of the more frequent users. (Some may believe this is desirable.) Because the survey is intended to identify the responses of different users, however, no individual should be interviewed more than once. Users can be asked not to complete another form if they have completed one during the survey period.

Frequency and Timing of the User Survey. The survey should obtain interviews from a representative cross section of the users. Because the type of user is likely to vary by the time of the day, the day of the week, and season, the survey should cover all periods that a facility is open. Some library systems may have to restrict their survey coverage because of lack of resources. For example, if the library system has to limit its surveys to a two-day period (once each season), it might choose the days of the week so that one day is of high use and the other, low use. The days can be selected after consultations with library staff and an examination of daily circulation statistics.

To cover seasonal differences, periodic surveys, such as quarterly, can be conducted. Seasonal surveys are likely to be more useful than annual surveys for two reasons. First, the resulting information will be more timely, and staff can detect problems and assess more quickly the results of previous actions (such as procedural changes). Second, asking respondents about their past twelve months of experience rather than, say, the past three months, will tax their memories. Citizen recall is most troublesome for factual data, such as the number of visits and length of stay. Memory is probably less important for "perception-type" information, such as ratings of library operations, but recent experiences are likely to influence replies more than remote experiences.

Survey Flexibility. If a library wants information on mobile services or telephone reference services, a revised questionnaire and set of interview procedures will be needed.

The survey can be used also to obtain other feedback from clients. For example, the survey can be used to query users about the days of the week they find most convenient to use the library, the hours of operation they favor, the types of media they would like to see added to the particular library, and what they consider to be the greatest need for improvement in the particular library. The questionnaire in Appendix 7 asks users about changes they would like to see made in the library (Question 23), their length of stay when visiting the library (Question 6), and the activity that brought them to the library (Question 3).

Who Should Undertake the Survey? Library personnel should be involved in the selection of the questions included in the user survey (as well as the library questions included in the household survey discussed in the next section). Not only do they have firsthand knowledge of the issues, but also they are likely to be the principal users and interpreters of the responses.

Most library systems will need outside professional advice, particularly in the first survey, for determining the final wording, pretesting questions, and training interviewers (for situations where the questionnaire is not self-administered). Local government library staff, assisted by central management personnel, can probably handle most aspects of later surveys themselves.

Special Validity Considerations

Much of the discussion of validity of customer surveys in Chapter 13 applies here. However, three specific issues are raised.

Refusals. Some individuals may refuse to complete the survey questionnaire. The most likely reason given for refusal is that the person is "too busy" or has "no time." Others may refuse because they came in to the library to "use the phone" or "use the toilet."

Refusals from many persons threaten the validity of the findings because those who refuse may have different views and behavior patterns from those who complete the questionnaire. An effort should be made to keep the refusal rate low, below 20 percent if possible. The use of pleasant and experienced or well-trained persons to encourage survey completions can help reduce refusal rates. Also, the questionnaire should be short, no more than two pages long, and should be clean and attractive.

Survey Bias. There are two sources of potential bias.

First, in face-to-face interviews the library personnel may intentionally or otherwise encourage responses along lines that correspond to their own perceptions. Second, library visitors, even if they complete the questionnaire themselves, may respond more favorably if they suspect that the library personnel will see their individual responses.

This problem can be alleviated if the respondent understands before completing the questionnaire that it must not be signed and must be placed in a secure receptacle such as an anonymous "ballot" box. Also bias can be eliminated if persons known not to be library employees—such as members of the League of Women Voters, an appointed library board, clubs such as Friends of the Library, other local government personnel, or paid professional personnel—handle the questionnaire distribution and collection or conduct the interviews. It is not recommended that respondents complete the questionnaires at home and mail them to a nonlibrary office—another option—because many of the questionnaires will not be returned.

Sampling Error. In terms of sampling, the validity problem is less severe in user surveys. Sampling and finding respondents is easy. Fewer biases are introduced by sampling because the sample population is the persons who actually visit the facilities. Also, because library users are more likely to be interested in the library questions, they may provide more thoughtful answers. But sampling problems still occur. Users at various times of the day, days of the week, and seasons of the year should be properly represented.

Library User Survey Cost and Staffing

The number of library facilities covered in the survey and the number of survey hours and days, as well as the sample size in any given facility, determine cost and staffing requirements.

An estimate of the amount of staff time required is given in the last section of this chapter. Costs can be reduced substantially by using existing library staff and volunteers.

A survey may require an overall survey coordinator, a staff coordinator at each facility, and someone to process and analyze the survey responses.

Although most library systems should be able to conduct a user survey with limited outside assistance, library staff assistance and top management support is needed.

The Household Survey

An annual survey of a sample of citizens in a community can obtain data on the measures listed in Exhibit 5-4. The household questionnaire presented in Appendix 1 illustrates questions that might be used to collect these data. Exhibit 5-4 matches questions on that questionnaire with relevant measures. Alterations to questions in Appendix 1 may be desirable to meet the needs of individual library systems.

Survey Procedures and Special Validation Issues

Because customer survey procedures are detailed in Chapter 13, they are not repeated here. However, some validation problems and related procedural issues that are especially pertinent to libraries are discussed.

Reaching the Right Respondent. For questions on use and nonuse of libraries, the least expensive approach is to request information covering all members of the respondent's household (see Questions 22, 23, and 25 of Appendix 1). But how accurately can a respondent answer for the experiences of the others in the household? Research in the fields of health and crime suggests that persons speaking for all household members tend to understate actual occurrences. We know of no research concerning this issue in public library use.

Ideally, each person in a household would be interviewed, but this procedure is too expensive for

---

Exhibit 5-4

Measures of Effectiveness Data Collected by Household Survey

Service quality	Measure[1]	Survey question[2]
Overall citizen satisfaction	1	21
User satisfaction	2	21
Usage by households	3	23
Nonuse—by reason	3	25
Use as indicated by registration card	4	22
Availability of material—user rating	7b	24b
Availability of material—nonuser rating	7c	25a
Speed of service	9	24f
Helpfulness—courtesy of staff	10	24e
Comfort—user rating	13	24c
Comfort—nonuser rating	14	25i
Convenience—user rating	15	24d
Accessibility—nonuser rating	16	25h
Hours of operation—user rating	18	24a
Hours of operation—nonuser rating	19	25g
Ease of parking—user rating	15	24g
Ease of parking—nonuser rating	—	25k

[1]See Exhibit 5-1.
[2]See Appendix 1.

most jurisdictions. Some survey experts believe that the adult who remains at home (if there is such) is the best person to respond for the family on questions such as library use. However, other questions—especially rating questions and questions on other local government service areas—should be addressed to a cross section of all adults interviewed. (The household survey cannot interview children as to their satisfaction levels. The user survey, however, can include older children.)

Survey Period. Questions on the uses of library facilities rely on the memories of the respondents, which can be a problem if respondents are asked about their use of libraries during the past twelve months. If the household survey is administered once a year, the questionnaire should probably ask the respondents only about the past three or six months at most. Memory is less important for questions that ask for the respondent's *current* perceptions as to the rating of a specific aspect of the library service. Fortunately, precise information on the number of uses is not required. The suggested response categories for Question 23 of Appendix 1 have wide ranges.

Defining Users. Questions that rate specific aspects of the quality of library services (such as speed of service and helpfulness of staff for Measures 9 and 10) should be asked only of those respondents who indicate that they have used the library. Thus, the question arises as to how many visits during the past three, or twelve, months should be considered sufficient experience to provide a rating. A good case can be made for even one visit. Question 23 in Appendix 1 illustrates how this question could be handled procedurally; some answers can direct the interviewer to proceed with user ratings and others to skip those ratings. This choice is judgmental; we know of no significant data bearing on this question.

Library Recognition. In communities where there are a variety of libraries (public, private, school, and university), the problem arises as to whether the respondent knows which are public libraries. One way to check whether there is confusion is to include Question 23a of Appendix 1, which asks for the name of the library facility the respondent uses most often.

Household Survey Cost and Staffing Requirements

The cost of a household survey of a representative sample of the community's population is likely to be impractical for most communities if undertaken solely for the library system, especially if it is to be conducted regularly. If library questions are included as part of a multiple-service, multiple-agency survey,

the costs to the library system and the added cost to the local government should be small.

If a city or county library system sponsors its own community survey, it will probably require in total about one hour per completed interview, including set-up, interview, and tabulation time. The actual interview time should be about five minutes. The questionnaire could consist of questions such as 21–25 and 66–73 of Appendix 1. The latter questions permit the library system to identify measurement data for various client groups identified by characteristics such as area of residence, age, sex, race or ethnic group, and income group.

Whether a household survey is conducted by volunteers or local government personnel, expert advice and direction will be needed. Assistance is available from private survey firms and many universities.

Overall Costs and Staffing Requirements

The staff time required to pursue an effectiveness measurement system as outlined in this chapter will

---

Exhibit 5-5

Estimated Annual Cost of Library Effectiveness Measurement Procedures for a Medium-Size City (Four Library Facilities)

Task	Annual number of employee-days
Data collection	
Household survey (once a year)[1]	Negligible
User survey (administered quarterly at each facility—50 per day over 2 days at each)—total sample of 1,600 each year[2]	
Train staff	4
Conduct survey—1 person half time over 2 days each at each facility each quarter	16–32[3]
Enter data—1 day each facility each quarter	16
Analyze and review data—1 day each quarter	4
In-library measurements (registration, circulation, visitation, fill rates, document delivery, reference completion rate), at 1 day per library per quarter[4]	16
Data analysis and review at 4 days per quarter	16
Total data collection and analysis	72–88 (14.4–17.6 staff-weeks)

[1]Assumes that library questions are included as part of a community-wide, multiservice survey at negligible cost to library.
[2]Assumes that a questionnaire similar to Appendix 7 is used. Assumes 50 per day for two days each at four facilities.
[3]The lower number is likely to be ample for most libraries; the higher number may be required for large facilities.
[4]Assumes that data for registration, circulation, and visitation are already collected, and that data for document delivery and reference completion rate can be collected by staff as part of normal duties.

depend on the size of the library system, the number of branches, the type of measures used, the frequency with which they are used, the accuracy desired, and other factors. A medium-size public library system (four facilities) should require about 14–18 staff-weeks per year.

Exhibit 5-5 estimates the time by major component. These estimates assume that the user survey and in-library measurements will be handled by the library and that any citywide, multiple-purpose household survey that includes library services will be conducted at no cost to the library. Exhibit 5-5 assumes that the data for the in-library measurements, except for the fill rates, are readily available or can be collected by the staff as part of their normal duties. These resource estimates include time for data collection, tabulation, limited analysis, and documentation.

Exhibit 5-5 includes 16 staff-days for data integration, analysis, and documentation. To be fully useful, the data obtained from the measurement procedures should be given some in-depth analysis.

To the degree that a library system already collects the data needed for effectiveness measurement, or can use currently available staff or outside volunteers, out-of-pocket costs will be minimal.[8]

1 Van House et al., *Output Measures for Public Libraries*.

2 Van House et al., *Output Measures for Public Libraries*.

3 D'Elia, "Materials Availability Fill Rates."

4 See note 2.

5 See note 2.

6 Lancaster, *If You Want to Evaluate Your Library....*

7 McDonald and Willett, "Interviewing Young Children."

8 Zweizig and Dervin, "Public Library Use, Users, Uses"; Childers and Van House, "Dimensions of Public Library Effectiveness."

T his chapter focuses on the role of police in crime prevention and deterrence and apprehension of offenders. Measures for corrections, prosecution, and adjudication are not included except to the extent that they are reflected implicitly in the suggested measures.

Crime control is a police responsibility, but it is influenced by other local government agencies, including those responsible for street lighting, drug treatment, recreation, and, in the long run, city planning, housing programs, and job development programs, as well as corrections and the courts. Crime control is also influenced by factors outside local government control, such as the community's population characteristics. The crime control measures therefore reflect the impacts of more than just police activities, and many police activities, such as traffic control and emergency medical aid, do not involve crimes and are not treated in this chapter. Police involvement in traffic control is partially reflected by measures in Chapter 8, on transportation. Some jurisdictions might wish to have a special set of measures that show police contribution to this important service.

Crime Control Objectives

For purposes of the development of effectiveness measures, the overall police objective in crime control is assumed to be the following:

> **To promote the safety of the community and a feeling of security among the citizens, primarily through the deterrence/ prevention of crime and the apprehension of offenders, providing service in a fair, honest, prompt, cooperative, helpful, sensitive, and courteous manner, to the satisfaction of the citizens.**

Principal Measures and Measurement Procedures

The following principal measurement procedures are suggested as possibilities for regular tracking. The specific measures are listed in Exhibit 6-1.

- A regular "victimization" survey of representative samples of citizens and businesses should be conducted, perhaps annually but preferably quarterly, to provide timely, seasonal information to police officials. Information from this survey can correct the current inadequacy of information on the total incidence of crime due to the reliance on data pertaining to *reported* crimes. (In this chapter the term "reported crime data" refers to the number of criminal incidents reported to a police department. Some studies prefer the term "recorded crime data" because police may not always record all incidents that are reported to them.) Victimization surveys will yield estimates of the number of unreported crimes in various categories. These estimates can help show whether changes in the reported crime rates result from changes in the degree of reporting or represent true changes in actual crime rates. The survey also can identify locations and characteristics of those parts of the population that are victimized the most often to help police develop better crime prevention programs. Because it is difficult to obtain fully accurate information from respondents, these data should be regarded as imprecise estimates. They will be valuable primarily for making comparisons over time and among various groups within the community. The same survey can be used to obtain other information.

- Common apprehension measures such as clearance rates and number of arrests do not consider the quality of arrests, so the use of some form of the measure "percentage of arrests that survive preliminary court hearing" is suggested. This measure can provide an important check on the quality of arrests. Moreover, if the reasons for dropping arrests are identified and tallied, the "number of arrests dropped, by reason for being dropped," provides additional useful information to police and courts. These measures require de-

fining procedures for obtaining data from the court or prosecution offices. Tests indicate that such procedures are feasible, but methods and definitions must be developed carefully.

A related improvement is to count the "percentage of 'person-crimes' committed that are cleared," so that if more than one suspect is identified, credit would be given when (or withheld until) the other suspects are brought to justice. Better yet would be a more complicated measure of the "percentage of

---

Exhibit 6-1

Measures of Effectiveness for Crime Control Services

Overall Objective: To promote the safety of the community and a feeling of security among the citizens, primarily through the deterrence/ prevention of crime and the apprehension of offenders, providing service in a fair, honest, prompt, cooperative, helpful, sensitive, and courteous manner, to the satisfaction of the citizens.

Objective	Quality characteristic	Specific measure	Data collection procedure
Prevention of crime	Reported crime rates	1. Number of reported crimes per 1,000 population, total and by type of crime.	Incident reports
	Victimization rates	2. Number of reported plus unreported crimes per 1,000 households (or residents or businesses), by type of crime.	Household survey
	Different households and businesses victimized	3. Percentage of (a) households, (b) businesses victimized.	Household survey, business survey
	Physical casualties	4. Number and rate of persons (a) physically injured, (b) killed in course of crimes or nontraffic, crime-related police work—including victims and police.	Incident reports
	Peacekeeping in domestic quarrels	5. Percentage of domestic quarrels and other disturbance calls with no arrest and no second call within x hours.	Dispatch records, incident reports
		6. Number of injuries to (a) citizens (after police arrival), (b) police per 100 domestic quarrel calls.	Incident reports
Apprehension of offenders	Crimes "solved" at least in part	7. Percentage of reported crimes cleared, by type of crime and whether cleared by arrest or by "exception."	Incident reports
	Completeness of apprehension	8. Percentage of "person-crimes" cleared, by type of crime.[1]	Incident reports, arrest reports
	Quality/effectiveness of arrest	9. Percentage of adult arrests that survive preliminary court hearing (or state attorney's investigation) and percentage dropped for police-related reasons, by type of crime.	Arrest and court records
		10. Percentage of adult arrests resulting in conviction or treatment (a) on at least one charge, (b) on highest initial charge, by type of crime.	Arrest and court records
	Stolen property recovery	11. Percentage of stolen property that is subsequently recovered: (a) vehicles, (b) other property.	Incident reports, arrest or special property records
Responsiveness of police	Response time	12. Percentage of emergency or high-priority calls responded to within x minutes and percentage of nonemergency calls responded to within y minutes.	Dispatch records
	Perceived responsiveness	13. Percentage of (a) citizens, (b) businesses that feel police respond fast enough when called.	Household survey, business survey, complainant survey
Feeling of security	Perceived safety	14. Percentage of (a) citizens, (b) businesspersons that feel safe (or unsafe) walking in their neighborhoods at night.	Household survey, business survey
Fairness, courtesy, helpfulness/ cooperativeness, honesty[2]	Fairness	15. Percentage of (a) citizens, (b) businesses that feel police are generally fair in dealing with them.	Household survey, business survey, complainant survey

'person-crimes' committed leading to an arrest that survives a preliminary hearing."

- The household survey that collects victimization data can also obtain representative citizens' perceptions of the adequacy of various aspects of police service, including feelings about security in their neighborhoods and about the speed of response, courtesy, cooperativeness, helpfulness, concern, honesty, and fairness of the police. In addition, a telephone or mail survey (if properly followed up) of persons who have requested help enables the local government to assess its performance on nonserious requests for assistance—the majority of all calls.

Because a major goal for police in the 1990s is to contribute to the quality of life in the neighborhood, as well as to control crime, a set of citizen perception measures even more detailed than those suggested here might be needed.

Exhibit 6-1, continued

Measures of Effectiveness for Crime Control Services

Objective	Quality characteristic	Specific measure	Data collection procedure
	Courtesy	16. Percentage of (a) citizens, (b) businesses that feel police are generally courteous in dealing with them.	Household survey, business survey, complainant survey
	Helpfulness/ cooperativeness	17. Percentage of (a) citizens, (b) businesses that feel police are generally helpful, cooperative, and sensitive to their concerns.	Household survey, complainant survey
	Honesty	18. Number of reported incidents or complaints of police misbehavior, and the number resulting in judgment against the local government or employee (by type of complaint (civil charge, criminal charge other service complaints), per 100 police.	Police and mayor's office records
		19. Percentage of citizens who feel police are in general honest and can be trusted.[2]	Household survey, complainant survey
	Citizen satisfaction with police handling of miscellaneous incidents	20. Percentage of persons requesting assistance for other than serious crimes who are satisfied (or dissatisfied) with police handling of their problems, categorized by reason for dissatisfaction and by type of call.	Complainant survey
	Citizen satisfaction with overall performance	21. Percentage of (a) citizens, (b) businesses that rate police performance as excellent or good (or fair or poor), by reason for satisfaction (or dissatisfaction).	Household survey, business survey, complainant survey
	Police safety	22. Number of injuries to police officers (a) per 100 officers, (b) per 100 calls.	Police injury reports
Vice and Drug Offenses[3]			
Apprehension	Level and focus of arrest activity	23. Number of arrests for vice- and drug-related crimes, by type of crime and by "big fish" or "little fish."	Booking records
	Quality of arrests	— Measures 10 and 11.	Arrest and court records
	Illegal materials seized	24. Quantity and street value of illicit drugs seized.	Police property records
	Drug usage	25. Percentage of arrestees who test positive for illegal drugs.	Arrest records
		26. Street price of illegal drugs.	Special data collection effort
Citizen satisfaction	Citizen perception of seriousness of problem	27. Percentage of citizens who feel that (a) pornography, (b) prostitution, (c) gambling, (d) "soft" illegal drug usage, (e) "hard" illegal drug usage, (f) sale of illegal drugs is a major problem in their neighborhood or community.	Household survey

[1]One person committing four crimes or four persons committing one crime would be four "person-crimes." When the number of offenders involved in a crime is unknown, as may frequently happen with such crimes as burglary, "one" criminal can be assumed for this statistic (or the historical average number of offenders for that type of crime could be used).

[2]A satisfactory approach to measuring the degree of corruption, malfeasance, or negligence is lacking. Data on the number of complaints received by the city on these problems should be examined, particularly when their number increases substantially.

[3]These offenses have special measurement difficulties, so measures for them have been grouped separately. Deaths from drug overdoses per 1,000 population might also be considered as part of this family of measures that indicate the magnitude of the local drug problem—only in part a reflection of police work.

- The measures in Exhibit 6-1 should be disaggregated by key operational characteristics such as the neighborhood where incidents occur and the category of crime. These breakouts can make the measurement information more useful to police officials and other users of the reports.

- Some small but potentially helpful refinements can be made to current reported crime statistics. These include providing crime rates separately for businesses and for households, and considering transient populations (daytime work force, visitors) as well as residential populations in determining crime rates.

    Local governments can also consider groupings of violent crimes, crimes against property, and other crimes with direct victims, in a manner different from the FBI Uniform Crime Reports (although the latter's measure should be collected also to allow consistent intercity comparisons and national aggregation).

- The impact of police on illegal drug use and drug-related crime continues to resist direct measurement, despite decades of attention to this high-priority area of police work. The measures suggested here are the street price of drugs, the extent to which drugs appear in persons arrested, and the number of arrests made for illegal drug activity, although none of these approaches is wholly satisfactory. The impact of the drug problem is also reflected in the crime rate statistics themselves; that is, the war on drugs can be viewed as a major crime prevention approach, along with other approaches such as neighborhood patrolling.

- Measures for local communities with special concerns can be added to the list in Exhibit 6-1, for use either from time to time or on a regular basis. For example, in some communities where college students traditionally vacation during spring break, the number of arrests for public disorder and citizen perceptions of rowdyism may be of local concern. Although such incidents are reflected in measures in Exhibit 6-1, a community can measure this aspect more explicitly. Other local concerns may be rates of nuisance crimes and crimes against visitors in tourist areas, attacks against students on local college campuses, vandalism against religious or ethnic institutions, drug arrests and perception of drug activity near schools, and clearance rates of high visibility or high public interest crimes (e.g., savings and loan embezzlement, serial murders, or subway crimes).

Individual Measures and Data Collection Procedures

The measures in Exhibit 6-1 and the procedures for collecting data are discussed in this section under four major headings:

- Measures of crime prevention (Measures 1–6)
- Measures of apprehension success (Measures 7–11)
- Measures of police responsiveness and citizen satisfaction (Measures 12–22)
- Measures of performance on vice, drugs, and similar offenses (Measures 23–27).

Measures of "Crime Prevention" (Measures 1–6)

Measure 1:   Number of reported crimes per 1,000 population, total and by type of crime.

This is the standard crime control measure. Several variations should be considered, in addition to the standard procedures required for FBI crime reporting.

Type of Crime. Aggregate crime rates can be reported using three groupings: FBI "index" crimes, FBI "Part I" crimes, and a locally defined group of all crimes that are considered serious. The first two groupings allow intercity comparisons. The last grouping, tailored to local judgments, might include (1) all Part I crimes: the seven index crimes (homicide, rape, robbery, aggravated assault, burglary, larceny, motor vehicle theft, and arson) plus negligent manslaughter and (2) those Part II crimes with direct, unwilling victims: forgery and counterfeiting, fraud, embezzlement, vandalism, child neglect or abuse, kidnapping, blackmail, extortion, stolen property trafficking, and other related crimes. The local definition of serious crimes might exclude the following: Part II sex offenses, narcotics possession, gambling, nonviolent offenses against the family, liquor law violations, drunkenness, disorderly conduct, vagrancy, runaways, loitering, and so forth. The additional crime categorization would not require any additional data collection, just another computer tabulation of data.

Populations at Risk. To the extent feasible, crime rates should be computed for various populations at risk, such as businesses and nonresidents (e.g., commuters). Crime rates based only on residential population (crimes per 1,000 population) can be misleading. For example, crime rates will seem high in those jurisdictions or portions of a jurisdiction that have proportionately more businesses with employees and shoppers commuting from outside.[1] To better reflect the populations at risk, the following separate crime rates might be calculated:

- The "number of reported crimes against residents (or residences) per 1,000 residents (or residential units)" defined to include all crimes against the person when the person is a resident and all property crimes involving residential property. Property crimes against businesses owned by residents could be counted here and also in the next measure; the double counting that would result from some incidents is not inappropriate.[2] Residential population estimates between censuses are often available from the local planning department.

- The "number of crimes against businesses per 1,000 businesses" or the "number of crimes against businesses per 1,000 employees." The latter version reflects the increased population at risk presented by larger establishments and reduces the problem of defining a single business. An estimate of the number of businesses is often available from the license department, the treasurer's office, or one of the local government's offices that is responsible for inspections, such as for fire and safety conditions. The measurement data might be categorized by type of business (banks, motels, and so forth).

- The "rate of crimes per 1,000 equivalent daily population," defined as the total number of residents and nonresidents in the city on an average day. The "equivalent daily population" is likely to change with the season for communities with large visitor populations or with seasonally varying employment, and averages should be computed for annual figures. The Chamber of Commerce often has estimates of visitor populations, but because they are estimates, they should be investigated before use. They may cover only visitors staying in hotels or motels. Better estimates of "average daily population" might be developed by the planning department, inasmuch as they will be useful to many agencies (for example, police, fire, transportation).

Other populations at risk are commonly reflected in crime rates by disaggregating them by age, race, and sex of the victim, by neighborhood where the crime occurred (for nonbusiness crimes), and by general type of business and neighborhood (for business crimes). This practice can identify more clearly those groups with the most severe problems and can provide clues as to the direction needed for prevention procedures. Of special concern may be crimes against the elderly, crimes against children, crimes against women, and crimes against minorities.

Special Validity Considerations. One problem with the use of reported crime rates is that many crimes are unreported. Surveys by the federal government indicate that more than 60 percent go unreported.[3] Measures 2 and 3 are included to counteract this problem.

If the degree of underreporting remains nearly the same from year to year, Measure 1 still can be a reliable indicator of crime trends. However, total victimization should be measured occasionally to determine if the counts are reliable. Also, because underreporting varies from community to community, comparisons based only on reported crimes can be misleading.

Another problem with reported crime rates is the differences that develop among police officers or from year to year in the definitions of various crimes. For example, practices may differ in recording crimes involving youths, especially the lesser crimes. To minimize differences in defining crimes, a local government can provide officer training that emphasizes the importance of accurate records and clarifies confusing categories. It can also conduct regular supervisory review of incident reports, establish clear departmental policies on reporting (when the law affords discretionary choice), and have an independent agency periodically check the accuracy of tabulations of a sample of incidents.

Measure 2:   *Number of reported plus unreported crimes per 1,000 households (or residents, or businesses), by type of crime.*

Underreporting crimes causes at least three measurement problems. First, it may mislead officials and the public about the magnitude of crime. Second, when a local government undertakes activities that lead to increased crime reporting by citizens, the higher *reported* crime figures will seem to indicate a real crime increase. And third, as discussed earlier, differences in underreporting confound comparisons over time and between communities.

Evidence from federal and local victimization surveys indicates that underreporting is common for incidents involving little or no loss or harm, such as attempted forcible entry, attempted robbery without injury, and personal larcenies where the value of the stolen goods was small. However, rape and other crimes of violence also have unreported rates of about 50 percent.[4] The degree of underreporting may also vary as citizens gain or lose confidence in the police and as they are encouraged to report, or are dissuaded from reporting, crimes.

Data Collection. Obtaining reliable estimates of unreported as well as reported crimes is not easy. Many local governments can survey periodically a random sample of households and businesses to provide estimates of the number and percentage of households (or individuals) and businesses that have been the victims of unreported crimes.

Another approach is to use insurance data on crimes with property loss or injuries to estimate total crime trends. However, this presents other validation problems such as lack of insurance for the poor (who are often heavily victimized), underreporting of even insured losses to the insurance companies themselves, and the lack of full information on nonproperty crimes, plus the difficulty of obtaining data from insurance companies. Victimization survey questionnaires are regularly used by the U.S. Department of Justice in nationwide surveys, and the questionnaires can be used by local communities as well.[5] These surveys ask detailed questions about many types of crimes to aid the memory of the respondents and to avoid relying on citizens' knowledge of the legal definition of each type of crime. For example, a layman might call a burglary a robbery. Few local governments, however, are able to afford the lengthy interviews and large sample size of the U.S. Department of Justice surveys (about 49,000 households are contacted nationally).

The victimization surveys proposed here pose fewer questions, use smaller samples (500 to 1,000 households), and use less sophisticated procedures than those of the Department of Justice. The smaller sample size reduces the accuracy of the estimates, but the results are still useful, even if the survey is undertaken only occasionally (such as every two or three years), especially if the degree of underreporting is found not to change much from year to year. The survey is designed to be part of a household survey.

This approach has been used by St. Petersburg, Nashville, Palo Alto, and other cities. Questions 31–36 in Appendix 1 are examples of victimization queries. The questions generally follow the wording of the Department of Justice questions but inquire about fewer categories of crime and obtain fewer details about each crime. Interviewers must be trained to understand the definitions of the categories of crimes included in the wording of the questions (such as when assault is "serious" or "not serious"; for example, see Question 34 in Appendix 1). Moreover, survey questions must be matched with the categories of reported crimes already in use in the jurisdiction if victimization information yielded by the survey is to be compared with the crime rates reported by the police.

Businesses as well as households can be surveyed to discover the extent of their unreported victimization, as has been done by the U.S. Department of Justice surveys. For annual data collection by local governments, however, it is recommended, as with the household survey, that victimization questions be included on a multiservice business survey. Surveys of businesses are discussed in Chapter 14; an illustrative questionnaire is presented in Appendix 2; Questions 14–18 could be used to estimate the number and percentage of unreported criminal acts against businesses.

Victimization rates can be computed directly from a household survey. If desired, the estimate of the total number of reported plus unreported crimes can be calculated in several ways; three are outlined here:

- Estimate total residential victimization by multiplying the per capita (or per household) victimization rate calculated from the survey by the total population of the jurisdiction. The number of commercial crimes could be estimated similarly from the business survey. (Less satisfactorily, business crimes could be estimated from police records, although this would omit unreported business crimes from the overall total.) This calculation will not include an estimate of victimizations of transients or homeless persons, who are not covered in the household surveys. Perhaps the number of reported incidents involving transients could be determined from police records.

- Estimate the number of unreported residential incidents (and commercial incidents, if the survey of businesses is used) by multiplying the per capita (or per household) nonreported crime rates obtained from the survey by the total population. Add this to the number of crimes reported in police records. (The resulting estimate will include no estimate of the underreporting of crimes involving transients because, as noted earlier, these incidents are not covered by the household surveys, but it will include reported crimes involving transient victims. Usually this is a small proportion of the total crime rate.)

- Multiply the ratio of unreported/reported residential incidents (from the survey) by the number of crimes reported (from police records) to estimate the number of unreported incidents. Add this number to the number of crimes reported in police records. This method assumes that the nonreporting rate will be nearly the same for transients as for residents.

There is no evidence to suggest which approach is most accurate. Regardless of which approach is selected, the procedures should be used consistently to permit meaningful comparisons from one time period to another.

Finally, tallies of the reasons for nonreporting are desirable. This information—such as frequent mention of "fear of retaliation"—can provide the jurisdiction with clues as to necessary corrective action. Question 31c in Appendix 1 illustrates how such data might be collected.

Special Validity Considerations. The potential problems with the sample survey approach are discussed in Chapter 13, but one particular concern for this measure is the ability of respondents to recall accurately their victimization experiences.[6] The memory problem has two major components: respondents may forget incidents or they may include incidents that occurred before the period they are being asked about. The questions shown in Appendix 1 ask about a six-month period (to be comparable to federally collected victimization data).

Another problem concerns the validity of responses in cases in which one person in a household is asked to recall crimes committed against anyone in the household. This problem can be eliminated if the more expensive survey procedures are used in which each member of the household is interviewed—perhaps including school-age children. Those efforts to check on the validity of crime victimization responses suggest that surveys have problems but yield data accurate enough for gross monitoring.[7]

By using proper survey procedures, estimating the total crime rate is likely to be a more accurate guide to a community's overall progress than relying solely on reported crime data. However, less detailed (and less expensive) victimization survey procedures, estimates of the number of unreported crimes for a given type of offense, are likely to be imprecise because of the occasional difficulty of determining the proper category of crime for a given incident. Thus, these abbreviated victimization surveys are not likely to collect enough information on each crime to estimate reliably the crime rate by type of crime.

If the same survey questions are used from year to year, the survey should help indicate relative changes in the magnitude of the crime rate as well as possible changes in the degree of underreporting over time.

Measure 3: *Percentage of (a) households, (b) businesses victimized.*

Victimization measures are usually calculated as a per capita rate, as shown in Measure 2 (the *total* number of crimes divided by the total population or number of households). A useful variation is Measure 3, which indicates the proportion of the population

that was victimized one or more times during the reporting period. The total number of crimes divided by the number of households is *not* equivalent to this measure, because many households are victims of more than one crime. For example, in 1985, according to the National Crime Survey, 25 percent of all U.S. households were touched by at least one crime; the number of victimizations divided by the number of households, however, was 0.40.[8]

Measure 3, if broken out by population characteristics such as age, sex, race or ethnic group, and geographical segment of the jurisdiction, is useful as an estimate of possible inequities in the provision of crime prevention services. It is helpful for the police to know if a particular segment of houholds or businesses is experiencing a disproportionate share of the crimes. If characteristics of the frequently victimized households and businesses can be identified, local authorities may be able to use such information to redesign and retarget crime prevention programs.

Data Collection. The number of households and businesses victimized at least once can be estimated from household and business surveys using the same questions as those used for Measure 2. The "number victimized more than once" also can be estimated.

Special Validity Considerations. This measure is generally more reliable than Measure 2 (estimated total crime rate) because it is easier for a respondent to remember whether there were any crimes at all than the exact number of crimes for a given period.

Measure 4: *Number and rate of persons (a) physically injured, (b) killed in the course of crimes or nontraffic, crime-related police work— including victims and police.*

Except for the deaths by murder and manslaughter, statistics on other citizen injuries or deaths related to crime are rarely compiled.

There are problems in defining what constitutes an injury. It can be argued, for example, that all crimes—or at least all crimes against the person and most robberies—cause some degree of psychological, if not physical, injury. For this measure it is suggested that only those physical injuries requiring medical attention be included. (This allows comparability with fire and traffic accident injuries, for which similar definitions are used.)

Although tempting, it is inappropriate to estimate this measure by summing the number of "crimes against persons." Many jurisdictions make no distinction between assaults that result in injury and those that do not. For example, aggravated assault may be an attack resulting in serious injury or a threat with a gun that is not fired. Also, injuries associated with crimes such as robbery and injuries to bystanders, whether caused by offenders or police, often do not result in separate formal charges for assaults.

Data Collection. Data can be grouped by the following categories:

- Role of person injured (victim of crime, bystander, suspect, or police)

- Cause of injury (actions of suspect, police, bystander, or victim; or accident associated with the crime—for example, a fall)

- Severity of injury (death, injury that required hospitalization, other injury likely to require medical attention).

For recording these data, a format such as the one in Exhibit 6-2 might be used.

Special Validity Considerations. Because it represents a reformulation and summary of existing data, often reported in narrative form on incident reports, this measure presents few special validation problems—except for the definition of injuries, which is a longstanding problem in fire and traffic statistics.

Measure 5: *Percentage of domestic quarrels and other disturbance calls with no arrest and no second call within x hours.*

Domestic quarrels, quarrels among acquaintances, and disturbances are often precursors of serious crimes. They often result in violence, sometimes with injuries to the officers responding. How well police defuse such situations is a key aspect of police effectiveness in deterrence. No other measure directly addresses this police activity.

This measure makes the assumption that, in many cases, police are able to defuse the situations that prompt these types of calls, without the need to make an arrest *and* in such a way as to prevent second calls for at least a certain period of time. This period (the value of x in the measure) might be the duration of a tour of duty, 24 hours, or perhaps even a week—the selection is left to local judgment.

There will, of course, be occasions when an arrest is appropriate on the first call. On other occasions, a police officer may, exercising reasonable judgment, avoid making an arrest on the initial call, but the circumstances beyond his or her control could prompt a second call. To the extent that such uncontrollable circumstances are prevalent, this measure might be less meaningful, although if the percentage of such situations is small or remains fairly stable from year to year, the measure will still meaningfully track trends.

Data Collection. Special procedures are needed to keep track of "family quarrel situations reported to the police." Each dispatcher might log such calls; the frequency of calls to the same address could be tallied (perhaps by computer). Records of the previous calls can show whether arrests were made. Calls discovered on arrival of police officers to involve felonies (thus making arrest more likely) should be grouped separately.

Measure 6: *Number of injuries to (a) citizens (after police arrival), (b) police per 100 domestic quarrel calls.*

One of the principal goals in responding to domestic quarrels is to keep the situation nonviolent after the police arrive. This measure represents the injuries to citizens and police on these calls.

Exhibit 6-2

Format for Recording Crime-Related Injuries or Deaths

	To victim(s)	To police	To suspect(s)	To bystander(s)/others	Cause
Number of injuries					
Number of deaths					

Data Collection. This information normally is recorded in the narrative section of police reports. Civilian injuries may not always be recorded explicitly on the form and may be identified in the text. Recording them explicitly makes data analysis much easier and more reliable, especially if the police incident reports are computerized.

Measures of Apprehension Success (Measures 7–11)

Measure 7:   Percentage of reported crimes cleared, by type of crime and whether cleared by arrest or by "exception."

This measure is the clearance rate, the traditional measure of apprehension effectiveness. This is the percentage of crimes for which at least one suspect has been arrested and charged, or for which an "exceptional clearance" has been made. ("Exceptional clearances," as defined by the FBI Uniform Crime Reporting (UCR) System, include cases where an arrestee confesses to other crimes, the accused dies, the victim refuses to cooperate in the prosecution, the suspect is transferred to another jurisdiction to face other charges, and so forth). The number of exceptional clearances should be presented separately. Exceptional clearances may constitute a substantial proportion of total clearances, and they present special measurement problems: (1) the degree to which police attempt to get apprehended criminals to admit to other crimes may change over time, (2) difficulties in using a consistent definition of exceptional clearance can cause inconsistent application, and (3) the number of exceptional clearances reported by suspects will vary with their willingness to confess to other crimes.

Clearance rates should be presented for each crime category so that performance on each type of crime can be assessed. Clearance rates on Part II crimes with victims (such as kidnapping) should receive the same treatment as clearance rates on Part I crimes.

Clearance rates vary considerably among types of crimes. For example, the nationwide clearance rate for aggravated assault was 57 percent in 1989 versus 14 percent for burglary.[9]

Consideration of clearance rates by individual crime categories also enables officials to determine if an improvement or degradation in the overall clearance rate was caused by a change in the crime mix. For example, if an unusually large number of "hard to solve" crimes are committed in a given year, a decrease in the overall clearance rate might result even though clearance rates for some individual crime categories increased.

Case "difficulty" within crime categories should

also be considered. Incidents might be classified for any given crime category by the quality of evidence available to the immediately responding police officer. Clearance rates could then be calculated for each category of case difficulty. Many police departments note on their incident reports whether there was an eyewitness, physical evidence, or a confession. This information is used to prioritize investigation and prosecution resource allocation. It also can be used as a "quality of evidence" (i.e., case difficulty) indicator.

Unfortunately, as has already been mentioned, clearance rates as currently defined have major validity problems, and the measure provides only a rudimentary indication of success in "solving" crimes.

Data Collection. Clearances are reported monthly by type of crime in most jurisdictions as part of the FBI UCR System. FBI definitions should be used consistently, especially those for exceptional clearances.

A local government should consider tallying clearances for each police unit that accomplishes clearances, including "assists" (cases in which one unit helps another). If this is done, fair ground rules for "assists" should be established to avoid misuse of the data and promotion of unhealthy rivalries. Clearances can also be categorized by how they were made. Some suggested categories are "response to a call of a crime in progress," "preventive patrol," "follow-up investigation by patrol," "follow-up investigation by detectives," and so forth.

Special Validity Considerations. Using clearance rates as indicators of "solution" success poses some problems:

- The validity of an exceptional clearance is sometimes questionable. For instance, arrestees may admit to multiple crimes in exchange for leniency because they know they are unlikely to be prosecuted for them in the absence of evidence other than their confessions. Also, definitions of exceptional clearances are complex and not always adhered to.

- Clearances as defined by the UCR reflect only the first arrest on a case and give no credit to subsequent arrests. A crime is considered cleared when only one offender is arrested—even when multiple offenders were known to have participated in it. A department that apprehends only one of the offenders involved in a crime would have as high a clearance rate as one that arrested all offenders involved in a similar crime. (Measure 8 addresses this problem.)

- The "clearance" is usually counted even if the

arrest does not pass preliminary court hearing, regardless of the reason it is dropped. Most jurisdictions have little systematic feedback from the court system to the police concerning disposition of arrests. A clearance is not removed from the total if the suspect is released. Thus, the clearance rates may not indicate the percentage of offenders who are successfully brought to justice or even the percentage of crimes that have been "solved." (Measures 9 and 10 address this problem.)

- Usually the clearance rate is computed as the number of clearances in a year, quarter, or month divided by the number of crimes in the same period. Because some time usually elapses between crime and arrest, some clearances in a given year will relate to crimes committed in the previous year, and some clearances for crimes in the current year will not show up until the next year. If elapsed time is generally short or if crime and clearance rates are constant, this practice presents little problem. If the lag is considerable and crime clearance rates vary, clearance rates computed the usual way will be somewhat different from the actual clearance rates. Local governments should estimate the distribution of times required to clear various types of crimes to determine the severity of this problem for various types of crimes.

Measure 8:   Percentage of "person-crimes" cleared, by type of crime.

As noted earlier, the clearance rate counts a crime as cleared after the first arrest on a case. The extent to which *all* offenders are apprehended can be reflected by a new measure, the percentage of "person-crimes" cleared. Although this measure may seem strange, it is more natural than the commonly used "clearance" definition.

A "person-crime" is defined as one person committing one crime. One person committing four crimes or four persons committing one crime would each mean four person-crimes have been committed. Each time a person is arrested for a crime or charged with an additional crime, one person-crime would be counted as cleared. Exceptional clearances of person-crimes would be handled the same as for FBI crime clearance. For example, one person committing four offenses during the same incident would count as only one person-crime and *not* four.

Data Collection. The known number of offenders is usually recorded on incident reports. An additional space on the report form for the estimated number

of offenders could expedite tallies. The total could be compared with the total number of arrests and exceptional clearances for the reporting period. When a case is classified as "unfounded," it may be necessary to look up the number of person-crimes in the case file to determine how many to subtract from the total number of person-crimes. As information becomes available to indicate that more (or fewer) persons were involved than previously estimated, the tallies should be revised. This process can be computerized easily.

Special Validity Considerations. The chief difficulty is the accuracy of the information on how many offenders were involved in individual crimes. The data are likely to be most accurate for crimes against the person (because the number of offenders is more likely to be known) as distinguished, for example, from burglaries. When the number of offenders is not known, "one" offender might be assumed.

Even with this limitation, this measure is more accurate in reflecting apprehension success than the traditional clearance rates. Its importance depends on whether there are many crimes known to involve multiple offenders. Some jurisdictions might wish to consider this measure only for crimes against the person, where the number of perpetrators is more likely to be known, and the importance of catching all of them is greater.

Measure 9:   Percentage of adult arrests that survive preliminary court hearing (or state attorney's investigation) and percentage dropped for police-related reasons, by type of crime.

Many arrests never lead to conviction, and others fail to survive even the preliminary court hearing. Thus, arrest and clearance rates may overstate apprehension effectiveness.[10] In addition, an ineffectual arrest may waste much police, prosecution, and judicial time before it is dropped from the system. Also, arrests are restrictions of personal liberty. Without some measure of the quality of arrests, there may be a perverse incentive for officers to make questionable arrests to increase arrest or clearance totals.

A suggested approach to measure the effectiveness of arrests is to determine the percentage that passes judicial screening or screening by a state attorney's office. Another approach is to measure the percentage of arrest reports that are judged of acceptable quality by a panel of attorneys. Both the quality of the report itself and the quality of the arrest as described by the report are considered.[11] The quality of police performance may have more influence on whether a case passes screening than it does on the final court disposition, although the latter is also important (see Measure 10).

For many jurisdictions, the judicial screening that can be used as the test for this measure is the preliminary hearing in a court of limited jurisdiction. "Preliminary" hearings are usually the second hearing in the process of an arrest. The first is usually an advisory hearing held within 24 hours after arrest, depending on the state, to set bail or appoint a public defender if necessary. Usually the advisory hearing is not a sufficient test of probable cause.

The preliminary hearing usually includes a presentation of evidence before a judge. Prosecution and defense are present. The basic test of the arrest at the hearing is whether a crime probably took place as charged, and whether there is "probable cause" to assume that the person arrested was one of the offenders. The arrestee may not be "bound over" if the evidence seems insufficient, if legal procedures in making the arrest and preparing the case were not properly followed, or if police and other key witnesses do not appear. Cases also may be dropped because of crowded court dockets and many other reasons that have no bearing on police effectiveness.

The measure should be subdivided to indicate the "percentage of arrests dropped for police-related reasons." This better reflects the police role, and it also provides feedback to the police on specific areas for improvement. The overall measure, however, is of interest because it is less dependent on value judgments than the subdivided version and because it is meaningful as a measure of apprehension effectiveness in relation to the criminal justice system of which the police are but one component.

Police-related reasons might include any deficiency in police preparation or procedures that is responsible for the unsatisfactory disposition of the case. Examples might be improper recovery of evidence, mishandled evidence, unintelligible reports, improper search and seizure, and similar problems that can be corrected by appropriate training and instruction. Some governments may choose to include cases dropped because witnesses were unwilling to testify.

Jurisdictions with no preliminary hearings sometimes substitute investigations by the state attorney's office, which perform a similar function, with one important difference: The prosecution's investigation purposely considers the likelihood of successful prosecution, and not just the likelihood that a crime took place and that probable cause existed for making the arrest. Thus, cases may be dropped that would have survived a preliminary hearing. Nevertheless, the "percentage that pass the state attorney's hearing," and the "percentage that do not pass the police-related reasons" seem satisfactory arrest effectiveness measures.

Measurements of the quality of felony arrests should be separated from misdemeanor arrests. Preliminary hearings often are not held for misdemeanors when the defendants waive their rights to jury trials. Instead, cases proceed directly to trial by a judge. The arrest effectiveness measure for misdemeanors, therefore, might be "the percentage that pass a preliminary hearing (or state attorney's investigation) or that are turned over to another court for further prosecution." This is a stricter test than that for felonies because a trial requires tighter standards of proof than does a hearing.

It seems desirable also to provide arrest "survival" rates by the major category of offenses for felonies and misdemeanors to direct attention to specific categories with low survival rates. It may also be useful to distinguish survival rates for arrests made (1) by an officer who either observes a crime in progress or who otherwise responds to a crime call, (2) after a warrant has been issued at the request of the police or prosecution, and (3) in response to a warrant obtained by a citizen. In one sample of arrests, there were striking differences among these categories in percentages of arrests surviving hearings.

"Survival" of an arrest past preliminary hearing should be defined as continued legal processing of at least one charge. Up to this point we have referred loosely to preliminary hearings for arrests. Actually, hearings are held for specific charges and not for arrests. One individual may be arrested on several charges, which may be heard either at the same time or at separate hearings. Several individuals may be arrested for the same crime and the charges against them heard simultaneously or separately. The intent of the proposed measure is to determine whether individuals are arrested needlessly. Thus, attention should focus on the percentage of arrests for which *at least one charge* survives preliminary hearing. If any one charge survives, the arrest can be considered of satisfactory quality.

Juvenile arrests can be excluded from the measure. In many jurisdictions, juvenile arrests are handled separately and differently from adult arrests for most noncapital offenses. The processing of a juvenile arrest often focuses on what is best for the juvenile rather than on the validity of the charges. The preliminary processing and decision for a juvenile arrest may be made by social workers rather than the courts. Also, juvenile arrest records are held in greater confidence than adult arrest records, which could make initial data collection and subsequent audits more difficult. This exclusion of juvenile arrests leaves a gap in the measures.

Does Measure 9 really reflect the quality of the arrest? Only in part. It reflects the quality of the arrest itself *and* the follow-up processing of the arrest and associated investigation for additional evidence and witnesses. It is conceivable that the arrest itself might have been made on insufficient grounds even though subsequent investigation turns up supporting evidence. The measure also does not reflect "quality" aspects of arrests such as whether the amount of force used was appropriate or whether the officer was courteous; nor does it reflect arrests that were not made when they should have been. Conversely, arrests for good cause may be disposed of improperly by prosecution or courts.

Despite these difficulties, this measure represents the effectiveness of apprehensions more accurately than do clearance rates and gives insights into how to improve arrest procedures and processing.

Data Collection. The principal data collection problem is to establish a procedure for police to receive regularly, or have access to, court disposition data.

Data on dispositions of preliminary hearings and state attorney's investigations are usually available in a centralized source, either a court docket book or a computer file. When different courts handle different types of cases, two or more sources may be needed. The number of arrests corresponding to the dispositions for a particular time period can be obtained either from arrest records or booking entries—or from the court records themselves, if the number of arrests dropped before the preliminary hearing is very small.

Each jurisdiction should develop definitions and ground rules for classifying specific arrest dispositions to determine which dispositions should be counted as successfully surviving the preliminary court prosecution test. For example, misdemeanor arrests with guilty dispositions could be defined as "successful" arrests. Those involving dismissal by the judge, withdrawal by prosecution, or a not-guilty verdict could be categorized as "unsuccessful" arrests. Those involving forfeit of bond, not-guilty plea coupled with paid fine, dismissal on (court) costs, capias warrant, or referral to another jurisdiction could be categorized as "ambiguous" arrests. Such definitions and ground rules should be adhered to so that the measurement findings will be fairly comparable from one time to another.

In general, the number of arrests is not equivalent to the number of preliminary hearing dispositions because cases may be dropped before the hearing for a variety of reasons. Each local government should make at least an initial examination to see if a significant number of cases are being dropped before the hearing. If not, court (or prosecution office) disposition data can be used also to obtain the number of arrests. If many arrests are dropped before the

preliminary hearing, the jurisdiction should use the arrest records or booking reports to calculate the number of arrests. In a sample of 112 arrest reports in one city, 3 resulted in no bookings, and 2 others could not be traced to a disposition (a total of 5 percent of the arrests). Of 79 felony arrests in a second city, 1 suspect escaped, 3 had charges dropped, and 1 case could not be tracked (6 percent of the arrests). The effect of dropouts on the measure thus was small. If these rates for dropouts before court disposition are representative, they can be ignored, and the added work of tallying arrest records or number of bookings can be avoided.

Similarly, jurisdictions probably can ignore the lapse between the time of arrest and the preliminary hearing. In the cases sampled in two cities, the lapse was small (about one to seven days for the majority of the cases). Thus, the number of arrests surviving the court test in a period (year, quarter, or even month) could be divided by the number of arrests booked in that period; or the number surviving could be divided by the number of cases heard, with both figures coming from the court disposition. It is recommended, however, that each local government check the time lag to determine if there are many cases that involve significant delays, and if so, whether they are uniformly distributed.

Care must be taken to avoid recording each charge as a separate arrest and to see whether each arrest resulted in at least one charge that survived the hearing. Even if data are recorded manually and the charges are not recorded consecutively, it seems feasible to attempt to relate charges to an arrest.

Felony arrests are frequently downgraded to misdemeanors either before or during preliminary hearings. In a sample of felony arrests in one test city, 11 percent were downgraded to misdemeanors. Care should be taken that these arrests are neither unintentionally recorded twice (once as a felony, once as a misdemeanor) nor neglected. A charge reduced to a misdemeanor may be recorded as one type of disposition of a felony arrest; alternatively, the arrest may be considered a misdemeanor arrest that was incorrectly labeled. In the latter case, it would be counted with misdemeanors and subtracted from felonies.

A major data collection problem involves persuading the courts or the state attorney's office to agree to specify reasons for dropping cases so that the percentage of arrests dropped for each major reason can be measured. It is often difficult to determine if the reason was "police-related." Also, it may be embarrassing to admit that cases are dropped for reasons such as crowded court calendars. One way to resolve this problem is to have representatives of the attorneys, judges, and police reach a consensus on how to classify reasons for dropping cases. This may not be accomplished easily.

Special Validity Considerations. Because parts of the criminal justice system other than police have a role in the outcome for Measure 9, this measure reflects more than just police apprehension effectiveness. Also, there are numerous data collection details, such as developing and adhering to category definitions, that can cause inaccurate data. Thus periodic, independent checking of the tallies is advisable for this measure.

Yet this measure has some significant validity advantages over traditional crime "solution" measures such as clearance rates. If a jurisdiction finds that a significant percentage of arrests for a particular category of crime does not survive the preliminary hearing, the validity of clearance rates as indicators of satisfactorily solving these crimes should be questioned.

Measure 10: *Percentage of adult arrests resulting in conviction or treatment (a) on at least one charge, (b) on the highest initial charge, by type of crime.*

The ultimate test of the effectiveness of an arrest and its associated police work is whether the arrest leads to conviction or treatment of those arrested. This is not to say that it is in the best interest of society to convict every person arrested. Some of those arrested will be innocent, and some arrests that the police officer knows to be on shaky evidence nevertheless can have a beneficial effect on guilty parties in discouraging future criminal activity. Nor is it implied that conviction and subsequent disposition in corrections are always correct and effective. However, ideally only the guilty would be arrested, and all those arrested would be convicted or provided treatment in lieu of conviction. This measure thus more closely reflects the ultimate effectiveness of arrests than does the previous measure ("percentage of arrests passing preliminary hearings"), but it also involves to a greater extent the work of the prosecutor's office and court system.

An arrest may stand the test of probable cause, which is adequate for preliminary hearing, but the evidence may not be strong enough to withstand the test of reasonable doubt at trial. The courts, prosecution, judge, and jury all have a major say in whether an arrest results in a conviction. Given the same evidence and quality of police work, different judges and juries may arrive at different conclusions.

Nevertheless, the quality of evidence obtained by the police, the proper legal handling of the arrested person, the competence of the police in giving court testimony, police lab work, and other factors are all important contributions to the likelihood of conviction and should be considered part of apprehension effectiveness.[12]

Conviction may be for the original charge, a lower charge, or less frequently, a higher charge. Sometimes a reduced charge results from plea bargaining. The strength of the case prepared by the police (and later the prosecutor's office) probably influences the extent of plea bargaining, but many other factors are also involved that are not controllable by the police (such as court work load or failure of prosecution witnesses to appear).

Various forms of the measure may be used, including the "percentage of arrests resulting in conviction for some charge," the "percentage resulting in conviction for the highest original charge," and "the percentage of charges that result in conviction." Each of these might be computed as successively more stringent tests of arrest effectiveness. Changes in these quantities provide somewhat ambiguous information on police effectiveness, but they should be interpreted as signals of possible problems or evidence of success in improving arrest and investigation procedures.

Conviction rates should be reported separately for adult felonies and misdemeanors and by specific type of crime, for the same reasons as noted in the previous measure.

In some situations the outcome of a trial may not be a finding of guilt but will imply strong evidence of guilt. For example, not-guilty pleas may be accepted and fines imposed. Such disposition may be made when a judge or jury feels it is warranted to expedite the case or to protect the record of the person arrested. Whether these outcomes should be counted with the "guilty" outcomes for assessing quality of arrest is a judgment that each jurisdiction will need to make.

Data Collection. Prosecuting attorneys' offices and courts often compile statistics for their own use on the percentage of cases resulting in various dispositions. These data may not be fed back to the police, may include results for several local jurisdictions using the same court mixed together, and are rarely categorized according to percentage of arrests resulting in each disposition. As with the preceding measure, the largest data problem is to establish regular reporting of court data to the police, or to get the prosecutor or courts to make the necessary computations. For states with reliable offender-based transaction information systems, the data collection problems may be alleviated considerably.

A significant number of arrests may drop out of prosecution after the preliminary hearing but before the trial. This may result from "nol-prossing" or any of the number of legal options that, in essence, put the case into limbo from which it may be recalled at a later time. Thus the overall percentage of arrests resulting in conviction cannot be obtained by simply multiplying the "percentage of those cases that were tried and resulted in conviction or treatment" by the "percentage of arrestees that passed preliminary hearing."

Another data collection problem results from the long delays between felony arrests and trials, which make it difficult to link arrests to dispositions. These delays may run into many months (although some states have "speedy trial" legislation that requires trial within a fixed period after arrest). Usually misdemeanors are disposed of more rapidly because the preliminary hearing is often waived and the case goes directly to trial before a judge.

To develop an approximate measure that partially circumvents the delay, the percentage of arrests that result in conviction might be computed using the convictions for the current time period divided by the arrests for some earlier period. For example, if felony trials usually take place between three and six months after arrest, then the convictions in one quarter might be divided by the arrests from the quarter ending three months earlier. Although there will still be some "edge effects," the resulting statistic may be a more reliable indicator than using convictions and arrests for the same month (or tallying arrests regardless of their outcome). The reliability will depend on how sharply the arrest rate is changing, whether it varies from season to season, how the times between arrest and trial are distributed, and whether the measure is computed annually or more frequently.

Measure 11: Percentage of stolen property that is subsequently recovered: (a) vehicles, (b) other property.

Part of the apprehension objective is recovery of stolen property, to help reduce losses from crime. (This measure, however, does not include doctor's bills for victims, repair of damaged goods, and reduced economic activity through fear of crime.) Because property may be recovered without apprehension of the offenders and vice versa, both should be measured for a full picture of apprehension effectiveness.

Because search and recovery methods that involve stolen vehicles are different from those that relate to most other stolen property—and the recovery rates are often different—vehicle recovery should be measured separately from the recovery of other property. Police attempt to recover all stolen vehicles regardless of value, so the "percentage of vehicles recovered" might be reported rather than the "percentage of vehicle value recovered." This statistic also is likely to be more practical and reliable than the percentage of dollars recovered because of the inherent problems in valuation. For stolen property other than vehicles, either the value recovered or the items recovered might be counted. Here the value is probably easier to track than the "pieces." Alternatively, for cars and other property, the percentage returned in still usable condition might be tracked.

Because stolen property—especially vehicles—often is returned damaged, the value of recovered property preferably would be assessed as the "value when stolen" reduced by the "estimated cost of damages," but this may be more detail than practical.

Year-to-year comparisons should be made in terms of dollars adjusted for changes in price levels.

Data Collection. Many departments already keep records of the number and percentage of vehicles recovered. Sometimes total value of recovered property of all types is also reported, but it is not usually stated as a percentage of property stolen. Damages to recovered property, especially vehicles, are often noted on reports but seldom deducted from value when stolen.

Value of stolen property may be either exaggerated or underplayed at the time of loss because of insurance claims or estimation errors or other reasons. Even if the absolute loss and absolute recovery value are inflated or deflated, using the same values for recovery as were listed for the loss will improve the accuracy of the "percentage recovered." Matching values is somewhat easier to do for automobiles, expensive jewelry, and other types of readily identifiable property than for other stolen items. To improve consistency in valuations, book values for new and used items might be used to estimate values for recovered property for which the value was not listed at the time of loss. Police do not usually record estimates of the value of recovered property, so instituting such record keeping may be the greatest change required to implement this measure.

Special Validity Considerations. Property recovered in one period may be from crimes in earlier periods. Similarly, when the measure is computed, "property recovered in one's own jurisdiction from crimes committed in others" may not offset "property recovered in other jurisdictions from crimes in one's own." Instead of going to great lengths to adjust for special calculation problems—such as when an important fencing operation is broken or when one jurisdiction is a dumping ground for stolen cars—it should suffice to note any large recoveries from previous periods or other jurisdictions. If these problems involve significant dollar values and cannot be corrected for, the measure would be of limited value as a gauge of the jurisdiction's police performance on property recovery.

Measures of Police Responsiveness and Citizen Satisfaction (Measures 12–22)

Measure 12: *Percentage of emergency or high-priority calls responded to within x minutes and percentage of nonemergency calls responded to within y minutes.*

Promptness in responding to calls for assistance is a direct service objective as well as a factor that contributes to prevention and apprehension effectiveness. Citizens want local government to respond quickly to calls for service; this particularly applies to police services—and not just to crime calls.

The value of reducing response times is not fully clear but for emergency calls there is much professional opinion, supported by some evidence, that for at least the first few minutes, quicker response time is associated with higher clearance rates.[13] Response times should be reported separately for calls of different priorities. Because of tight local government budgets, some communities have weaned citizens from the notion that police must respond quickly to every call. In some communities, the response time goal is stated as arrival within some predetermined amount of time, rather than arrival as fast as possible, with the goal varying by type of call. For crimes in progress, it might still be as fast as possible, say within three minutes; for other serious emergency situations, within five minutes, and for minor or non-time-dependent calls (e.g., report of a crime that took place the day before), twenty minutes or longer. In some communities, citizens report minor crimes entirely by phone, or even by appointment. Response time is usually defined as the "time from receipt of a call by the police to the time the first unit arrives at the scene." It is preferable to note the time from the moment the phone starts ringing. Jurisdictions should consider this refinement if telephone lines to the department's emergency number are frequently overloaded.

In addition to measuring the percentage of calls responded to in less than *x* minutes, the mean, median, and range of response times are also useful indicators of response time.[14] The mean (or average) response time should not be used alone because it can be misleading; a few extremely long response times can sharply affect the average.

Data Collection. The time when a call is received and the time when police are dispatched are recorded by most police departments, frequently by computer or by a punched card run through a time clock in the dispatch (communications) office. The time of arrival at the scene may be radioed in by the officers responding or signaled to a control computer at the touch of a button in the patrol car. Some jurisdictions do not collect this information because they want to avoid delaying the start of "service" at the scene or clogging the air waves. As communication systems improve and are computerized, more departments are collecting this information, because it is vital for monitoring operations and designing patrol sectors.

Special Validity Considerations. The accuracy of response time data depends on the diligence with which the dispatcher's office and the officers in the field report promptly and accurately. An appropriate definition for response time should be established and adhered to. If arrival times are called in before the officers' actual arrival at the scene, the data will not give a valid measure.

Measure 13: *Percentage of (a) citizens, (b) businesses that feel police respond fast enough when called.*

Citizen satisfaction with the service rendered is a major service objective, and perceived speed of police response to citizens' calls is likely to be a prime component determining that satisfaction. It can be argued that the more "objective" previous measure is superior for measuring promptness of response and, thus, that Measure 13 is secondary. However, if citizen satisfaction is considered a principal issue in nonemergency calls, this measure assumes greater importance.

Citizen perceptions of response time should be reported separately for those who have called for assistance (or at least been present when someone else has called) and for the general public—to distinguish firsthand experience from other types.

Data Collection. Perceptions of response times of citizens who have called for service can be obtained best by using a survey of a scientifically drawn sample of those callers. For the general public, questions on perceived speed of response can be included as part of a household survey of police issues only or a survey of a number of local government services.

The multiservice survey has the disadvantage that only a portion of the respondents will have had firsthand contact with police during the period of interest. (As noted earlier, about 25 percent of U.S. households were victims of at least one crime in 1985; additional households are likely to call the police on some other concern, such as traffic accidents or presence of suspicious persons in the neighborhood.)

An example of a question to use is "Would you rate the speed of the police in responding to calls as Excellent, Good, Fair, or Poor?" Question 30 in

Appendix 1 would be appropriate to distinguish the responses of those who had direct contact with police from those who had not. A similar question for surveys of businesses is Question 20 in Appendix 2.

The random household survey has one advantage over surveys of those who have called for services. Not all calls for service result in an incident report. The random household survey is likely to include some of these callers.

Survey procedures are discussed at greater length in Chapter 13. The survey of callers ("complainant survey") is discussed in more detail under Measure 20.

Measure 14: *Percentage of (a) citizens, (b) businesspersons who feel safe (or unsafe) walking in their neighborhoods at night.*

An important police objective is to help establish and maintain an atmosphere of security for residents, the business community, and visitors.

Apparent risk and true risk are not always the same. It is seems desirable to measure the perceptions of citizens as well as actual crime rates.

Feelings of security will not always change when true risks change. The reporting of crime in the mass media and the actions of civic leaders can affect citizens' perceptions. Feelings of security may vary considerably by age group, sex, race or ethnic group, and neighborhood; results should be reported for each of these breakdowns.

Data Collection. Data on citizens' feelings of security can be obtained using the same random household survey and business survey used for obtaining data on other measures.

Question 28 of Appendix 1 can be used for residents. Questions regarding areas of the city into which the citizen would like to go but does not for fear of crime (Questions 29 and 29a of Appendix 1) help measure the atmosphere of security and also suggest specific areas of the community where the problems are worst. Illustrative questions that might be used for businesses are presented in Appendix 2 (Questions 11 and 12).

Measure 15: *Percentage of (a) citizens, (b) businesses that feel police are generally fair in dealing with them.*

Measure 16: *Percentage of (a) citizens, (b) businesses that feel police are generally courteous in dealing with them.*

Measure 17: *Percentage of (a) citizens, (b) businesses that feel police are generally helpful, cooperative, and sensitive to their concerns.*

The fairness and courtesy with which police services are delivered concern citizens and businesspersons. Moreover, police are expected today to go beyond being civil (courteous), to being helpful, cooperative with individuals and various citizen and civic groups, and sensitive to the feelings of the citizen. Some police departments emphasize the quality of the response and the extent of community cooperation as much as end results in measuring police effectiveness.[15]

Although response time, clearance rates, and so forth can be measured by more objective data, fairness, courtesy, helpfulness, cooperativeness, and sensitivity seem to be measured best by obtaining direct citizen feedback.

Fairness has several aspects, including evenhandedness in dealing with different clientele groups and individuals, respect for civil rights, use of reasonable force in apprehension, and neither overzealousness nor underenforcement of the law. Each of these aspects may be separately addressed, but considering them as a group—at least at first—usually will suffice. If problems develop, supplemental questions could be added to the same or to later surveys. An alternative measure is "the number of complaints reported regarding police fairness," but the probable lack of reporting of complaints makes it difficult to know how representative reported figures are.

Courtesy is related to fairness, but one can be fair and not courteous, and vice versa. Whether citizens can distinguish between these two qualities is questionable. It may be sufficient to include only one or the other measure, but both are recommended.

Likewise, "helpfulness, cooperativeness, and sensitivity" are likely to correlate with perceptions of fairness and courtesy. But they have been raised in so many descriptions of the role of police today versus one or two decades ago that it is wise to include this third set of qualities as well. Including their measurement itself may be perceived as contributing to achieving them in the eyes of the citizens who see the survey results. The measurement also may contribute to sensitivity to these elements by police personnel.

Data Collection. The random household survey can be used to obtain data on citizen perceptions of fairness and courtesy. Examples of questions that have been used are presented in Appendix 1 (Questions 38 and 39).

If the department wants also to assess "helpfulness, cooperativeness, and sensitivity," a question might be added such as "How would you rate the police in your neighborhood as to their helpfulness, cooperativeness, and sensitivity to your community:

Excellent, Good, Fair, or Poor? If less than good, why do you say this?" Questions regarding the number and possibly the nature of contacts with the police should also be included so that perceptions of persons who have had firsthand experience can be reported separately from the general public's perceptions (see Question 30 of Appendix 1).

As discussed earlier, an alternate data collection procedure is to survey a sample of those persons who have called the police department for service, rather than the general public.

Questions on fairness and courtesy applicable to businesses are presented in Appendix 2 (Questions 21 and 22).

All these citizen and business perception measures should be disaggregated by neighborhood, race or ethnic group, age group, and complainants versus the general public.

Measure 18: Number of reported incidents or complaints of police misbehavior, and the number resulting in judgment against the local government or employee, by type of complaint (civil charge, criminal charge, other service complaints) per 100 police.

Measure 19: Percentage of citizens who feel police are in general honest and can be trusted.

At least crude measures should be used to indicate the extent of problems with corruption, malfeasance, and negligence such as the "number of reported incidents or complaints of police misbehavior." The total number of complaints and the number resulting in judgment (as by police internal investigation) should be included.

The number of citizens likely to have firsthand information regarding police honesty is smaller than the number likely to be informed about other police service qualities. It is also questionable whether respondents with firsthand information will be candid about police honesty because of the sensitivity of the issue and potential criminal liability. Questions on police honesty can be included in random household surveys, but they are intrinsically less valid than are questions on fairness and courtesy. Nevertheless, citizen perceptions are valued and considered important; perceptions of honesty and trust (police image) can be extremely important to the police agency.

Data Collection. Data on complaints are routinely collected in some cities. Data on citizen perceptions of honesty and trust can be collected by another question on random household, complainant, and business surveys. The latter two qualities are important because they can indicate the extent of at least petty dishonesty. The question might take the form "How would you rate the honesty and trustworthiness of the police: Excellent, Good, Fair, or Poor?"

Special Validity Considerations. As indicated earlier, this measure is far from satisfactory. Obviously, not all incidents of dishonesty are reported. Incidents invalidated by police internal investigations and police review boards may be questioned by outsiders. More complaints are likely to be made during periods when police misbehavior receives much publicity than during periods when the level of honesty is not necessarily better but there is little attention to the issue.

The major problem on the validity of citizen perceptions is that it is hard to say whether citizens report what they hear from the media and hearsay or what they know themselves. Comparisons across neighborhood, age, and race or ethnic group may indicate problems, but they may be problems of alienation and distrust rather than corruption.

Measure 20: Percentage of persons requesting assistance for other than serious crimes who are satisfied (or dissatisfied) with police handling of their problems, categorized by reason for dissatisfaction and by type of call.

Most calls for service in most jurisdictions do not involve serious crimes. This measure can provide an indication of overall satisfaction with police services among those who called for help on nonserious crime matters.

Separate measures could be used for each type of minor complaint, such as noise, disorderly conduct, animals, and so forth. However, the many types of miscellaneous complaints preclude a separate measure tailored to each, at least for regular measurement.

The approach suggested here is to consider together all miscellaneous calls for service and to assess the effectiveness of the police in handling them on the basis of the satisfaction of those making the calls. Did the police, in the opinion of citizens who called for assistance, help remedy the situation for which they were called or otherwise effectively supply the service desired, or refer the caller to the appropriate agency if the matter was outside police jurisdiction?

Data Collection. A survey of a random sample of those calling can be used to obtain caller satisfaction levels. (Data for other measures could be obtained at the same time.) Reasons for any reported dissatisfaction, such as response delay or discourtesy, should be requested. This will help identify how to improve service and give some indication of the validity and seriousness of a reported problem. Results could be tallied separately for calls responded to in person or only by telephone to assess the relative effectiveness of the two modes.

The random household survey is another way to collect data. But the small samples involved for these surveys (typically 500 to 1,000 households) will yield even smaller samples of complainants. The household survey, however, may be adequate to obtain a general idea of overall complainant satisfaction, even if inadequate for reporting results by type of call.

A survey of persons who have requested services (complainants) can be made using either a random sample of complainants surveyed by telephone or a survey of all complainants reached with a short questionnaire sent by mail.

Five to ten minutes are probably enough to obtain the data necessary from each person interviewed—whether by phone or mail. Because the complainant survey surveys complainants who had called the police department, addresses for a mail survey or phone numbers for a telephone survey are likely to be available from the original incident reports or from computer or tape records of telephone numbers of incoming calls. The success of this procedure depends on the availability of correct addresses or telephone numbers for most of the persons who have called the police department; otherwise, the sample of responses may be biased. Therefore, department personnel should carefully record callers' names, addresses, and telephone numbers.

A mail survey will be less expensive than a telephone survey but low response rates may call into question the representativeness of the responses. Response rates can be increased by second and even third mailings or perhaps by the use of telephone interviews for nonrespondents. As discussed in Chapter 13 on customer surveys, we recommend that response rates of at least 50 percent be sought for any survey.

Out-of-pocket survey expenses can be reduced considerably if local government personnel do the mailing and interviewing. To avoid influencing respondents who might fear retaliation for unfavorable responses, interviewers should not come from within the police department; they should come from a special office within the department that can guarantee anonymity to respondents. Similarly, if a mail survey is used, questionnaires should not be mailed back to the police department; they should be mailed to a special office within the department that is not identified with any of the field offices.

Measure 21:   Percentage of (a) citizens, (b) businesses that rate police performance as excellent or good (or fair or poor), by reason for satisfaction (or dissatisfaction).

An overall measure of citizen satisfaction with police services can provide insight into the composite perceptions of citizens about police services.

Data Collection. The random household survey and survey of businesses are the primary sources of data. As with other perception questions, citizen ratings should be reported separately for those with first-hand contact with the police, by type of contact, as opposed to those from citizens with no contact during the period covered by the survey. Categories for "types of contact" could include callers for assistance, witnesses, persons stopped for traffic violations, and persons stopped for other reasons by the police.

As for previous measures reflecting citizen perceptions, a multiservice household survey and, for citizens who have called for assistance, a complainant survey can be used to obtain the data. Question 41 of Appendix 1 could be used for residents; Question 23 of Appendix 2 for businesses.

Measure 22:   Number of injuries to police officers (a) per 100 officers, (b) per 100 calls.

This measure reflects the frequency of injuries to police officers normalized per 100 officers and per 100 calls.

The measure should be disaggregated by organizational assignment (uniformed patrol, investigations, traffic, and so forth), by extent of injury, activity and/or type of call when injured, age, and sex.

Data Collection. Most police departments keep excellent records on police injuries. Only on-duty injuries should be counted. Probably only injuries requiring medical attention (whether or not given) should be counted.

Measures of Performance on Vice and Drug Offenses (Measures 23–27)

Measuring police effectiveness in controlling crimes against public morals and crimes relating to drugs (the so-called "victimless" crimes) poses special difficulties. The objectives of the laws concerning vice crimes are ill-defined and continually changing with public attitudes. Also, most vice crimes are not reported to the police, and there are no data on the incidence of such offenses equivalent to reported crime data. (Incidents are counted when arrests are made.) Thus even the approximate total incidence of such events is seldom known and we know of no appropriate procedure for obtaining such information.

Measures 23 through 27 in Exhibit 6-1 should be considered as a group. Together they can help provide an overall indication of effectiveness in controlling vice and drug crimes.

Measure 23: *Number of arrests for vice- and drug-related crimes, by type of crime and by "big fish" or "little fish."*

In many communities, police can make as many vice arrests as they want to by arresting prostitutes and other drug purchasers and sellers. The number of these arrests, therefore, may not be a very useful indicator of effectiveness.

The measure is more useful when coupled with Measures 9 and 10: the percentage of arrests that survive preliminary hearing, and the percentage of arrests that lead to conviction. These indicate arrests that stick.

Measure 23 is also more meaningful when presented by type of crime (especially severity) and type of illegal drug. For example, reporting arrests for possession versus sales, and separating arrests for marijuana sales from arrests for crack or heroin sales, is recommended.

Finally, to the extent possible, Measure 23 should break out the arrests of bigger fish—dealers or possessors of large amounts of cocaine; pimps controlling large numbers of prostitutes, and so on. (Again, the quality of arrest and conviction measures should be applied.)

Data Collection. The arrest data is readily available. The type of drugs and the big fish/little fish information may be routinely recorded, but it is usually in narrative form. The importance of the arrestee may have to be estimated. Nevertheless, vice squad commanders should be able to supply that information at least with some special analysis.

Special Validity Considerations. It is easy to rate this measure by simply commanding a crackdown on known drug sales or vice areas. The arrests are made, but the activity tends to reappear almost immediately in the same areas or nearby areas. Some crimes—especially prostitution and pornography—the community may be satisfied to see contained to a small redlight district rather than eliminated. Arrest levels may vary with desired degree of crackdown, media stories, and other factors that make the absolute measure not useful by itself.

Some measures should reflect total drug activity (Measures 24–26) and citizen satisfaction with the level of enforcement (Measure 29).

Measure 24: *Quantity and street value of illicit drugs seized.*

Measure 25: *Percentage of arrestees who test positive for illegal drugs.*

Measure 26: *Street price of illegal drugs.*

This group of measures reflects the magnitude of the illegal drug problem in the community. Police are only one of many factors that influence the magnitude of the problem. The national-level interdiction of drugs, community mores, health officials, school authorities, drug prevention programs, and many other forces can be as important or more important than local crime control. But the measures are important, even if they are not purely reflective of police efforts.

The amount of drugs seized, Measure 24, reflects supply available as well as diligence in apprehension. Nevertheless, seizure of large lots continues to be an objective of police.

Measure 25, the percentage of arrestees who test positive, reflects illegal drug use among the criminal population. Arrestees are more likely to be users, and more likely to be driven to crime by their use. This measure reflects to some extent the tie between crime and drugs, although special studies are needed for credible conclusions.

Measure 26, the street price of drugs, is commonly used by law enforcement officers in urban communities to indicate the effects of law enforcement on the supply and demand for illegal drugs. Although factors outside the local police department, such as efforts by the FBI and DEA, can have an important effect, so can local police activity.

Data Collection. Drug seizures (Measure 24) are recorded by police in most places. Arrestees are routinely tested for drugs in many communities (Measure 25), but the data may not be routinely tabulated.

Data on street drug prices (Measure 26) are usually available from undercover police as well as from reports from drug users.

Special Validity Considerations. Obviously the validity of the data and the validity of its interpretation are open to question. Not all drug services are recorded; not all tests for drugs are reliable; the street price of drugs is affected by many external factors. Nevertheless, drug activity measures should be included, especially when viewed as trends and considered together.

Measure 27: *Percentage of citizens who feel that (a) pornography, (b) prostitution, (c) gambling, (d) "soft" illegal drug use, (e) "hard" illegal drug use, (f) sale of illegal drugs is a major problem in their neighborhood or community.*

Ultimately, for vice crimes, it is community opinion that decides the tolerable level. Police can crack down and maintain pressure, or occasionally hit particular problems (e.g., rousting prostitutes or dispersing drug markets), or ignore a problem (e.g., sex films rented or sold by video stores in suburbia).

The degree of effort to put on vice is one of the hardest managerial decisions in policing and local government management. Measure 27 reflects whether the citizens judge various aspects of vice as major problems. Because some citizens may want even minor problems aggressively pursued, a second question or alternative question might be, "Do you feel the police should devote more, less, or about the same level of effort as at present?" Although few citizens know the current level of effort, their responses will reflect their attitude toward the problem.

Summary of Suggested Additions to Incident Reports

Some additions to the discrete, computerized information generally collected on incident reports have been suggested in the previous sections. Some may already be used in some jurisdictions. Most information is available in narrative form.

- *Type of victim:* Resident, nonresident, business, or other (for example, institutions) (for Measure 1).

- *Number of casualties, by cause:* Number of injuries or deaths to (a) crime victims, (b) bystanders, (c) suspects, and (d) police associated with the particular crime. It is also useful to indicate whether the casualty was inflicted *by* (a) crime victims, (b) bystanders, (c) suspects, (d) police, or (e) accidents not caused directly by a person, such as a fall (for Measures 4 and 22).

- *Number of offenders:* The probable number of participants in the crime (for Measure 8).

- *Disposition of arrests* (from court or state attorney's records) (for Measures 9 and 10).

- *Response time information:* The time each call for assistance is received and the time the first police unit arrived at the scene (for Measure 12).

Costs and Staffing Requirements

The principal additional costs in staff time or dollars for use of the procedures discussed in this chapter are for the following:

- Household survey, to obtain data on household victimization, feeling of security, and citizen attitudes to such aspects of police performance as speed of response, fairness, and courteousness (for Measures 2, 3, 13–17, 19, 21, and 27).

- A survey of businesses to obtain the same data as described for the household survey but from the business community's perspective (for Measures 2, 3, 13–16, and 21).

- A survey of persons who have called for assistance to obtain their perceptions as to the helpfulness, speed of response, fairness, and courteousness of the service (for Measures 13, 15, 16, 20, and 21).

- Data from the courts or prosecutor's office on disposition of arrests (for Measures 9 and 10).

Household Survey

Costs are likely to run $12 to $15 (1990 prices) per telephone interview (for a 10- to 15-minute interview). For annual samples of 300 (small jurisdictions) to 1,000 households (large jurisdictions), this would mean $3,600 to $15,000. These costs can be much higher if more detailed, elaborate, and larger surveys are undertaken. However, if these crime questions are included as part of a multiservice survey, the costs can be spread over a number of local government services and should be much smaller.

Survey of Businesses

Business respondents may be more difficult to reach and interview by telephone. With proper groundwork in obtaining the business community's cooperation, however, a mail survey can achieve a high business response rate, so the cost should be lower than that for the household survey. Without such groundwork, the unit costs would probably be about the same. However, sample sizes can usually be smaller: perhaps 50 for small jurisdictions and 200 for large ones. If these crime control questions are included in a multiservice survey of businesses, as described in Chapter 14, the survey costs to the police department should be quite small.

Survey of Persons Who Have Called for Service

A telephone or mail survey, if adequately followed up to obtain a reasonable response rate and if undertaken by current local government personnel (perhaps those from the local government's "service and information" office), would require little out-of-pocket expense. The length of the interview should be held to a maximum of five to ten minutes. An annual sample of 100 to 500 callers would probably cost $12 to $15 per completed interview, even if done by an outside organization.

This survey can readily be split into seasonal, quarterly samples (about one-quarter each quarter) at little, if any, extra cost to provide more timely and seasonal information.

Disposition-of-Arrest Data

Costs will depend on the number of different courts, the number of cases, and the extent to which police and court cases are computerized and linked to a common data base. In tests in two cities, a junior city employee required two or three days to record manually data on preliminary hearing dispositions from court docket books for 900 cases to measure the percentage of adult arrests surviving the preliminary court hearing. The additional cost for also recording data on final dispositions should be lower because the basic arrest information will already have been collected and court dispositions are usually tabulated by courts or prosecutors' offices.

Analysis Costs

Analysis is an important step after the data have been collected. In many jurisdictions, analysis capability already exists. Local governments without such capability within their police departments should consider acquiring it; analysis of effectiveness measurement data would be only one activity for their analysts.

---

1 For example, a sample of 100 Part I crimes in one city found 18 were against businesses and 7 against nonresidents. The overall crime rate as usually computed was thus one-third higher than the actual rate of crimes against residents. However, some of the businesses may have been owned by residents.

2 An assault against a resident that occurs within a business would be counted as against resident. If a store was robbed, the crime would be counted as against both business and resident if the owner is a resident. Note that for crimes against the person, each person victimized constitutes a separate crime by FBI definitions, so that mixtures of residents and nonresidents involved in those crimes need not involve double counting.

3 For example, in 1988 only 36 percent of all crimes were reported to the police. See U.S. Department of Justice, *Criminal Victimization in the United States, 1973–88 Trends*, p. 82.

4 See, for example, U.S. Department of Justice, *Criminal Victimization in the United States, 1987*; *Report to the Nation on Crime and Justice*; and "Criminal Victimization 1988."

5 For a general description of the National Crime Survey of the U.S. Department of Justice, see their two-page flyer, "The Nation's Two Crime Measures." For more details, see U.S. Department of Justice, *The National Crime Survey: Working Papers*, and any recent copy of their *Criminal Victimization in the United States*. The National Crime Survey is conducted by the U.S. Census Bureau for the Department of Justice.

6 A study by LEAA in 1970 in Santa Clara County, California (U.S. Department of Justice, *San Jose Methods Test of Known Crime Victims*), reported a 74 percent recall rate when the inquiry was for "the past 12 months" and concluded that "a reference period of 12 months is not worse than one of 6 months for simply assessing whether a crime occurred." LEAA used 12-month recall periods for victimization surveys of 26 large central cities in the 1970s, but the Department of Justice now uses 6 months for its National Crime Survey.

7 See Tuchfarber and Klecka, *Random Digit Dialing: Lowering the Cost of Victimization Surveys*.

8 Derived from data in U.S. Department of Justice, *Report to the Nation on Crime and Justice*, pp. 12 and 14.

9 U.S. Department of Justice, *Crime in the United States: Uniform Reports 1989*.

10 In one city, a sample of 60 consecutive Part I arrests found that only 48 percent passed the preliminary hearing. A second sample of 52 consecutive Part I arrests found that only 38 percent passed the preliminary hearing. A sample of 870 misdemeanor arrests in one month showed that 21 percent resulted in a guilty verdict; however, 49 percent of the cases resulted in dispositions that could be classified as "ambiguous." For example, the defendant paid a fine, court costs, or forfeited a bond but was not found guilty. In a second city, a sample of 76 consecutive felony arrests showed that 68 percent passed the state attorney's hearing, and another 12 percent were certified for trial as a misdemeanor, for a total of 80 percent receiving further prosecution. Of a sample of 23 consecutive misdemeanor arrests, 61 percent passed state attorney's hearings.

11 See Schnelle et al., "Evaluation of the Quality of Police Arrests by District Attorney Ratings."

12 For further discussion, see Forst et al., "Arrest Convictability as a Measure of Police Performance." Convictions are shown to be more likely when the arresting officer received tangible evidence, found cooperative witnesses, and made the arrest soon after the crime.

13 See, for example, Bertram and Vargo, "Response Time Analysis Study."

14 The cumulative frequency distribution for response times should be examined. It shows the percentage of calls responded to in less than x minutes for various values of x and not only for the single value used in the measure.

15 See ICMA, "Community-Oriented Policing."

F ire protection is the reason for the existence of fire departments, but fire protection requires the cooperation and efforts of many other municipal departments: the police department for arson investigation and traffic control, the building department for code enforcement and control of vacant buildings, the planning department for street layout, public works for water supply and street maintenance, the school system for fire safety education, and health services for counseling of juvenile fire setters.

Likewise, many modern fire departments provide a wide range of services beyond fire safety. These services include emergency medical care, emergency management, disaster assistance, "cat-in-the-tree" calls, and many others. Many fire departments are now called "fire and rescue service," or a similar name to reflect the expanded role. The majority of calls for service in fire departments nationwide are for these "other" services and not for fires.

In this chapter the focus is on the fire protection, and not on the other services provided by fire departments. The multidepartmental, integrated efforts required for fire protection are reflected in the suggested measures.

Fire protection is surprisingly difficult to measure well. The main purpose of fire protection is to reduce loss of life and property, and it is difficult to measure or even estimate what was averted. There are two key measurement strategies: (1) measuring losses that occur, how they change over time in light of outside explanatory factors such as socioeconomic conditions and weather, and how the losses compare to those in other like municipalities and (2) measuring intermediate fire protection efforts that are known to contribute to the desired goals. Citizen satisfaction measures are also suggested, but they tend to reveal little since most citizens love their fire fighters; anything short of top ratings should be taken as dire warnings here.

Measuring fire protection effectiveness lies partly with the choice of appropriate measures, which is discussed below, and partly with the proper analysis of the seemingly straightforward data, which is discussed in other works.[1]

Fire Protection Objectives and Measurement Approaches

Fire departments have a long tradition of monitoring the outcomes of fire protection. Annual reporting of fire rates, fire losses, fire deaths and injuries, and even response times is commonplace. In most communities, detailed records are kept on every fire call and every commercial inspection. Usually these records are available from computer systems. In 1990, about 14,000 of the 34,000 or so fire departments in the United States collected data on each incident in a form compatible with the National Fire Incident Reporting System (NFIRS) of the U.S. Fire Administration. Nevertheless, important information gaps remain, even in departments with advanced data systems.

A set of suggested measures of effectiveness for fire protection is presented in Exhibit 7-1. The measures are based on the assumption that the objective of fire protection services is:

To minimize casualties and losses of property from fire by helping to prevent fires from occurring and to reduce losses and casualties from fires that do occur.

The modern fire department increasingly emphasizes prevention activities. "Prevention" usually includes preventing ignitions, as well as mitigating losses and casualties by encouraging use of built-in fire protection systems such as automatic sprinklers and smoke detectors, educating the public on what to do when fire occurs, inspecting buildings, reviewing plans, and so forth.

The list of measures is grouped into several sets:

- Measures of overall loss minimization (1–3)

- Measures of prevention effectiveness (4–15)

- Measures of suppression effectiveness (16–21)

- Number of false alarms (22)

- General citizen satisfaction (23).

The measures and their data collection procedures are discussed below, along with any special difficulties in collecting or interpreting the data.

Measures of Overall Loss Minimization (Measures 1–3)

Measure 1: Number and rate of civilian injuries and deaths per 100,000 population.

Civilian injuries and deaths are among the most commonly used measures, but not always in rates per 100,000 population (or per capita).

Deaths should be counted if they occur within some period after the fire (such as a year) and if they result from an illness or injury directly related to the fire.

Injuries should be counted if they require medical attention (whether or not the attention is given). This is a judgment call and makes injury data more

---

Exhibit 7-1

Summary of Principal Effectiveness Measures for Fire Protection Service

Overall objective: To minimize losses to persons and property by helping to prevent fires from occurring and to reduce losses from fires that occur.

Objective	Quality characteristic	Specific measure	Data collection procedure
Overall loss minimization	Civilian casualties	1. Number and rate of civilian injuries and deaths per 100,000 population.	Incident reports, census
	Fire fighter casualties	2. Number of fire fighter injuries and deaths per 100 fire fighters and per 1,000 fires.	Casualty reports
	Property loss	3. Direct dollar loss from fires per $1,000 property served and per 100,000 population.	Fire department or insurance company estimates
Prevention	Reported fire incidence	4. Number of reported fires per 1,000 population, total and by type of residential occupancy.[1]	Incident reports
	Reported building fire incidence	5. Number of building fires per 1,000 occupancies, by type of occupancy and fire size.	Incident reports, planning department records
	Reported plus unreported building fire incidence rate	6. Number of unreported plus reported building fires per 1,000 households (or businesses).	Household and/or business survey
	Preventability of fires	7. Percentage and rate of fires that are relatively preventable by inspection or education.[2]	Incident report (special addition)
	Inspection effectiveness	8. Rate of fires in inspected versus uninspected (or frequently inspected versus infrequently inspected) occupancies of a given type.	Fire inspection files linked to incident reports
	Deterrence effectiveness for arson	9. Number of incendiary and suspicious fires per 1,000 population.	Incident reports, police and court records (for arson motive)
	Apprehension effectiveness for fire-related crimes	10. Clearance and conviction rates for incendiary and suspicious fires.	Fire incident and inspection data linked to police arrest records and fire department case records
	Juvenile fire setter recidivism	11. Percentage of juveniles sent to treatment programs who set fires again within two years (recidivism rate).	Juvenile treatment program records

difficult to compare than death data. Many injuries occur in fires that are not reported to fire departments, and some injuries are discovered by victims of reported fires after the fire department leaves. A focus on the most serious injuries, such as major burns, can give a clearer picture. Death and injury data should be disaggregated by age group, especially the groups under 6 years old and 65 and over, the highest risk groups. Data also should be tabulated by area of the municipality. If there are significant numbers of casualties to nonresidents (commuters, visitors, through traffic), they should be reported separately.

Data Collection. Counts of deaths and injuries are available from fire department incident reports.

Population data are available from the U.S. Census Bureau or the planning department. For making comparisons across jurisdictions or over several years, it is crucial to match casualties to the population protected. Sometimes the boundary for provision of fire protection services is not the same as a political boundary; the total population protected may then have to be estimated.

Measure 2: *Number of fire fighter injuries and deaths per 100 fire fighters and 1,000 fires.*

Fire fighting is one of the most hazardous professions. This measure reflects fire fighter casualties. With number of fires as a denominator, the measure

Exhibit 7-1, continued

Summary of Principal Effectiveness Measures for Fire Protection Service

Objective	Quality characteristic	Specific measure	Data collection procedure
	Inspection outreach	12. Percentage of occupancies inspected within x months.	Inspection records
	Inspection violation "clearances"	13. Percentage of building violations "cleared" by removal of hazard or imposition of penalty within x days.	Inspection records
	Detector and sprinkler usage/maintenance	14. Percentage of homes or businesses with (a) sprinklers, (b) working smoke detectors.	Household survey, inspection records
	Public education outreach	15. Percentage of citizens reached by public fire education.	Household survey, public education contacts
Suppression	Fire-fighting effectiveness—dollar loss	16. Average dollar loss per fire not out on arrival, by size on arrival and type of occupancy.	Incident reports (including estimate of size on arrival)
	Fire-fighting effectiveness—spread	17. Number or percentage of fires (not out on arrival of first unit) in which spread after arrival is limited to x square feet or z steps of the extent-of-flame scale.	Incident report (including estimate of size on arrival)
	Fire-fighting effectiveness—time	18. Time to control or extinguish the fire.	Incident reports or dispatch center
	Speed of providing service	19. Percentage of response times that are less (or more) than x minutes.	Incident reports or dispatch center
		20. Average response time.	Incident reports or dispatch center
	Rescue effectiveness	21. Number of "saves" versus number of casualties.	New data element for incident report
	False alarms	22. Number of false alarms.	Incident reports
Overall	Citizen satisfaction	23. Percentage of population rating fire protection services as satisfactory.	Household or "client" survey

[1]The term "occupancy" refers to a piece of property in terms of its use, for example, detached houses containing only one household, apartments, drug stores, or warehouses. There may be more than one type of occupancy in one building, and some occupancies—for example, garbage dumps and piers—are not buildings at all.

[2]For example, fires started by flammables stored near ignition source, or in buildings with fire-code violations relevant to the fire start, would be "relatively preventable." Fires started by hidden equipment defects not common to that equipment would be relatively "unpreventable."

reflects safety relative to the amount of action seen (the risks). With number of fire fighters as a denominator, the measure reflects the risk per person—the likelihood that a fire fighter was hurt. The risk per employee should be computed for different ranks, for different ages, for volunteers versus paid employees, and, perhaps, for different bureaus. Personnel assigned to fire fighting operations usually have a much higher casualty rate than those in prevention bureaus. Adding in prevention employees, secretaries, and administrators could make the true risk to fire suppression personnel seem smaller. Data should also be disaggregated by type of activity at the time of injury: in training, en route to a call, at the scene, or other.[2]

Data Collection. Data on fire fighter injuries are readily available from incident casualty records and from fire fighter casualty records and/or personnel records. Whatever the combination of sources, make sure all on-duty injuries are counted and all off-duty injuries and illnesses not directly traceable to on-duty exposure or activity are excluded.

Sometimes the effects of work on health do not appear immediately. Judgments are needed on whether to count a heart attack a fire fighter suffers at home after having a heavy work load at a fire and exposure to toxic fumes. These decisions have to be made for worker's compensation and liability and pension issues, so the data will be available for effectiveness measurement purposes too.

Some departments (for example, New York City) are tracking *exposures* of fire fighters to toxic fumes as if they were injuries, on the grounds that cumulatively they cause damage that might not otherwise be traceable to work-related problems. Often exposure cases must be reviewed by doctors before the fire fighters are released. Exposures are considered at least as damaging to the lungs as a cut is to a finger—an injury that gets counted.

Measure 3:   Direct dollar loss from fires per $1,000 property served and per 100,000 population.

This measure is perhaps most appropriately computed per $1,000 property served. It shows the proportion of property at risk that is damaged; however, the value of all property at risk may be difficult to estimate. The measure on a per capita basis shows the losses per citizen and is at least grossly reflective of the size of the community too.

The measure should be broken out by type of property (residence, nonresidence, vehicle, outside, and other), by specific type of property (for example, apartment, single-family dwelling), and by area of the community.

Data Collection. Data on fire losses usually are estimated as part of fire incident reports. Sometimes the data can be improved with insurance company estimates by professional appraisers.

Given the importance of data on fire loss in indicating the success of fire protection, fire departments should try to improve the accuracy of these data by providing documented procedures for collecting data in the most common situations and by providing training in the use of these procedures. Establishing consistent estimates within a department would be a major step forward.

No single method of estimating loss can be recommended with confidence. One of the more promising approaches uses standardized estimates of the current cost per square foot for different types of construction and different occupancies. The dollar value of the property served also can be estimated from assessed property values available from the assessor's office. Rough estimates of the value of *nontaxed* property should be added to the denominator to obtain a more meaningful measurement.

Because a few major fires could dominate the amount of loss in a given year, the measure might be calculated both with and without such fires.

Constant dollars should be used in comparing loss rates from one year to the next. Note that direct dollar loss does not include lost wages, lost taxes to the community, medical expenses, and many other costs that should be considered when evaluating the total magnitude of the fire problem. A measure of total losses—direct and indirect—might also be used, but it would add considerable complexity to the procedures.

Measures of Prevention Effectiveness (Measures 4–15)

Measure 4:   Number of reported fires per 1,000 population, total and by type of residential occupancy.

The paramount goal of fire prevention is to prevent fires in the first place. Fire prevention effectiveness is partly reflected in the fires reported to the fire department (Measure 4) and partly in the number of unreported fires (Measure 6).

The data should be disaggregated by general and specific occupancy type, population group, and area, as discussed for Measure 3.

The data also should be broken out by major cause of fires to reflect the successes and failures of different programs and to provide insights for future programs.

Data Collection. The main problem in collecting these data is the definition of a fire and what is reported.

Communities should include chimney fires and zero-loss fires in their counts to be comparable to other communities following National Fire Protection Association (NFPA) and NFIRS standards. Not counting these latter fires can radically distort the measures because these fires are so numerous.

One step communities can take is to ensure that fire fighters are using a standard definition of a fire ("any uncontrolled burning," according to NFPA and NFIRS standards). Communities also might want to tabulate only those fires with dollar loss. A histogram of fires by dollar loss groupings is useful and instructive.

Measure 5: Number of building fires per 1,000 occupancies, by type of occupancy and fire size.

The number of building fires relative to the number of occupancies of a given type (for example, single-family dwelling, duplex, apartment, mobile home, store and office) shows how preventive activities are working in relation to the population of a particular type of building at risk.

Adding the dimension of fire size to the measure provides a check or alternative to Measure 3 (property loss). "Size" can be measured roughly in terms of what the fire spread was contained to, using the common NFIRS/NFPA scale of "contained to" object of origin, area of origin, floor of origin, building of origin. "Size" can be measured more accurately by recording the approximate square footage of the burned area. The measure would be, for example, the number of fires not confined to the room of origin per 1,000 buildings.

Data Collection. The size of fire is recorded on the incident report. Size is usually in the "contained to" scale and rarely in square feet; the former probably suffices here.

The number of buildings by occupancy type can be estimated from planning department and pre-fire inspection records.

Measure 6: Number of unreported plus reported building fires per 1,000 households (or businesses).

Previous national studies of unreported fires found that 90–96 percent of household fires are not reported.

As noted above, one problem in interpreting rates of reported fires is that they may appear to change significantly from year to year because of changes in the percentage of small fires with minimal or no damage that are reported. Changes in the tendency to report fires may affect the rate of reported fires more than any other factor. If, for ex-

ample, the percentage of small household fires that were reported increased from one year to the next by ten percentage points, which might occur after a new fire prevention program calls attention to the fire problem, the number of reported fires could double or triple, even though the actual number of fires had not changed at all.

Data Collection. The degree of underreporting can be estimated by adding a question in a survey of households or in a random telephone survey conducted by the fire department. The question can be like Question 43 in Appendix 1. It is not necessary to ask why the fire was not reported—usually the answer is simply that there was no need to report it.

The person taking the survey should make clear to the person being interviewed whether the question concerns fires in the home *or* any fires the person was involved in. (Both are reasonable approaches. Large workplace fires might be over-reported if two or more people from the same workplace happened to be included in the sample, but usually this will be a minor problem.)

Measure 7: Percentage and rate of fires that are relatively preventable by inspection or education.

The most important measures of prevention success are Measures 1-6, which show the changes in the magnitude of the fire problem. A supplemental approach is to consider the "number of fires that are relatively preventable by inspection or education per 1,000 occupancies," or "per 1,000 households," for a residential inspection program. Changes in this measure over time would indicate a change in inspection or education impact, because the rate of "relatively preventable" fires would presumably decrease or remain stable if these programs are effective.

In using this measure, however, it is important to realize that the principal preventive effect of inspections is achieved through education of the owners, managers, and staff of inspected properties. Therefore, it is best not to make too much of the split between inspection and education and better to treat the measure as a measure of fires susceptible to prevention by a range of specific programs.

St. Petersburg, Florida, which used such a measure for perhaps longer than any other department, found it useful in making strategic decisions on prevention and in making budget decisions to support more public education.

Data Collection. The officer responsible for reporting the fire cause on the incident report can also make the judgment as to whether the fire was preventable by education or inspection. St. Petersburg used a simple checkoff box added to the incident report. The department should establish clear guidelines to reduce variations in judgments among fire officers.

Measure 8:   *Rate of fires in inspected versus uninspected (or frequently inspected versus infrequently inspected) occupancies of a given type.*

The effectiveness of inspections can also be measured by comparing relative fire rates (per 1,000 occupancies) for inspected versus uninspected properties. This can be done for commercial occupancies and for residential occupancies.

Since inspections are intended to improve life safety as well as reduce the likelihood of fires, a similar comparison can be made for deaths and injuries, though their numbers will be much fewer than fires and make it harder to find statistically significant results.

Data Collection. The first procedure described here is for residences that have recently started an inspection program or whose inspection program is of limited scope. The second procedure is for fire-code inspections of commercial occupancies or other situations in which inspections have been done for all properties for many years.

For residences, take a list of all residences contacted (whether residences were inspected, residents were not home, or residents refused inspection) during one year's operation of the residential inspection program. For each residence, find out whether one or more fires occurred there within a year of the contact. Compare the rate of fires in inspected residences to the rate of fires in the other residences contacted—those whose occupants had not been home for inspection, or had refused inspection.[3]

A major problem with this procedure is that the "comparison" group—the households that are not inspected—may differ in their propensity to have fires from the households that were inspected. It is possible that households not available for inspection, in some cases because units are unoccupied, are inherently high-risk areas for fires. To check on this possibility, compare the fire rate in the inspected households for a few years *before* they were inspected to the fire rate in the households in which residents were not home when called on for inspections for the same number of years before they received those calls. If the fire rates are about the same, the concern can be ignored; if not, the test results may have to be considered inconclusive.

Unless inspections cut down substantially on incidence of fires, communities with smaller numbers of homes contacted may have difficulty obtaining statistically significant results for any single year. Such communities might undertake the analysis every few years.

A different procedure is needed for residential inspection programs in communities where most residences are inspected, and for commercial inspection programs in which all or most occupancies of a kind are inspected at least every two years. This is because there is no comparison group of uninspected similar occupancies. Instead, it is necessary to compare the fire rate for recently inspected buildings to the rate for those not recently inspected. If the fire rate for recently inspected buildings is less than for those not recently inspected but of similar type, this would suggest that a policy of more frequent inspections would make a difference. The general procedure is as follows:[4]

Match the records of fires during the period of study to the inspection files and determine what percentage of fires occurred in buildings that had their last inspection x months ago, for all x up to two years. Draw a random sample of inspection files (assuming one file per establishment) and use the inspection histories during the period being studied to determine what percentage of time a building spends, on the average, in the position of having had its last inspection one month ago, two months ago, up to 24 months. If the two distributions look about the same, it means that a recent inspection offers no more protection than an old one. If the two distributions do not look the same, the ratios of corresponding percentages can be used to see how much the likelihood of fire increases as the time since last inspection increases. An example of such an analysis in chart form is shown in Exhibit 7-2.

To use the procedure, a community should have reasonably complete files in a centralized location or on a computer on inspections dating back several years (at least a period considerably longer than the time between inspections). If a community does not have complete files going back some years, it can begin keeping files and use the procedure in the future. The reliability of the inspection file data on addresses of fires and inspected buildings must be sufficient to give accurate inspection information on most fires.

Even if the chances of a fire do not increase as a building's last inspection gets more remote, the chance of a fire may be lower just because there is an inspection program. The knowledge that inspections are conducted periodically may produce a continuing level of fire prevention awareness, and corresponding actions. This ongoing effect can be estimated by comparing fire rates before and after a program is initiated, if records go back that far, or by comparing communities with and without inspection programs, if comparable communities can be identified. This procedure is useful for evaluating new community-wide residential inspection programs, but it is not likely to be applicable to most commercial inspection programs because most communities have inspected commercial buildings regularly for years.

Measure 9:   *Number of incendiary and suspicious fires per 1,000 population.*

Measure 10: *Clearance and conviction rate for incendiary and suspicious fires.*

These two measures show how well the community prevents arson and apprehends arsonists, and they reflect the combined results of community awareness and education about arsonists, private building se-

curity measures, and police and fire efforts. The definition of arson varies; here it includes both incendiary and suspicious fires.

Data Collection. Data on fire causes, arrests, and convictions usually are readily available, though it takes some effort to link them.

Perhaps the principal data problem here is estimating whether fires of "unknown" cause were intentionally set or not. Some departments may include them in the "suspicious" category if there is no hard evidence, and some may include them in the unknown category. Some fires of "unknown cause" are undoubtedly arson. For Measures 9 and 10, only the fires of known cause should be counted, but it should be kept in mind that Measure 9 understates the problem because of the unknowns. Alternatively a por-

---

Exhibit 7-2

Example of Estimating Fire Inspection Effectiveness

Suppose there are only ten buildings subject to inspection in the community. Their inspection histories for a year might look like the chart below.

Building number	Jan	Feb	Mar	Apr	May	Jun	Jul	Aug	Sep	Oct	Nov	Dec
					Number of months since last inspection							
1	8	(9[a])	10	0[b]	1	2	3	4	5	6	7	8
2	3	4	5	6	7	(8)	0	1	2	3	4	5
3	2	3	4	5	6	7	8	9	10	11	12	(13)
4	6	0	1	2	3	4	5	6	0	1	2	0[b]
5	5	6	7	0	1	2	3	4	5	6	7	0
6	10	11	(12)	0	1	2	3	4	5	6	7	8
7	(9)	0	1	2	3	4	5	6	7	8	0	1
8	1	2	3	4	5	6	0	1	2	3	4	5
9	7	8	9	10	11	12	13	14	(15)	0	1	2
10	3	4	0	1	2	3	4	0	1	2	3	4

[a] A circled entry indicates that building had a fire in that month. For example, Building No. 1 had a fire in February and at that time Building No. 1 had not been inspected for nine months.

[b] A "0" entry means that building was inspected in that month. Note that the inspection frequency varies considerably among the ten buildings, and in some cases (such as Building No. 4) the inspection frequency varies for the same building.

Summary analysis

Number of months since last inspection	Number of entries showing that many months since last inspection	Number of fires in buildings that many months from last inspection	Incidence of fire in buildings that far from last inspection
0–2	40	0	0 = 0/40
3–5	37	0	0 = 0/37
6–8	24	1	.05 = 1/24
9–11	11	2	.18 = 2/11
12–15	7	3	.43 = 3/7
All entries	120	6	.05 = 6/120

The fire incidence ratios shown in the last column indicate that a considerable increase in fire incidence occurs when buildings have gone without inspections for a long time. Of all fires, for example, 83 percent (5 of the 6) occur in buildings that have gone at least nine months without an inspection, but buildings are in that position only 15 percent of the time (18 of the 120 entries). In practice, the exact fire incidence likelihood numbers will not be known because data on all months will be collected for only a random sample of buildings in the program; however, the percentage increases in the ratios computed will be the same as the percentage increases in the underlying fire incidence values. Also in practice, some adjustments have to be made to reflect the possibility that, when a fire and an inspection in the same building occur in the same month, the fire may have preceded the inspection and thus not have been affected by it.

tion of the unknowns might be considered arson; or the unknowns can be reported along with the known arson incidents. In any event, the department needs to state how unknowns are treated before attempting comparisons.

Another major problem in monitoring arson rates is the community's treatment of juvenile arsonists. Nationwide, identified arsonists include a far larger proportion of children under age 10 than do groups responsible for any other crime. However, fire departments recognize that some children are too young to understand the nature of their fire-setting activities, so the category "child playing with fire" exists as an alternative to the category "juvenile incendiary act." Departments may differ as to the age threshold or other criteria they use to distinguish fire play from incendiary acts. A firm policy should be adhered to in defining these types of fires. If the policy changes over time, it will affect the numbers and should be considered in any comparisons made.

Measure 11: Percentage of juveniles sent to treatment programs who set fires again within two years (recidivism rate).

Most arson nationwide involves juveniles who intentionally set fires. A major element of many prevention programs is a juvenile fire setter program that educates the child or refers the child for treatment.

Data Collection. Most juvenile fire setter programs follow up on each child's treatment, using surveys of parents, guardians, and institutions, and also police records, to track the child's behavior for at least a year or two.

The recidivism data should be reported separately based on the child's degree of disturbance when first referred, using a typology such as the three-part risk classification used by the U.S. Fire Administration. Degree of disturbance tends to be correlated with age. Results are markedly different for the different groups, and the programs are different as well.

Measure 12: Percentage of occupancies inspected within x months.

Measure 13: Percentage of building violations "cleared" by removal of hazard or imposition of penalty within x days.

The end result of inspections is reflected implicitly in many of Measures 1–10. However, the immediate purpose of inspecting is to reduce or eliminate fire hazards. Often the law requires local governments to conduct inspections at a certain rate and to take remedial action for violations found. These two mea-

sures reflect those responsibilities directly.

Both Measures 12 and 13 should be tabulated by detailed types of occupancies. They can also be reported as the percentage of occupancies no*t* inspected, and the percentage of violations *not* cleared. These versions may be as important or even more important to report, especially as part of the budget process, to provide evidence of the need to reduce deficiencies.

Data Collection. Inspection records contain data needed for both measures.

Measure 14: Percentage of homes or businesses with (a) sprinklers, (b) working smoke detectors.

A major mission of the fire service of the 1980s was to help get at least one smoke detector in every home. In the 1990s that mission is to get detectors into the homes that still do not have them, to ensure that there are an adequate number of detectors in each home, and to ensure that all detectors are working. It has been shown that detectors reduce calls for service, reduce losses, and reduce deaths. While these effects are all reflected in other measures, the use of smoke detectors is important enough to be singled out for measurement. A refinement on the measure is the percentage of homes with at least one working detector on each living level.

Use of sprinklers in homes as well as public occupancies is more feasible today as a result of technical breakthroughs in sprinkler design and cost in the late 1970s and early 1980s. The presence or absence of sprinklers and detectors is not an either-or matter. They may be present but insufficient or not working. Therefore, it is desirable to use as measures both (a) percentage of properties using any system and (b) percentage of properties using systems up to the level required by codes and standards. For example, for hotels the measure would be the percentage of hotels that have at least partial sprinklering versus the percentage sprinklered to the extent required by current local code.

Data Collection. The standard NFIRS/NFPA incident report calls for data on the existence and performance of detectors and sprinklers. This report provides data for places that have reported fires.

Inspection records and pre-fire inspection plans can provide information on detectors and sprinklers in all but private dwellings. A household survey could include a question as to the presence and operability of detectors, but telephone responses on detector operability are less reliable than actual inspections of the equipment (unless the telephone surveyor asks for the detector to be tested while the surveyor waits on the line). Home sprinklers are still extremely few and far between; data on their numbers can also be obtained from local dealers or installers or water companies.

Measure 15: Percentage of citizens reached by public fire education.

Another major trend in fire protection of the 1990s is renewed emphasis on public fire education. To be effective, a program must not only communicate but shape behavior through well-targeted, high-quality messages that have wide if not universal coverage. For purposes of effectiveness monitoring, the percentage of citizens reached by at least one message from the fire department may suffice. A fire department, however, may want to have more detailed measures of public education effectiveness. A number of publications provide more detail.[5]

Data Collection. The data for this measure can be obtained from questions included in a survey of households. Persons can be asked whether they have heard any message or received any literature from the fire department. If they answer yes, they can be asked what it was, what they remember, and what their resultant behavior was relative to fire safety. It also may be useful to ask questions to test citizen knowledge regarding fire safety.

Measures of Suppression Effectiveness (Measures 16–21)

These measures address the effectiveness of fire suppression activities. Measures 16-18 reflect the control of property losses; Measures 19-20 address response times; and Measure 21 addresses rescue effectiveness.

Measure 16: Average dollar loss per fire not out on arrival, by size on arrival and type of occupancy.

The dollar loss per fire extinguished by the fire department reflects a combination of how fast the fire fighters arrive, how fast they extinguish the fire and evacuate the smoke, and how well they minimize damage by not using excessive water or causing fire-fighting damage and by taking positive salvage actions such as vacuuming water.

A new concern in fire protection is the degree to which the fire or fire fighting causes damage to the environment. A historic fire in a paint storage facility in Dayton, Ohio, in 1987 endangered the city's water supply and therefore was allowed to burn to the ground, causing a $30 million loss. The fire chief set an international precedent by making this decision, even though the loss added enormously to the city's average loss per fire. The approach for a case like this, as mentioned earlier, is to note such extraordinary losses separately, and not include them in the averages.

Because a few very large fires can greatly affect the average dollar loss, a measurement report should be made of the number of fires with losses falling into different ranges. Similarly, the dollar loss per fire preferably should be tabulated for *each* category of size of fire upon arrival of the first unit (see Measure 17 below). Dollar loss per fire will vary depending on how large a fire is when the fire department arrives. Dollar loss is also affected by the nature of the occupancy, type of construction, built-in building defenses, and fire-fighting actions taken by occupants. All of these factors except occupancy type can be affected to some extent by fire department actions but not by the fire-fighting crew who arrives to put the fire out.

Data Collection. The data for this measure can be obtained from incident report data.

Measure 17: Number or percentage of fires (not out on arrival of first unit) in which spread after arrival is limited to x square feet or z steps on extent-of-flame scale.

Fire-fighting effectiveness is not adequately quantifiable in terms of dollar loss and casualties, partly because much loss and many casualties occur before arrival of the first unit. A measure more closely tied to fire department actions at the scene is the spread-of-flame damage *after* arrival. "Spread" can be measured in terms of the difference between the approximate area of the fire on arrival and the area it was confined to at extinguishment. Each of these areas can be described in terms of approximate square feet or in terms of grosser scales indicating the number of rooms, floors, or buildings involved, or in terms of the familiar *NFPA 901* "extent-of-flame-damage" scale indicating whether the flame damage was confined to area, room, floor, or building of origin. Whichever scale is used, the important point is that it be used to describe the extent of the fire both on arrival and at extinguishment.

Exhibit 7-3 shows how such data might be presented. This example shows that fire size on arrival increased from 1990 to 1991, but spread after arrival decreased.

The square-foot version of this measure was tested experimentally in the mid-1970s in one fire department, but it is used by few if any departments today. It continues to hold some promise for departments willing to make the effort involved (which can be considerable) and able to reduce the interoffice variability in size estimates (which was considerable in the original feasibility test). Use of the NFPA extent-of-flame-damage scale on arrival as well as at extinguishment is easier.

Data Collection. The key to the feasibility of this procedure is how reliably the size of the fire can be estimated in spite of smoke and the pressures that accompany any fire emergency. Great precision is neither possible nor necessary, but poor precision will make the measure useless for identifying any but the grossest of changes.

The first-in officer or fire fighter usually is in the best position to estimate the size of the fire. In some fires it will not be clear how many floors are on fire, let alone the square-foot size. But most fires are relatively small and are stopped in their tracks, and for most fires fire personnel can provide at least a rough estimate of fire size on arrival.[6]

As an alternative to this measure, the department might undertake a careful analysis of the extent of fire damage just at extinguishment, comparing different areas, types of occupancies, and communities.

Measure 18: Time to control or extinguish the fire.

"Time to control" can be defined as the time from the arrival of the fire apparatus at a fire to the time when fire fighters confirm that the fire has been contained and spread stopped, although the fire may not necessarily have been extinguished. "Time to extinguishment" can also be used. The measure might be expressed in a number of variations such as the median time, average time, or percentage of fires with control time greater than a given value.

Data Collection. Data can be collected by having the officer in charge radio the dispatcher (or signal the computer) upon arrival at the scene and signal when control is confirmed. The times are then obtained from the dispatcher (or computer) after the reporting officer returns to the station house. Reporting of control time is greatly facilitated when the officer in charge has a portable radio or other data input device.

The necessary raw data for estimating control times are already reported in many departments, often under other names such as "knock-down" or "tap-out" time. But the data are not summarized for the purpose of periodic reporting, and definition of "control" is not always consistent from officer to officer. Estimation of time to control for large fires may be subject to considerable uncertainty because of the difficulty in judging precisely when control is achieved. Yet summary, perhaps annual, statistics on time to control still seem likely to show how fire burn times are being reduced (or not reduced), resulting in more (or less) damage averted.

An example of the information obtained is the following:

- 66 percent of fires were controlled in 0 to 5 minutes
- 17 percent of fires were controlled in 6 to 10 minutes
- 12 percent of fires were controlled in 11 to 20 minutes
- 5 percent of fires took more than 20 minutes to control.

To maintain the quality of the data, fire departments planning to use time-to-control data should consider at least some spot checks of time to control, possibly by having senior officers attend a sample of fires and compare notes concerning the reported time. In addition, follow-ups should be undertaken on any reports that seem unusual. Fires out on arrival should be reported separately from others and not included in this measure, regardless of the time taken to confirm that the fire was out.

Measure 19: Percentage of response times that are less (or more) than x minutes.

Measure 20: Average response time.

These measures are used by many fire departments. Usually the time of arrival of the first fire unit is used: it can be the time of arrival of the first engine or truck company.

Some departments use more complex variations that measure the time to arrive with *x* gallons per minute pumping capability, the time for the first engine and first truck to arrive, or the time *x* fire fight-

---

Exhibit 7-3

Illustration of How to Present Data on Fire Spread

Fire size at arrival	Percentage of fires		Percentage of fires that spread to next size after arrival of first unit	
	1990	1991	1990	1991
Up to 50 sq. ft. or confined to object	60	30	5	0
51–250 sq. ft. or confined to room	34	45	30	25
251 sq. ft. and up or confined to floor	6	25	80	75
All fires	100	100	18	30

ers arrive at the scene—each by type of call. These measures are all variations of a general form: the time required to reach the location with all the suppression resources considered necessary to fight a reference fire at that location.

Measure 21: Number of "saves" versus number of casualties.

"Saves" data may help provide proper credit to the fire department for a major outcome of its service. The basic concept is to estimate the number of people saved from death or injury by arriving fire fighters.

For credibility, "saves" should be reported in terms of the danger posed by the fire to the person "saved" (for example, the person's location in relation to the fire), and the degree of the person's mobility (for example, unconscious, can walk but trapped, and so forth). Thus, a warning to a healthy person able to evacuate a floor below a fire would not be treated the same as the rescue of an unconscious victim from a burning room. The practice should help provide a clearer description of outcomes, reduce perverse reporting incentives, and improve credibility with the public. A sample "Fire Saves Report" is presented in Exhibit 7-4.

Data Collection. Data would be collected as part of incident reports by the officers in charge at the fires, based on their personal observations and debriefing of fire fighters, and victims or witnesses if necessary.

Either notes or a blank version of Exhibit 7-4 can be used to record the data. Narrative descriptions on incident reports should provide more details, for verification of the counts.[7]

Other Measures (Measures 22 and 23)

Measure 22: Number of false alarms.

False alarms are of two types: malicious alarms, made by telephone calls or by pulling fire alarm boxes, and mechanical failures or fooling of sensors associated with automatic alarm systems.

Both types of alarms cause public nuisance, nonproductive expenditure of fire department resources, and risk to the public and fire fighters from needless emergency runs. Virtually all fire departments have an explicit or implicit objective of minimizing false alarms through public education, elimination of call boxes, inspection of alarm systems, apprehension of offenders, and other measures. Measure 22 indicates the success of these approaches.

Data Collection. Most fire departments routinely record false alarm runs.

False alarms should not include good faith no-fire calls in which the caller thought there was a fire or potential for a fire, based on seeing or smelling smoke or suspicious odors or feeling an usually hot wall or switch.

False alarms should be reported as mechanical

Exhibit 7-4

Example of Report on Fire Saves (Data from 17 Fires)

Fire hazard for victim	Victim mobility — Fire dept. action	Unable to walk — Unconscious — Carried	Unable to walk — Other	Can walk only with assistance — Aided	Can walk — Pinned/trapped — Released	Can walk — Path blocked — Provided path	Can walk — Unaware of fire — Directed	Totals
1. Fire in room		1	1	2		1		5
2. Fire on same floor								
a. Smoke/heat hazard in room				1		10	9	20
b. No smoke/heat hazard in room							2	2
3. Fire on next floor below								
a. Smoke/heat hazard in room		1				24	2	27
b. No smoke/heat hazard in room						2	2	4
4. Fire more than one floor below								
a. Smoke/heat hazard in room					3	13	7	23
b. No smoke/heat hazard in room						2		2
5. Within danger zone of hazardous materials fire							1	1
6. Below fire floor								
Totals		2	1	3	3	52	23	84

(unintentional) or human (intentional), since prevention approaches to the two types are different.

Intentional false alarms also might be reported by whether they were initiated by children or by adults (if known), method of alarm (telephone or alarm box), and area of origin—all of which give clues as to the success in remedying different aspects of the problem.

Measure 23: Percentage of population rating fire protection services as satisfactory.

Ratings by citizens with firsthand knowledge of a community's fire services will provide fire personnel feedback on citizen perception of the quality of the service. In most communities, however, the majority of citizens have no firsthand contact with the fire department during a given year and no other valid source of knowledge about its services.

Data Collection. To obtain data for this measure the fire department can either undertake its own survey (by telephone or mail) of households that have had contact with the fire department, particularly households that have reported fires, or include questions in a survey of a random sample of households and/or businesses in the jurisdiction. In either procedure, only respondents that had firsthand contact with fire services during the period would be asked to rate fire protection services.

Question 45 in Appendix 1 could be used to obtain these data. For a survey of a random sample of households, Question 44 can be used to identify those with some firsthand contact. Data can be disaggregrated by area of the community and other groupings to identify specific problem areas. Changes in the level of satisfaction over time may indicate successes or problems in community relations.

If the community is already conducting a regular survey of its citizens, there will be little added expense and effort to include questions on fire services. The first procedure, surveying all, or a sample of, households who have had contact with the fire department, need not be costly, especially if a mail questionnaire is used.

These survey procedures are discussed at length in Chapter 13 on customer surveys.

Effects of Community Characteristics on the Measures

Physical and socioeconomic characteristics of a community over which the fire department has no control have a profound effect on fire protection. For the measurement data to be fair and to provide proper insight, these characteristics should be considered in making comparisons over time, between areas of the community, or between communities—as is generally the case for all services discussed in this book.

Among the important community variables to consider are weather, terrain, poverty, age profile, ethnic group, education level, owner-occupied housing, and apartments versus single-family homes.

Fire analysts should identify and consider community characteristics relevant to fire prevention in order to help distinguish changes in fire rates due to prevention activities from changes attributable to other factors. For example, areas that lack the characteristics associated with high fire rates might be given more demanding targets for prevention programs (that is, they might be expected to achieve lower fire rates) than those areas with characteristics associated with high fire rates.

The analysis would indicate what fire rate would be "expected" in each census tract based on its characteristics; these projections could be compared against actual rates to identify which tracts had rates that were higher or lower than expected. The comparisons would give an approximate picture of performance in the light of conditions faced.

A similar attempt could be made for characteristics that affect suppression.

---

1 See, for example, ICMA, *Managing Fire Services*; Hall, *Fire Protection Handbook*; and U.S. Fire Administration, *Fire in the United States.*

2 National Fire Protection Association, *Fire Reporting Standards (901)*, provides a dictionary of terms for this and many other measures in this chapter.

3 For details of this procedure, see Chapter 5 of Schaenman et al., *Procedures for Improving the Measurement of Local Fire Protection Effectiveness*, and the supplemental technical report by Hall, "Measuring the Effectiveness of Fire Inspections"; as well as Hall et al., *Fire Code Inspections and Fire Prevention— What Methods Lead to Success?*

4 Again, the specific procedure for undertaking analysis is presented in Chapter 5 of Schaenman et al., *Procedures for Improving the Measurement of Local Fire Protection Effectiveness*, and the supplemental technical report by Hall, "Measuring the Effectiveness of Fire Inspections."

5 See, for example, Schaenman et al., "Proving Public Fire Education Works"; National Fire Protection Association, "Evaluation Instruments" and *Fire Safety Educator's Handbook.*

6 For a fuller discussion of this measure and its testing, see Chapter 1 in Schaenman et al., *Procedures for Improving the Measurement of Local Fire Protection Effectiveness.*

7 The procedure is more fully described in Schaenman et al., *Procedures for Improving the Measurement of Local Fire Protection Effectiveness.*

Chapter 8

General Transportation Services

E ffectiveness measures for local transportation services should address a municipality's public transit system and general transportation services. General transportation measures are discussed here separately from mass transit measures because the responsibilities for these two areas are usually separated and it is desirable to examine transit performance by itself.

Hence, this chapter focuses on measures for such transportation concerns as street maintenance, traffic control and safety, pedestrian safety, accessibility, and environmental quality. Chapter 9 discusses public mass transit. The approach taken for both general transportation and mass transit is described here. This report does not cover air and water transportation, intercity transportation, or peripheral services such as taxi regulation.

Local Transportation Objectives and Measurement Approaches

The set of effectiveness measures presented here assumes that the objective of a jurisdiction's transportation services is:

To provide access to desired destinations such as employment, shopping, and community services or other facilities in a quick, convenient, safe, and comfortable manner for all population groups in the community with a minimum of harmful effects on the environment.

Although the following discussion focuses on the movement of people, some of the measures and data collection procedures can be adapted readily to assessing the movement of goods. Examples are the measures of travel times and safety.

Major Features Recommended

A number of transportation characteristics merit attention for annual monitoring. Measures for each of the following characteristics are recommended:

- Accessibility of citizens to their desired destinations
- Rapid movement
- Safety
- Comfort
- Convenience
- Air and noise pollution levels
- Overall citizen satisfaction with local transportation services.

The measures suggested for regular monitoring by local governments are presented in Exhibit 8-1.

A measurement approach proposed here is the use of annual surveys of citizens within the jurisdiction to obtain their opinions of local transportation services. The surveys can be used to obtain feedback on citizen perceptions of the following:

- The overall ability of citizens to get where they want to go, such as to work, recreation areas, and shopping centers
- The "rideability" of streets in their neighborhoods
- Parking convenience
- Visibility of street signs and signals
- Level of traffic noise in citizens' neighborhoods
- Adequacy of sidewalks and street lighting near their residences
- The transit service's convenience, reliability, comfort, speed, and general acceptability.

Data should be collected regularly on travel times between representative origins and destinations within the community, and on the severity and duration of automobile and other congestion in the most crowded areas. Local governments do not always monitor these characteristics, possibly because of the technical problems involved in obtaining reliable information at a reasonable cost. However, even small periodic samples of travel-time-related information can be valuable to public officials who want to know how travel times vary among parts of the community and over certain periods.

It is suggested that road rideability conditions be sampled regularly in various sections of the community either by a mechanical device such as a "roughometer" or by trained observers using a combination of photographic and written rating scales. If a trained observer approach is used, other conditions such as visibility of street signs and signals and sidewalk conditions can be rated simultaneously at little added cost. (In addition, ratings of street cleanliness, as discussed in Chapter 2, could also be obtained simultaneously, further increasing the value of the trained observer procedure.)

For some measures it is important to group the data to determine levels of service for persons with ready access to cars and for those without, especially the aged and handicapped. For most measures, the data should be grouped for different residential areas. Such data shed light on equity of service and whether the needs of special groups are being met.

One deficiency in these measures is that they do

Exhibit 8-1

Effectiveness Measures for General Transportation Services

Objective: *To provide access to desired destinations such as employment, shopping, and community services or other facilities in a quick, convenient, safe, and comfortable manner for all population groups in the community with a minimum of harmful effects on the environment.*

Objective	Quality characteristic	Specific measure	Data collection procedure
Vehicular travel			
Accessibility	Accessibility	1. Percentage of citizens rating their ability to get where they want to go in the jurisdiction in a reasonable time as satisfactory.[1]	Household survey
Rapid movement	Travel times	2. Average peak and off-peak travel times between key or representative origins and destinations.	Timed runs on selected routes
	Severity of congestion	3. Ratio of peak travel time to a "base" travel time between selected pairs of points.	Timed runs on selected routes
	Duration of congestion	4. Length of time that peak travel times exceed x percent of the "base" travel time.	Timed runs on selected routes
Safety	Frequency of accidents	5. Number of reported traffic accidents and the rate per 1,000 population.	Police accident reports
	Casualties from accidents	6. Number of deaths and number of injuries from traffic accidents and the rate per 1,000 population.	Police accident reports
	Property losses from accidents	7. Dollar property loss from traffic accidents and dollar loss per 1,000 population.	Insurance data or police reports
	Preventability of accidents	8. Rate of accidents involving a contributing factor that can be influenced by a local government agency.	Police accident reports
	Extent of hazards	9. Number and percentage of streets with pavement driving hazards.	Trained observer ratings
	Response time to remove hazards	10. Average time to repair potholes or other hazards reported by citizens.	Street department records
	Feeling of security in driving—driver perceptions	11. Percentage of drivers who feel driving conditions are generally safe (or unsafe) (a) in the community, (b) in their own neighborhoods.	Household survey
Comfort	Street rideability (surface condition)	12. Percentage of streets with rideability (street surface conditions) rated as satisfactory.	Roughness-measuring instrument or trained observer ratings
	Street surface condition—citizen ratings	13. Percentage of (a) citizens, (b) businesspersons rating street rideability as satisfactory.	(a) Household survey (b) survey of businesspersons

not measure the effects of transportation on employment, property values, neighborhood cohesiveness, and aesthetics. These secondary impacts of transportation are outside the scope of this report because they seem inappropriate for regular monitoring. Special in-depth evaluations are needed to measure these important impacts of local transportation.

Individual Measures for General Transportation

The remainder of this chapter discusses vehicular and pedestrian transportation measures—those

shown in Exhibit 8-1—and how data for these can be obtained regularly.

Measure of Overall Accessibility, All Modes (Measure 1)

Measure 1:   Percentage of citizens rating their ability to get where they want to go in the jurisdiction in a reasonable time as satisfactory.

This measure attempts to provide an overall assessment of citizen perceptions of the transportation system's accessibility, considering all modes jointly

Exhibit 8-1, continued

Effectiveness Measures for General Transportation Services

Objective	Quality characteristic	Specific measure	Data collection procedure
Convenience	Parking convenience—driver perception	14. Percentage of (a) drivers, (b) business-persons, (c) handicapped drivers who feel that finding a parking space is usually (or sometimes or infrequently) a problem, by area of the community.	(a) Household survey (b) survey of businesspersons (c) survey of handicapped drivers
	Visibility and condition of traffic control and street name signs	15. Percentage of streets with one or more (a) stop signs, or other traffic control, or information signs, (b) traffic signals, (c) street pavement markings, and (d) street name signs that are missing, blocked, or in otherwise unsatisfactory condition.	Trained observer ratings
		16. Percentage of citizens rating the understandability, visibility, and overall adequacy of traffic and information signs, traffic controls, street pavement markings, and street name signs as satisfactory.	Household survey
Environmental quality	Air pollution	17. Air-pollutant levels attributable to transportation sources; number of days air pollution exceeded "hazardous" threshold; and number of persons possibly exposed to hazardous levels.	Air samples and pollutant dispersion models
	Noise pollution	18. Percentage of street miles with traffic noise above x decibels, by residential (or nonresidential) area and type of street.	Noise-monitoring equipment or estimates based on HUD noise assessment guide.
		19. Percentage of citizens stating that they are bothered by traffic noise in their neighborhoods frequently, occasionally, or rarely.	Household survey
Pedestrian travel Convenience/ safety	Sidewalk walkability (surface condition)	20. Percentage of blocks with sidewalks in satisfactory condition.	Trained observer rating
	Sidewalk availability and walkability	21. Percentage of citizens satisfied with the adequacy and condition of sidewalks in their neighborhoods.	Household survey
	Adequacy of street lighting	22. Percentage of citizens who feel street lighting in their neighborhoods is insufficient, about right, or too bright.	Household survey
	Handicapped access	23. Percentage of handicapped persons who feel they can get around streets satisfactorily.	Special handicapped citizens survey

[1]Measures calling for "satisfactory" ratings may use the term "unsatisfactory" when officials believe that emphasis would be more meaningful.

(that is, automobile, bus, rail, and walking). Chapter 9 presents a separate measure of accessibility to public transit services, based on the proximity of residents to transit stops. That measure, however, does not indicate whether citizens *perceive* themselves as being able to get where they want to go, nor does it consider all modes of local transportation.

Data Collection. Data on this measure can be obtained by the household survey recommended for other government service areas discussed in other chapters. Covering a number of services in this survey will make the approach both more useful and more economically feasible, as costs can be divided among the several services. The household survey procedure is discussed at length in Chapter 13. To obtain data for Measure 1, a question such as the following can be included in the survey: "In general, how would you rate your ability to get where you want to go in (name of city or county) in a reasonable amount of time, considering all forms of transportation, including automobiles, buses, and walking: excellent, good, fair, or poor?"

In addition, respondents might be asked about their ability to get to specific types of destinations such as work opportunities, recreation sites, and shopping areas. A question such as the following might be included: "For each of the following destinations, please tell me whether, over the past twelve months, it was usually easy, sometimes difficult, or often difficult to get to the following locations (whether by car, bus, or walking): (a) your place of work; (b) stores where you do your weekly shopping; (c) recreation areas within the city (or county); and (d) hospital or medical facilities."

When respondents give negative responses (for example, "fair" or "poor" or "often difficult") to any of these questions, it is useful to ask them to identify reasons for their dissatisfaction.

Citizens also might be asked if they feel they have an adequate choice of transportation alternatives. Some people can get where they want to go at present, but they strongly desire alternatives, especially adequate public transit service.

If police traffic control is not measured separately, a question might be added on the degree of satisfaction with that service. The enforcement of speed limits and handling of traffic accidents affect all transportation but rail.

Measures of Rapid Movement (Measures 2–4)

Measure 2:   *Average peak and off-peak travel times between key or representative origins and destinations.*

This measure indicates the combined effect of such factors as traffic volume, speed limit, traffic control devices, and directness of available routes on the time required to travel by automobiles within the community. Travel times for this measure can be determined by regular monitoring of "typical" trips within the community, perhaps fifteen to thirty. The average time can be reported separately for each trip or class of trips.

The calculation of travel times is a familiar activity for many local government transportation agencies. Few, however, regularly make measurements to provide regular comparisons along key routes. The measurement may be, for example, to prepare maps that depict equal travel-time contours for trips from the central business district.

A major problem in this measure is selecting the "typical" trips. Types of trips to consider for regular measurement include:

- Those from residential areas to destinations such as the central business district, large shopping centers, employment centers, medical centers, and major recreation sites

- Business or commercially oriented trips such as those between commercial districts or between important local cargo depots and points in business or manufacturing districts (to monitor times for goods shipments)

- Trips with special social value, such as from neighborhoods with high unemployment to industrial districts

- Trips to and from areas of likely future residential or commercial development.

Selected trips should include cross-community as well as radial trips from the central business district.

Origins and destinations should be chosen carefully to minimize the number of origin-destination pairs to be measured. For example, some of the selected points might simultaneously represent residential areas and medical centers, or residential areas and shopping areas. The more paths used, the greater the coverage of the measure, but also the greater the costs of data collection and analysis.

Whenever possible, the paths selected for general transportation travel-time measurements should also be usable for measuring transit travel times so that auto and transit travel times can be compared. If a city identifies ten residential area origins and twelve commercial-medical-entertainment destinations, these identifications define 120 (10x12) paths for which transit travel times can be calculated. (The nearest transit stop might be identified for each selected origin and destination.)

Data Collection. For each path included, an average travel time can be computed from the results of a number of runs made on the prescribed route. Drivers should attempt to move at the "average" speed of the traffic, keeping within posted speed limits. Separate measurements should be made for peak-hour trips between residential and employment centers, off-peak trips within the business district, and off-peak trips between residential and commercial or recreation areas.

Several runs, at least four to six, should be made under similar driving conditions (for example, peak periods or off-peak periods) to provide a basis for computing the averages. If there is a wide variation among the times, additional runs should be made. Runs should not be made in inclement weather. Runs during which other unusual traffic conditions are encountered (for instance, a traffic accident or stalled car) should not be counted. Averages can be severely distorted by such circumstances.[1]

Seasonal differences can be determined by sampling the runs throughout the year and tabulating them for each season. This procedure is a variation of the more common approach of measuring travel times for a number of radial routes emanating from the central business district of a metropolitan area, in order to provide maps showing equal-time contours.

Data can be collected by regular employees or temporary staff members, such as summer interns hired specifically for the task, or by street repair crews and supervisory employees who regularly travel throughout the city. The latter may be able to adjust some of their trips to include a specified path to record off-peak travel times. Alternatively, city employees can record data on routes that lie generally within their normal travel patterns. For example, office employees might gather data on rush-hour trips. In all cases, the employees should be adequately instructed. A sample of their runs should be checked to ensure that correct procedures are being followed. If these problems can be surmounted, costs may be reduced and more frequent measurements may be possible throughout the year.

Special Validity Considerations. There are drawbacks in using the same routes each year. While it enhances the validity of trends, the selected routes may no longer be "typical." Thus, it may be necessary to revise some of the route selections from time to time, with resulting loss in comparability.

A second potential problem is that government agencies might give special attention to the particular routes included in the measurements, at the expense of paths not included. Again, annual review of the selected paths is desirable and changes should be made if it is suspected that this is occurring.

The small number of travel-time runs likely to be economically feasible for each route limits the representativeness of the results for estimating conditions for each season and for the entire year. Also limited is the accuracy of the averages calculated for each route. Ideally the routes should be covered at various times of the year, and many runs should be made for each route to increase both the accuracy of the travel-time estimates and the likelihood that the averages calculated are representative of conditions throughout the year. Of course, congestion and long travel times are greatly affected by factors that, at least in the short run, are beyond the control of a transportation agency—such as population growth and development. However, transportation agencies have a major role in at least alleviating these conditions.

Measure 3:   *Ratio of peak travel time to a "base" travel time between selected pairs of points.*

Measure 4:   *Length of time that peak travel times exceed x percent of the "base" travel time.*

These two measures are intended to indicate the severity and duration of congestion at peak travel times. Changes such as staggered work hours may decrease the severity of peak congestion but spread the rush hour over a longer time. Such measures should be considered at least for the most heavily traveled arterials.

Data for several arterials presented together can help provide a picture of overall congestion in the community.

"Congestion" can be defined for this measure as a condition where the travel time between two points on an arterial route exceeds a "base time" by some minimum, such as 25 percent. This base time can be either actual travel-time measurements at off-peak hours or a standard such as the number of minutes needed to travel between two points at the legal speed limit. The "severity" of congestion would be the ratio of the maximum travel time to base time (for example, 35 percent greater than the "base time"). The "duration" of congestion would be the length of time that travel times exceed the threshold percentage, for example, one hour at 25 percent or more over the base.

Data Collection. The first steps in data collection are selecting the arterials of interest and identifying points on these arterials between which congestion is to be measured (for example, one-half to three miles apart). Travel times between these two points might be measured during peak traffic flow periods on each of at least three, and preferably more, weekdays. The number of observations needed varies with the desired level of precision and the number of seasons for which the measurements are needed.[2] If the worst congestion on a road occurs on weekends during the summer (for roads leading to beaches, for instance), then summer Saturdays and Sundays should be used rather than weekdays.

Two observers, one stationed at each measurement point, can record the times and license numbers or other identification of vehicles as they pass; a two-way radio link helps. The vehicles used for the routes to be measured could be city vehicles, if they are normally driven on the route and circle back to the start for subsequent measurements; buses, if the measurement points lie along a bus route segment with frequent service (but not "bus-only" lanes) and there are no bus stops on that segment; or private vehicles that happen to be traveling the route.

Note that Measure 3 should be considerably less expensive than Measure 4 because it requires estimates at only two points in time per route.

Special Validity Considerations. Measures 3 and 4 are affected by the same concerns of number and timing that were described under Measure 2.

Measures of Safety (Measures 5–11)

Measure 5: *Number of reported traffic accidents and the rate per 1,000 population.*

Measure 6: *Number of deaths and number of injuries from traffic accidents and the rate per 1,000 population.*

Measure 7: *Dollar property loss from traffic accidents and dollar loss per 1,000 population.*

Accident rates (Measure 5) provide an indicator of frequency of problems, whereas casualty rates and dollar value of property damage (Measures 6 and 7) are indicators of the severity of the incidents.

Rates of traffic accidents, deaths and injuries, and property loss are commonly used as measures of a transportation system's safety. These rates reflect traffic control efforts and road network design as well as conditions substantially beyond local government control, including the design and condition of private vehicles, the quality of driver education, and the physical condition of the drivers—intoxicated, aged, poor eyesight.

Accident, injury, and property damage information should be presented in summary form and should include the following categories: mode of transportation (for example, automobile, bus, pedestrian, or rail); apparent reasons or contributing factors for the accident; location; driver characteristics; and victim characteristics. A special subject of the data should be "accidents involving city-owned or leased vehicles," which are more controllable by the city and which open it to liability.

Data Collection. The number of traffic accidents is reported universally, but not all communities compute accident rates. The rates in Measures 5, 6, and 7 are computed by dividing the number of accidents, deaths, injuries, or dollar loss by estimates of current population, which are usually available from local planning departments.

The residential population is commonly used as the denominator for these measures. That normalization provides a useful overall indicator, especially for comparisons over time and with other communities, or for comparisons among various residential areas of the jurisdictions. However, residential population does not reflect the effects of nonresidential (that is, visitor and business) traffic on a community.

To allow for this problem, the estimated nonresident (daytime) population should be included in the denominator. Or, the number of accidents, deaths, and injuries of *resident* drivers per 1,000 *residents* could be stated as separate measures. Accident reports usually include addresses of the drivers involved, thus allowing computation of accident rates separately for residents and nonresidents.

Two other denominators might be used in computing the rates in Measures 5 and 6. First, the number of accidents or deaths and injuries per 1,000 vehicle-miles driven would reflect safety in terms of vehicle usage. Second, the number of accidents or deaths and injuries per 1,000 passenger-miles could be used to compare the relative safety of various transportation modes. Both vehicle-miles driven and passenger-miles are difficult to estimate accurately. Rough estimates of the former can be made using areawide gasoline consumption.

The numerator of Measure 5, number of reported accidents, currently is tabulated by most jurisdictions, but this figure is likely to be underestimated because not all accidents are reported to the police. Household surveys or possibly insurance company records could be used to estimate the degree of nonreporting and thus provide a more accurate estimate of total accidents. The same applies to measures of injury and dollar loss.

In many communities, police take no accident report at all if no one is injured and there is no damage to public property. This becomes a problem if different communities, with different reporting practices, are being compared.

The type of injury to be counted in Measure 6 needs to be defined. The state of Florida has categorized injuries into three classes, based on what is visible at the scene:

- Physical signs of injury such as bleeding wounds, a distorted limb, or a victim who has to be carried from the scene
- Other visible injuries such as bruises, abrasions, swelling, or limping
- No visible injuries, but complaint of pain or momentary unconsciousness.

For Measure 6, at least the first two categories of injury should be included. Whatever definition of injury a community chooses, it should be made clear to those compiling the tabulations and be used consistently.

The numerator of Measure 7 is the total dollar amount of property loss from traffic accidents. Police accident reports in some communities indicate property damage, but dollar estimates of damage are made infrequently. Police officers generally lack training for making damage estimates in any event.

Several methods for gathering accident cost data are available, including the following:

- Professional appraisers used to estimate damages at the scene of a sample of accidents
- A follow-up survey of victims of a sample of accidents to ascertain the costs of repairing property damage
- Summary data obtained from insurance companies, on the cost of all or a sample of accidents, provided such data are not confidential. This procedure would not, however, pick up costs of accidents involving uninsured drivers.

When data from Measure 7 are compared over time, they should be expressed in constant dollars (adjusted for price changes) or plotted against changes in indices for automobile prices and repair costs.

Measure 8: *Rate of accidents involving a contributing factor that can be influenced by a local government agency.*

Many local government activities affect accident rates to some extent. These activities include police traffic control and law enforcement, street engineering and repair, traffic signing and signaling, and street lighting. This measure attempts to separate accidents involving contributing factors that could be affected by local government from those that would

not. Exhibit 8-2 lists a number of contributing factors and the agency likely to have prime responsibility for each.

Data Collection. Many communities routinely record data regarding conditions at the time of the accident. Some police accident reports contain a checklist of possible contributing factors, such as apparent traffic violations, physical condition of the driver, obstructions to vision, unreasonably high speed limit, absence of traffic control, pavement defects, and little advance warning of intersection. Checklists such as these provide a starting point for gathering data for this measure.

Reporting forms and data displays should describe relevant conditions as "possible contributing factors" rather than "causes." Rarely is it possible for a police officer to identify causes with certainty during the investigation at an accident scene. There also are liability considerations in the choice of wording on the form—it should be reviewed by the city attorney.

Police officers should be instructed on the proper preparation, intended use, and importance of acci-

---

Exhibit 8-2

Factors Contributing to Accidents and Related to Local Government Functions

Contributing factor	Typical agency with prime responsibility
a. Street surface condition by type (e.g., pothole, severe bump) b. Ice or snow on road	Streets
c. Traffic control (signal, sign, or pavement marking) malfunction, missing, not visible, confusing, by type of control and type of problem d. Traffic control lacking where needed (in judgment of police officer reporting)	Traffic
e. View obstruction (e.g., buildings, hedges)	Parks (possibly streets)
f. Driver under influence of alcohol or drugs g. Moving violation, by type of violation h. Vehicle malfunction or defect in violation of the law (e.g., no lights)	Police
i. Other vehicle malfunction or defect j. Driver's health or physical condition (other than alcohol or drugs)	Not usually local government responsibility, but probably of concern to other levels of government.[1]
k. Other (specify government-related factors)	Various agencies

[1]Local governments may use these data to help inform state governments of problem areas that are usually state responsibilities, such as vehicle inspections and driver licensing (including testing).

dent reports. Sample accident reports should be reviewed periodically by supervisors to ensure that they are being filled out properly.

In communities where accident report data are computerized, periodic tallies of the number of accidents involving various factors can be accomplished at a small incremental cost.

Otherwise, manual tallies can be made for a sample of accidents.

Measure 9:   Number and percentage of streets with pavement driving hazards.

Hazards in the roadway are accidents waiting to happen. They are extremely annoying to drivers, not only because of riding discomfort but also because they can cause accidents. They also expose the community to liability suits.

"Hazards" need to be defined. They are generally large potholes or other sharp bumps, drops, or tilts in the driving right-of-way.

Data Collection. The data for this measure can be collected as part of the surveys of road conditions used for Measure 12. If Measure 12 is not used, the criteria specified for a level 4 problem in Measure 12 can be used, with drive through of community streets. (In most communities few streets have hazards, and the sampling is much faster than when rating rideability.)

Measure 10:   Average time to repair potholes or other hazards reported by citizens.

This measure reflects the responsiveness of street maintenance to citizen calls. It also reflects how long a hazard is left exposed.

Measure 10 could be limited to road hazards or broadened to include sidewalk hazards, broken stop signs, and other high priority transportation problems reported by citizens. Note that this measure reflects only facilities and equipment already built or installed. Citizen complaints about perceived hazards such as lack of a traffic light or lack of a stop sign probably should not be included.

Data Collection. Street maintenance records usually include the time of a complaint and the time the complaint was addressed (or the records department can be asked to include them).

Measure 11:   Percentage of drivers who feel driving conditions are generally safe (or unsafe) (a) in the community, (b) in their own neighborhoods.

Driver perceptions of unsafe conditions may make travel unpleasant or even unhealthful for them. When such perceptions are intense, they may cause

persons to avoid driving on particular roads, or even at all.

A local government's potential influence on driver perceptions of safety is limited. Driver perceptions probably are influenced by clear and ample traffic control, nighttime markings, shoulders, railings, and the like; police enforcement of traffic laws; driver education programs; and safety campaigns that encourage courteous, careful driving behavior. The measure is used to gauge the "feeling" of security; it may or may not be correlated with the actual extent of driver safety.

Data Collection. Data for this measure can be gathered from the multiservice household survey using a question such as "How safe from traffic accidents do you generally feel while driving in your neighborhood: very safe; somewhat safe; somewhat unsafe; very unsafe?"

A follow-up question might identify the sources of perceived danger, such as defective road surfaces, inadequate traffic law enforcement, confusing traffic control devices, actions of other drivers, inadequate pavement marking for night driving, construction, or other factors. This question might be used as a separate measure in the form of "percentage of respondents who cite (specific problem areas)." Although not included in the list of measures, the "percentage of citizens who feel there is relatively low (or high) danger to *pedestrians* (especially children or the elderly) from traffic in their neighborhood" also might be obtained through the household survey.

Measures of Comfort (Measures 12 and 13)

Road maintenance is a major activity of local transportation. The construction and maintenance of street surfaces affect the comfort, safety, and time involved in local travel. The two measures below are of particular importance because they provide indicators of road maintenance.

Measure 12 uses an "objective" approach to measuring road conditions that is directly related to riding comfort or rideability. Measure 13 uses a subjective approach by obtaining ratings from citizens on their perceptions of road conditions.

Measure 12:   Percentage of streets with rideability (street surface conditions) rated as satisfactory.

The concern here is with the rideability for road users, whether they are using automobiles, trucks, buses, or bicycles.

Local street maintenance agencies regularly examine streets and roads to rate their surface conditions from an engineering viewpoint. They then determine priorities for maintenance and repair programs, such as resurfacing, and try to prevent rideability from becoming a problem. (This is essentially preventive maintenance.) Here, however, the concern is with measuring current rideability—the quality of the "ride" on existing roads. Bumpiness may be considered by a street maintenance agency as a superficial blemish on a road but rideability or bumpiness is of direct concern to citizens using the roads.

Measure 12 (and Measure 13) can be used to help assess the success of preventive street maintenance programs as manifested by current conditions.

Data Collection. Basically, there are two approaches for obtaining "objective" assessments of street rideability: using mechanical roughness-measuring devices and using "trained observers" to make visual ratings.[3]

Several mechanical devices exist for measuring road surface conditions. These include the Portland Cement Association (PCA) Roadmeter and the Mays Ride Meter (developed by the Texas Highway Department). Some of these devices are mounted on a trailer and towed along the streets at about 20 mph. Others are mounted inside a test car, connected to the suspension, and can be used at speeds up to 55 mph.[4]

These devices were developed primarily for measuring the smoothness of newly constructed roads and high speed roads, but they can be used for urban streets as well. They require technicians for calibrating and operating the equipment. Many state highway departments have used these devices (sometimes called "profilometers"). Local governments wanting to make periodic effectiveness measurements but not wanting to build or buy their own devices can borrow or rent these devices.

To relate the results obtained from such devices to citizen perceptions of discomfort, a bumpiness scale should be developed from the mechanical readings. This can be done by correlating data gathered mechanically with ratings of road bumpiness made by a panel of citizens riding over the same streets.

When instruments for measuring roughness are not available or are considered too expensive or unwieldy, street surface conditions can be assessed by trained observers who use preestablished visual ratings or "seat-of-the-pants" bumpiness ratings.

These measurements can be made by a driver or passenger in a car cruising at a fixed speed. Ratings of street surface conditions can be made simultaneously with those for street litter (see Chapter 2), conditions of street signs (Measure 15), pavement markings (Measure 15), and sidewalks (Measure 21). This methodology has been used successfully by a number of jurisdictions, such as the state of Massachusetts to measure street conditions before and after maintenance cutbacks, the cities of Charlottesville and Alexandria, Virginia, for routine annual effectiveness measurements, and by Nashville and St. Petersburg. Side benefits of using raters drawn from various departments include better interdepartmental cooperation and greater awareness of the community's problems. Serving as a rater has been viewed in some locations as professional development. Bumpiness ratings are influenced by the vehicle's suspension system, so the same type of vehicles should be used for all test runs.

Visual ratings normally should be from the center line of the street to the right curb, because it is hard to observe both sides of the street simultaneously and because the observer has not experienced the quality of the ride on the other side. This gives a 50 percent sample unless each block is traversed twice, once in each direction.

The visual ratings should be based on a scale described both photographically and in writing. The intent is to reduce the subjectivity of the ratings so that different observers using the rating guidelines would give the same rating to given street conditions.

A set of photographs should be established to show various levels of "rideability." Exhibit 8-3 shows photographs representing four levels of ratings used first in Nashville, and subsequently in several other communities, to help trained observers standardize their field observations. It is difficult to find a satisfactory picture of a "4" (worst) condition because of the difficulty in distinguishing pothole depths in photographs; level 4 therefore relies on physically measurable conditions, using a ruler if there is any doubt.

Exhibit 8-4 gives definitions of the four condition levels based on a scale of 1 to 4. Half-level ratings, such as 1.5, can be used to indicate conditions that fall between two levels. Numbers on the four-point scale describe certain conditions and are not part of a continuous, equal-interval rating scale. Therefore, the results actually should be presented as "the percentage of streets within each level" or "the percentage of streets that are worse than some level (such as 2.5)" rather than as "average" ratings. "Average" ratings technically are not correct because the scale is not uniform from 1 to 4. Although it is tempting to use averages, and no great distortion seems likely to occur from them, averages vary less than do the percentages of streets with poor or fair conditions and they are more difficult to interpret.

Rideability ratings should be made at least once a year, and preferably more frequently, to help identify seasonal distortions in the measurement. The timing will depend on the local climate and the street maintenance schedule. Communities that experience cold winters might record conditions at the time of year when the worst street conditions are present (for

Exhibit 8-3

Examples of Street Rideability Conditions

Condition 1, smooth

Condition 2, slightly bumpy

Condition 3, considerably bumpy

Condition 4, potential safety hazard, severe jolting

example, after thawing) and at the "best" time of the year (for instance, the dry season or immediately after the conclusion of repair programs for the year). If ratings are not spread throughout the year, they should be made at about the same time(s) each year to avoid seasonal distortions.

The number of streets to be rated depends on the desired range of accuracy, the variation in street surface, conditions within the jurisdiction, the size of the jurisdiction, the intended use of the ratings (rough measure or detailed street and neighborhood feedback) and the resources available for doing the ratings and their analysis. A large community might, for example, use trained observers to rate 500 streets with a random sample of 50 streets in each of 10 areas. Other communities might rate 100 percent of the streets.

In communities where public works departments visually rate streets at regular intervals for engineering purposes, the rideability ratings can be added readily, thus providing these data on a potentially large sample of streets at small additional cost.

Exhibit 8-4

Rating Scale for Street Rideability (Visual Rating from an Automobile)

Condition	Description
1	**Smooth** a. No noticeable defects. This could be split off as a separate "perfect rating" category if desired or b. One or two minor defects, such as a small open crack, minor bump, small hole less than 2 inches across; or cracked surface with no perceived bumpiness (e.g., Condition 1 on the photographic exhibit)
2	**Slightly bumpy** a. Several minor defects or small potholes, but none severe or b. A sizable single bump or several minor bumps or c. Gravel or dirt road in good condition[1]
3	**Considerably bumpy** At least one section of the street is broken up or with easily visible bumps, but no single safety hazard (as defined below) present
4	**Potential safety hazard or cause of severe jolt** One or more large potholes, "steps," or other major defects 3½ inches high or deep. (This category could be divided into parts to distinguish streets with only one hazard from those with more than one.) Types of hazards should be noted.

[1] Unpaved roads and roads with rough surfacing for aesthetic reasons (such as bricks or cobblestones) might be rated along with other types of roads using this rating scale with 2c included. Alternatively, such roads might be rated apart from paved roads, using the scale from 1 to 4 with 2c deleted. The percentage of roads that are unpaved and the "percentage by special surfacing type" might also be reported as a separate measure.

The accuracy of the visual rating system is not perfect, but based on results in several jurisdictions, it appears that adequate consistency among observers can be obtained with proper initial training, periodic retraining, and monitoring of a sample of ratings by a second "judge," who gives the raters feedback on rating problems. The following points are important for proper use of the procedure:

- The rating scale for each measure should be pretested in each municipality prior to its use, to assure that persons with proper training will give reliable ratings. Some of these procedures are discussed in Chapter 12 (for example, the requirement that 75 percent of the ratings by a new inspector be in exact agreement with, and that 90 percent be within one-half grade of, the ratings by an independent judge). If a municipality uses the rating scales included in this report, it should test them for local conditions prior to use and adjust definitions as needed to accommodate local street features.

- Adequate training in the use of the rating scales must be provided. This means both initial training for new observers and refresher training for experienced observers before ratings begin again. Without periodic refresher training, there is a tendency for raters to deviate from the scales. Training should include both classroom and field work. Initial training requires approximately two days; one or two half-day sessions are enough for refresher training.

- A fraction (10 to 25 percent) of the ratings made by each trained observer on each measure should be replicated by an independent judge. If significant deviations between ratings occur, refresher training or other action is needed. Any rater whose ratings deviate significantly from the others should be given special attention or be dropped from the team.

- If, to keep down measurement costs, only a sample of the streets is rated periodically rather than all streets in the jurisdiction, proper sampling techniques must be used to assure that the sample is reasonably representative. This is basic good practice and, along with the rating replications, will help yield proper ratings and give credible results.

- Another alternative to save costs is to rate some streets or areas only once every year or two *if* the ratings show street condition to be excellent *and* this has been the case one or more previous years, *and* there is no known reason for expecting a sharp change in the situation. The cities of Alexandria and Charlottesville both independently elected to do this when year-to-year ratings found few streets in poor condition (2.5 or higher scores). However, they had to retrain raters when they started up again. Another option to save costs is to rate alternate sides of the street in alternate years.

- To keep trained observer ratings useful for comparing conditions over time, the rating scales and key procedures should be kept stable. Changes in those scales and procedures can affect the comparability of findings and degrade the usefulness of the rating effort. Careful pretesting of the procedures, as suggested above, will help avoid the need for subsequent revisions.

- Ratings preferably should be stored in computer-readable form, street by street. This facilitates a variety of analyses and year-to-year comparisons. On the other hand, simple hand tallies can yield a wealth of information, and a lack of computers should not affect the decision to use these measures.

More details on trained observer procedures are presented in Chapter 12 and Appendix 1.

Studies in 1975 by Indiana University indicated that ratings by trained observers using a four-level scale were highly correlated with those gathered by mechanical devices on the same roads. The ratings of mechanical roughness measurement devices have two important advantages over ratings by trained observers: the measurements generally are more reliable (if the equipment is suitably calibrated and working properly), and some devices produce a printed record of each road's bumpiness, which allows management to identify specific spots needing attention. On the other hand, trained observers also can note problems requiring immediate attention, and mechanical readings include only the portion of the roadway touched by the wheels of the device or test vehicle and may miss bumps or hazards, especially those near curbs. In addition, costs for operating some devices may be higher than costs for measurements by trained observers. However, with the advent of inexpensive devices such as the PCA Roadmeter or the South Dakota Profilometer, which can be operated by one technician at speeds up to 50 mph, mechanical roughness measurements are economically feasible for local governments. If a reliable, low-cost mechanical device is available, possibly on loan from a state highway department, the use of a mechanical device is warranted. Otherwise, the

trained observer approach seems adequate, provided suitable training and periodic replications are assured. Some state highway departments have decided that mechanical measurements are the most economical approach to meet their needs, but somewhat different conditions, such as higher speeds, exist in the areas under state jurisdiction.

Pavement Condition and Distress Indicators. In addition to roughness, engineers use a variety of pavement condition and distress measures to evaluate maintenance, rehabilitation, and reconstruction needs. Common condition and distress indicators include rutting and various types of cracking such as alligator, block, and longitudinal cracks. These indicators have been assessed mainly by walking, windshield surveys, or photologging. Automated methods, involving pattern recognition techniques, are being developed to identify different types of pavement distress and determine their extent and severity. Numerous agencies have developed composite indices of these condition and distress indicators to help determine the proper level of roadwork on each section of road. Some of these indices can be used to convey the change in road conditions over time. These composite indices capture more than roughness; they can be considered a proxy for rideability, and they provide warnings of future road distress.

Measurements of both roughness and road surface condition and distress can be a major help to the jurisdiction in determining needs and priorities for its road maintenance and rehabilitation activities for specific road segments.

Measure 13: Percentage of (a) citizens, (b) business-persons rating street rideability as satisfactory.

A key concern is whether the users of a jurisdiction's roads perceive them as comfortable to ride on. Whether or not citizen or businessperson ratings are "accurate" in a technical sense, the public's perceptions are important to public officials. Individuals will differ in their sensitivity to road problems, but the resulting data on the distribution of ratings should be useful for assessment purposes, especially when compared across major areas of the community and from one time period to another.

Citizen perceptions may include factors beyond those considered in trained observer or mechanical ratings and can add a dimension to those ratings by, in effect, "weighting" or "summing" various quality characteristics.

Data Collection. The household survey suggested for Measure 1 and for a number of other measures throughout this report can be used to obtain data on the citizen's perspective. Question 9 in Appendix 1 is an example of a question that can be used to ask respondents about the condition of streets in their neighborhoods. Respondents also might be asked to rate streets in the community as a whole or perhaps in the central business district, but they are likely to be most familiar with conditions in a more limited area, such as their own neighborhoods.

Respondents also should be asked their reasons for negative ratings to identify the particular nature of street problems and perhaps their location. Finally, the views of business officials on street conditions in their areas can be obtained from a question in a survey of businesses, such as Question 4 in Appendix 2.

Mechanical Ratings of Street Conditions Compared to Citizen Perceptions. Research comparing citizen perceptions of street roughness to mechanical ratings shows some correlation.[5] However, the relationship is not strong enough to indicate that one adequately reflects the other.

Street maintenance officials generally believe themselves considerably more capable than citizens of identifying road rideability. From a technical viewpoint, this is correct. Nevertheless, citizen perceptions of road rideability, even if not in agreement with the more technical measurements such as those in Measure 12, are likely to be of major concern to public officials.

The best approach seems to be to use a combination of "objective" mechanical device ratings or trained observer ratings and citizen surveys.

Measures of Convenience (Measures 14–17)
The measures in this group reflect various aspects of driving convenience. Many of them also reflect safety.

Measure 14: *Percentage of (a) drivers, (b) business-persons, (c) handicapped drivers who feel that finding a parking space is usually (or sometimes or infrequently) a problem, by area of the community.*

The supply of on-street and off-street parking spaces can be inventoried, and the "percentage of capacity used" can be obtained. It is difficult, however, to develop an estimate of demand for parking spaces that can be compared to the number of spaces available and that is appropriate for regular monitoring. It is even more difficult to formulate a measure that encompasses specific convenience characteristics such as location, price, security, and shelter from weather. Utilization rates for available parking facilities are also ambiguous. For example, underutilization of available parking could indicate that there is either sufficient parking in the area or that such parking is unsuitable for citizens' needs.

Citizen perceptions of the overall convenience of existing parking, although probably not as "objective" as transportation officials might like, provide important input. The household survey, if undertaken regularly, provides a convenient way for a municipality to obtain these data. A question such as Question 3 in Appendix 1 might be used. Because customer parking convenience is of special interest to businesses, the local government undertaking a periodic survey of businesses can include a question on parking. An example is Question 9 in Appendix 2.

The convenience of parking for handicapped drivers can be determined by a special survey of handicapped drivers, or, if the household survey is large enough, by identifying respondents that are handicapped and analyzing their responses separately.

Measure 15: *Percentage of streets with one or more (a) stop signs, or other traffic control, or information signs, (b) traffic signals, (c) street pavement markings, and (d) street name signs that are missing, blocked, or in otherwise unsatisfactory condition.*

The principal effect of obscured, defaced, damaged, or missing signs is likely to be inconvenience, but such defects also can be dangerous (for example, an obscured stop sign at a dangerous intersection). Damaged signs also are unsightly, and like litter, they give the neighborhood a bad image.

Traffic signs and signals fall into two categories: *regulatory* and *advisory*. Regulatory signs and traffic lights control or limit driver actions in ways enforceable by legal penalties. Regulatory signs include such traffic signs as: stop, yield, one way, do not enter, no left turn, no parking, and speed limit. Advisory signs provide information to the driver on exits, route numbers, school or bicycle crossings, the location of specific facilities, and street names. The condition of stop signs is of paramount importance here. The condition of street name signs tends to be the most neglected.

Four characteristics of traffic and street signs are important:

- Visibility: Positioning, lack of tilting or twisting, lack of obstruction, lack of defacement, size of lettering, and cleanliness. Ideally, the visibility factors of daytime and nighttime conditions and poor weather also should be considered. Obviously it is important for traffic signals and electronic advisory signs to be in good working order.

- Understandability: Clarity and lack of ambiguity in the message.

- Sufficiency: Whether the number of signs and signals is adequate to keep drivers advised of regulations and hazards, to control traffic, and to make it convenient for drivers to get around.

- Oversigning: The extent to which the number of regulatory signs makes it difficult to drive about conveniently. Too many signs can be confusing and may dull the impact of important signs; this profusion also is aesthetically unpleasant.

To identify specific problems, ratings can be separated into four subjects: traffic control signs, traffic signals, street name signs, and street markings. Several jurisdictions using these measures have decided to split out a separate measure of the condition of stop signs, or both stop and yield signs, because they pose imminent danger if they are not visible.

It would be too complicated for a trained observer rating system for signs to include the rating of streets as to the need for signs not already present, the sufficiency of signs for directing drivers to various destinations, or the need to eliminate some signs if there are too many signs present. These additional conditions can be reflected, at least grossly, by surveys of citizens' perceptions of the adequacy of signs. (See discussion of the next measure.)

For traffic signals, the frequency of repairs and related downtime, at least as measured from the time the first report of the problem was received, can be used in place of trained observer ratings, if desired. Traffic signals cause such immediate problems when they fail that they tend to be repaired the same day. Trained observers tend to see few failed signals during a once-a-year sample. Also, the signals often fail as a result of thunderstorms, and the occurrence of failed signals shortly before sampling would skew results.

Data Collection. Based on experience in Alexandria, Charlottesville, and Nashville, the use of trained observers appears to be a feasible procedure for making standardized ratings of the visibility of traffic control and street name signs. These ratings can be made concurrently with ratings of other street characteristics such as road rideability (Measure 12) and perhaps street cleanliness (see Chapter 2). Chapter 12 sets forth procedures for rating several types of street conditions simultaneously and suggests rating scales for stop, yield, and street name signs.

The ratings for this measure can be made by either the driver or the rider from a car driven slowly down the block. The car should be stopped short of intersections to allow time for the rater to note the condition of street name signs, traffic lights, if any, and other equipment.

Both a written rating scale and photographs illustrating the various conditions corresponding to each level on the scales should be employed. An example of a written rating scale is provided in Appendix 10. Illustrative photographs used in rating stop signs and street name signs are shown in Exhibits 8-5 and 8-6.

Adequate training and retraining are needed. As discussed in Measure 12 and in Chapter 2, part of the ratings should be replicated, and retraining should be given when the replications indicate significant differences in ratings.

Nighttime ratings and bad weather ratings of traffic signs and pavement markings also are desirable. They can be developed using photographic rating scales similar in concept to those already discussed for daytime ratings. An alternative approach is to use comparison standards. Pieces of reflectorized material, chosen because the degree of their reflectivity is considered desirable for important signs, are held next to a sample of existing signs at night. The brightness of the test material is compared to that of the sign sample being tested. These ratings can be done using a flashlight at close range or headlights from a distance. A panel of citizens might be used to make the initial selection of materials considered bright enough. Alternatively, subjective ratings by trained observers or from citizens on household surveys can be used.

Rating pavement markings at night and in the rain, using similar principles, also should be considered by local governments.

Measure 16: *Percentage of citizens rating the understandability, visibility, and overall adequacy of traffic and information signs, traffic controls, street pavement markings, and street name signs as satisfactory.*

Citizen perceptions directly indicate whether "users" view signs and signals as satisfactory. After all, these are the persons who use the signs, signals, and markings.

Data Collection. A survey of drivers, obtained either by the household survey or a special driver survey, could be used to gather data on this measure.

Questions in Appendix 1 such as Question 4 (on pavement markings such as center lines), Question 5 (on traffic signs), and Question 7 (on street name signs) can be used to obtain these data. Questions 5

Exhibit 8-5

Examples of Stop Sign Conditions 2 and 3

Condition 2

Condition 2

Condition 3

Condition 3

Exhibit 8-6

Examples of Street Name Sign Conditions 1, 2, and 3

Condition 1

Condition 2

Condition 3

Condition 3

and 7 measure the adequacy of both traffic and street name signs in terms of the rating "easy to see and understand quickly." Question 5a illustrates how, when a problem is indicated in a response, an attempt can be made to identify the specific nature of that problem (for example, blocked view, missing signs, or signs that are too small).

Note that these questions should be asked only of those survey respondents who indicated in a previous question that they had driven an automobile in the jurisdiction in recent months.

The perceived degree of undersigning or over–signing and the comprehensibility of signs are difficult to measure objectively on a regular basis except by such surveys.

Measures of Environmental Quality (Measures 17–19)

Air and noise pollution are important problems for transportation systems. Regular monitoring of air quality and noise levels can be important to community mental and physical health. This highly specialized area is not discussed here in detail, but a few suggestions are given below. For the most part, these are general air and noise pollution measures related to transportation sources.

Measure 17: *Air-pollutant levels attributable to transportation sources; number of days air pollution exceeded "hazardous" threshold; and number of persons possibly exposed to hazardous levels.*

Air pollutants of concern include hydrocarbons, nitrogen oxides, ozone, and carbon monoxide. Carbon monoxide is primarily a vehicle-related pollutant. The other three types of gases are generated by both vehicles and other sources, and separating out the contributions from transportation alone is a problem. To minimize the influence of nontransportation sources, these measurements should probably focus on geographical areas most affected by vehicle emissions.

Pollutant levels can be expressed in terms of the following:

- The average levels of various pollutants in the air at various times of the year and, if possible, the approximate amount generated by transportation sources

- The number of days when various pollutants exceed designated "hazardous" thresholds (as defined by federal, state, or local standards)

- The number of persons exposed to hazardous levels of pollutants.

Data Collection. Local governments have been improving steadily the number and precision of air pollution measurements, using both stationary and mobile monitoring stations. The latter are especially useful for measuring along heavily traveled arterials. It is desirable to calculate the number of persons exposed to air pollution. Maps showing the distribution of various levels of pollution over a geographical area can be overlaid on a population density map to estimate the number of persons affected by various pollution levels. Few communities now make enough measurements to develop such overlays.

Rather than using actual measurements, some communities employ pollution dispersion models based on such factors as traffic counts, the local mix of automobiles of various ages, and meteorological conditions that can be used to make estimates of pollution contours, and the population affected.

Governments with a regular household survey might want to obtain the percentage of citizens who state that they are bothered by polluted air in their neighborhoods (frequently, occasionally, or rarely).

Citizen perceptions of the severity of pollution in their neighborhoods reflect the aesthetically objectionable and often physically irritating aspects of pollution, such as visible smoke, haze, and bad odors. But citizens are not likely to be able to distinguish transportation-caused pollution from other causes; nor can they identify the extent to which individual transportation modes are responsible, or changes in the levels of non-odorous invisible components of pollution. Therefore, the physical measurements are recommended.

Measure 18: *Percentage of street miles with traffic noise above x decibels, by residential (or nonresidential) area and type of street.*

Measure 19: *Percentage of citizens stating that they are bothered by traffic noise in their neighborhoods frequently, occasionally, or rarely.*

These two measures are intended to be complementary. The first provides "objective" measurements of the amount of noise, while the second offers subjective measurements, citizens' perceptions of the extent to which citizens are bothered by noise.

Data Collection. Noise levels can be measured physically using some version of an "A-weighted" noise meter at selected points along a sample of streets. Streets might be selected to indicate the different conditions in business and residential areas and along some of the most heavily traveled arterials with an adjacent residential or work population. Depending on local traffic conditions, physical measurements might be made at various times of the day, days of the week, and seasons of the year in order to reflect noise fluctuations. To adapt this method for gathering data on different areas of a community, it is desirable to designate measurement points at a standard distance from the roadway and certain height above the ground (for example, 5½ feet).

An alternative to physical measurement is to estimate noise based on traffic volume and other factors by a method described in the Department of Housing and Urban Development's noise assessment guidelines. Although developed to assess alternate sites for proposed public housing, this method seems applicable to regular monitoring of noise levels. Its estimates are based on the volume and composition of traffic on selected streets, and on the existence of barriers between the observation point and roadway. The noise level is estimated by using a series of nomographs and charts.

For Measure 19, Question 8 and 8a in Appendix 1 can be used. The first question elicits information on the percentage of respondents bothered by traffic or construction noise with various frequencies over the previous twelve months. Question 8a elicits information on the perceived major cause of the noise; this is an effort to distinguish various transportation modes from other causes.

Measures of Pedestrian Travel (Measures 20–22)

Measure 20: Percentage of blocks with sidewalks in satisfactory condition.

Measure 21: Percentage of citizens satisfied with the adequacy and condition of the sidewalks in their neighborhoods.

Measure 22: Percentage of citizens who feel street lighting in their neighborhoods is insufficient, about right, or too bright.

Pedestrians also have concerns relating to local government transportation services. In addition to safety from traffic accidents (Measures 5 and 6), the adequacy of sidewalks (Measures 20 and 21) and of street lighting (Measure 22) are also of concern.

Measure 20 is an "objective" rating of sidewalk conditions, using the trained observer procedure already discussed for road conditions and the condition of signs and signals. An illustrative scale for rating sidewalks as to their convenience for pedestrians is included in Appendix 10. For further discussion of the procedures, see Chapter 12.

The basic idea is to rate sidewalks on a scale of

1 to 3, where "3" means a hazard to walkers exists, "2" means some discomfort to walkers or visible sidewalk decay, and "1" means a generally smooth and safe walking surface.

For Measure 21, data can be obtained from the household survey shown in Appendix 1 using Questions 11 ("Would you say there are enough sidewalks in this neighborhood?") and 12 ("Are the sidewalks in this neighborhood generally in good condition?"). A question similar to Number 5 in Appendix 2 might be used in a survey of businesses to rate the condition of sidewalks in front of their establishments. For Measure 22, the adequacy of street lighting, data also can be obtained from the household survey using Question 10 of Appendix 1.

Another approach to assessing street lighting is to measure the amount of light on a sample of streets with a photoelectric meter. Past work has indicated some but not very good correlation between citizen perceptions and physical readings. If a household survey is undertaken on a regular basis, that approach seems to offer a better way to measure citizen satisfaction with street lighting.

Measure of Handicapped Access

Measure 23: Percentage of handicapped persons who feel they can get around streets satisfactorily.

The key aspect to be measured here is accessibility of streets to devices such as wheelchairs. (Access to public transportation vehicles is covered in the next chapter.)

Data Collection. Data can be collected from a citizen survey of handicapped persons, using questions such as those discussed in Measure 1, or by observation of the presence of accessible sidewalk crossing areas at intersections in various parts of the community.

---

1 An excellent example of an ad hoc study, whose procedures are also likely to be applicable to *regular* travel-time measurement, is presented in Williams and Mohammed, "Arterial Travel Time Survey" prepared for the Metropolitan Washington Council of Governments. They selected 16 routes: 11 routes were examined in one direction only; the other 5, which had balanced peak flows, were examined in both directions. "Test" cars traveled along each route at the posted speed limit unless impeded by actual conditions. Travel data were collected during the 4 p.m.–6 p.m. peak period. No runs were made in the morning peak hours; it was felt that the p.m. peak had higher traffic volumes. Stopwatches were used to determine the total elapsed travel times and delay times (for example, at red lights). At least four runs were made for each route (based on recommendations given in the Institute of Transportation Engineers, *1976 Manual for Traffic Engineering Studies*).

2 For instance, using license-plate-matching techniques on congested, signalized urban streets, at least 36 observations would be needed for a two-lane facility and 102 for a multilane facility in order to achieve an estimation error of no more than 5 percent and a 95 percent confidence level. See Walker, "Speed and Travel Time Measurement in Urban Areas." However, fewer observations will be needed if the acceptable confidence level is, say, 80 to 90 percent.

3 The Federal Highway Administration (FHA) requires pavement roughness data on many of the nation's urban and rural roads, data usually collected by state agencies. FHA provides specifications for such measurements in terms of inches of roughness per mile. See the latest version of FHA's *Highway Performance Monitoring System Field Manual (HPMS)*.

4 For a description of some state-of-the-art devices and cost information, see Hudson and Uddin, "Future Pavement Evaluation Technologies: Prospects and Opportunities," and Ronald W. Carmichael, "State-of-the-Practice of Roughness and Profile Measuring Technology," both in *Second North American Conference on Managing Pavements: Proceedings*.

5 See Ostrom, "Multi-Modal Approaches to Measurement of Government Productivity," p. 11.

This chapter identifies effectiveness measures and data collection procedures for public mass transit, both bus and rail. A general statement of transportation objectives and a summary of the principal measurement approaches applicable to public mass transit and other local government transportation procedures is presented at the beginning of Chapter 8.

Individual Transit Measures

A suggested comprehensive set of transit measures is shown in Exhibit 9-1. The measures are discussed primarily as they relate to bus travel. A subset of the same measures would be appropriate for rail. The discussion indicates where adjustments to the measures are needed for rail. Some of the measures also are relevant to other forms of public transportation (such as taxis and dial-a-rides) that are not considered in this work.

For government officials primarily concerned with a general picture of transit services in their jurisdictions, the overall measures of citizen satisfaction (Measures 18–21) may be sufficient. The other measures discussed here permit an examination of many of the major components likely to affect this satisfaction.

Rapid Movement (Measures 1–3)

Measure 1:   Travel times between selected key origins and destinations.

Travel times are an important factor influencing citizens' use of and satisfaction with mass transit. Especially important is the comparison of transit travel times with private automobile travel times. To emphasize this comparison, transit times can be expressed both in minutes and as a percentage of automobile travel times for the same trip.

Most of the discussion of travel times covered in Chapter 8 on general transportation also applies here. Origin-destination pairs should be selected for which travel times can be estimated. Preferably these should be a subset of the trips used to assess vehicular transportation in general (see General Transportation Measure 2). The emphasis of Public Transit Measure 1 is on area-to-area rather than door-to-door travel times. Vehicle times from one transit stop to another should be used. The accessibility to residences and reliability of transit stops is covered by Measures 4–9.

Travel times should be of particular interest for period-to-period comparisons of the same trips and for measuring the combined effects of changes in road network and traffic controls, transit vehicle routing, and special expediting features such as transit-only lanes and transit-controlled traffic signals. Weather and traffic volume also affect the time measurements; these factors can be discussed in reports containing the measurement data, to place the measurements in better perspective.

Data Collection. If they are reliable, transit schedules can be used to estimate travel times for selected origins and destinations. Reliability, however, should be checked periodically by the transit department, using data compiled by drivers or inspectors on starting, midroute, and end times for samples of runs. Schedules also can be checked independently by trained observers riding a sample of runs. Volunteers from among local government employees who normally ride the bus might be used as a third source.

For trips requiring transfers, the waiting time between legs of the trip should be included in the trip time. Using transit schedules, the scheduled arrival time of the next available vehicle reaching the transfer point would be used to compute the time for the final leg(s) of the trip. When there is a choice of routes, the one that would produce the shortest travel

		Exhibit 9-1	

Effectiveness Measures for Public Mass Transit

Overall objective: *To provide access to desired destinations in a quick, convenient, safe, and comfortable manner with minimum harmful effects on the environment.*

Objective	Quality characteristic	Specific measure	Data collection procedure
Rapid movement	Travel times	1. Travel times between selected key origins and destinations.	Transit schedules and test runs
Convenience/ reliability	User satisfaction	2. Percentage of users who rate travel times as satisfactory.[1]	Household or user survey
	Nonuser dissatisfaction	3. Percentage of nonusers who state that travel time is a reason for nonuse.	Household survey
	Accessibility of service	4. Percentage of (a) residents, (b) work force within x feet of a transit stop.	Calculations based on maps of transit stops and population distribution
	Frequency	5. Average time between runs.	Schedules or direct observation
	Reliability (dependability)	6. Percentage of runs that (a) are missed altogether, (b) vary from schedules by more than x minutes.	Transit inspector or other independent trained observer for a sample of runs
	User satisfaction	7. Percentage of users who rate factors related to convenience and reliability as satisfactory.	Household or user survey
	Nonuser dissatisfaction	8. Percentage of nonusers who state that factors related to convenience or reliability of transit are reasons for nonuse, tabulated by factors cited.	Household survey
	Handicapped access	9. Percentage of buses (or trains and stations) with adequate handicapped access.	Transit equipment records
Comfort	User satisfaction	10. Percentage of users who rate factors related to comfort as satisfactory.	Household or user survey
	Nonuser dissatisfaction	11. Percentage of nonusers who give factors related to comfort as reasons for nonuse, tabulated by reason.	Household or user survey
Safety	Frequency of traffic accidents	12. Number of accidents involving transit vehicles per 1,000 vehicle-miles.	Accident reports
	Casualties from traffic accidents	13. Number of (a) deaths, (b) injuries per 1,000 passenger-trips and per 1,000 vehicle-miles.	Accident reports
	Property loss from accidents and crimes	14. Dollar loss from (a) accidents, (b) vandalism and other crimes, per 1,000 vehicle-miles.	Accident and crime accident reports
	Crime rate	15. Number of crimes committed against persons (a) on board, (b) at stops (or stations), per 1,000 passenger-trips.	Crime incident reports: victimization surveys
Environmental quality	Air pollution	16. Percentage of transit vehicles that do not comply with local air pollution standards (or, preferably, the percentage of vehicle-days of noncompliance).	Periodic testing of vehicles
	Noise pollution	17. Percentage of transit vehicles that do not comply with local noise standards (or, preferably, the percentage of vehicle-days of noncompliance).	Periodic testing of vehicles using noise meters
Overall citizen satisfaction/ usefulness	Usage	18. Total and per capita number of passenger-trips.	Fares collected
	Usage	19. Percentage of population using service more than x times per month.	Household or user survey
	Mode choice	20. Percentage of all motor vehicle passenger-trips made by transit.	Origin-destination surveys
	Citizen satisfaction	21. Percentage of citizens who rate transit service as satisfactory, tallied by extent of transit use.	Household or user survey

[1]"Satisfactory" ratings may be changed to "unsatisfactory" when that appears more meaningful to local officials.

time should be used, although this may not be the shortest trip in length. (The inconvenience of transferring is reflected in Measure 7 and the overall effect of transferring convenience and travel time should be reflected in Measure 21, overall citizen satisfaction.)

All stops may not be listed on transit schedules. When an origin or destination point is not shown on a schedule, the time of arrival at the selected stop can be estimated from arrival times at the closest up-route and down-route stops appearing on the schedule.

If staff has access to a computer program that has reliable schedules entered, calculating travel times requires little staff time. The manual procedure described below was used by the St. Petersburg Transit Department and required two person-days. A summer intern, guided by a transportation analyst, worked from bus schedules to estimate travel times between 120 origin-destination pairs. The transit department felt the schedules were reasonably reliable, based on their checks. The selected pairs were origin-destination connections of ten residential areas (origins) and twelve business, shopping, or hospital areas (destinations) chosen in coordination with the traffic department.

Each trip was computed from the same starting time each day. Other jurisdictions may wish to compute different types of trips for different times of day—for example, residential to shopping areas at off-peak times and residential to work areas at peak times.

As a by-product, the analysis of travel times may reveal scheduling problems, such as long waits to make certain transfers.

Measure 2: *Percentage of users who rate travel times as satisfactory.*

Measure 3: *Percentage of nonusers who state that travel time is a reason for nonuse.*

Measure 1 provides an "objective" measure of travel times. Another important gauge is the perceived satisfaction level of users and potential users in terms of travel times. Measure 2 provides information on user ratings, and Measure 3 focuses on travel times as a reason for nonuse.

Data Collection. Surveys of a random sample of households can be used to collect data on Measures 2 and 3. For Measure 2, a survey of transit riders is preferable to a survey of households in communities where only a small fraction of residents use mass transit, to obtain a large enough sample of respondents who can assess transit travel times.

A question such as Number 15c in Appendix 1 can be used to obtain the data for Measure 2. Questions 18 and 19 in the same appendix can be used for Measure 3. One option is to use a question worded as follows: "For each of the following possible reasons why you do not ride city/county buses/trains more often, please indicate whether it is (a) a major reason, (b) a minor reason, or (c) not a reason: (1) service not frequent enough, (2) bus stop too far from home, (3) bus takes too long, (4) too many transfers required, (5) buses do not run on schedule, (6) fares are too high, (7) waiting conditions at bus stops are poor (no shelters or benches, areas muddy or dusty), (8) danger of crime at bus stop, (9) cannot find out when and where buses run, (10) buses are overcrowded, and (11) riding conditions too unpleasant." It is recommended that "prefer to go by automobile" not be permitted as a preference to the exclusion of other responses. Trials in Nashville indicated that this response predominates when it is permitted in this way and this response hides the many reasons *why* the respondents prefer to go by automobile. If "prefer to go by automobile" is included, it is important to ask respondents to indicate why they prefer the automobile.

The number of "bus takes too long" responses to the question just cited would yield the data for Measure 3. Other measures, such as Measures 10 and 11, use data from other responses to the same question. A similar set of questions can be used for rail transit. If the relative importance of the reasons for nonuse of public transit service is not explored in these surveys, the reasons given for nonuse should be considered only as rough indications of problems.

One problem is in defining the term "nonuser of transit." A nonuser might be defined as a respondent who did not use buses at all in the previous twelve months or who used public buses less than once a month. This choice is a matter of judgment and the individual jurisdiction's preference.

Convenience and Reliability (Measures 4–9)
These measures cover five aspects of the convenience and reliability of transit services. Measure 4 focuses on the proximity of transit stops to the population. It includes a variation that reflects transfer frequencies, the assumption being that transfers can be a major inconvenience. The frequency of service is often cited as a major factor for nonuse, and it is the subject of Measure 5. Reliability or dependability is another major concern for transit users and is the focus of Measure 6.

Although Measures 4–6 can be considered "objective," ultimately it is the users' and potential users' viewpoints on convenience that are important.

Therefore, Measure 7 focuses on user ratings of convenience and Measure 8 focuses on nonuser ratings of inconvenience as a reason for nonuse.

Measure 4:   *Percentage of (a) residents, (b) work force within x feet of a transit stop.*

Variation A: *Percentage of residents within x feet of a transit stop from which they can travel to within y feet of key destinations in less than z minutes.*

Variation B: *Percentage of residents within x feet of a transit stop from which they can travel to within y feet of key destinations with one transfer or fewer.*

This measure attempts to gauge the degree to which public transit is physically convenient to the population. But the proximity of citizens' residences to transit stops does not mean that transit vehicles go where citizens want to go within a reasonable time; thus Variation A is included. Also, because the need to transfer is likely to be a special inconvenience, Variation B is included.

Data Collection. Measure 4 can be estimated using a computerized geographic information system or by using a map of transit stops overlaid on a population density map. The population density map can be obtained from U.S. Bureau of Census data and updated by city or county planning department estimates. A circle is drawn around each stop, with a radius equal to one-fourth or one-eighth of a mile, or whatever walking distance is chosen as the criterion for x in the measure. (Lower values of x—that is, shorter walking distances—can be used as criteria for areas where the elderly are concentrated.) The population within the circles is then estimated and divided by the total population.

A simplified procedure, tried in St. Petersburg, can be used as an approximation for areas of the community in which stops are close together and circles overlap. All persons residing within a quarter mile (or whatever value is chosen for x) of the transit line would be counted as near a stop.

Some communities do not have maps of every transit stop for buses. Such maps must be prepared as a first step in the data collection procedure, unless the stops are close enough together that the approximation described above can be used.

When possible, barriers in citizens' paths to bus stops (such as freeways, streams, or railroads) should be considered, in addition to the straight-line distance; this consideration will complicate the computation.

In St. Petersburg, Measure 4 took two person-days to compute, with Variation A requiring an additional person-day. The computations were made by a summer intern in the transit department.

Measure 4 is particularly useful for determining the before-and-after conditions of a change in the design of routes for the entire system.

The accuracy of Measure 4 is limited primarily by the accuracy of population estimates by block or area. The validity of Variation A also is limited by these population estimates, and by a local government's ability to select an adequately representative set of destinations.

For Variation B, the procedure is similar to that for Variation A, except that instead of computing travel times, the analysts count the number of transfers for each origin-destination pair. The measure requires some additional time to obtain—perhaps one-half person-day.

An option in this process is to calculate Variation A allowing only one transfer per trip.

Measure 5:   *Average time between runs.*

The average time between buses (or trains), known as headway, affects the convenience of using transit. Most users, particularly commuters, want to go to a transit stop and board the next vehicle after a short wait, without consulting schedules.

A related level-of-service concern is the number of hours of operation, which also might be included as a measure, or the average headway can be reported by time of day.

Data Collection. This measure can be computed from the schedules, unless there is reason to believe they are grossly inaccurate. Data collection in connection with Measure 6 (on reliability) can be used to check the scheduled frequency.

Measure 6:   *Percentage of runs that (a) are missed altogether, (b) vary from schedules by more than x minutes.*

A particularly important aspect of convenience in transit service is dependability. Dependability spares transit users excessive waiting and gets them where they are going, as scheduled.

Transit officials obviously do not have complete control over punctuality and reliability. Variations in weather, traffic conditions, number of passengers, and driver illnesses can play a major role. However, punctuality and reliability also are affected by other factors that transit managers do control. These include vehicle maintenance, proper scheduling, safe driving, and management of substitute drivers and buses.

Runs that are missed altogether, that is, dropped from the schedule without advance notice, might be reported separately from the percentage that are early or late. On routes with relatively infrequent service, missed runs represent greater inconvenience to riders than do early or late arrivals. Typically, missed runs constitute a much smaller number than early or late runs, so these particularly irritating incidents might be lost in the overall statistics if they are not reported separately. Likewise, breakdowns of vehicles with passengers on board, which can be especially vexing and even frightening (in subways), may be lost in overall averages; some communities report them as a separate statistic.

Data Collection. The raw data for Measure 6(a) are usually collected routinely by transit dispatchers or inspectors, although they may not be summarized.

Measure 6(b) can be computed by arrival times at one or more midroute points and the route terminus for a sample of routes. These times would then be compared with schedules. Times might be gathered by trained observers stationed at measurement points, or volunteers who normally ride buses. Data should be collected on several days, preferably throughout the year.

Probably the main data collection difficulty is in choosing a representative sample of routes and measurement points along each route. The sample of routes monitored for this measure might be the same as those used to compute travel times in Measure 2; or a random sample of routes might be selected, perhaps with extra weight given to those carrying heavier passenger loads.

Measure 7: *Percentage of users who rate factors related to convenience and reliability as satisfactory.*

Convenience and reliability are basically subjective qualities. Both this measure and the next one are based on citizen perceptions. Measure 7 focuses on the views of citizens who have used the service within some length of time, such as the last twelve months. Measure 8 focuses on nonusers.

Convenience and reliability factors that users can be asked to rate in terms of satisfaction include: frequency and reliability of service, hours of operation, ability to obtain schedule and route information, correctness of signs on vehicles and at stops, ability to reach desired destinations without transferring, closeness of bus stops, and waiting conditions at bus stops.

Data Collection. Data can be obtained through the same household survey used for other measures or by a special survey of transit users, as discussed under Measure 2. Questions such as 15a, b, d, f, g, and h in Appendix 1 can be used to obtain the data.

Measure 8: *Percentage of nonusers who state that factors related to convenience or reliability of transit are reasons for nonuse, tabulated by factors cited.*

Respondents identified in a survey of a random sample of households as not using transit services can be asked about their reasons for nonuse—some, but not all of which may be correctable by the transit agency. Such information will suggest problem areas.

Data Collection. Data can be obtained through the same household survey used for other measures. As discussed under Measure 3, respondents should be asked to rate various possible reasons for not using the public transit systems. For Measure 8, respondents should be asked about the following: (1) service not frequent enough, (2) bus stop not close enough to home, (3) too many transfers required, (4) buses do not run on schedule, (5) cannot find out when and where the buses run, and (6) hours of operation are not long enough. The wording suggested here and under Measure 3 is preferred to the wording in Questions 18 and 19 of Appendix 1.

Measure 9: *Percentage of buses (or trains and stations) with adequate handicapped access.*

Physically handicapped persons (and many elderly persons) have problems getting onto a bus or down the stairs or escalator of a subway stop—neither accommodates wheelchairs. Federal law now requires such access. Many transit systems have, and others will increasingly have, handicapped accessible buses and trains.

This measure reflects the degree to which the transit system is accessible for handicapped persons, not just its equipment but also the adequacy and condition of the equipment and process.

Data Collection. These data can be obtained by periodic trained observer ratings of public transit vehicles. Volunteer handicapped persons might be used for such ratings.

The reliability and adequacy of the special equipment that affects special groups of handicapped people (for example, the blind) also can be asked about in a survey of handicapped citizens. That survey also could be used to obtain feedback on other transit characteristics, such as those reflected in Measures 3, 7, 8, 10, 11, 19, 20, and 21.

Comfort (Measures 10–11)

Measure 10: Percentage of users who rate factors related to comfort as satisfactory.

Measure 11: Percentage of nonusers who give factors related to comfort as reasons for nonuse, tabulated by reason.

Comfort is clearly a concern to both users and potential users of transit services. These measures include such aspects as crowding (including having to stand), temperature, noise, odors, cleanliness, smoothness of ride, seat comfort, and driver helpfulness and courtesy. Both on-board and waiting conditions at stops are relevant.

Measure 10 provides users' ratings of various aspects of comfort. Measure 11 indicates the percentage of nonusers who cited the lack of certain aspects of rider comfort as a reason for their nonuse.

Other means to measure these characteristics include: using trained observer to rate on-board conditions such as cleanliness, noise, crowding, and smoothness of ride; and tallying the percentage of transit stops where there are no benches or shelters.

Data Collection. The household survey (Appendix 1) can be used to obtain the data for both of these measures. For Measure 10 the survey includes Questions 15e (driver helpfulness and courtesy), 15h (waiting conditions at bus stops), 16a (vehicle temperature), 16b (on-board odors and cleanliness), and 16c (smoothness of ride), 16d (crowding), 16e (seat comfort), and 16f (noise).

For Measure 11, as for Measures 3 and 8, nonusers can be asked to rate possible reasons for their lack of use—if comfort-related reasons are included. Various comfort reasons such as those listed above can be addressed. In a St. Petersburg survey, for example, "Poor waiting conditions at bus stops (no benches or shelter)" was cited as often as most of the convenience factors (see Measure 8).

Safety (Measures 12–15)

Measure 12: Number of accidents involving transit vehicles per 1,000 vehicle-miles.

Measure 13: Number of (a) deaths and (b) injuries per 1,000 passenger-trips and per 1,000 passenger-miles.

Measure 14: Dollar loss from (a) accidents, (b) vandalism and other crimes, per 1,000 vehicle-miles.

Measure 15: Number of crimes committed against persons (a) on board, (b) at stops (or stations), per 1,000 passenger-trips.

Measures 12–14 are the rates of accidents, deaths and injuries, and property losses, which indicate the safety of transit operation. Most of the discussion in the previous chapter under General Transportation Measures 5 to 7 also applies here. However, somewhat different denominators are needed for transit vehicles. Public Transit Measures 12 and 14 call for the number of accidents and dollar loss per 1,000 transit vehicle-miles, and reflect safety from the viewpoint of the reliability of the vehicle-driver system. Measure 13 considers safety from the viewpoint of the rider; it is stated as a rate per 1,000 passenger-trips or passenger-miles. Measure 15 relates transit-related crimes to the number of passenger-trips.

These tallies should reflect all incidents involving a transit vehicle, even when other modes of transportation are involved.

Losses from vandalism and other crimes, included in Measure 14, often are significant in public transit and should be measured to indicate the intensity of the problem and the government's effectiveness in preventing these crimes.

Measure 15 is included to reflect the occasional problem of crimes involving mass transit passengers, or people waiting at stops or stations. These crimes may deter usage, especially at night or in certain areas. Operating procedures such as requiring drivers not to carry cash on buses may reduce some types of crime, such as robbery. Patrols of stations and on board vehicles, camera surveillance, and good emergency alerting systems also can help.

Data Collection. Data on vehicle-miles traveled, the number of passenger-trips, and estimates of passenger-miles traveled are already routinely available in most transit agencies. (The number of passenger-trips is usually estimated for Urban Mass Transit Authority Section 15 reports by making a count of passengers entering and exiting vehicles for a statistical sample of bus trips throughout the year.) Also routinely collected are data on the number of accidents (Measure 12), the number of deaths and injuries (Measure 13), and the cost of repairing damage due to accidents and vandalism (Measure 14).

For Measure 15, crimes committed against the transit service itself (for example, robberies or assaults against the driver, refusal to pay the correct fare, and disorderly behavior) might be tabulated separately from crimes committed against riders. Data for Measure 15 might be obtained either from driver reports or police department records. The transit agency should maintain and tabulate these data.

Another approach is to obtain ratings from respondents to the household survey as to their "feeling of security" about transit services, with respect to crime and accidents. The percentage of respondents indicating that a reason for nonuse of public transit was "danger of crime at bus stop" (see discussion under Measure 3) can be used as an additional measure.

Environmental Quality (Measures 16 and 17)

Measure 16: *Percentage of transit vehicles that do not comply with local air pollution standards (or, preferably, the percentage of vehicle-days of noncompliance).*

Measure 17: *Percentage of transit vehicles that do not comply with local noise standards (or, preferably, the percentage of vehicle-days of noncompliance).*

General Transportation Measures 17–19 provide estimates of air and noise pollution levels from all sources, along with rough estimates of amounts resulting from individual transportation modes. They indicate changes in *overall* pollution levels after changes in the mix of transportation modes.

In addition, it is desirable to monitor the pollution generated by each mass transit vehicle, especially pollution that is visible, smelly, and likely to offend and harm motorists and pedestrians. Air and noise emission levels from each vehicle can be compared to standards in order to provide tallies of the percentage of vehicles that do not meet the air (Public Transit Measure 16) or noise (Measure 17) emission standards. If such measurements are taken often enough, estimates of the number and percentage of vehicle-days of noncompliance can be obtained.

Data Collection. For air pollution, the exhaust from transit vehicles can be rated for its "blackness" or opacity by using trained observers and a smoke density rating scale similar to the Ringlemann Charts, which rate emissions from smoke stacks. Even simpler, the observer can note on a possible four-part scale whether there is an extreme amount of obnoxious exhaust smoke, a considerable amount, a small amount, or none at all. This scale might be based on a photographic rating guide, showing the various exhaust conditions.

Transit vehicle conditions can be tested with vehicle engines at idling, accelerating, and cruising speeds, since these states affect the amount of pollu-tion. Transit vehicles should be tested with devices for making pollution measurements directly from vehicle exhausts at least once a year to see if they are within local and federal standards.

With regard to noise, sound generated by transit vehicles while idling, while accelerating from zero to some specified miles per hour, and while operating at cruising speed can be measured and compared to locally set standards for tolerable noise levels. The location of sound meters in the test is a matter for expert judgment. Consideration might be given to choosing meter placements that will correspond to a typical distance between pedestrians on the sidewalk and a bus on the street. Noise meter levels might be calibrated by using a panel of citizens to distinguish degrees of unpleasantness in transit noise.

Overall Citizen Satisfaction (Measures 18–21)

Measure 18: *Total and per capita number of passenger-trips.*

Measure 19: *Percentage of population using service more than x times per month.*

Measure 20: *Percentage of all motor vehicle passenger-trips made by transit.*

Measure 21: *Percentage of citizens who rate transit service as satisfactory, tallied by extent of transit use.*

Overall citizen satisfaction is a major issue in measuring transit effectiveness. Two basic types of measures seem appropriate: the degree to which the service is actually used (Measures 18–20) and citizen perceptions of the adequacy of that service (Measure 21).

Usage is a common gauge of transit performance. (Of course, the revenues obtained are also critical to government officials, especially as compared to expenditures. However, amount of revenue is not a measure of "effectiveness" as defined here.) It can be argued that many users, such as the poor and the elderly, are captive audiences, however, and that usage alone is not an adequate indicator of satisfaction.

Measure 18, the number of passenger-trips, is the traditional measure. Measure 19, the percentage of the population who have used the transit service (that is, the number of different users), is not now in general use because of the lack of data for it, but it can be determined as part of a survey of households. Measure 20 is a direct attempt to measure the proportion of motor vehicle passenger-trips made by public transit; this can be considered an effectiveness measure if one assumes that it is important to shift vehicle trips from the automobile to transit vehicles. Measure 21 provides ratings of citizens' overall levels of satisfaction with transit service.

Transit measures described earlier addressed citizen perceptions of individual service qualities. Measure 21 attempts to measure overall satisfaction. In effect, this measure provides an integrated rating of all elements. A respondent might rate individual elements as poor but service overall as satisfactory, or vice versa.

Measure 21 will provide more insights if the information is disaggregated by the extent of respondent transit usage (for example, transit used at least weekly, less than weekly, rarely, or not at all). A typical issue is: Do regular riders rate the overall service higher (or lower) than do those who rarely use the transit system?

Data Collection. Data on the number of passenger-trips made by transit (Measure 18) are available in most jurisdictions. The data are often approximations based on total fares divided by the average fare, and they may not include passengers who ride free of charge.

Data for Measure 20, the percentage of trips made by different modes, probably requires origin-destination studies (that is, special household surveys in which passenger-trips per household are analyzed). Household surveys can be used to collect data for Measures 19 and 21.

For data on the percentage of the population using transit services with various frequencies, Measure 19, Question 13 (usage by respondent), and Question 14 (usage by others in the respondent's household) can be used. Answers to the latter question will be less accurate because the respondent is asked to answer for other members of the household. A local government might want to interview each member of the household above a certain age, but this practice raises survey cost.

For further insights, usage information might be grouped by the number of cars in the household, using a question such as Number 68 in Appendix 1.

For Measure 21, a question such as Question 20 in Appendix 1 can be employed to obtain the citizens' overall ratings of satisfaction with local transit service. Cross-tabulation of these data by amount of usage (Measure 19) and by access to private automobiles, can provide insights into how satisfactory the service is for persons with various levels of usage and degrees of dependency on it. Question 13 (frequency of riding buses) and Question 68 (number of automobiles in the household) in Appendix 1 can be used for these cross-tabulations.

In addition, the data on Measures 19 and 21 should be cross-tabulated by geographical area; by size and type of household; and by age group, sex, and racial or ethnic group of the respondents. This will provide the agency with information as to its service as perceived by different population groups (thereby suggesting, for example, whether helpful activities—such as providing more information on the transit system—should be targeted to specific groups).

Notes on the Household Survey Procedure

A number of measures in this chapter and the preceding one call for data obtained from a survey of a representative sample of households in the community. Such a household survey is discussed at length in Chapter 13. Exhibit 9-2 identifies the transportation measures that use data obtained from household surveys.

Exhibit 9-2

Transportation Measures Calling for Data from the Household Survey

Quality characteristic	Measure	Illustrative question for obtaining the data (Appendix 1)
General transportation	Exhibit 8-1	
Accessibility	1	—[1]
Safety: Feeling of security in driving	11	—[1]
Street rideability conditions	13	9
Parking convenience	14	3
Visibility of traffic signs and signals	16	4, 5, 7
Noise pollution	19	8
Sidewalk conditions	21	11, 12
Adequacy of street lighting	22	10
Public transit	Exhibit 9-1	
Satisfactory travel times— users	2	15c
Satisfactory travel times— nonusers	3	18, 19
Convenience—users	7	15a, b, d, f, g
Convenience—nonusers	8	18, 19
Comfort—users	10	15e, h, 16
Comfort—nonusers	11	18, 19
Use by different households	19	13, 14
Overall citizen satisfaction with transit services	21	20

[1]Appropriate questions for these measures were not included in the questionnaire that is reproduced in Appendix 1. However, illustrative questions are contained in the text.

A principal obstacle to the use of surveys on a regular basis is the cost. In other chapters, the household survey has been recommended as a procedure for obtaining feedback on many other local government services. Performance information on those other services and on transportation should be obtained in the same survey, where possible. Thus the cost of the survey is allocated among a number of services so that no individual agency carries too large a financial burden. In addition, as discussed in Chapter 13, various "bargain basement" approaches can make the survey reasonably practical without unduly sacrificing precision or accuracy.

Finally, it is suggested that the annual household sample size be divided into four (quarterly) segments to enable the agency to obtain more rapid, seasonal feedback on citizens' perceptions and how they are changing over time. The measurement data also can be accumulated over the year to provide annualized data.

ocal governments are involved in water supply activities in a variety of ways. They are frequently:

- Operators of water supply and treatment systems
- Purchasers of water from regional authorities and operators of distribution systems
- Participants in metropolitan or regional water authorities and water districts
- Funders and underwriters of water supply construction projects and water treatment facilities
- Users of water for schools and other public institutions, fire fighting, irrigation, and other municipal purposes
- Inspectors and regulators of the water delivered to citizens and in many cases to institutional users.

Local governments are concerned with the purity, safety, availability, and flow adequacy of water as well as a wide range of water characteristics affecting aesthetics and citizen satisfaction such as taste, odor, color, turbidity, hardness, and mineral content of the water delivered to customers.

This chapter provides a set of measures and an evaluation framework to help agency officials, other senior local government officials, and the local legislature to do the following:

- Understand the progress of their public water systems in meeting water quality standards and monitoring provisions
- Provide water services that satisfy customers
- Pinpoint deficiencies in the water supply
- Monitor progress in addressing problems.

The types of analytical monitoring systems installed and the remedial actions taken in response to problems will vary widely depending on the roles of the local government in providing water and the magnitude of the system. It is beyond the scope of this chapter to detail how water quality measurements should be made.

General Objectives for Water Supply

The following general statement of water supply objectives has been used in formulating the list of measures of effectiveness. It is appropriate for consideration by all local agencies involved in supplying or overseeing water supply and distribution.

> **To provide an adequate supply of water that is free of health hazards, meets applicable federal and state standards, is aesthetically acceptable, and is of adequate quality for household, municipal, commercial, and industrial use. To provide prompt, courteous, reliable service.**

Local governments monitor extensively the quality and levels of specific characteristics such as chemical and biological contaminants and pH and hardness. However, local governments rarely develop impact measures of the type stressed throughout this book to assess the quality of services. Major recommendations for filling this gap are presented briefly here and discussed in detail in the rest of the chapter. The full set of measures is presented in Exhibit 10-1.

Health Hazards

The principal concern regarding the water supply is that it be as free as possible of health hazards and that it not exceed applicable maximum contaminant levels established by the federal government or by the state government.

Under provisions of the 1974 Safe Drinking Water Act (PL 93-523) and the 1986 Amendments to the Safe Drinking Water Act (PL 99-339), the federal government must establish standards for a large number of contaminants in four categories:

- Organics (including pesticides, herbicides, and volatile organics)

- Inorganics (including arsenic, barium, copper, iron, lead, manganese, mercury, sulfate, and zinc)
- Radionuclides (including beta particle and photon radioactivity, alpha particle activity, radium)
- Microbials (coliform and turbidity).

Exhibit 10-1

Measures of Effectiveness for Water Supply Service

Overall objective: To provide an adequate supply of water that is free of health hazards, aesthetically acceptable, and of adequate quality for household, commercial, and industrial use. To provide prompt, courteous, reliable service and to minimize injuries and damage associated with the system.

Objective	Quality characteristic	Specific measure	Data collection procedure
Health hazards	Presence of substances linked to health risks	1. Number of health-related water quality characteristics exceeding standards one or more times during reporting period, broken out by category.	Regular testing by qualified personnel using accepted procedures
	Evidence of waterborne diseases	2. Number of incidents of public notification during reporting period, by type of condition.	Reports issued by agency
Aesthetic quality	Presence of substances with adverse effects on appearance, taste, or odor	3. Number of days that one or more aesthetic characteristics failed to meet standards (testing for turbidity, color, and chemicals such as chlorides or sulfates that affect taste and appearance).	Regular testing by qualified personnel
	Citizen perception of water quality	4. Percentage of customers who rate their drinking water as satisfactory in appearance, taste, and odor.	Customer survey
	Rate of validated complaints about water aesthetics	5. Number of validated complaints per 1,000 customers about drinking water appearance, taste, or odor, by type of complaint.	Tallies of reported complaints
Household use quality	Levels of water characteristics with effects on household use	6. Estimated number of days that one or more of the following characteristics failed to meet its standard(s): hardness and pH (cleaning effectiveness) and iron and manganese (staining).	Regular testing by qualified personnel using accepted procedures
Flow adequacy	Restrictions on household or commercial usage	7. Number of days of restrictions on household and business water use, by type of restriction.	City and department records
	Citizen perceptions of flow problems	8. Percentage of (a) households, (b) businesses reporting problems with water pressure or flow, by type of problem.	Customer survey
	Rate of validated complaints about flow or pressure	9. Number of valid complaints about water flow per 1,000 clients, excluding complaints on matters shown to be private responsibility.	Tallies of reported complaints
	General flow adequacy	10. Percentage of fire hydrants surveyed that meet static water pressure standard of, for example, 40 pounds per square inch.	Annual testing of fire hydrants
Service adequacy and responsiveness	Rate of validated complaints	11. Total number of valid complaints and requests for nonroutine service per 1,000 customers, by type of complaint (including billing overcharge, water quality, broken or leaking pipe or meter).	Tallies of reported complaints
	Customer perception of adequacy of response to calls	12. Percentage of persons complaining or requesting service who were satisfied with the handling of their complaints or requests, by type of complaint (for example, billing complaints).	Survey of a sample of persons complaining or requesting service
	Speed of response	13. Percentage of valid complaints and requests that were effectively responded to within an allowed period of time, overall and for each class of requests.	Revised forms for recording customer calls and actions taken in response to calls

Schedules have been established for the annual development of enforceable standards called maximum contaminant levels (MCLs) and for nonenforceable maximum contaminant level goals (MCLGs) for contaminants in these categories. State governments may adopt regulations more stringent than those of the federal government.

A specific checklist of health-related water quality characteristics should be identified and acceptable standards agreed upon for each. In most cases these will be the U.S. Environmental Protection Agency (EPA) Safe Drinking Water Standards, and in any case are expected to include the contaminants listed in Exhibit 10-2 plus new ones being established by EPA. Accepted biological, chemical, and physical testing procedures are established.[1]

Adequate Supply

The measure "Number of days when household or business water use is restricted" is recommended. Restrictions include such limitations on the public as restrictions on watering lawns and washing vehicles as well as restrictions resulting from interruptions in service due to failure of water mains, closure of the system, and so forth. The information for this measure is normally available from the water department.

Exhibit 10-2

Organic and Inorganic Contaminants to Be Regulated and Monitored Periodically under PL 99-339

Inorganic contaminant	Volatile organic contaminant	Pesticide/Herbicide/PCB
Asbestos	cis-1,2-Dichloro-	Alachlor
Barium	ethylene	Aldicarb
Cadmium	1,2-Dichloropropane	Aldicarb sulfone
Chromium	Ethylbenzene	Aldicarb sulfoxide
Mercury	Monochlorobenzene	Atrazine
Nitrate	o-Dichlorobenzene	Carbofuran
Nitrite	Styrene	Chlordane
Selenium	Tetrachloroethylene	Dibromochloropropane
	Toluene	(DBCP)
	trans-1,2-Dichloro-	2,4-D
	ethylene	Ethylenedibromide
	Xylenes (Total)	(EDB)
		Heptachlor
		Heptachlor epoxide
		Lindane
		Methoxychlor
		PCBs
		Pentachlorophenol
		Toxaphene
		2,4,5-TP (Silvex)

Source: "USEPA Proposed National Primary and Secondary Drinking Water Regulation Tables," American Water Works Association, Denver, Colo., 1990. This list may change over time.

Customer Satisfaction with Water Quality

Few communities seek regular feedback from their customers as to their satisfaction with such qualities of the water as taste, odor, appearance, and flow. If the community undertakes periodic multiservice telephone surveys of a representative sample of households (as suggested in other chapters), this information could be obtained readily at slight additional cost. It can be collected somewhat less reliably by mail surveys—perhaps in conjunction with billings to customers.

These aspects of water quality also can be measured by established test procedures for color, turbidity, odor, and taste to supplement citizen satisfaction responses.[2]

Responsiveness to Customers

A survey of a sample of persons who have requested service or who have complained should be undertaken periodically. Each household surveyed should be asked about the quality of the agency's response, whether the service was provided courteously and promptly, and overall satisfaction with the agency's handling of the report or complaint. Billing problems, which typically constitute a large share of all complaints, should be distinguished from service complaints. Illustrative questions that might be used for such surveys are provided in Appendix 8.

Additional Measures

Agency officials may want to develop additional measures of system quality, such as: amount of water loss in the system, broken out by leakage and by unauthorized use of water; number or percentage of customers using accepted water conservation procedures; storage capacity and reserve capacity; quality of the distribution system indicated by the number and frequency of water main breaks; number of housing units not connected to a municipal water supply system; and number of housing units more than 500 feet from fire hydrants.

These are relatively straightforward measures with obvious data collection methods.

Individual Measures for Water Supply

The proposed measures are discussed under five categories:

- Health protection (Measures 1 and 2)
- Aesthetic quality (Measures 3–5)
- Household use quality (Measure 6)
- Flow adequacy (Measures 7–10)
- Service adequacy and responsiveness (Measures 11–13).

Health Protection (Measures 1–2)

Measures 1 and 2 assess the potential impact of the public water supply on health, in nontechnical terms readily understandable by elected officials and the public as well as by agency officials.

The 1974 Safe Drinking Water Act (SDWA: PL 93-523) mandated establishment of the first drinking water health and safety regulations that applied to all public water systems in the United States. The US EPA was authorized to set national drinking water regulations. Public water systems were responsible for meeting the regulations. States were to be responsible for enforcement of the regulations.

In 1986 Congress adopted significant amendments to the SDWA. These amendments (PL 99-339) mandated establishment of a variety of drinking water regulations according to specific timetables. They required setting maximum contaminant levels (MCLs) and maximum contaminant level goals (MCLGs) for 83 contaminants. Furthermore, they required the establishment of a subset of contaminants that were to receive highest priority in setting MCLGs and MCLs. Additional provisions specified monitoring frequencies for the contaminants and strengthened notification requirements both for inadequacies of the water supply in providing water meeting the requirements and for failing to comply with established monitoring requirements. PL 99-339 allowed the EPA to modify the set of priority contaminants as new information on prevalence and health-impacts became available.

In response to PL 93-523 and PL 99-339 and to state laws and regulations, local governments undertake extensive monitoring of a variety of characteristics, contaminants, and impurities with potential health significance. In the decade of the 1990s, they will have to monitor an increasing number of contaminants to meet requirements of these acts. In addition, new discoveries of the adverse health effects of various contaminants are likely to highlight the need for even more monitoring.

Measure 1:   Number of health-related water quality characteristics exceeding standards one or more times during reporting period, broken out by category.

Measure 1 is a count of all the contaminants or health-related water quality characteristics for which tests are conducted that exceed standards during the reporting period. It is recommended that the values for this measure be presented quarterly even though some characteristics may be assessed on a yearly or less frequent basis.

When Measure 1 exceeds zero, information should be provided as to the contaminants that ex-

ceeded standards, the dates of tests showing the conditions, and the actions taken in response. A listing of regulated substances for which no tests were required or conducted during the reporting period also might be provided.

Some communities might want to present information on the number of contaminants exceeding federal or state standards at the end of the reporting period.

Measure 1 does not indicate the duration of contaminant levels exceeding standards. To track the duration of such conditions, water supply agencies could employ a measure such as "Number of days during reporting period that water quality characteristic (or contaminant) exceeded standards."

With the exception of a few characteristics such as coliforms and turbidity, water systems do not test for contaminants on a daily basis, and precise information on the duration of nonconformance will not be available. The following method for estimating the number of days above standard is proposed.

An estimate of the number of days can be obtained by counting the number of days between the first test of the characteristic that shows it above standard (or the start of the reporting period if the characteristic ended the previous reporting period above standard) and the first subsequent test showing that the characteristic is within standard (or the current date if not yet within the standard). Exhibit 10-3 illustrates how the measure might be calculated for lead and iron content in water.

In this example, only the time following observation of a condition that fails to meet the standard has been counted. This measure indicates the speed of response to a problem once it has been identified. But it tends to understate the actual duration of the problem since the characteristic may not have met the standard for some days prior to the analysis. The measure could create incentives to do too little testing or to tamper with the scheduling of tests.

As a more conservative alternative, a government might prefer to count as not meeting standard all days back to the time the last test showed the characteristic meeting its standard. Or, it might split the difference.

Using both methods will show the government's speed in discovering problems and in responding to known problems, and it might create an incentive for more frequent testing to eliminate long delays in discovering violations.

It is suggested that violations be counted back only to the time the first test shows the contaminant exceeding the standard. Counting back to the last satisfactory test, which could be a year or more, would tend to overwhelm or conceal the length of time authorities take to respond to conditions.

Measure 2:   Number of incidents of public notification during reporting period, by type of condition.

Since the 1974 SDWA, owners or operators of public water systems have been required to notify customers when drinking water standards are violated. Notification can be by radio, newspaper, or television, or in writing to customers. Public notification requirements initially were established by the EPA in 1975. The 1986 SDWA amendments and subsequent regulations have increased the requirements and responsibilities for public notification.

Beginning in 1989, water system operators were required to notify customers for six types of conditions or violations:

1. Failure of the water supply system to comply with an applicable MCL
2. Failure to comply with a prescribed treatment technique
3. Failure of the system to perform water quality monitoring as required by the regulations
4. Failure to comply with testing procedures as prescribed by National Primary Drinking Water Regulations
5. Issuance of variances or exemptions allowing relief from meeting certain requirements
6. Failure to comply with any schedules associated with a variance or exception.

The revised public notification requirements distinguish between serious violations with possibly di-

---

Exhibit 10-3

Sample Calculation of "Number of Days That One or More Water Characteristics Failed to Meet Standards"

During January all tests except those for lead and iron were within standards.

A. Test on lead in water

January

Date	1	2	3	4	5	6	7	8	9	10	11	12	13	14	15	16	17
Test reading	.01						.06	.06	.04						.02		
Did test show satisfactory conditions?	Yes						No	No	Yes						Yes		
Cumulative number of violation days							1	2									

Scenario: Testing normally is performed weekly with a standard of 0.05 milligram per liter (mg/l). The test on January 7 showed a violation. Steps were taken to detect the cause and cure the problem. At the same time, the testing schedule was accelerated to monitor the success of corrective actions. The test on January 8 still showed a violation, but the test on January 9 showed that the standard was again being met. The days on which the last test showed a violation were January 7 and 8, a count of two days of violations.

B. Test on iron in water

January

Date	1	2	3	4	5	6	7	8	9	10	11	12	13	14	15	16	17
Test reading	.1							.4							.2		
Did test show satisfactory conditions?	Yes							No							Yes		
Cumulative number of violation days								1	2	3	4	5	6	7			

Scenario: Testing normally is performed weekly with a standard of 0.3 mg/l. The test on January 8 showed a violation. Steps were taken to detect the cause of the problem, but testing was not accelerated because this is a characteristic related only to household use, and hence not of critical concern. (This judgment is assumed only for purposes of this example; it is not recommended as a policy.) The next regular test was on January 15. It showed no violation. The days on which the last test showed a violation were January 8 to 14, a count of seven days of presumed violations.

C. Combined measure

For the combined set of water characteristics, there were eight days (January 7 to 14) when at least one characteristic showed a violation of its last satisfactory test. (On one of those days, January 8, two characteristics were in violation.)

Note: This example also applies to Measures 3 and 6.

rect health implications (such as numbers 1 and 2) and less serious violations (such as 3–6). Violations of numbers 1 and 2 are to be reported within 14 days while the rest have to be reported within 3 months.

A closely related performance indicator would be the findings of an annual audit of the water supply system showing whether the water system supply operator was in compliance with existing regulations for monitoring. Federal and state laws and regulations are establishing monitoring requirements for an increasing number of contaminants. Monitoring requirements vary according to the size of the system and the rate of violations. Monitoring is expected to become more complex in the future with the promulgation of many regulations. Even well-intentioned water supply agencies are likely to have difficulty in determining what and when to monitor.

The audit should be made by an independent organization such as a registered engineer, a professional society, a state health authority, an environmental monitoring authority, or some public accrediting board.

Other possible health measures are "Number of outbreaks of waterborne diseases in the community due to the ingestion of contaminated public water" and "Number of persons suffering from waterborne diseases."

Historically, significant waterborne diseases have included cholera and typhoid fever, but these diseases are very rare in the United States. From 1971 through 1985 there were only 502 known outbreaks of waterborne diseases due to contaminated public water. Given the rarity of such events, the extensive publicity such events receive, and the great public awareness of them, it does not seem advantageous to use these two measures on a periodic basis.

Aesthetic Quality (Measures 3–5)

Measure 3:   *Number of days that one or more aesthetic characteristics failed to meet standards (testing for turbidity, color, and chemicals such as chlorides or sulfates that affect taste and appearance).*

Measure 4:   *Percentage of customers who rate their drinking water as satisfactory in appearance, taste, and odor.*

Measure 5:   *Number of validated complaints per 1,000 customers about drinking water appearance, taste, or odor, by type of complaint.*

These measures provide three different perspectives on the aesthetic quality of drinking water. Measure 3 covers the duration of the failure of public water to meet standards. Measures 4 and 5 provide customer perspectives. Measure 4 provides representative, community-wide data from a statistically sound sampling of customers, whereas Measure 5 indicates episodes that customers deemed serious enough to report.

Procedures for collecting data for these measures are well established.[3] Frequent testing—perhaps weekly—of at least four basic factors of turbidity, color, taste, and odor seems warranted. Additional tests for specific dissolved minerals that contribute to taste and appearance can be made less often, since serious problems with any of these dissolved materials will show up as taste, odor, or appearance problems as well.

Problems affecting water quality can arise anywhere along the water distribution system—from its original source, through the public distribution system, and in the private distribution components, such as pipes in private homes, apartments, and other buildings. Thus, tests at various points in the distribution system are desirable to identify the locations of problems.

For Measure 4, data can be obtained from a survey of a representative sample of customers. A question such as Question 55 in Appendix 1 can be used to obtain the data for this measure.

Question 55 seeks a rating from customers of the overall satisfactoriness of the water supply in terms of taste, odor, appearance, and temperature. Question 55a asks those respondents who were *not* satisfied to identify the specific water characteristic(s) to which they objected. Question 55b asks about the frequency of the problem identified in Question 55a. Questions can be added about the *degree* of dissatisfaction with each particular problem.

These questions refer only to the quality of drinking water, not the adequacy of the water for other household uses. (Questions with regard to the latter are omitted because respondents are less able to separate problems in the water itself from problems caused by other factors such as the choice or amount of detergent.)

Question 55a, or a similar question, is desirable to help identify the specific reason for dissatisfaction, so that officials can better determine possible problems and corrective action. The primary cause for dissatisfaction is likely to be the taste of the water. Many taste complaints are attributable to the chlorine used to disinfect the water, particularly at dead ends of the distribution system where the chlorine may separate from the water, and to dissolved material dislodged by construction activity.

A regular household telephone survey is one way to obtain these data, but it is impractical if limited to questions on water quality. If a government undertakes a survey covering a number of government services, as is suggested here, the additional cost of questions on water supply issues should be quite small. The survey procedure is discussed at greater length in Chapter 13.

More feasible are periodic mail surveys of water customers. The agency can mail to a random sample of customers a short (one- or two-page) questionnaire, containing questions such as the Appendix 1 questions noted above. This could be done as part of a regular water bill mailing.

An important concern for these surveys is to obtain an adequate response rate from those mailed questionnaires, a rate that can give public officials confidence that the responses are representative of their customers' views (and are credible to persons outside the agency). Thus, the agency will need to follow up with a second mailing and a telephone reminder (or interview) to nonrespondents to achieve response rates of 50 percent or more. The data are much more likely to be valid if the agency achieves a high response rate from a small but properly drawn sample (of, say, 200 each quarter) than if questionnaires are sent to all customers and the *rate* of response is low (typically 10–20 percent for such single-mailing surveys)—even if much larger *numbers* are returned.

Customer surveys are discussed at greater length in Chapter 13.

Because citizens may become accustomed to the taste of their water and thus become insensitive to it, cross-community comparisons of survey results are risky. Nevertheless, even desensitized persons may detect significant adverse changes. For Measure 4, it may be particularly informative to compare the responses of citizens who have recently come to the community with responses of longer-term residents. A question such as Question 1 in Appendix 1 can be used as a basis for cross-tabulating the responses to Questions 55 and 55a.

For Measure 5, the number of validated complaints about the drinking water can be obtained by tallying complaints reported by customers. Although most jurisdictions have procedures for processing complaints, tallies by type to provide a record of the trends in complaints are less common. Complaints cannot be considered necessarily representative of the level of concern in the population because of the limited conditions under which citizens will complain. (This is why Measure 4 is needed; proper sampling procedures can provide representative information.) Reported complaints do, however, provide convenient data for tracking major drinking water problems of concern to a segment of the population. Procedures for examining complaints and validating them are presented in Chapter 11.

Levels of Water Quality That Affect Household Uses (Measure 6)

Measure 6: Estimated number of days that one or more of the following characteristics failed to meet its standard(s): hardness and pH (cleaning effectiveness) and iron and manganese (staining).

Measure 6 covers the quality of the water for household uses other than drinking. The arguments in favor of using the "estimated days of unsatisfactory quality" form of the measure are essentially the same as those indicated for Measures 1 and 3—to present test results in a manner understandable to public officials and to focus on problem areas needing attention. Frequent testing of these qualities is probably warranted, especially if the water is softened.

Procedures for the four tests are provided in the *Standard Methods for the Examination of Water and Wastewater.*[4] The procedure for translating the results of these tests into Measure 6 is the same as that illustrated in Exhibit 10-3. The additional cost for these tallies should be quite small.

Flow Adequacy (Measures 7–10)

Measure 7: Number of days of restrictions on household and business water use, by type of restriction.

Measure 8: Percentage of (a) households, (b) businesses reporting problems with water pressure or flow, by type of problem.

Measure 9: Number of valid complaints about water flow per 1,000 clients, excluding complaints on matters shown to be private responsibility.

Measure 10: Percentage of fire hydrants surveyed that meet static water pressure standard of, for example, 40 pounds per square inch.

These measures provide four different perspectives on the adequacy of water supply flow and pressure. Measure 7 tracks a major impact of inadequate flow—restrictions on water use in households or businesses. These restrictions generally reflect problems of access to supply that the water department cannot solve on its own. In most communities restrictions seldom occur. Flow problems still may show up for individual households and businesses. Measure 8 provides information on the water flow problems as perceived by a representative sample of households and businesses. Measure 9 uses tallies of reported citizen complaints on water flow problems.

Although data on reported complaints (unlike the information collected for Measure 8) cannot be assumed to be representative of problems occurring throughout the community, this information is readily available and likely to provide a rough indication of major flow problems of concern to at least a portion of the population. Measure 10 uses measurements of water pressure at fire hydrants to provide an indication of the adequacy of flow at a number of fixed points in the distribution system. (Since fire fighting is an important use for the water supply of every jurisdiction, this measure directly reflects the operational readiness of fire hydrants for fire fighting.)

Measure 7 tallies incidents of water restrictions weighted by their duration but not by the number of households and businesses affected, because that information generally is not available at reasonable cost. (If a jurisdiction can obtain reasonably accurate estimates of the number of households and businesses affected without excessive costs, such figures also could be used to weight each incident in terms of the scope of the restriction—that is, an outage affecting fifty families would be more severe than a similar outage affecting ten.) Measure 7 would include bans on watering lawns and outages due to broken water mains.

Changes in the annual rainfall should be taken into account in interpreting the occurrence of restrictions. Restrictions may reflect unusual weather rather than failure of an operating component of the municipal water supply system.

Measure 8 is important because interrupted or reduced water flow can be a considerable irritant to users in households and businesses. The frequency of such interruptions in service as perceived by users is a major indication of flow adequacy. A survey of a sample of households and businesses can be used to provide statistically reliable estimates of the perceived prevalence of these problems. Data for this measure would be obtained from the same survey used for Measure 4. Questions such as 56, 56a, and 57 in Appendix 1 can be used to obtain this information from a representative sample of households. For businesses, questions such as 37, 37a, and 37b in Appendix 2 can be used.

The procedures, and issues, associated with such surveys were discussed briefly under Measure 4. Household and business surveys are discussed in more detail in Chapters 15 and 14, respectively.

Although water pressure and flow are probably as important to citizens as water aesthetics (see Measure 4), they are harder to measure accurately because inadequacies in pressure or flow can take many forms, ranging from chronic low pressure to occasional short-term stoppages. The survey questions ask about the existence of any problem during the past reporting period (the assumed interval between surveys), then about the nature of the problem, and finally about the frequency of its occurrence. Tallies by type of problem are particularly important. Pressure and flow problems often originate in deficiencies in private plumbing or in demands upon the system for several simultaneous heavy uses. Identification of the types of problems encountered is intended to provide at least some evidence of whether the responsibility for the problems is public or private. The checklist provided in Question 56a (Appendix 1) can be supplemented by using more probing questions about the nature of problems to pinpoint sources.

Measure 9, the number of complaints, may be of limited value in reflecting the perceptions of all citizens (as discussed under Measure 5), but data for it are usually readily available and worth tracking for that reason. Usually complaints about flow or pressure adequacy can be tallied readily to provide a gross indicator of major problems for at least the "vocal" citizens.

The information for Measure 10 is based on regular (at least annual) inspections of fire hydrants already performed by many local governments in order to maintain their fire insurance ratings. Thus the additional cost of this measurement is likely to be very small. Water pressure for fire hydrants is relevant to fire-fighting usage and indicative of the pressure provided for nearby homes and other buildings.

Different goals or standards of pressure can be set for different water uses. A pressure commonly used for fire-fighting purposes, which places the highest demand on flow, is 40 pounds per square inch (psi). For domestic purposes, a lower standard such as 30 psi might be appropriate. Below 30 psi, some machinery requiring water, such as washing machines and dishwashers, may not receive the pressure they require. At pressures below 20 psi, there is danger of backwashing—that is, water moving opposite to the intended flow in places—and associated water contamination. A standard somewhere between 30 and 40 psi will be in accordance with established practices.

The use of fire hydrants as test points, rather than some sample of household taps or a sample of points leading up to households but short of the private property line, is recommended for two reasons. First, measurement at the tap would present significant access and measurement procedure problems, and it would be difficult to determine public and private responsibilities. Second, measurement at points just outside the property line would be more difficult to do and would cost more than the hydrant test, which must be done anyway for fire insurance purposes.

Service Adequacy and Responsiveness (Measures 11–13)

Measure 11:   *Total number of valid complaints and requests for nonroutine service per 1,000 customers, by type of complaint (including billing overcharge, water quality, broken or leaking pipe or meter).*

Measure 12:   *Percentage of persons complaining or requesting service who were satisfied with the handling of their complaints or requests, by type of complaint (for example, billing complaints).*

Measure 13:   *Percentage of valid complaints and requests that were effectively responded to within an allowed period of time, overall and for each class of requests.*

These measures cover three aspects of adequacy and responsiveness of providers of water supply service, with "service" used in the limited sense of government maintenance of the system and response to customers' requests. Measure 11, the rate of valid complaints (not shown to be private responsibility) per 1,000 customers, is a measure of service effectiveness in preventing problems. Measure 12 reflects the customers' own perceptions of how well the government responds to their requests. Measure 13 provides information on the government's response time in resolving requests for assistance, an aspect of service quality that lends itself to the collection of "objective" information.

Measure 11 can be used to track problems of the vocal segment of water supply customers, as discussed with regard to Measure 5 (complaints on drinking water quality) and Measure 9 (complaints on water pressure and flow). However, reported complaints cannot be considered to represent reliably the views of all water customers. The rate of unreported complaints is likely to vary markedly over time and from place to place within the community. Yet, when reported complaints are tallied by subject, they enable the government to identify patterns of problem areas that need attention.

Although most governments have some provision for handling citizen complaints, few actually tally complaints as a monitor of performance. Tallying is complicated by the fact that complaints may be reported to a variety of places, such as the chief executive's office, the council, or the water supply agency. Procedures may not be in place to bring all complaints together and to tabulate the valid ones. A more extensive discussion of the processing of complaint data is presented in Chapter 11.

The measure is expressed as a rate per 1,000 customers to permit fairer comparisons over time, on the assumption that the more customers there are, the more complaints will be received. Use of the rate is important chiefly to jurisdictions with significantly changing populations. Rates also are needed in making comparisons of the numbers of complaints from various segments of the population (such as those living in different neighborhoods) to reflect different numbers of customers in each population segment.

Measure 12 provides feedback on the quality of government response to a citizen complaint or request for routine service—the degree of customer satisfaction with the government response. (Some governments may choose to separate "complaints" from other "requests," such as new hookups. See Chapter 11 for discussion of this distinction.) Surveys of the whole population of customers are probably not the most efficient way to provide this information, because most customers will not have reported complaints or requested services in the past year. Much more efficient is to ask customers who have received such service to rate it.

In addition to ratings for overall level of satisfaction, ratings on specific aspects of quality, such as the promptness and courtesy of government employees, can be obtained.

The procedure suggested here is to survey a sample of persons who actually have called the government for water supply service or who have made a complaint. A series of questions such as those shown in Appendix 8 can be used. The questions seek ratings on the convenience, promptness, courtesy, and satisfactoriness of the response to the complaint or request. Concerns over billing also are encompassed in the questions in Appendix 8. For Measure 12, responses to Questions 13 or 14 in Appendix 8 suffice. The other questions focus on more specific aspects of the service quality, providing the water supply agency with more detailed information to act on.

Telephone surveys require five- to ten-minute interviews. Mail surveys have poor return rates, which make it difficult to assure that the final sample is representative of the population being surveyed. Mailings, however, can be used if the agency takes steps to obtain adequate response rates (50 percent higher) using a second mailing and telephone reminders or interviews of nonrespondents.

Telephone interviews are so expensive that a government will probably want to interview only a random sample of complainants, if there are many. Mail surveys cost relatively little. However, because of the need to follow up on nonrespondents, sampling is likely to be more practical. If a mail survey is used, a shorter version of the survey in Appendix 8 will be necessary.

The required sample size will depend on a number of factors as discussed in Chapter 13.

Interviews can be spread over the year or scheduled at specific times during the year. Because households should be surveyed soon after "completion" of the service, spreading interviews over the year is preferable. If surveying is done only periodically, some respondents might have trouble recalling how they felt at the time of their complaint.

Measure 13, the time it takes to respond to and complete requests for service, is important to those requesting service—whether the call is an emergency or not. Measure 12 takes care of this problem to some extent, in that ratings of overall satisfaction as perceived by the customers are likely to reflect response times. In addition, the survey can provide customers' ratings on promptness using a question such as Question 11 in Appendix 8.

More "factual" data can be obtained by keeping records of response times. This is likely to require some revision of the forms for recording customer calls and actions taken in response to them. It can be difficult to determine (and subject to different operational interpretations) when a request for service has been effectively resolved. (This issue is discussed further in Chapter 11.) Response times should be broken down by whether the calls were emergencies or nonemergencies and by nature of the complaint or request. The target response times should be different for each.

The costs are likely to be small unless a major effort is needed to determine when a service call has been resolved. Some start-up costs will occur as forms are revised.

Developing Measurement Data for Major Client Groups

Although water supply tends to be "equally" provided to all parts of a local jurisdiction, certain localized geographical conditions can affect the water quality at the receiving end, and different groups may have slightly differing tastes. Thus, as with most other local government services, some disaggregation of the measurement data by major client groupings seems desirable for some of the measures.

For most measures, computation of values for each geographical area of the community will permit useful comparisons of service levels. Groupings by age, sex, race or ethnic group, and income group can be made only when such data are available, as for the measures involving interviews with customers (see Measures 4, 8, and 12). Differences in values among these groups will usually reflect either residential patterns combined with varying levels of

service to different areas or differences in sensitivity that the agency cannot control and may not feel it necessary to consider. Two exceptions are the acceptability of water for household uses—in this instance, women may be more knowledgeable than men—and adequacy of responses to complaints.

Staffing Requirements

The major costs involved are those associated with the periodic testing of the various water characteristics (for Measures 1, 3, and 6), but such testing should be undertaken whether or not effectiveness is measured. The other sources of potentially significant costs are the customer surveys (for Measures 4 and 8) and the surveys of complainants and persons who have requested service (Measure 12). A survey of a sample of households will probably be undertaken only if several government services are included, in which case it would cost little more to obtain data for Measures 4 and 8. Customer surveys are likely to be the largest added cost for the measures presented here. A telephone survey of perhaps 100 clients quarterly would likely cost over $3,000 per year if contracted to an outside firm. Mailing questionnaires will probably cut this amount in half. If a government has persons available who can do the interviewing or mailing, this will greatly reduce the out-of-pocket expense. Some minimum professional survey assistance is needed to assure that reasonably sound technical procedures are used in these surveys and that interviewers are trained properly.

---

1 See American Public Health Association, *Standard Methods for the Examination of Water and Wastewater*.

2 These procedures are presented in Section 2000 of American Public Health Association, *Standard Methods for the Examination of Water and Wastewater*.

3 See Section 2000 of American Public Health Association, *Standard Methods for the Examination of Water and Wastewater*. Relevant tests are for turbidity, color, odor, taste, chlorides, sulfates, copper, and methylene-blue-active substances.

4 Tests for iron and manganese (as well as for hardness and pH) are included here because their suggested limits are based on the concentration required to stain laundry. Both substances may also have taste effects in larger concentrations.

Hardness is a measure of the propensity of water to form deposits on clothes washed in carbonate-based detergents (as opposed to phosphate-based detergents). The carbonate combines with calcium or magnesium to form deposits that precipitate onto clothes during the spin cycle. Hardness is a measure of calcium, magnesium, and other minerals available for precipitation. It is expressed in terms of calcium carbonate equivalents, as calcium carbonate is by far the most common precipitate. From the standpoint of cleaning, then, the softer the water is, the better it is.

The pH measures hydrogen ion activity. Many different ranges of acceptable pH levels exist and there appears to be no basis to choose among them. Scores of chemical processes are affected by pH, but their sensitivities to changes vary widely. A pH of 7.0 is neutral and so all ranges of acceptability are built around 7.0. (Measures of pH are expressed without units.) There is no generally accepted recommended range, but combining the recommendations of several sources leads to a possible range of 6.5 to 8.3. The prevailing practice in most local jurisdictions is to try to keep the pH fairly close to the natural level, whatever that may be, to avoid excessive costs and injury to local fish life. Hence, pH monitoring is employed only to assure that industrial wastes do not produce significant shifts.

Chapter 11

Handling Citizen Complaints and Requests

A t one time or another, nearly every household has occasion to contact its local government. The reason may be:

- *To complain about poor government service*—a missed trash collection, potholes, inadequate street lighting, or some other condition requiring corrective action

- *To seek service or assistance*—a special pickup of bulk refuse; health and social services; or intervention in some situation the government might be able to influence, for instance, a tenant-landlord dispute or a consumer problem

- *To seek information*—to find out about waste collection policies, a new tax provision, or a specific government program or facility

- *To offer a suggestion or comment*—an idea for improving a particular service, a word of praise or appreciation, or an opinion on a government issue or action.

Complaints, requests, and suggestions like these constitute an important part of the day-to-day communication between local governments and the public. They provide valuable feedback on government services in the absence of "market" signals, helping to hold agencies accountable to the public they serve. Increasingly, local governments are encouraging citizens to contact public agencies and officials directly with their complaints and concerns so that they can be dealt with quickly and constructively.

Complaints and requests often represent the only direct contacts citizens have with their local government. As a result, such contacts frequently become the primary basis for citizen perceptions of government efficiency, effectiveness, and responsive-

ness.[1] How well the government handles complaints and requests can thus be of considerable political—as well as operational—importance.

Jurisdictions differ in their approaches to dealing with citizen complaints and requests. Most local governments leave it to individual departments to process the complaints and requests they receive. Some governments also provide special centralized facilities such as complaint hotlines, citizen action centers, "little city halls," ombudsman offices, even computers in malls, for receiving, referring, and—if possible—resolving citizen complaints and requests.

The effectiveness measures identified in this chapter are applicable whether complaints and requests are handled by a central office or by individual line agencies. Agencies that process large numbers of citizen complaints or requests should use some or all of the measures presented in this chapter to supplement the effectiveness measures for their other responsibilities. (This chapter excludes citizen reports of crimes. The handling of complaints pertaining to crime is discussed in Chapter 6.)

Principal Measures and Measurement Procedures

For purposes of effectiveness measurement, it is recommended that citizen requests for services and information be distinguished from citizen complaints. (The implications of not distinguishing complaints and requests are discussed below.) For the convenience of the reader, complaint measure numbers are preceded by a "C," request measure numbers are preceded by an "R."

Eleven effectiveness measures are suggested for assessing the handling of citizen complaints. (These measures are listed in Exhibit 11-2). The complaint measures address the following:

- The satisfactoriness of the jurisdiction's responses to complaints from the perspectives of both the local government and the complainants (Measures C1 and C2)

- The quality of the treatment received from government complaint-processing personnel as reflected in response time, courtesy, helpfulness, and fairness (Measures C3–C5)

- The willingness and ability of citizens to make their complaints known to government officials as indicated by the accessibility of the government's complaint-handling machinery (Measure C6), and the number and percentage of legitimate complaints not reported to government officials (Measures C7 and C8)

- The degree to which the overall need for citizen complaints is reduced, as indicated, for instance, by the combined annual incidence of justifiable reported *and* unreported complaints (Measures C9–C11). Unreported complaints can be identified with a general household survey.

In assessing the degree to which the need for citizen complaints is reduced, it is important to ensure that the local government is not held responsible for frivolous matters or problems outside its jurisdiction. Moreover, the presence of such assessments must not tempt government officials to discourage citizens from reporting legitimate complaints in order to make the "need" for complaints appear to be falling. The first concern is addressed by focusing, whenever possible, on "justifiable" complaints. (A suggested definition of a "justifiable complaint" appears in Exhibit 11-1.) The possibility of discouraging citizens from reporting is reduced by monitoring citizens' willingness and ability to make their complaints known (Measures C6–C8).

The six measures proposed for assessing the handling of citizen requests are analogous to the first six complaint measures. They attempt to measure from various perspectives the satisfactoriness of the government's responses to requests for service and information (Measures R1 and R2), the speed and quality of the treatment received (Measures R3–R5), and the extent to which the public is inhibited from making such requests (Measure R6). (These measures are listed in Exhibit 11-4.)

To support these complaint and request measures, the following measurement procedures are suggested for regular usage—at least once a year and preferably quarterly or monthly to provide timely feedback to agency managers.

"User" Survey. A survey of citizens who have reported complaints or made requests for services should be conducted on a regular basis. At some specified interval after the citizen's initial complaint or request, the government should ask all or a sample of these citizens to rate the extent to which they were satisfied with the resolution of their complaints or requests and to evaluate various aspects of the service received. These aspects include the ease with which they registered their complaint or request, the timeliness of the government's response, the courtesy and helpfulness of government personnel, the fairness of the treatment received, and the absence of bureaucratic red tape or "run-around."

Such a survey could be conducted by telephone or by mail. Tallies made from the responses received provide the appropriate performance measures (for instance, "the proportion of respondents satisfied with the resolution of their complaints," "the proportion experiencing 'run-arounds' or red tape," and so forth). Much of the work connected with the user survey (including conducting interviews and preparing tallies) probably can be done by personnel from the local government's complaint/request office or by administrative support staff from line agencies as part of routine complaint follow-up procedures and at little additional cost to the community.

Household Survey. A household survey can be used periodically to canvass a random sample of citizens concerning their unreported complaints and their reasons for not reporting complaints and requests. The responses provide data for estimating the extent to which the local government's handling of complaints or requests encouraged and facilitated citizen reporting of legitimate matters. Survey data are the major source of information for estimates of both the number and percentage of previously unreported complaints and the percentage of persons inhibited from filing requests and complaints.

A household survey such as this is probably too expensive for a local government if used only for assessing the handling of complaints and requests. However, if the government regularly undertakes a household survey covering a variety of government services, questions on the extent of, and reasons for, unreported complaints can be added to the general survey without significant additional cost.

Data on the incidence of unreported complaints (obtained from the household survey) can be used to estimate the "total" incidence of justifiable citizen complaints—whether or not reported to the government. This figure is obtained by adding the estimated total number of unreported complaints to the number of reported complaints. Changes in the total from year to year indicate whether the "need to complain"—that is, the total number of perceived problems within the local government's jurisdiction—has increased or decreased and suggest the degree to which justifiable citizen complaints have been prevented.

The main problem with using survey data as a source of information on unreported complaints is in establishing whether the complaints elicited are legitimate and within the jurisdiction of the local government. Some of the unreported complaints identified by the respondents *are* likely to be invalid or outside the local government's jurisdiction. However, any exaggeration of the number of unreported complaints is probably partly offset by respondents' memory limitations. The problem of overcounting also can be alleviated (although at added expense) by screening the survey responses to eliminate clearly unjustifiable complaints. Although the validity of unreported complaints may be uncertain, their inclusion provides a better indication of the number of problems that need to be addressed than can be obtained by counting only reported complaints.

Existing Records on Complaints and Requests. To get data regularly for such measures as the number of justifiable complaints that *are* reported, the frequency of complaints on various topics, the median response time, the percentage of excessive delays, and the satisfactoriness of the responses received (as viewed from the perspective of the local government) may require some relatively inexpensive modifications of the forms, reporting requirements, and filing procedures used by the various offices. The computer software packages that many governments use to record and process citizen complaints and requests can often be used to extract and process data for performance measures.

Trained Observers. In some jurisdictions, the sheer volume of requests for information makes it impractical for staff to record the addresses or telephone numbers needed for conducting follow-up surveys of persons who requested information. An alternate measurement procedure under such circumstances is to have trained participant observers "test" the effectiveness of the government's responses by requesting information from a number of agencies. The requests must be chosen carefully to reflect the types and variety of information citizens typically seek from those agencies. Each caller uses prespecified rating scales and procedures to rate accessibility, response time, courtesy, the accuracy of the information (or referral) provided, and so forth. Such tests can be conducted by municipal staff or citizen volunteers, after suitable training.

The measurement data should be categorized and reported by *type* of complaint or request, such as the subject of the complaint and the neighborhood of the complainant. Exhibit 11-1 contains an illustrative listing of useful types.

The foregoing measurement procedures require that government personnel agree on specific practical definitions of complaints, as distinguished from requests for services, and the conditions under which a complaint should be considered justifiable. The formulation of and adherence to strict definitions and ground rules for tallying complaints are especially important for jurisdictions that do not handle complaints or requests on a centralized basis. Exhibit 11-1 presents illustrative definitions for "complaints," "requests for services and information," and "justifiable complaints." An operational definition of a "satisfactory response" (from the local government's perspective) is suggested in the discussion of Measure C1. (See also Exhibit 11-3.)

It is difficult to distinguish between complaints and requests (especially requests for service). The distinction often turns on phrasing or the citizen's tone of voice, meaning that the staff member must make a judgment as to whether a given item should be counted as a complaint or a request.

As a result, some jurisdictions do not distinguish between complaints and requests, using the two terms interchangeably or perhaps referring to everything as a request. Other local governments combine complaints with requests for service when reporting on performance. In such cases, requests for information (which usually can be identified unambiguously) are treated separately (or ignored) for statistical purposes.

Such practices limit the usefulness of the effectiveness measures discussed in this chapter. Most jurisdictions receive far more requests than complaints and many more requests for information than requests for service. As a result, if complaints are not distinguished from requests, measures of effectiveness will be dominated by the government's performance in handling requests, especially requests for information. And since the handling of complaints tends to be more difficult and controversial than the handling of requests (particularly requests for information), the lack of distinction between complaints and requests is likely to distort the effectiveness results by artificially elevating satisfaction levels and reducing response times.

Moreover, if complaints are lumped with requests, volume-based complaint measures such as C8–C11 lose their significance; no longer do they indicate emerging problems or the government's effectiveness in reducing or preventing such problems. Thus, a government should distinguish between complaints and requests, starting with definitions such as those in Exhibit 11-1 and supplementing them with rules for handling specific ambiguous cases. (For instance, some governments adopt the convention that any request for code enforcement is a complaint, or that repeat requests for a given service should always be treated as complaints.) Eau Claire, Wisconsin, provides its employees with a laminated card listing fifty topics to be used for classifying *all* citizen contacts. And Hillsborough County, Florida, has as part of its complaint/request software a "help" screen that lists all standard topic codes relevant to keywords entered by the operator.

Some computerized complaint/request packages make it possible for local government staff members to record at least limited information on *all* citizen contacts—including requests for information—and to code them by topic. By using detailed topic codes (facilitated perhaps by a "help" screen), it is possible to leave the complaint versus request decision to the manager or analyst preparing the effectiveness measures. The analyst can specify which topic codes will be counted as complaints and direct the computer to prepare appropriate performance measures based on that definition.

In the following sections, specific measures and related data collection procedures are discussed, first for complaints and then for requests for service and information.

The Handling of Citizen Complaints

The complaint-handling operation usually is concerned with three distinct objectives:

> **To respond to and, if technically and legally possible, to resolve satisfactorily reported complaints with speed, fairness, and courtesy.**
>
> **To encourage and facilitate the reporting of legitimate citizen complaints.**

This objective implies that the local government needs to have an accessible system that permits citizens to conveniently make their complaints known to the proper government officials.

> **To reduce or prevent the occurrence of circumstances that lead to justifiable citizen complaints, whether or not they are reported to government officials.**

Exhibit 11-1

Suggested Definitions and Policies for Distinguishing Complaints and Requests

---

Basic definitions

Request for information—A request explicitly seeking knowledge or data in symbolic form (for example, in terms of spoken or written words, pictures, maps). If the information is not readily available (for example, if data must be developed), the provision of the data probably should be interpreted as a service.

Request for service—A request that potentially involves action or activity on the part of local government personnel (other than the provision of readily available information) but which does not reflect any evidence of dissatisfaction on the part of the requester.

Complaint—An expression of annoyance, an indication of the presence of a problem (i.e., that something is wrong or unsatisfactory). The presence of explicit or implicit dissatisfaction (and a consequent need for corrective action) distinguishes a "complaint" from a "request for service or information."

Justifiable complaint—A situation in which the reported unsatisfactory condition does exist and the matter is within the jurisdiction of the local government (that is, the government has legal authority for correcting the problem). For purposes of measurement, some governments also may wish to classify as "unjustifiable" those complaints that are vague, unfocused, unrealistic (in the immediate future), or only indirectly relevant to the complainant.

A policy for handling ambiguous items

If an item exhibits characteristics of both a complaint and a request, it should be classified as a complaint to ensure an accurate tally of

complaints (for Measures C8–C11). Officials should establish clear policies for classifying the most common types of ambiguous items. Examples include requests for repairs or maintenance of existing municipal facilities (such as notification of the location of a pothole or a malfunctioning traffic light), requests that alleged code violations be inspected and rectified, requests that city officials intervene as a third party (for instance, to force a property owner to clean his lot), and long-range requests (such as those seeking the creation of a new park or installation of storm sewers).

Useful ways to characterize the type of complaint or request

"Type" refers here to any useful property of complaints or requests by which such citizen communications can be classified and analyzed. Potentially useful classifications include the following:
- Agency initially contacted
- Agency ultimately responsible for handling the matter
- Detailed subject of the complaint or request
- Source of the complaint or request (government employee versus other citizens)
- Neighborhood, ward, and/or district in which the complainant or requester lives
- Urgency of the matter (how soon a response is needed)
- Status of the item (closed versus pending; if pending, the number of weeks that have elapsed since the item was received)
- Uniqueness of the item (new or unique issues versus repeat or recurring issues).

Note: No matter how carefully these terms and policies are defined, there will always be borderline cases for which classification will be highly subjective. However, the procedures suggested will minimize the need for such judgments.

Although this is an important objective for the local government as a whole and for individual operating agencies, it may not be considered a specific responsibility of a central complaint office.

A local government's approach to handling complaints will reflect its priorities among these objectives. Some governments may be especially interested in encouraging citizens to speak out, for instance, by providing central referral facilities, mobile complaint centers, and other "outreach" programs. These jurisdictions may therefore be particularly concerned with measuring accessibility. Local governments with an ombudsman may be especially anxious to ensure proper treatment for all complainants and to prevent future recurrences of the problems reported. In most cases, the local government will be concerned only with "justifiable" complaints, those for which the reported conditions exist and lie within the jurisdiction and responsibility of the local government to correct.

Effectiveness measures for the foregoing objectives are summarized in Exhibit 11-2. The measures should reflect performance over a specific time span, such as a quarter or a year. Attention should be given not only to the absolute numbers but also to the changes in these measures over the period of interest.

Measures of the Satisfactoriness and Quality of Complaint Resolution (Measures C1–C5)

Measure C1: Percentage of justifiable complaints, by type, that were resolved satisfactorily (or unsatisfactorily), as determined by government personnel.

Measure C2: Percentage of complaints, by type, that were resolved satisfactorily (or unsatisfactorily), as judged by complainants.

These two measures focus on the final disposition or outcome of citizen complaints, as seen from two different perspectives— that of citizens and that of local government personnel. Data from both groups should be collected and presented, as citizens and government personnel may differ in their assessments of what constitutes a satisfactory outcome.

Data for Measure C1 can be derived from existing local government records if those records describe the nature and disposition of the complaints received. If the records do not describe the dispositions or give inadequate information for assessing the justifiability of the complaint, the government will need to modify its record keeping and begin collecting these data.

"Satisfactory resolution" must be defined with care. An approach for making such judgments is illustrated in Exhibit 11-3. Under the procedure given in this exhibit, complaints are judged satisfactorily resolved from the standpoint of the local government if correction has been completed *or* if resolution was impossible but an adequate explanation of the reason was provided to the complainant. Another way to assess the resolution of a complaint is to define several levels of "satisfactoriness," for example, "fully resolved," "partly resolved," and "some assistance provided." The outcomes of complaints for which action is pending or in process could be considered "ambiguous" and tallied separately.

Data for Measure C2 can be obtained as part of a household survey using, for example, Question 59C of Appendix 1. However, the number of respondents who have complained will probably be too small (less than 100) to allow comparison of responses between population subgroups or to determine how well a particular department has resolved the complaints directed toward it.

A better way to collect data on complainant satisfaction is to conduct a follow-up survey of a sample of the persons who have registered justifiable complaints. An illustration of such a survey is presented in Appendix 9. Questions 5a through 5d in the appendix provide the data needed for this measure. Questions 5b, 5c, and 5d elicit reasons for dissatisfaction with the government's response. These questions make it possible to track the number and proportion of dissatisfied complainants, classified according to the reason for dissatisfaction. Such data can provide clues to government officials as to possible corrective actions.

The validity of the information obtained from a complainant survey depends on the willingness of the complainants to respond completely and accurately, and on the quality of the survey process. Proper procedures for conducting a survey of complainants are described later in this chapter and in Chapter 13. Note that the perspectives of government employees and complainants, as indicated by Measures C1 and C2, should become more similar to the extent that unjustifiable complaints can be screened out when determining Measure C2.

Measure C3: Median response time for resolution of justifiable complaints, by type of complaint.

Measure C4: Number and percentage of excessively delayed responses (those for which the time to resolve exceeds, for example, 10 working days), by type of complaint.

These measures provide two perspectives on the time it takes the government to resolve a complaint. The median response time (Measure C3) indicates the time typically needed for processing a complaint.

Exhibit 11-2

Measures of Effectiveness for Handling Citizen Complaints

Objectives: 1. To respond effectively to and, if technically and legally possible, to resolve satisfactorily reported complaints with speed, fairness, and courtesy.
2. To encourage and facilitate the reporting of legitimate citizen complaints.
3. To reduce or prevent the occurrence of circumstances that lead to justifiable citizen complaints, whether or not they are reported to government officials.

Objective or quality characteristic addressed	Specific complaint measure	Data collection source or procedure
Satisfactory response to and resolution of complaints (from government's perspective [C1] and complainant's perspective [C2])	C1. Percentage of justifiable complaints, by type,[1] that were resolved satisfactorily (or unsatisfactorily), as determined by government personnel.[2]	Agency complaint records
	C2. Percentage of complaints, by type, that were resolved satisfactorily (or unsatisfactorily), as judged by complainants.	Either a follow-up survey of past complainants or a household survey
Speedy resolution of complaints	C3. Median response time for resolution of justifiable complaints, by type of complaint.	Agency records
	C4. Number and percentage of excessively delayed responses (those for which the time to resolve exceeds, for example, 10 working days), by type of complaint.	Agency records
Quality of treatment of complainants (speed, courtesy, fairness, etc.)	C5. Percentage of complainants satisfied (or dissatisfied) with the following aspects of their treatment by complaint-processing personnel: (a) speed and timeliness of response, (b) absence of red tape, "run-around," and similar bureaucratic inconveniences or complexities, (c) courtesy, helpfulness, and general attitude of government personnel, (d) fairness of treatment.	Complainant survey or household survey
Willingness and ability of citizens to make their complaints known to the government	C6. Percentage of citizens who (a) *filed* a complaint or (b) *did not file* a complaint who found it difficult or impossible to register their complaint(s) with the proper official, grouped by type of difficulty encountered.	Household survey Data from the perspective of persons who *have* filed a complaint also can be obtained from a survey of complainants
	C7. Number of unreported complaints, expressed as (a) jurisdiction total, (b) overall rate per 10,000 adults, (c) total for each type of complaint, and (d) rate per 10,000 adults, by reason for not having reported the complaint.	Household survey
	C8. Proportion of citizen complaints reported, expressed as (a) jurisdiction total and (b) total for each type of complaint.	Data collected for Measures C7 and C9
Reduction or prevention of justifiable citizen complaints	C9. Number of justifiable complaints received by the jurisdiction, expressed as (a) jurisdiction total, (b) overall rate per 10,000 adults, (c) total for each type of complaint, and (d) rate per 10,000 adults for each type.[3]	Agency records or household survey for number of justifiable complaints, planning department for population data
	C10. Number and rate of citizen complaints, including both reported and unreported complaints, expressed as (a) jurisdiction total, (b) rate per 10,000 adults, (c) total for each type, and (d) rate per 10,000 adults for each type.[3]	Data collected for Measures C7 and C9
	C11. Number of different complainants per 10,000 adults, expressed as (a) persons reporting complaints, per 10,000 adults, (b) persons with unreported complaints, per 10,000 adults, and (c) persons with reported or unreported complaints, per 10,000 adults.	Agency or central office complaint files and a household survey

[1]"Type" of complaint refers to the complaint classifications selected by the local government as being useful. Classifications might be by agency responsible for the problem or its resolution, by type of problem, or by degree of urgency (see Exhibit 11-1 for other potential groupings).
[2]"Satisfactorily resolved" includes those cases where corrections were completed and those cases where an adequate reason exists (and was given to the complainant) as to why no help was possible.

[3]Certain types of complaints also can be displayed as a rate per 10,000 *customers* (e.g., sanitation complaints per 10,000 garbage accounts) or per 10,000 *exposures* (e.g., water bill complaints per 10,000 bills issued).

Specifically, it is the length of time within which half of all the complaints received were handled, from receipt of the complaint to final disposition. Other ways to present response-time data include using the average response time, the time until *x* percent of all complaints are resolved (where *x* is selected by the jurisdiction and is perhaps 75 percent or 90 percent), and the percentage of complaints resolved within various time periods (for example, 5 days, 10 days, 30 days, and 90 days). Note that *citizen* ratings of the timeliness of the government's response also may be considered an important measure; this is discussed as part of Measure C5.

Information for this measure usually can be obtained from government records on the disposition of each complaint. The median is determined by putting all response times in increasing (or decreasing) order and finding the one that falls in the middle of the ordered list.

Many of the computerized complaint-tracking packages that are available calculate the response time for each complaint. Unfortunately, few complaint-tracking software packages compute *median* response times. When overall statistics on response times are provided at all, the *average* is the figure most commonly given. Averages, however, are very sensitive to a few extremely long delays in response times. The median is consequently a much better estimate of the response times *typically* experienced by citizens.

Local governments may find it useful to establish performance targets for response times. Measure C4 focuses on performance criteria defining "excessive" response times. Different time periods might be used for different types of complaints. Response time benchmarks used by local governments have ranged from 24 hours to 20 days, sometimes depending on the nature of the complaint. Note that in assessing the *effectiveness* of complaint-handling services, "response time" refers to the time needed to *resolve* a complaint, rather than the time needed to refer the complaint to the appropriate agency or to notify the complainant that the complaint is being addressed. Although many governments establish time standards for the latter efforts, such standards are measures of *process* rather than outcome or effectiveness. Measure 4 can be computed manually by maintaining a running tally of excessively delayed complaints in conjunction with a "tickler" file of pending complaints, often used to identify agencies that need prodding.

Ideally Measures C3 and C4 should be reported separately for different types of complaints. For instance, an agency is likely to find it useful to compute these response-time measures for each department receiving complaints, each major complaint topic, and complaints of differing urgency. (See Exhibit 11-1 for other potentially useful ways to differentiate complaints by type.) The following categories can be used for the urgency of complaints:

Exhibit 11-3

Assessment of "Satisfactory Resolution" of Complaints by Government Personnel: A Schematic Representation

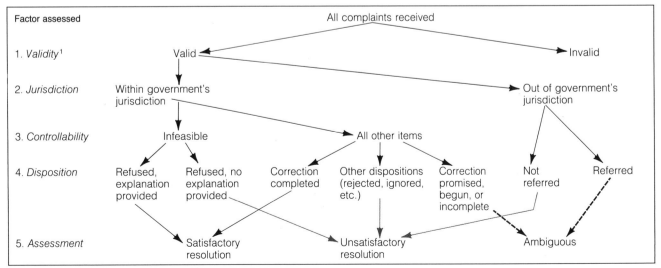

[1]A complaint is considered "valid" if the reported situation does seem to exist.

- *Priority 1*—Emergency, requiring immediate attention even if after hours and demanding interruption of any lower-priority activities.
- *Priority 2*—Serious, requiring attention as soon as possible but without interrupting a job in progress.
- *Priority 3*—Nonurgent, with action to be taken as time permits.

Two problems can affect the accuracy of Measures C3 and C4. One is the difficulty of deciding when a complaint has finally been resolved, especially when a citizen repeatedly contacts the municipality about a given item. In such cases the government might distinguish separate response times for each new contact made by the citizen (measured from the time of the contact to the next government response) and for the total length of time required for the overall disposition of the matter.

The other problem involves a department's reporting the resolution of a complaint when it has only been scheduled for action. The government should distinguish items that are "pending" or "in progress" from those that have been "resolved"; only items that have been "resolved" should be used in preparing Measure C3. (However, a variation of Measure C3, "the median or average number of days that *unresolved* complaints have been pending," should be monitored separately to ensure that long-delayed, unresolved complaints do not escape notice.) Measure C4, on the other hand, should include *all* items that exceed the given response time benchmark, whether or not resolved.

Measure C5: Percentage of complainants satisfied (or dissatisfied) with the following aspects of their treatment by complaint-processing personnel: (a) speed and timeliness of response, (b) absence of red tape, "run-around," and similar bureaucratic inconveniences or complexities, (c) courtesy, helpfulness, and general attitude of government personnel, and (d) fairness of treatment.

This measure (actually a group of measures) is designed to track several aspects of the quality of the service provided other than the satisfactoriness of the disposition of the complaint. It addresses such service characteristics as speed and timeliness, absence of red tape or evasiveness, general attitudes of government employees (courtesy, helpfulness, and concern), and fairness (the extent to which the complainant feels that public employees were biased toward the government's position or that other complainants have received better treatment).

The principal approach for obtaining these data is to survey complainants, as discussed under Measure C2. Questions 7 through 11 on the complainant survey in Appendix 9 can be used to obtain this information. A household survey also can be used, as illustrated by the response options to Question 59C in Appendix 1. As noted earlier, however, the disadvantage of using a household survey for obtaining this information is that only a small number of citizens who have used the government's complaint services are likely to be included in any given sample. Thus, there would be too few ratings to provide representative, statistically reliable data for assessing these aspects of the service. Survey results related to Measure C5 should be grouped by respondent characteristics such as age, education, income, race or ethnic group, and handicaps. Such an analysis can provide information on the equitability of the government's treatment of these groups.

Measures of the Extent to Which Reporting Legitimate Citizen Complaints Is Encouraged and Facilitated (Measures C6–C8)

Three measures address the degree to which citizens are willing and able to make their complaints known to government officials. The first is an assessment of the *accessibility* of the complaint system—the ease with which a citizen can file a complaint with the appropriate office or official. The second measure is an estimate of the number of *unreported complaints*. The third is the *percentage of complaints that are actually reported*. While versions of the first measure are routinely collected by some local governments, the other two are rarely prepared and require a household survey.

Measure C6: Percentage of citizens who (a) filed a complaint or (b) did not file a complaint who found it difficult or impossible to register their complaint(s) with the proper official, grouped by type of difficulty encountered.

Over the past two decades, many local jurisdictions have stressed the goal of making the government bureaucracy more accessible. The proliferation of centralized complaint offices and action centers is testimony to this desire. By helping—and even encouraging—citizens to file complaints, local governments address citizen demands for responsiveness and encourage "market" feedback on government services and accountability in a market sense. Where citizen complaints are an essential means for monitoring contracted services, it becomes even more important for a local government to make it easy for citizens to register their complaints.[2]

Consequently, improving the accessibility of a local government's complaint-handling mechanism is often an important concern. Improved accessibility is also likely to increase the number of complaints reported (see Measure C9); the more accessible the system seems to be, the more likely it is that people will use it.

Measure C6 focuses on the accessibility of the complaint processing system from the perspectives of two different groups of people—those who *did not file* a complaint because of the actual or perceived difficulty of doing so, and those who *filed* a complaint and thus are able to rate the ease (or difficulty) of the experience.

The ease with which a citizen can file a complaint depends on three key factors: the citizen's knowledge of how and where to register a complaint; the citizen's ability to access physically (or electronically) the complaint mechanism at any given time (which is a function of the hours the facility is open, its location, the number of telephone lines available, and so forth); and the difficulty of identifying and reaching a person or office that can help with the complaint. Persons who actually filed a complaint are in a position to assess all these factors, while those who did not file a complaint may not be able to assess the latter two factors.

Measure C6 focuses on *overall* accessibility rather than the detailed aspects described above. A household survey can be used to obtain data for persons who *have filed,* as well as persons who *have not filed,* a complaint (a random household survey is the *only* source of data for the latter group). The responses to Question 62b of the household survey questionnaire in Appendix 1 can be used to determine the percentage of persons inhibited from filing complaints because of accessibility problems, and Question 59C can be used to elicit accessibility information for persons who have filed complaints. Because a household survey will probably reach few respondents who have filed complaints, a survey focusing only on complainants is likely to be a better source of accessibility ratings from persons who *have* complained. Questions 2 and 2a in Appendix 9 can be used for that purpose.

When possible, the survey data should be broken out by type of problem experienced (did not know how or where to complain, unable to file the complaint, too much "red tape," procedures too complex or demanding, and so forth) in order to help identify what might be done to reduce the barriers to reporting complaints. In addition, if the sample size is adequate, the results should be grouped by respondent characteristics—such as age, education, income, race or ethnic group, and handicaps—to check for evidence of inequities in access.

Some governments may wish to focus more intensively on specific factors contributing to accessibility. For instance, knowledge of how and where to complain could be assessed by including an appropriate question on the household survey or by tallying the proportion of complaints that the complainant initially directed to the wrong agency. Measures of the physical accessibility of the complaint system include the number of hours per week that the complaint telephones are covered and various telephone statistics such as the average time on hold and the percentage of time when all lines are busy. The difficulty of identifying or reaching someone who can help with the complaint also can be assessed by tabulating the number of referrals or transfers needed, or the number of calls (or minutes) necessary to reach an individual or agency that will agree to handle the problem. Such information can be obtained by augmenting the user survey given in Appendix 9, or by placing a series of anonymous "test" calls to register common complaints. In the latter case, the caller acts as a trained observer, recording items such as whether the line was busy, the number of rings before the call was answered, the number of intra- and interagency referrals experienced, and so forth.

The measurements described in the preceding paragraph address certain specific aspects of the accessibility of the complaint system. However, they are too narrowly focused to be used in lieu of Measure C6. Only Measure C6 addresses the *overall* accessibility of the complaint-handling system from the citizen's perspective.

Measure C7: Number of unreported complaints, expressed as (a) jurisdiction total, (b) overall rate per 10,000 adults, (c) total for each type of complaint, and (d) rate per 10,000 adults, by reason for not having reported the complaint.

This measure provides an indication of the inaccessibility of the complaint-processing operation and the extent to which citizens feel that the government will not or cannot resolve their complaints. Data can be collected by using a household survey question similar to Question 62 in Appendix 1.

There are two problems with this measure and the proposed data collection procedure. First, because of the relatively small sample sizes expected to be associated with a household survey, the survey probably will provide only a rough estimate of the number of persons who have had specific reasons (such as not knowing where to complain) for not reporting their complaints. Second, respondents indicating unreported complaints actually may be referring to unjustifiable complaints (perhaps a problem outside the jurisdiction of the government) or to items that would be classified more correctly as requests for service. Inclusion of such items can overstate the number of unreported complaints.

To alleviate the latter problem, the questionnaire should provide an opportunity for respondents to describe the nature of their previously unreported complaint(s) (see Question 62b in Appendix 1). Such complaints can then be screened for justifiability before preparing Measure C7.[3]

Because memories are short, respondents probably tend to understate the number of complaints they had but failed to report. If a local government focuses more on *changes* in the number and percentage of unreported complaints (from one time period to another) than on the absolute number, there is less likelihood of being misled by tendencies to understate or overstate the number of unreported complaints.

Measure C8: Proportion of citizen complaints reported, expressed as (a) jurisdiction total and (b) total for each type of complaint.

The ratio of the number of complaints that *are* reported to the sum of those reported *plus* the estimated number of unreported complaints (as obtained in Measure C7) indicates the willingness of citizens to use the complaint-processing mechanism (and by implication, the accessibility of that mechanism).

Data on the number of reported complaints can be obtained from either local government records or a household survey (see Question 58a in Appendix 1). The pros and cons of each procedure are discussed later in connection with Measure C9. However, for estimating the *proportion* reported, the results of the household survey may be all that is needed. For instance, Questions 58a and 62 in Appendix 1 can be used to determine the numbers of reported and unreported complaints among the persons surveyed. The appropriate ratio can then be computed directly from these two quantities. (This procedure provides a means for preparing Measure C8 when no central records are kept of the complaints received by each agency.) Measure C8 would probably be more meaningful if both the reported and unreported complaints identified in the survey were screened for justifiability.

Breakouts of Measure C8 by type of complaint will indicate the degree to which some types of complaints are escaping the attention of local government officials. Such breakouts also can indicate whether, and for what types of complaints, reported complaints fail to indicate the full scope of citizen dissatisfaction. Breakouts by population subgroups (discussed later) might identify special problems concerning the inaccessibility of the complaint-receiving mechanism or the unwillingness of certain segments of the population to register complaints—potential indications of inequities.

An alternate form of Measure C8 is "proportion of persons with complaints who claim to have reported all of them." Since this form depends only on whether a respondent had *any* unreported complaints, it reduces the effects of respondent memory limitations regarding the *number* of reported and unreported complaints. Data for this alternate form would be obtained from the general household survey and computed by dividing the number of "yes" responses to Question 58 by the sum of the "yes" responses to Questions 58 and 62 in Appendix 1.

Measures of the Overall Level of Complaints (Measures C9–C11)

These measures are designed to reflect a government's desire to reduce or prevent the occurrence of circumstances leading to justifiable citizen complaints, reported or unreported. A jurisdiction may consider this an overall government objective rather than a specific responsibility of a central complaint-receiving agency.

Usually it is impossible to measure the number of problems prevented. What is measurable, however, is the number of complaints that have *not* been averted. The three measures presented here focus on various aspects of the number of complaints that *do* occur. Measure C9, "the number of reported justifiable complaints," is currently used by many local governments. A better estimate of the total number of citizen complaints that occur is one that incorporates unreported complaints. Measure C10 includes unreported incidents as estimated by a household survey. Finally, because complaints may come largely from a select segment of the population that complains frequently, a government may want an estimate of the number of different complainants as well as of the total number of complaints. Measure C11 provides this estimate.

Measure C9: Number of justifiable complaints received by the jurisdiction, expressed as (a) jurisdiction total, (b) overall rate per 10,000 adults, (c) total for each type of complaint, and (d) rate per 10,000 adults for each type.

This measure reflects the level of expressed citizen dissatisfaction. A justifiable complaint, as defined earlier, is one in which the reported condition existed and was within the jurisdiction and responsibility of the government to correct. Because many government departments routinely keep records of the complaints they receive, data for this measure are often readily available. Such information is a standard byproduct of most computerized complaint-tracking systems.

The "type" of complaint here refers to any or all of the complaint classifications the local government selects as being useful, such as the agency responsible for the problem or its resolution, the type of problem, or the urgency of the matter. For some types of complaints, it may be more appropriate to calculate complaint rates relative to the number of potential sources of a complaint (for instance, sanitation complaints per 10,000 households served or water bill complaints per 10,000 bills issued) in order to adjust for different levels of exposure. The rate of reported complaints on certain specific topics also can be used to assess the effectiveness of specific municipal services such as solid waste collection.

Several factors affect the accuracy of this measure. Complaints usually are received by a number of different government officials or agencies. A complaint about a missed refuse collection, for example, might be made to the mayor, a city council member, the chief administrator's office, the sanitation department, or to several of these offices. Complaints may be lost or counted more than once. Some matters (a missed refuse collection is a good example) may be referred to a government unit for immediate action without being recorded. And some departments may not keep good records on the number of complaints received, especially if complaints are perceived as indicators of poor performance.

A number of jurisdictions have addressed the above problems by standardizing the form that all agencies *must* use to record a complaint (or request) and requiring that a copy always be forwarded to a central complaint office. The use of computerized complaint-tracking systems—where all agency complaint activities are logged and linked via a local area network—can greatly reduce such difficulties.

There is also a potential definition problem. To make a department's record on justifiable complaints look better, some departments may liberally classify citizen complaints as unjustifiable (that is, as not within the responsibility of the department to correct) or as not being complaints at all but requests for service. A set of specific definitions, perhaps based on those in Exhibit 11-1, should be established and applied consistently. In addition, periodic audits could be conducted to verify the accuracy of the classifications used.

Some of the record-keeping inaccuracies might be overcome by estimating the total number of reported complaints from the responses to an appropriate household survey question such as Question 58 in Appendix 1. However, there are problems with this procedure (including memory and sampling errors), as discussed later in this chapter in the section on the household survey. Because government records at present are likely to have greater credibility than complaints reported in a survey, the former may be preferable for preparing Measure C9.

This measure does not include unreported complaints. Thus, changes in the value of Measure C9 could stem from changes in citizen awareness and the accessibility of the complaint system, rather than from any change in the number of complaint-provoking incidents. For example, improvements in handling complaints may lead to more reported complaints because citizens feel that the government has become more responsive. To alleviate these ambiguities, Measure C10 is presented.

Measure C10: Number and rate of citizen complaints, including both reported and unreported complaints, expressed as (a) jurisdiction total, (b) rate per 10,000 adults, (c) total for each type, and (d) rate per 10,000 adults for each type.

A comprehensive picture of citizen problems and dissatisfaction cannot be obtained by looking only at reported complaints (Measure C9). Findings in St. Petersburg, Nashville, and elsewhere have indicated that sometimes more than half of the complaints are not reported (see Measure C8). Thus, a more thoroughgoing assessment of the level of citizen problems and dissatisfaction—and changes in that level over time—can be obtained by looking at the sum of reported and unreported complaints.

The estimated number of unreported complaints can be obtained as discussed under Measure C7, and the number of reported complaints as discussed under Measure C9. Measure C10 will be subject to the potential accuracy problems discussed in connection with each of those measures. However, if the focus is on tracking relative changes over time rather than the absolute number of reported plus unreported complaints, Measure C10 should be less vulnerable to these problems. The values of Measure C10 will also, inevitably, reflect the influence of external factors such as the emergence of new problems, changes in citizen expectations, and similar influences that the local government may not be able to control entirely. Whenever possible, such factors should be identified and their likely effects should be noted in reporting and interpreting this (and any other) measure. As with Measures C7, C8, and C9, the accuracy of Measure C10 will be enhanced if respondents to the household survey are asked to describe briefly their reported or unreported complaints, and if these descriptions are subsequently screened to delete clearly unjustifiable items.

The use of complaint rates per 10,000 adults, exposures, or clients will help produce "fairer" comparisons between different years or client groups (for example, in situations in which the sizes of the populations differ significantly). Rates for individual types of complaints can be calculated if the data on unreported complaints obtained in the general household survey provide enough detail to categorize them by type.

Measure C11: *Number of different complainants per 10,000 adults, expressed as (a) persons reporting complaints, per 10,000 adults, (b) persons with unreported complaints, per 10,000 adults, and (c) persons with reported or unreported complaints, per 10,000 adults.*

In contrast to previous measures that focus on the number of complaints, this measure indicates the number of *different persons* who have complained.[4] Measure C11 can be used to provide a supplementary perspective—or even an alternative—to Measures C7, C9, and C10. Measure C11 may actually be more accurate than these measures, as it avoids the details on the *number* of reported or unreported complaints from persons with more than one complaint. Measure C11 also helps to compensate for the presence of chronic complainers. Unlike Measures C7, C9, and C10, however, it provides less information about the frequency with which problems are being encountered. The latter information can be quite useful to a government for tracking progress in the prevention of complaint-provoking situations.

The data for this measure can be collected from the household survey using Questions 58 and 62 in Appendix 1. Alternatively, estimates of the number of different people who have *reported* complaints can be made by analyzing complaint records from the past year, if the records show the names of complainants. (Complainants, however, should not be *required* to provide their names; introducing such a requirement could discourage citizens from reporting legitimate complaints to government officials.) One way to do this would be to keep an alphabetical file of complaints by complainant and to divide the total number of complaints received in a year by the number of names in the file. Anonymous complaints should be filed separately and not included in the computation; the errors introduced by their exclusion should be small. Some computerized complaint-tracking systems keep track of whether a complainant has filed previous complaints. Such information can serve as a convenient basis for preparing Measure C11.

The accuracy of Measure C11 can be improved by screening out unjustifiable complaints, as described in conjunction with other complaint measures. The measure will, however, be affected by changes in the accessibility and perceived effectiveness of the complaint-processing system.

The Handling of Citizen Requests for Services and Information

Responding to requests for service and requests for information is a key responsibility for most local governments. Requests represent an important—perhaps *the* most important—way for citizens to access municipal services. Officials of one large city have estimated that citizen requests generate between 20 and 30 percent of the city's work.

The processing of citizen requests for services and information generally addresses the following objective:

> **To provide a convenient and effective mechanism for receiving, responding to, and, when technically and legally possible, satisfactorily fulfilling citizen requests for service and information with speed, fairness, and courtesy.**

This objective is similar to those suggested in connection with citizen complaints except that the volume of requests (and its increase or decrease) is not considered to be an aspect of request-processing effectiveness. Although the volume of requests for service and information is clearly important for planning and budgeting, neither increasing nor decreasing the volume of those requests appears to represent an explicit government objective.

The relevant effectiveness measures for handling requests are summarized in Exhibit 11-4. Although the following discussion is primarily in terms of requests for services, the measures also can be used for assessing the handling of requests for information. Measures for requests for service probably should be computed and displayed separately from measures for requests for information because the two activities have significant operational differences (including the volumes handled, the response times involved, the efforts required, and the completeness of the records maintained).

The request measures (R1–R6) are similar to the complaint measures C1–C6. Since much of the discussion of those complaint measures and the associated data collection procedures applies to the request measures presented here, it will not be repeated. See the discussions of the corresponding complaint measures for more detailed information.

One important difference between complaint and request measures is that the latter depend on an analysis of *all* types of citizen requests—not just those considered justifiable. The stated objective includes good treatment for *all* citizen communications, even those that seem irrelevant or unjustifiable. Because quality treatment includes appropriate referrals for matters beyond the government's jurisdiction and adequate explanations even when unreasonable requests must be refused, the measures should cover the disposition of all requests.

A number of jurisdictions use computerized complaint/request-tracking systems to record *all* citizen communications, including requests for information. Such a system can greatly facilitate the preparation—and accuracy—of the request measures described here. Local governments that do not have such a system, and have too many requests to track, can instead collect data on a random sample of requests or certain types of requests of special significance.

Measure R1: Percentage of requests for (a) service, (b) information that were (or were not) disposed of satisfactorily, as judged by government personnel, by type of request, and, when appropriate, by type of unsatisfactory response.

A practical procedure for defining requests disposed of satisfactorily from the standpoint of the local government is to include only those cases in which the original request was fulfilled or, if fulfillment was infeasible, an "approved" reason was given. Such reasons might include the following: requested service not provided by the government; government

---

Exhibit 11-4

Suggested Objectives and Measures of Effectiveness for Handling Citizen Requests for Services and Information

Objective: To provide a convenient and effective mechanism for receiving, responding to, and, when technically and legally possible, satisfactorily fulfilling citizen requests for service and information with speed, fairness, and courtesy.

Objective or quality characteristic addressed	Specific request measure	Data collection source or procedure
Satisfactory response to, and fulfillment of, requests for service and information (from government's perspective [R1] and citizen's perspective [R2])	R1. Percentage of requests for (a) service, (b) information that were (or were not) disposed of satisfactorily, as judged by government personnel, by type of request, and, when appropriate, by type of unsatisfactory response.	Government records of citizen requests, perhaps incorporating some modifications
	R2. Percentage of requests for (a) services, (b) information that were (or were not) disposed of satisfactorily, as judged by requester, by type of request, and, when appropriate, by major reason for dissatisfaction.	A survey of requesters (Questions 5a, 5b, 5c, and 5d in Appendix 9) or, less desirably, a general household survey (see Appendix 1, Questions 59c, 60c, and 61c—especially Responses 2, 3, 4, and 8). For data on requests for information, "test" requests by participant observers can be used.
Speedy disposition of requests for service and information	R3. Median response time for each type of service and information request received.	Government records
	R4. Number and percentage of (a) requests for service received during the past year for which the response time exceeded, for example, 10 working days, (b) requests for information received during the past year for which the response time exceeded, for example, 1 day (grouped or identified by type of request).	Government records
Quality treatment of persons requesting service or information	R5. Percentages of persons who have requested service or information who rate the following aspects of their treatment as satisfactory (or unsatisfactory): (a) speed and timeliness of response, (b) absence of red tape, "run-around," and similar bureaucratic inconveniences or complexities, (c) fairness of treatment, (d) courtesy, helpfulness, and general attitude of government personnel.	Household survey (Appendix 1, Questions 59c, 60c, and 61c, especially Responses 5–7) or survey of requesters (Appendix 9, Questions 7–11). "Test" requests by participant observers can be used for data on requests for information.
Convenient intake of citizen requests	R6. Percentages of citizens who (a) *filed* a request or (b) *did not file* a request who found it difficult or impossible to request services or information, grouped by type of difficulty encountered.	Household survey (Appendix 1, Questions 59c, 60c, and 61c [Responses 5 and 6] and Question 63). Data from the perspective of persons who *have* made a request also can be obtained from a survey of requesters (Appendix 9, Questions 2, 2a, and 8) or from "test" requests for information made by participant observers.

regulations or ordinances prohibit complying with the request; circumstances make the requester ineligible to receive the service; or the service already has been scheduled for delivery at a future date (as in the case of major road improvements or other planned facilities). Requests that were still pending or referred to other organizations because of the local government's lack of jurisdiction in the matter should be considered ambiguous; all other dispositions can be assumed to be unsatisfactory.

The results for Measure R1 should be reported separately for different types of requests, for example, according to the nature of the request, the department responsible, and the urgency of the matter.

To help officials identify what remedial efforts are needed, jurisdictions should group requests not responded to satisfactorily by the kind of unsatisfactory response, for example, no information available (but should have been); refusals without adequate explanations or referrals; promises made and ignored; or incorrect responses (provision of the wrong service, erroneous or out-of-date information, or faulty or ineffective service).

Pending requests cannot be considered to have been disposed of satisfactorily *or* unsatisfactorily. However, for purposes of Measure R1, a separate analysis should be made of the percentage of pending requests—by type—to ensure that poorly handled items are not concealed from Measure R1 by remaining in the "pending" category indefinitely.

The accuracy of this measure depends largely on the extent to which the request and its outcome are accurately documented. When the accuracy of the recorded information is in doubt (or records of requests are not maintained), the government may want to flag a sample of requests as they come in and follow them up using other government records and interviews with both the requesters and the government personnel who handled the matters.

Measure R2: Percentage of requests for (a) service, (b) information that were (or were not) disposed of satisfactorily, as judged by requester, by type of request, and, when appropriate, by major reason for dissatisfaction.

Data for Measure R2 can best be obtained by a special survey of requesters, using a question such as Question 5a in Appendix 9. Obtaining the names and telephone numbers of requesters for such a follow-up poses complications. For some requests, the government will need to record this information to satisfy the request. In other cases, this will not be so. If the government undertakes a household survey, citizens' satisfaction with the responses to their requests

for services or information can be measured using a question such as Question 59C of Appendix 1. However, as discussed previously in connection with the complaint measures, only a small portion of those sampled in such a survey are likely to have requested services or information in the previous twelve (or three) months. The small number of requesters in the sample limits the possibility of comparing responses by type of request, client group, or reason for dissatisfaction. Jurisdictions may want to experiment with both data collection approaches to determine which is more practical for their own circumstances.

When surveying requesters, the government also should identify the reasons, if any, for the citizens' dissatisfaction with the handling of their requests by including questions such as Question 5b, 5c, and 5d from Appendix 9 in a survey of requesters, or Question 59C from Appendix 1 for a household survey. This information can help officials to identify correctable problems.

Follow-up surveys of persons who have requested information may be especially difficult because of the impracticality of collecting names, addresses, and telephone numbers of requesters. One alternative is to use participant-observers trained to assess the satisfactoriness of the government's responses to "test" requests made by the observer. The test requests must be selected with care to ensure that they adequately reflect the type and variety of requests for information usually received.

Measure R3: Median response time for each type of service and information request received.

The median response time indicates the interval likely to be required for processing a request, from initial receipt to final fulfillment or other disposition. Median response times should be broken down by type of request (such as the urgency or nature of the request) and by agency responsible. As discussed under Measure C3, the primary data collection procedure would be the analysis of government records. Many of the computerized complaint/request-processing packages used by local governments to track requests also compute the response time associated with each item. This feature can greatly facilitate the preparation of Measure R3 (although few packages actually determine the median; at most they provide the *average* response time, a figure that tends to be overly sensitive to a few extreme cases).

Measure R4: Number and percentage of (a) requests for service received during the past year for which the response time exceeded, for example, 10 working days, and

(b) requests for information received during the past year for which the response time exceeded, for example, 1 day (grouped or identified by type of request).

The determination of what constitutes an "excessive" response time will depend on the nature of the request for service or for information—ten working days may be appropriate for some services, one day for some information requests. The same records and procedures used to collect information for Measure R3 can be used as the basis for calculating this measure.

Measure R5: Percentages of persons who have requested service or information who rate the following aspects of their treatment as satisfactory (or unsatisfactory): (a) speed and timeliness of response, (b) absence of red tape, "run-around," and similar bureaucratic inconveniences or complexities, (c) fairness of treatment, (d) courtesy, helpfulness, and general attitude of government personnel.

This measure is designed to profile information on various specific attributes (other than the actual disposition of the request) associated with the quality of the local government's request-handling process as perceived by the requester. Such attributes include the timeliness of the process, the absence of red tape or run-around, and the fairness, courtesy, helpfulness, and attitude of the government personnel with whom the requester has dealt. As discussed under Measure C5, Questions 7 through 11 in Appendix 9 can be used in a survey of requesters; if a household survey is undertaken, a question such as 59C in Appendix 1 can be used. The problems with surveys of requesters, as well as the possible alternative of using "participant-observers," were discussed under Measure R2.

Measure R6: Percentages of citizens who (a) filed a request or (b) did not file a request who found it difficult or impossible to request services or information, grouped by type of difficulty encountered.

Measure R6 provides information on the accessibility of the request system and reasons for inaccessibility, some of which the government may be able to ameliorate. Accessibility is evaluated from two perspectives—that of citizens who *have* requested services or information, and that of citizens who *have not* made such requests.

The best method for collecting data on Measure R6 is a household survey. (Indeed, a household survey seems to be the *only* way to obtain accessibility ratings from persons who have not filed requests.) Questions from Appendix 1 can be used to provide such information—Question 59C, Response 6 (for requesters) and Question 63, Responses 3-6 (for persons inhibited from filing a request).

Two other alternatives for obtaining accessibility information from the perspective of persons who *have* made requests are a survey of requesters and a selection of "test" requests made by trained participant-observers. As discussed previously with other measures, a survey of requesters is usually a better way to obtain detailed information on reasons for inaccessibility than a household survey since the latter is likely to include few respondents who actually requested services or information. Questions 2, 2a, and 8 from the survey of requesters in Appendix 9 can be used to learn about accessibility.

The participant-observer approach to collecting information on accessibility involves rating government responses to carefully selected "test" requests. These requests are made by persons trained to rate various features of the government's response using precisely defined scales (for example, how easy it was to get through, the number of intra- or interagency referrals experienced, how long it took to get someone to accept responsibility for providing assistance). Such tests may be especially useful in connection with requests for information, since the volume or nature of such requests prevents many governments from obtaining the requester's address or telephone number, thus precluding the use of a follow-up survey.

The results for Measure R6 should be broken out by type of difficulty reported, for example, did not know how or where to file a request, unable to file (for example, no telephone, local government offices too far away), lines always busy, filing procedures too demanding, too many referrals, and so forth. Such information can help identify barriers faced by citizens and areas needing improvement. Survey results also should be grouped by respondent characteristics—age, education, income, race or ethnic group, handicaps, and so forth—to check for potential inequities in accessibility.

Note that if a survey of households is used to prepare Measure R6, the government can compute the *overall* percentage of persons who found it difficult or impossible to file a request (including both requesters and those who have not made requests). Computational procedures are described under Measure C6.

Special Data Collection Considerations

The suggested measures of effectiveness for the handling of citizen complaints and requests for services and information depend on data from three major sources: a household survey of citizens, a survey of a sample of persons who have complained or requested services or information, and government records of the complaints and requests processed. "Tests" by participant-observers are suggested as an alternate approach for collecting data on the handling of requests for information. Readers are referred to Chapter 13 for a more extensive discussion of the procedures and problems associated with undertaking household surveys. This chapter discusses some additional considerations especially pertinent to the examination of complaint and request handling.

The Household Survey

Ten of the seventeen measures proposed in this chapter rely on at least some data from a household survey. A household survey seems to be the only practical way to obtain certain information such as the incidence of unreported complaints or reasons for not reporting complaints or requests for services.

Appendix 1 contains an illustrative set of questions for obtaining information on the handling of citizen complaints and requests for services and information, using a multiservice household survey. The specific measures addressed by each question are noted in the left margin.

Open-ended questions (such as Question 59 in Appendix 1) asking the respondent to describe the complaint briefly will complicate the coding and analysis of the data. Yet such questions provide information for at least a rough verification of whether the complaints are justifiable. The information obtained also can be used to provide a useful breakdown of the nature of the complaints and requests. Questions such as Question 59a provide data for determining where citizens tend to take their complaints or requests and, when cross-tabulated with the responses to other questions, also permit limited analysis of the performance of each office.

Citizens may be dissatisfied if told that the local government has no authority to handle their concerns. Question 59b provides information to check for such a situation. Cross-tabulations of these questions with the corresponding questions on citizen satisfaction (such as Question 59C) can indicate if dissatisfaction is related to whether or not a problem is within the local government's jurisdiction.

One persistent unresolved issue is how long citizens can accurately remember complaints or requests. For instance, will persons tend to remember only complaints and requests from the last several months, thus underestimating the number of items in a twelve-month period? One way to alleviate this problem is to reduce the recall period to six months or three months and to conduct surveys more frequently.

Another approach is to focus on the number of persons or households that complain rather than the number of complaints (that is, on Measure C11 rather than Measures C7, C9, and C10) since data on complainants is probably less affected by memory lapses. It is important to keep the same time period, whatever it is, from survey to survey so that changes will be attributable to different conditions rather than to variations in how much respondent memories are taxed.

Household surveys generally should be contracted to a professional survey firm. To keep down the cost for any one agency, the surveys should cover more than one government service—as suggested in other chapters. Appendix 1 is an example of such a multiservice survey questionnaire.

Other special issues in implementing a household survey for collecting data on the handling of citizen complaints and requests are discussed below.

Special Interviewer Instructions. Interviewers should be given special instructions for administering the survey regarding citizen complaints and requests. For instance, they should be taught:

- How to count distinct problems or matters (see Question 58a in Appendix 1). Repeated calls on the same item should not be counted as separate problems. For example, three calls to rectify a single missed trash collection is one situation, but three calls to rectify three separate missed trash collections should be counted as three situations. One call to report three separate problems (noise, water bill, missed collection) equals three situations.
- Which offices or organizations are and are not part of the local government
- When multiple responses (such as several reasons for dissatisfaction) may be recorded
- How to define each of the response options (for instance, how to distinguish "took too long" from "too much run-around" in Question 59C in Appendix 1).

Analyzing and Presenting the Survey Findings. The local government should prepare the cross-tabulations needed to make full use of the information obtained (for instance, to analyze citizen satisfaction in terms of the department initially contacted, the subject of the complaint or request, or the demographic characteristics of the complainants and requesters—where available). Any of a number of widely available computerized statistical packages can be used to ease the computational burdens. An analyst should review, classify, and encode the various open-ended responses according to the definitions and distinctions agreed upon by government officials. Information on survey results from other jurisdictions also can be helpful in interpreting the data.

Survey of Complainants and Requesters of Services

As noted earlier, a "client" survey can be especially useful for obtaining information on government services, including satisfaction with the government's responses, ratings of various aspects of the service, and client characteristics. The complainant-requester survey can be administered by telephoning a randomly selected sample of persons who have contacted the local government to complain or to request service or information, if the telephone numbers of such persons are available. Alternatively, a questionnaire can be mailed to all (or a sample of) clients. If a government wants to use such a survey to identify operating conditions needing correction, frequent polls (monthly, if possible) of complainants and/or requesters would be needed.

Client surveys often can be administered at low cost. If existing government personnel have time to serve as interviewers (a total of about 250 employee-hours would be required for an annual sample of about 800 "clients," calling 200 clients every quarter), the survey could be conducted without significant additional outlays. Mail surveys require less time but to achieve reasonable response rates (at least 50 percent), second mailings (and perhaps telephone calls) will be needed.

The data from a client survey may be subject to subtle biases to which a household survey would not be subject. Records on complainants or requesters (from which the sample is drawn) may not include complaints or requests from all the departments that have actually received them. Those records that *are* available may reflect various degrees of screening by government personnel who perhaps chose not to record what they viewed as "unjustifiable" requests. Sometimes numerous anonymous complaints or requests may be encountered. Systematic biases such as these should be identified and corrected, where possible.

An example of an appropriate client survey for complainants and requesters is presented in Appendix 9. It requires about ten minutes to complete. Note that at the end of the interview, the interviewer asks demographic questions similar to those on a household survey, for cross-tabulating the results by population subgroups.

Some additional considerations in implementing a survey of complainants and requesters are discussed in the following sections.

Sample Selection. The sample should be drawn from a listing of all the persons who have made complaints or requested services or information in the time period of concern. Enough names should be drawn to provide 50 to 100 *responses* for each category of concern—for example, for each department whose effectiveness is of special interest, for each specific problem about which the government wants detailed information, and so forth. Separate samples should be drawn for complaints, requests for service, and requests for information (if each is to be examined). One option is to sample requests and complaints in each department by using the relevant files. The government might begin with the departments that handle the most complaints or requests.

Central complaint or request files also may constitute an adequate listing. But if some departments are not included in those files or if individual departments vary in their thoroughness in reporting complaints to the central office, a sample of central files may not be representative of all citizens who have had contacts with the local government. Perhaps the best way to obtain a satisfactory sample is to implement uniform record-keeping procedures for all departments handling complaints or requests. Such procedures, however, must not be so demanding as to interfere with the servicing of the complaints or requests received.

A related issue in drawing the sample is the *age* of the records. Contacting persons about a week after the government has disposed of their complaint or request is most desirable. This period gives the citizen time to reflect on the results but not to forget. Such a procedure requires spreading the interviews over a number of weeks. To avoid biases, the sample should not be limited to persons who contacted the government during one particular week but should include citizens who contacted the government throughout the year.

If some subjects tend to crowd out items of special interest, the local government can oversample the less common complaints. However, care must be taken in analyzing such a stratified sample; results cannot be simply lumped together and averaged to obtain an overall effectiveness measurement.

In view of the complexity of drawing a client sample, sample selection and the establishment of a detailed sampling procedure should probably be done with the help of a person with statistical sampling experience.

Anonymity of Citizens Who Make Complaints or Requests. Follow-up surveys of complainants and requesters require information on the identity of citizens making complaints and requests so that they can be contacted. A significant proportion of anonymous complaints or requests may bias the survey sample in unknown ways.

Government Records of Citizen Complaints and Requests

The third important data collection procedure is the use of local government records. Although complaint and request files in many jurisdictions contain considerable information, they probably will not include certain kinds of data—especially on dispositions— needed for some of the suggested effectiveness measures. Revisions in the forms used, changes in filing procedures, and implementation of certain special data collection procedures may be needed to improve the description and classification of requests and complaints, permit tallies of the number of complaints and the determinations of response times, and encourage consistent assessments (by local government personnel) of the disposition of complaints and requests.

Revisions of Forms and Records. Local government officials must first determine what information is to be collected and for what purpose each piece of information is needed. The officials also must agree on and formalize the many definitions and distinctions needed. What constitutes a complaint, a request for service, or a request for information? When is a complaint justifiable? How should various types of complaints be defined? What will be accepted as a "satisfactory" disposition? Exhibit 11-1 presents some suggestions for such definitions.

The use of a single form by all agencies for reporting complaints and requests for services would simplify the paperwork and reduce the burden on personnel for making accurate distinctions. Forms for recording complaints and service requests should contain at least the following information: the citizen's name, address, and telephone number; identification of the matter as a complaint or a request; the general subject; a description of the specific complaint or request; an indication of its urgency; the location of the matter; the agency receiving the complaint or request; the agency responding to it; a judgment as to the justifiability of a complaint; the government's jurisdiction over the matter; the disposition of the complaint or request; and the response time.

Revised Filing Procedures. Alphabetical and tickler files for government complaint and request records can be helpful in gathering data for the proposed measures, as well as for other management purposes.

Filing procedures and data retrieval methods will be somewhat different from those described here if the local government's record keeping is computerized, in which case the computer will be able to do most of the work. The two types of files are as follows:

- Alphabetical files of complaints and service requests. Complaint records should be filed alphabetically (by the last name of the complainant). A high percentage of anonymous complainants will complicate this approach. Care should be taken not to violate client confidentiality; the filing of complaints by the last name of the complainant should be used only to provide a means for conveniently computing the average number of complaints per complainant for Measure C11. Separate files should be kept for complaints and for service requests. Requests need not be filed alphabetically since no estimates of the number of requests per requester are needed. New files should be started every fiscal year and retained for at least twelve months after the end of that fiscal year to facilitate annual data analysis. A complete file probably will not be feasible for requests for information because of the large numbers involved; instead, only a random sample of the information requests received might be retained in the files.

- Tickler files. Copies of all pending complaints and requests should be filed in a "tickler file" by the date the matter was first reported or the date when a response is due. When the complaint or request is resolved, a summary of the disposition of the matter should be returned by the various offices involved, at which time the corresponding complaint or request record should be removed from the tickler file. These copies can then be held in special files such as "complaints by type" or "requests by agency responsible" until the appropriate periodic tabulations can be prepared. Regular examinations of the tickler files can serve as a basis for prodding agencies about tardy responses and for conveniently preparing Measures C4 and R4 ("items delayed longer than x days").

Special Data Collection Procedures. Running tallies prepared on a daily or weekly basis (and subtotaled monthly) are a convenient way to routinely collect the information needed for reporting on measures that require data only from government records (Measures C1, C3, C4, C9, R1, R3, and R4). An important advantage of using running tallies is that the preparation—and perhaps the use—of the measures becomes a regular activity, rather than the focus of a concentrated effort once or twice a year; the latter approach is often disruptive and may use personnel inefficiently.

If a high volume of complaints and requests presents a problem for preparing running tallies or storing records, the local government might retain only randomly selected samples of the records for measurement purposes.

The classifications made by government personnel should be monitored periodically to ensure consistency with the definitions that have been established. If deviations are noted, additional (or refined) definitions, guidelines, or training may be necessary.

Reporting the Findings

Much information will be generated by the proposed measures, particularly if some are categorized by complaint and population characteristics.

Exhibit 11-5 illustrates a format for summarizing the effectiveness information for complaints and requests. If the local government decides to set annual performance targets, the format of Exhibit 11-5 can be modified to provide a comparison of "actual" versus "targeted" achievements.

If measurement data are categorized by various population subgroup characteristics, a local government will be able to detect whether certain groups seem to be getting better services—or having more problems—than others; such information might indicate inequities and a need for service revisions. For many of the proposed measures, data on the location and sex of the complainant or requester will be available, permitting disaggregation by neighborhood of residence and by sex. Other demographic characteristics (such as age group, income group, and race or ethnic group) are likely to be available only for certain measures (those utilizing survey procedures routinely collect such information).

A special case occurs for Measure 8, "the proportion of complaints that are reported." If the necessary data on reported complaints are obtained from local government records, information on characteristics such as income or race or ethnic group will not usually be available. Breakouts by such characteristics can be made, however, if the alternate data collection procedure for Measure C8—a household survey—is used.

When analyzing effectiveness measures that use sampling techniques, government personnel will need to consider the statistical accuracy associated

---

Exhibit 11-5

Illustrative Format for Exhibiting Measures of Effectiveness for Complaint and Request Handling

Objective and measure	City-wide total			Neighborhood area (current period)				
	Prior period	Current period	Percentage change	Central	North-east	North-west	South-east	South-west
Reduction or prevention of justifiable citizen complaints								

Number of justifiable complaints received during the past year (Measure C8), expressed as:
a. City total
b. Total for each type:
    Problem 1
    Problem 2
c. Overall rates:
    Per 10,000 adults
    Sanitation complaints per 1,000 garbage accounts
    Utility bill complaints per 1,000 accounts
d. Rate per 10,000 adults, for each type								

Willingness and ability of citizens to make their complaints known to the government								

Total number of reported and unreported complaints during the past year (Measure C9), expressed as:
a. City total
b. Total for each type:
    Problem 1
    Problem 2
c. Rate per 10,000 adults								

with the particular sample sizes used. This step determines the degree to which observed differences might have been due to the "luck" of the sample drawn rather than to real differences in the entire population of interest. Some of these issues are discussed further in the chapter on customer surveys.

Business Community Coverage

The business community is a special clientele group receiving many local government services (see Chapter 14). The same basic service quality considerations of interest to private citizens regarding government handling of complaints and requests apply to the business community. The local government can easily distinguish those complaints and requests that come from the business community. Procedures similar to those used for complaints and requests of private citizens (for record keeping, household surveys, and complainant/requester surveys) can be used for complaints and requests from the business community. A survey of a random sample of businesses, for example, would replace the survey of households. Questions 40 through 43 of the business community survey questionnaire in Appendix 2 constitute an appropriate set of questions on complaints and requests for a survey of business officials.

Staffing Requirements

Staff time will vary according to the volume of complaints and requests, the frequency of conducting client surveys (and the sample sizes chosen), the availability of computer facilities, and the degree of centralization among the complaint- and request-processing operations. Because it is not generally practical for local governments to undertake a household survey solely for the complaint- and request-handling function, it is assumed here that any such survey will cover numerous local services and that the additional cost for including questions on complaints and requests will be very small.

A part-time coordinator will probably be needed to supervise the data collection for the complaint and request measures and the computation of the various measures, to deal with departments that have their own units for handling citizen complaints and requests, and to help analyze and interpret the results. This work should take about four employee-days per month; a few additional employee-days will

be needed occasionally to prepare quarterly and annual measurement reports.

For telephone surveys of clients, one or two part-time interviewers should be trained; they should be expected to administer about three surveys per staff-hour. (With 300 interviews per quarter, this would require about 100 hours of interview time per quarter.) Some evening survey work is likely to be necessary. Mail surveys require considerably less staff time—primarily clerical time for processing two or three mailings, with a small amount of telephone time to bring response rates to acceptable levels.

For either telephone or mail client surveys, an outside expert will probably be needed to instruct the interviewers in survey techniques, and an analyst will be required from time to time to handle computer runs, prepare measurements, run cross-tabulations, and the like. Also, a person with knowledge of survey sampling will be needed to help determine sample sizes and develop procedures for drawing the sample of clients to be interviewed. The length of time needed to draw the sample depends largely on the way the records are kept.

---

1 There is a growing body of research on the nature and significance of citizen-initiated contacts (including complaints and requests) involving local governments. See, for instance, Coulter, *Political Voice: Citizen Demand for Urban Public Services*; Sharp, *Citizen Demand-Making in the Urban Context*; Percy and Scott, *Demand Processing and Performance in Public Service Agencies*; and Jones, *Service Delivery in the City*.

2 A four-state survey of 184 midwestern cities and towns with populations over 10,000 found that complaints constituted the most popular method for monitoring contracted services (65 percent of the respondents used complaints for that purpose). See Rehfuss, "Contracting Out and Accountability in State and Local Governments—The Importance of Contract Monitoring."

3 Examination of the results of a 1973 St. Petersburg survey indicated that of 232 unreported complaints, 70 percent appeared to be valid and within the city's jurisdiction, while 25 percent did not (validity could not be established for 5 percent). In addition, 31 percent of the justifiable complaints cited no specific city problem or objectionable action; many, for instance, indicated a general dislike of certain city policies. Under some definitions of "justifiability" (see Exhibit 11-1), general complaints like these, which are nonspecific or unrealistic, or for which action is either not required or impossible, might be classed as "unjustified" for measurement purposes.

4 Surveys conducted in Nashville and St. Petersburg in 1973 and 1974 indicated that there were approximately 1½ reported complaints per person complaining.

Chapter 12

Trained Observer Rating Procedures

his chapter presents basic procedures for using specially trained observers to obtain objective rating data for particular conditions. For example, trained observers can rate street and alley cleanliness, road and traffic control maintenance, housing conditions, community appearance, park and school building maintenance, and the condition of food establishments. The examples in this chapter are taken from Chapters 2 ("Solid Waste Collection"), 3 ("Solid Waste Disposal"), 4 ("Park and Recreation Services"), and 8 ("General Transportation Services").

Trained observer ratings enable local governments to quantify conditions from either a sample of locations or all locations in the community. Comparisons can then be made among conditions in different neighborhoods at any given time, or among conditions in the same neighborhood or the whole community at different times, to measure changes. After appropriate training, different persons acting at different times and using the same photographic and/or written guidelines and rating procedures are able to produce comparable ratings. Photographic guidelines consist of several preselected photographs showing typical conditions that define a rating value. The ratings are made by the trained observers while they are walking or riding in an automobile moving at a slow speed. Observers compare the actual condition under observation to the photographic or written guidelines to determine which rating to assign. Other persons can readily understand these ratings, particularly if shown the guidelines used for making them.

If trained observer ratings of a number of measures are undertaken simultaneously, the costs of collecting data for each measure are substantially reduced. If more than two or three conditions are to be measured from a moving vehicle at every inspection point, however, it is usually necessary to have another observer in the vehicle to share the rating tasks.[1]

A number of factors should be considered in making decisions on using trained observers and in implementing and supervising a trained observer program. These factors are discussed below.

Reliability: Can Independent Observers Consistently Arrive at the Same Ratings?

All ratings should be made following carefully developed written guidelines and photographic standards that enable observers to assign discrete grades to conditions (such as 1.0, 2.0, 3.0, or 4.0 with intermediate 0.5-point ratings when an observer cannot decide on a whole number rating). Agencies should seek about 70 percent of second ratings of the same condition to be in exact agreement with the first and 85 percent of the second ratings to be within no more than one point on a scale with four or fewer whole number grades. Experience in training programs in Nashville, St. Petersburg, and Washington, D.C., showed that in most cases two or more persons applying the guidelines and standards could achieve these agreement levels. Greenville, South Carolina, in 1991 achieved an 87 percent agreement within one point of each other.

Several factors that can cause observers to rate conditions improperly include:

- Forgetfulness—observers may inadvertently apply modified guidelines if they fail to refer frequently enough to the standard. Or, observers who have several different conditions to rate at once may forget to record one of the ratings.
- Boredom or fatigue—these can cause observers to fail to examine all the characteristics that need to be considered in assigning a rating.
- Excessive speed, visual obstructions, parked vehicles, or traffic—these can cause observers to miss conditions.

- Inability to take the strain of driving and rating, or perhaps inability to read maps or to navigate.
- Cheating—observers falsify ratings to avoid the rigors of inspection.

How well these problems can be avoided or overcome will depend on the quality of the inspection personnel, the adequacy of the training program, and the comprehensiveness of supervision. A high degree of accuracy can be maintained only if the supervisors repeat a sample of ratings made by observers for quality control (perhaps 5 percent of each observer's ratings) and discuss any differences the same day the ratings are made. Corrections (retraining or replacement) should be made quickly, and supervisors should have latitude in selecting and removing persons for the inspection task; not everyone makes a good trained observer.

Establishing a Trained Observer Rating System

Four steps are needed to establish an operational trained observer rating system.

Step 1. Develop and Document Explicit Definitions for the Grades for Each Condition to Be Measured

The heart of the trained observer rating system is a set of written and photographic guidelines that enables observers to assign a grade or numerical rating to each condition being evaluated. The guidelines should be specific, thorough, and clearly documented. All observers should have their own copies for use when making their ratings. The guidelines will, in general, consist of several photographs of typical scenes with litter (or whatever condition is being rated) and/or a written description of the conditions that constitute a particular rating. The guidelines should:

- Define the area to be inspected
- Identify the items or conditions that determine the ratings
- Cover the entire range of conditions likely to be encountered
- Be sufficiently precise and detailed that the trained observer using the guidelines can make accurate ratings with a minimum of guesswork and a high degree of consistency
- Provide at most four or possibly five major rating points (1.0, 2.0, 3.0, 4.0, and, perhaps, 5.0)
- Cover conditions that are of concern to the particular department. A combined rating that includes the cleanliness of the street (responsibility of the sanitation department) and the cleanliness of the front yard (responsibility of zoning for enforcing an antilittering ordinance) would be of less value to either department than separate ratings
- Be in a looseleaf notebook, or similar device, for easy updating and quick reference during inspection.

Examples of guidelines for street cleanliness and various street transportation-related conditions are presented in Appendix 10. (Examples for solid waste disposal and parks maintenance are shown in the chapters on those subjects and Appendices 3 and 6.) Communities that adopt guidelines such as these should modify them to make them conform to their own conditions. A procedure for developing guidelines is illustrated in Exhibit 12-1.

Step 2. Develop and Document Procedures for Selecting Inspection Locations, Directing Inspectors, Recording Data, and Transcribing and Processing Data

Inspections based on rating only a sample of blocks, or street lanes (or whatever) require a method for selecting the sample at random. The planning department or some other government agency may have assigned numbers to the blocks or block faces in the jurisdiction, from which a random sample can be selected. If no such numbering exists, it will be necessary to assign numbers to each unit to be rated, perhaps numbering them in each census tract. For litter, it is preferable to number each block face and each alley, rather than each block (the number of block faces and alleys is likely to vary substantially from one block to another). This practice ensures that each block face (or alley) has an equal probability of being selected and that ratings of the sample will be statistically representative of the conditions in an entire area.

Good maps are needed for marking the locations for inspection and for laying out routes for inspectors to follow before they go into the field. In Washington, D.C., maps with a scale of approximately 1 in. = 650 ft. were most appropriate for directing inspectors rating all blocks; maps with a scale of 1 in. = 1,400 ft. were most appropriate for a sampling inspection. The maps should be current and should show alleys as well as streets.

Observers can enter rating data on a written form or they can dictate the data into a small cassette recorder for later transcription. The recorder facilitates further notations observers should make of any unusual conditions or situations requiring immediate agency attention. Thus, these trained observer ratings also can provide the agency with "needs assessment" information. As the technology develops, direct entry of findings into a hand-held computer will enable more efficient and much quicker data processing.

In addition to recording street and alley cleanliness ratings, the observers also can identify abandoned autos, dead animals, evicted families, illegal dumps, exceptionally littered vacant lots, overflowing public refuse containers, and missed collections. These conditions can then be reported to appropriate government agencies for prompt attention. Transcribing tapes requires more clerical labor than handling written forms. Moreover, unless observers refer frequently to a checklist for the items to be rated, they are apt to forget to record some data at inspection points where more than one condition is being rated.

The data should be transcribed within 24 hours so that any unusual conditions—health or fire hazards or other problems noted above—can be handled promptly. This transcription can be done by clerical personnel or by the observers; such work provides a break from the routine of making inspections and seems to encourage trained observers to record ratings in an orderly manner. If automatic data processing is being used, the forms should be set up to aid input. Otherwise, the ratings can be summarized on ledger sheets, giving values of each measure by census tract, by service area, or by the geographic or clientele groupings that have been decided upon.

All procedures should be documented carefully, first, to help the trained observers in their work and, second, to assure that identical or compatible procedures are used for all inspections, thus allowing meaningful comparisons among areas and over long periods of time.

Step 3. Select and Train Observers

Inspecting is not difficult, but it can be tedious. Candidates should be reliable, capable of sustained motivation, and able to work alone for long periods when necessary. They must read maps well and be observant of details. Most applicants can learn to make inspections, but those who find the work difficult and distasteful should be replaced by others who enjoy

---

Exhibit 12-1

Suggested Procedure for Developing Trained Observer Guidelines

A. *Determine government responsibilities and set boundaries for inspections*

The responsibilities and jurisdictional limits of the government and individual departments need to be spelled out to assure that the trained observer system is used to rate conditions controllable by the government or particular department. For example, if street cleanliness is being measured and the particular department is responsible for cleaning only from curb to curb, the condition of the sidewalk would not need to be included in the litter rating. Ordinances and departmental regulations defining specific areas of responsibility should be reviewed.

B. *Document the full range of conditions throughout the areas of responsibility*

Two or three observers should travel throughout the jurisdiction to photograph and describe the full range of conditions that occur in the areas for which their department is responsible. Individual alleys, for example, should be photographed to illustrate gradations from the cleanest to the dirtiest; different types of litter should be noted. Any difficulties in distinguishing public from private sidewalks or in differentiating between blocks that have more than one alley should be noted, so that procedures can be developed to handle such situations consistently. The observers might take as many as 100 to 200 photographs of littered streets and alleys in a variety of neighborhoods and 25 to 50 photographs to illustrate other problems such as broken sidewalks or street sign problems.

C. *Select representative photographs and develop measurement guidelines*

The photographs should be examined to ascertain whether they cover the full range of conditions. If any gaps are discovered, additional photographs should be taken. Five to ten persons not associated with the project should independently review and classify each photograph as representing one of significantly different condition gradations, such as those running from excellent to poor. A four-category, or four-point, scale will usually be sufficient for grading photographs of street pavement conditions or litter, although a five-point scale might be appropriate in some jurisdictions with areas that have extremely rough pavement or exceptional amounts of litter. A three-point scale will generally be sufficient for rating street and traffic signs and sidewalk pavement conditions. Three to five photographs that are generally agreed on as representative of each category should then be selected to be the rating standard for the category.

Persons responsible for developing the measurements should then review the photographs to confirm that they cover the range of conditions. Additional photographs should be taken if required to distinguish further between the two middle-range categories, in which judgments are most difficult. Definitions to accompany the different photographic groups should also be prepared.

D. *Test the photographic categories and guidelines; document the rating scales*

The photographs and tentative guidelines must be tested to make sure they produce consistent ratings and to determine if additional guidelines or photographs are needed for handling unusual situations. For each measure, several persons should independently make from 50 to 60 ratings at randomly selected locations throughout the community. Because the extreme ratings are easiest to make, particular attention must be paid to the middle categories. The test of the procedures is whether the raters, working independently and using the guidelines, agree on at least 90 percent of the ratings.

In evaluating the system, the following questions should be asked: (1) Did the raters agree? If not, were the disagreements caused by errors in judgment, inability of the raters to discriminate among conditions, or inadequate guidelines? (2) Were there conditions that the proposed system could not cover adequately? The system should provide a consistent procedure for rating every situation that arises. (3) Do the guideline definitions make sense? Are they practical in application? Once a scale has been developed, it should be clearly documented and reproduced in large enough quantities to provide individual sets to each trained observer and to all other persons concerned with the system.

the relatively independent field inspections and find the rating process interesting.

A variety of types of personnel can be used. St. Petersburg used environmental and sanitation inspectors; Nashville used summer interns from a local university; Washington, D.C., used existing

---

Exhibit 12-2

Sample Training Schedule for Trained Observers

Monday:	Instructors provide an overview of the rating system and the uses of the information collected. Distribute an inspection manual to each candidate. Verify drivers' permits. Discuss visual inspection rating procedures using photographic standards and written descriptions of conditions to be rated. Introduce maps and map routing. Discuss all items to be observed and recorded. Discuss data recording (using sheets or tape recorders) and explain codes for special items. Allow time for candidates to read inspection manual and ask questions.
Tuesday:	Instructors and candidates visit an inspection area, preferably in one vehicle. Make trial inspections together. After each inspection, discuss ratings in detail so that each candidate understands why the scene has a particular rating. Drive to different areas to rate a variety of conditions. Explain hazards in driving and reporting.
Wednesday:	Candidates travel again to the field in one or two vehicles. Each candidate makes independent ratings on a sample of streets and alleys selected to provide a variety of conditions. Give practice in map reading and navigation. Make reports on the same forms or tape recorders that will be used in regular inspections. Review ratings and discuss any problems. Reinspect any sites where there was substantial disagreement in ratings (off by one or more points). Discuss any problems or ways to handle unusual situations.
Thursday:	Candidates make independent inspections under conditions to be used in actual inspections. (If one person per vehicle is to be used for the actual inspections, then use one person per vehicle here.) All candidates rate the same set of streets and alleys. Compare the ratings. Review data recording procedures.
Friday:	Leaders review performance of each inspector candidate and discuss any problems. Review or retrain as necessary. By this time, at least 75 percent of the cleanliness ratings of each candidate should be in *exact* agreement with those of the trainer, who is the master judge, and 90 percent within one-half grade. At least 95 percent of the special conditions to be counted (such as health hazards and abandoned autos) should have been noted by each observer.

Note: For periodic retraining of inspectors a reduced version might consist of only the Tuesday and Wednesday sessions. Approximately six hours each day are needed.

Source: This training schedule is based on a schedule developed for the District of Columbia and described in Operations Analysis Division, Department of Environmental Services, *Supervisor's Manual for Visual Inspection and Report System* (Washington, D.C.: District of Columbia Government, January 1973).

---

sanitation department personnel; and New York City has employed ex-drug addicts. A sample training program and schedule are depicted in Exhibit 12-2. Alexandria and Charlottesville, Virginia, and Greenville, South Carolina, have used personnel from several city departments to work in the field, such as police, fire, parks, community development, and public works departments.

Step 4. Set Up a Procedure for Systematically Checking the Ratings of the Trained Observers
To maintain the reliability of the trained observer system, it is essential that observers understand that a randomly selected portion of their ratings will be checked by a supervisor and that if their ratings are inaccurate or incomplete they will be retrained or replaced. Replication is conducted by the supervisor, who reinspects sample blocks already graded by the observers, without the latter's knowing when or where the replications are to be made. About 5 percent of the ratings of each observer should be replicated. The supervisor then compares his or her ratings with those of the observers and calculates the percentage of agreement. Any inaccuracies should be discussed with the observer. The observers and the supervisor should reexamine any scene over which there was a rating disagreement of one or more points. If the rating system is to be valid, observers who cannot maintain specified rating accuracy levels (70 percent of ratings in agreement and 90 percent within one grade) should be retrained or replaced.

In addition to replicating ratings, the supervisor periodically should examine the rating sheets (or listen to the tapes) of the observers to make sure that observers are keeping to their routes and maintaining orderly notes on the rating information.

Cost of the Trained Observer Program

Costs vary according to the type and frequency of trained observer ratings and the geographical layout and flow of traffic in the community.

Principal cost elements include the following:

- *Sample versus complete inspections.* If a random sample is selected, travel time between points and perhaps some navigation problems will limit inspections to about fifty locations per day under the most favorable conditions. If a continuous inspection program is conducted with ratings made on every block, and there is virtually no extraneous travel time, up to 250 inspection points can be rated in a day by a single inspection team. However, overall, complete coverage will require considerably more personnel time than sampling.

- *Number of conditions to be rated on each block.* If more than two or three conditions are to be rated every time (street cleanliness, street pavement conditions, sidewalk pavement conditions, street signs on each block), two inspectors per vehicle will probably be needed.

- *Frequency of inspection and total number of locations inspected.* Some localities may want to make frequent inspections, perhaps every other week, as New York City does for street litter. Frequent inspection enables sanitation agencies to allocate their crews based on their most recent findings. For other services where conditions are not expected to change rapidly, less frequent observation (such as quarterly to obtain seasonal perspectives) will suffice. The timing of inspections also can be varied depending on the area of the community and on previous ratings. (For example, problem locations might be rated more frequently and locations with past good ratings, less frequently.)

- *Inspectors' time.* If these observations are considered part of employees' regular work, and can be fitted in with current staff availability, out-of-pocket costs will be nil. Similarly if volunteers or low-paid interns can be used for at least some of the inspection, costs will be reduced.

- *Clerical time.* About one employee-day of clerical personnel support time for transcribing rating data for data processing or for hand analysis, laying out routes, preparing maps, and the like, will be required for every two days of observer time; this estimate will be slightly less for multiple measurements.

- *Supervisory personnel wages.* About one employee-day of supervisory time for training and supervising observers including regularly replicating some of their inspections will be required for every four to six employee-days of inspection time.

- *Vehicle costs, including fuel and vehicle depreciation.* These costs can be estimated on the basis of the projected mileage for observers and supervisors.

- *Data processing costs.* Computer analyst time will be required to develop programs for processing data and developing user-friendly data printouts (tables and maps) to be used in periodic reports. Costs for individual reports should be small once the programs have been written.

- *Report preparation.* Trained observer data should be examined and interpreted.

Exhibit 12-3 presents estimated times for different trained observer rating operations. Multiple ratings produce some shared savings in clerical support and vehicle usage and report preparation. The costs of any of these inspection systems should be small compared to the annual costs of the activities being rated.

Exhibit 12-3

Time Estimates for Trained Observer Inspection Options

(Approximate annual time requirements for quarterly inspections in a locality with: 5,000 blocks; 1,500 alleys; 6 service areas)

Quarterly inspection options		Inspection for street and alley cleanliness only (1-person crew)	Inspection for street and alley cleanliness, street and sidewalk pavement condition, stop signs and other traffic signs, street name signs (2-person crew)
Sample: 50 blocks and 30 alleys inspected per service area (30 alleys or 40 blocks inspected per day)	Inspector	54 days	108 days
	Clerk	27 days	40 days
	Supervisor	18 days	20 days
	Total	99 days	168 days
Complete: (200 blocks or 75 alleys inspected per day)	Inspector	180 days	360 days
	Clerk	80 days	140 days
	Supervisor	36 days	60 days
	Total	296 days	560 days

Note: The first column (street and alley cleanliness) provides time for a single service (in this case, street cleaning). The times in the second column cover two services (street cleaning and road transportation); the two departments plan to share the costs.

Many agencies might choose a strategy not shown in Exhibit 12-3: To do even more frequent inspections (to help use inspection crews) but focus on only certain sections of the community—areas where most of the problems (e.g., litter) occur (these might be major commercial areas and high density population areas served by the agency).

1 During initial phases of development of the multiple trained observer rating procedure in Nashville, the driver and the rider each tried to rate five different items. Even when the observers stopped their vehicles at the end of blocks to allow time for completing the ratings, they suffered undue strain, frequently failed to record all data, and produced inconsistent ratings. Traffic in New York City was so congested that it was not considered prudent to have drivers make ratings. In other cities, however, traffic congestion, even in commercial areas, has not been so great as to prevent drivers from making ratings.

Chapter 13

Surveying Customers

A number of aspects of government service performance are nearly impossible to measure without obtaining direct feedback from the agency's customers. Surveys can provide *customer ratings* of various service characteristics. They can indicate the views and perceptions of citizens on such matters as security from crime, accessibility of particular services, timeliness of government actions, and the responsiveness of government employees to citizen requests and complaints.

Customer surveys also can yield certain types of *factual data* that are otherwise very difficult to obtain. Examples of such data include crime victimization rates (permitting the estimation of unreported as well as reported crime incidents); household participation rates in such services as recreation, library, and public transit (which permit an estimate of the number of different persons or households using and not using particular government programs—and estimates of the incidence of various reasons for nonuse); and the frequency of unreported citizen complaints. Of the performance indicators suggested for the various government services included in this volume, approximately one-third seem best obtained through customer surveys.

Local governments can use two kinds of customer surveys:

- Surveys that question persons who have used a particular service ("user" surveys)
- Surveys that question samples of households in the community about more than one service ("household" surveys).

Both have important advantages and disadvantages. The user survey is usually administered by the agency responsible for the service. This type of survey can:

- Obtain more comprehensive information on the service (the key advantage of user surveys)
- Be less complicated to administer since, for example, addresses and telephone numbers for the service's clients are likely to be available or clients can be readily surveyed at a public facility such as a library or recreation facility
- Achieve higher response rates, because the potential respondents, being service clients, have a personal interest in the service and are likely to respond.

Household surveys have the advantages that:

- They can obtain information from households that have not used the service, to identify reasons why those households have not used the service and to calculate the percentage of households using, and not using, such services as public transit, libraries, and recreational facilities, by reason for non-use if desired
- Their costs can be shared by several services and thus will be lower for each service
- Control of survey quality is easier because these surveys will be administered centrally (otherwise each agency must do or sponsor its own survey).

This chapter discusses procedural issues involved in customer surveys and their costs and accuracy. Appendix 1 contains an example of a multiservice household questionnaire. Appendix 4 is an example of a questionnaire for a household survey that focuses on only one service, parks and recreation (and, thus, can explore the service in considerable depth). Appendices 5, 7, 8, and 9 are examples of questionnaires for user surveys. Appendix 11 provides guidelines for local governments that contract for surveys for the purpose of effectiveness measurement.

Detailed survey methodology is not discussed in this report as there are numerous works available on conducting surveys.[1]

Fortunately, modern survey techniques permit governments to obtain generally valid and reliable information at reasonable cost. These techniques make possible the interviewing of small portions of the population (perhaps only a few hundred persons) to obtain rough, but generally adequate, estimates of conditions representative of a community's total population. The use of sampling procedures can help keep survey costs down.

The surveys described here should be repeated by the government on a regular basis, at least annually, and preferably at more frequent intervals, such as quarterly, to permit seasonal and timely feedback to agency managers for their action, and to enable comparisons of one time period with another. Comparisons can indicate whether progress has been made, whether problems have arisen, and whether past changes in government programs or policies have affected service effectiveness and quality.

To facilitate comparisons, the majority of the survey questions should remain the same from one time period to the next. Inevitably, some questions will be added and some deleted from one period to the next, but the overall questionnaire content should remain fairly stable. Even seemingly minor changes in the wording can elicit substantially different responses and invalidate comparisons.

The surveys described here and throughout this report are not public opinion surveys. Respondents are not asked to set priorities among services or to express opinions about what they would like. Such questions are not appropriate for assessing the effectiveness of government services.

A number of local governments have undertaken regular surveys to measure effectiveness, including Aurora, Colorado; Charlotte, North Carolina; Dallas, Texas; Dayton, Ohio; Nashville-Davidson County, Tennessee; Palo Alto, California; Randolph Township, New Jersey; St. Petersburg, Florida; Sioux City, Iowa; Sunnyvale, California; Washington, North Carolina; and Zeeland, Michigan.

Procedural Issues

Basic Steps
Generally, five overlapping steps are required to develop customer surveys, particularly surveys to obtain service effectiveness information.

Step 1: Prepare a Draft Questionnaire. The questionnaires provided in this volume can be used as a starting point, but it is highly desirable that operating agencies participate in a local government's development of its own questionnaires.

Step 2: Identify the Major Population Subgroups for Which the Local Government Wants to Obtain Data. The number of subgroups and the number of categories within each are needed to determine the size of the sample. As a rule of thumb, the sample size should be large enough to provide approximately 100 (or more) respondents in each category. For example, if the local government has funds for a total sample of 600, then it should, in general, have no more than six geographical areas, six age groupings, and so on, on which it expects to obtain data. The local government may need to combine some groups or provide for "stratified" sampling to assure that each group will be covered by an adequate subsample.

Step 3: Determine the Mode of Administration and Who Will Be Responsible for Each Survey Task. The agency will need to determine whether the survey will use mail, telephone, or in-person surveying, or some combination. This choice is discussed later. The agency also needs to decide who will undertake such tasks as questionnaire design, administration, data tabulation, and report preparation. If a professional survey organization is to administer the survey, a request for proposal must be designed. Elements to include in contractual arrangements for a customer survey are discussed in Appendix 11.

Step 4: If the Survey Is to Be Contracted, Select the Contractor and Undertake the Survey. Universities and survey firms should be included in the bidders' list. Try to find organizations that have had experience with local government surveys.

Step 5: Provide for Analysis and Reporting of the Data. Prepare a summary of findings for use by public officials, the council, and citizens. (This step and some illustrative formats are discussed further in Chapter 16).

Content of the Questionnaire
Customer survey questionnaires should include four types of questions:

- Questions that ask about specific service characteristics, so that the responses can be used to calculate individual measures of service effectiveness or quality

- Questions that solicit demographic information on the respondent that can be used to group responses by particular customer characteristics

- "Diagnostic" questions that can help the agency understand why respondents gave the ratings they did

- Questions asking for suggestions for improving the service, usually placed at the end of the questionnaire.

Numerous examples of questions are given throughout the text and appendix of this volume.

The organization that undertakes the interviewing should pretest the questionnaire to work out the final wording. Exhibit 13-1 provides general criteria that may be helpful in deciding whether a particular question or question topic is appropriate for a government customer survey that is used to measure service effectiveness.

Method of Administering the Questionnaire

Local governments can use in-person, telephone, or mail surveys, or combinations of these.

Exhibit 13-1

Criteria for Customer Survey Questions

1. The information cannot be obtained as accurately by other practical means.

2. The information cannot be obtained as inexpensively by other means.

3. The information is sufficiently important to merit the time and expense of inclusion in the survey. Interviewing time and cost are not the only considerations. Each additional question generates added data to be tabulated, displayed, and analyzed. Marginal questions can overload the government's capacity to consider the data.

4. The question is of direct relevance to measuring service effectiveness; that is, it provides information on (a) service effectiveness, (b) respondent characteristics, or (c) conditions that can help to explain why the level of effectiveness is as it is.

5. The question will be understandable to respondents.

6. Enough respondents will answer the questions asked in the sample size chosen to provide useful information. Some questions are asked only of those in a particular category. For example, only those who have made a complaint to the government would be asked how satisfied they were with the handling of complaints. If the local government estimates that only a very small number of respondents (e.g., under 20 percent) will have complained, questions about satisfaction with the handling of the complaint probably should be dropped.

7. Citizens are competent to respond to the questions so that their information will be meaningful; that is, they can be expected to make a reasonably informed response on the question. (In general, questions encouraging "hearsay" evidence and questions that presume special or technical knowledge should be avoided.)

Note: Some local governments also may want to include questions that seek citizen opinions on current issues. Because such questions are particularly susceptible to unintentional bias and lack of respondent knowledge, special care should be given to how they are worded.

In-Person Interviews. Interviews at the home of respondents usually will be too expensive for regular surveys. These surveys require a great deal of interviewer time for travelling and interviewing. In-person questionnaires can be appropriate, however, for user surveys in which customers can be interviewed at a public facility (for example, a library or recreation facility). If questionnaires can be administered at a facility, a low-cost option is to hand out the questionnaires and ask customers to complete them before leaving the facility. This "self-administration" option is likely to be more efficient than interviewing customers (if the questionnaire is short and easy to read and if special effort is made to encourage customers to complete and return the questionnaire).

Telephone Interviews. Telephone interviews have become the favorite mode for most professional survey firms. They are less costly than at-home interviews, and most families in the United States can be reached by telephone. Techniques called "random digit dialing" and "plus one dialing" can be used to cover communities with unlisted telephone numbers as alternatives to drawing samples from telephone books. For user surveys, telephone interviewing is feasible if the service agency has access to its customers' telephone numbers. (Agencies that serve substantial numbers of customers who do not have phones—the homeless or very low-income persons—will need to use in-person interviewing to reach these groups.) To achieve adequate interview completion rates, telephone interviewers can make multiple callbacks if no one answers. Furthermore, this interview method allows greater access to respondents in areas where people are reluctant to allow strangers in their home. And it does not require interviewers to travel into dangerous locations. The effect of answering machines on telephone response rates and costs does not seem to be significant.

Mail Surveys. Generally mail surveys are by far the least expensive type of survey. The major problem is that response rates are much more likely to be unacceptably low, too low for reliable information. However, steps can be taken to achieve acceptable response rates. For example, second and third mailings and telephone reminders or telephone interviews can be used to increase response rates.

Mail surveys have other disadvantages: the questionnaire must be shorter and simpler, probably no longer than two to four pages. For performance monitoring purposes, this length should be adequate if the questionnaire covers only one or two services. A mail survey questionnaire cannot probe for information as a telephone or in-person interviewer can. The mail survey is, of course, not useful when mailing addresses are not available (or do not exist, such as with the homeless).

To increase response rates in mail surveys, agencies can:

- Include in each mailing a stamped, self-addressed return envelope
- Keep the questionnaire as short and simple as possible, to no more than 3 or 4 pages
- Make the questionnaire attractive, uncluttered, and easy to handle. Avoid using simply typed questionnaires
- Include a brief transmittal letter from the mayor or manager emphasizing that the responses are to be used to improve the local government's services
- Guarantee the confidentiality of responses, that is, that responses will not be reported in any way permitting identification of individual respondents.

Recommendations on Mode of Administration. To achieve acceptable response rates, certain modes of administration are better than others. Some recommendations are as follows:

- For household surveys, telephone interviews are likely to be needed, especially if the survey covers multiple services. In such cases, the questionnaire length will probably preclude mail surveying.
- For regular user surveys, mail surveys probably can be used, as long as multiple mailings or telephone reminders are used. Customers of a particular service are more likely to return a mailed survey about that service than the general population receiving a household survey.
- Local governments should seek at least a 50 percent response rate in surveys (thus achieving a response from a majority of those from whom the survey seeks responses).
- For services with substantial numbers of non-English-speaking customers, the questionnaires should be translated into the principal foreign languages.

Development of the Questionnaire

The questionnaire should be developed to be of use to both operating managers for improving programs and higher-level officials for accountability purposes. To avoid unclear and biased wording, the final wording of questions, and their arrangement on the questionnaire, should be left to an expert in questionnaire development.

One useful procedure is to form a working group to develop the questionnaire. The group might include the service manager from the service area being evaluated, selected members of the manager's staff, a representative of the department head's staff, a representative of the local government's chief administrative officer, and a survey expert. The group also might include someone representing the service's customers to increase the likelihood that the questionnaire covers the service characteristics of importance to customers.

As noted earlier, several appendices in this volume give sample questionnaires for both household and user surveys. These questionnaires can serve as starting points. However, each local government will want to modify the existing questions, delete some, and add others to cover aspects of local concern. (Exhibit 13-1 presents a list of criteria for deciding whether a question should be included in the survey.)

Before conducting the survey, each local government should have its questions pretested to check for possible bias and to ascertain local citizens' interpretation of the wording. The pretesting should screen out: long, awkwardly worded, or ambiguous questions; local language usage that requires a special choice of words; confusing or incorrect instructions to interviewers regarding "skip" patterns; redundant questions; wording that may offend or sound foolish to respondents; illogical or awkward sequence of questions; and difficulties encountered by interviewers in recording responses. The pretest also can be used to help establish the categories for responses to open-ended questions that will be asked of respondents in the full survey. For instance, if respondents are asked for specific reasons why they did not use a particular service, the pretest can identify the most common reasons, which can then be used by the interviewer to record responses on the final questionnaire.

Respondents who give negative ratings to specific service characteristics should be asked to indicate, in their own words, why they have given the negative rating. (Such a question sequence is illustrated in Question 17 of the library user questionnaire in Appendix 7.) These responses should be compiled and provided to service personnel since they may indicate service changes that are needed.

Frequency of Survey Administration

Most local agencies should try to survey customers on a quarterly basis. Most local governments that survey do so at most once a year. Unfortunately, this does not provide information frequently enough to help operating managers improve service delivery. To avoid excessive costs, the annual survey budget can be split into four parts, and one quarter of the total year's sample can be surveyed each quarter. For example, if a city plans to survey 600 clients during the year, it can survey 150 each quarter.

This approach will provide more timely feedback to service managers. If a service modifies its programs during the year, it obtains feedback more quickly as to the impact of that change. Also, quarterly surveys enable a service to identify seasonal differences and seasonal problems.

The major drawback to quarterly samples is that the sample size each quarter is smaller, providing statistically less precise information each quarter. However, the data from each quarter should be reported both for the quarter and for the year to date. Thus, at the end of the year the cumulative findings will represent the findings for the full year. The agency should recognize, however, that the year's cumulative totals are from four quarterly samples and have not all been obtained at one point in time.

For user surveys, an appropriate survey strategy is to mail a questionnaire to each customer or interview each customer by telephone, at a predetermined interval after the service was provided to the customer. The findings from customers' responses to date can be tabulated at any desired interval, such as monthly.

For surveys administered to customers at public facilities, such as libraries and parks, the timing should be chosen so as to be representative of the times clients use the facilities—various times of the day and days of the week.

Size of Sample
The size of the sample affects both the accuracy of the survey findings and survey costs. Sample size is affected by such factors as: the desired confidence level, the number of breakouts (for example, neighborhoods) for which the agency would like separate information, the resources available to do the survey, and the mode of questionnaire administration.

For household surveys, it will seldom be feasible to obtain performance measurement feedback from all households (likely to number in the thousands). The local government could mail out questionnaires to each household, for instance, with tax or water bills, but the response rate from such mailings is typically well under 20 percent, yielding inadequate levels of confidence that the findings represent community experience. Instead, the agency should seek a representative sample of households and make the effort needed to obtain an adequate response rate so the findings can be used with reasonable confidence.

Mathematics show that small samples can yield usable findings. (The large national polls, for example, typically interview only 1,600 households to yield findings representative of the whole population of the United States.)

With properly drawn samples of about 400, for example, the percentages obtained should be within plus or minus five percentage points with a probability of about 95 percent. If a probability of 90 percent is acceptable (as it should be for most government purposes), then a sample size closer to 300 is adequate. As indicated throughout this volume, however, local governments should identify the responses of various segments of their populations and not just measure aggregate responses. In general, public agencies should seek sample sizes of about 100 for each such segment. For example, if a jurisdiction has six geographical neighborhoods from which the government wants data, total sample size should be about 600. The confidence levels for each segment, however, will be lower than for the combined presentation. Samples of 100 randomly chosen customers should be accurate to plus or minus ten percentage points with a 95 percent probability, and plus or minus about eight percentage points with a 90 percent probability.[2]

While these levels of accuracy are not ideal, they are probably adequate for most government purposes.

The same considerations and statistics apply to user surveys if the service has large numbers of clients. However, if a service does not have a large number of clients, the agency should consider surveying all clients, preferably on an ongoing basis (by mailing a questionnaire at some fixed interval of time after each client has received service). If all clients (or, at least, most clients) respond to the survey, there will be no sampling error.[3]

Who Should Undertake the Surveys?
Because of the many technical, specialized aspects of handling household surveys, local governments probably should use an experienced survey firm. Only those governments with substantial in-house capabilities should consider undertaking such surveys by themselves. Even governments that have the technical capability to handle the surveys on their own may have difficulty in gaining public credibility for the findings if they do not use outside experts. (Appendix 11 provides suggested guidelines for local governments that contract for surveys.)

There are several cost-cutting alternatives. One is to hire outside technical consultants to direct the process while using citizens' groups or government employees to conduct the actual survey. As long as outside expertise is used to provide adequate training and oversight, the technical quality can be obtained and public credibility maintained. However, governments using employees for interviewing have found that this imposes a considerable strain on employee resources. Thus, this option is not suggested for regular use.

Other survey activities that local governments can undertake, rather than contract, to reduce out-of-pocket costs include preparation of the list of persons from which the sample will be drawn, various data processing activities such as preparation of cross-tabulations, and preparation of reports on the findings.

Which government office should coordinate the activity? For household surveys that cover a number of services, a central staff office is likely to be most appropriate. However, surveys limited to one service (such as user surveys or the recreation household survey of Appendix 4) can be administered by that agency. Some central oversight is desirable to ensure that adequate quality is maintained for the survey work.

Large operating agencies probably can handle the mailing, tracking, and tabulation of responses for user surveys. Surveys for small agencies might better be undertaken by some central office. The unit that actually delivers the service should generally not be the unit that administers the survey—for two important reasons: the added operating effort is likely to place too much burden on the operating unit's resources, and the reported findings are likely to be less credible outside the unit.

Analysis of Survey Findings

The amount of information yielded by customer surveys can be considerable. Analysis of survey information should include:

- Examination of the responses to each question for each category of respondent. This information indicates which service elements are doing well, which not so well, for different categories of clients. (The tables of findings should show both the percentage of respondents giving each response rating and also the number of respondents in each category so that analysts can consider the relative size of each category.)

- Examination of the responses to open-ended questions, such as why the respondents gave certain answers or suggestions to improve the service. This information can provide clues as to problems and ways to correct them.

- On occasion, more sophisticated statistical approaches, such as special analyses that consider simultaneously the relationship among the responses to multiple effectiveness indicators and multiple respondent characteristics. This information can provide a picture of the interaction of multiple factors and provide an improved understanding of the effectiveness indicators.

Use a multiple cross-tabulation summary form, such as the one shown in Exhibit 16-4 of Chapter 16, to present survey results. This form permits users to work with about one-fourth of the paper that would otherwise be necessary. It also makes it easier for users to spot major differences in responses among respondent groups on individual questions. Computer software is available for formatting findings into such a form. In addition, standard statistical computer programs such as SPSS (Statistical Package for the Social Sciences) or SAS can be useful for a variety of special data analyses.

Reporting the Results

Chapter 16 provides suggestions for reporting the findings from measurement procedures, including customer surveys. Here are some suggestions and concerns that are especially associated with findings from customer surveys:

- The results from each question should be presented in a concise, easy-to-interpret format. Clear labels should be provided for all rows and columns. In general, the principal form of presentation of survey findings should express the findings as the *percentage* of the sample that gave each response. Exhibit 16-4 in Chapter 16 shows a format useful for service managers and other officials.

- Results should be presented for the whole sample and should be *broken out by key categories of customers*. As emphasized throughout this volume, the survey information will be much more useful to service managers if the data are reported by key types of clients: geographical area (residence of respondents), race or ethnic group, income group, age group, sex of respondent, and household composition. These categories will vary somewhat among services. Public transit agencies, for example, probably will want to distinguish responses of those who have automobiles from those who do not. Solid waste collection agencies may want to distinguish responses of persons who live in various types of housing.

- A summary of highlights should be provided, preferably one developed with the service manager or program manager.

- The specific wording used in the questions should be provided in the survey report so that readers can better interpret the findings.

- The total number of persons responding to each question should be identified so that readers can see the basis for the findings (as illustrated in Exhibit 16-4). When highlights are singled out that involve small sample sizes (less than 100), this fact should be noted. Statistical significance levels and confidence intervals for selected findings might be included as footnotes, although this type of information may be unfamiliar to many readers.

- The government should make the findings from household surveys easily available throughout the community. Copies of the report containing the complete survey results can be placed in public libraries, for instance.

- Survey results should not be released just before an election, lest the data become a political football—with the survey team and operating agencies getting kicked around in the process.

Operating Agency Role

Involving operating agencies in the survey process is crucial. Within operating agencies are the employees who can respond most directly to survey findings. Local governments should involve individual agencies and the appropriate program managers both in the initial preparation of the questionnaires (especially in the development of the questions) and in the subsequent review of the survey findings. This advice is more easily given than taken. Three problems seem particularly troublesome:

- Interest in customer survey data is mixed. Some agency managers will be highly skeptical about the utility and meaningfulness of customer responses. Some managers ask questions such as, "Why do we need to ask for citizens' perceptions of road rideability when we are perfectly able to determine it ourselves through government employees?" Or they retort: "Let sleeping dogs lie," "Citizens are not capable of rating our services," and "We cannot control what customers think." Some managers feel they can take little action to improve customer satisfaction. However, each question included in a survey questionnaire should be subjected to this test: "Is there some government action that could improve customer ratings on this question?"

- Most agency managers have had little experience, or training, in the nature and use of performance information coming from their customers.

- Agency staff analysis time often is limited or nonexistent. Part of this problem stems from the absence of analysis within many local government agencies. Part stems from the pressure of day-to-day activities, which prevents existing staff members from spending much time reviewing survey data. Most agency managers can provide considerable insight in the examination of performance data relevant to their own area of responsibility, but trained analysts can improve understanding of the responses, for instance, by the simultaneous examination of responses to more than one question. Trained analysts can sometimes be made available from a central staff to help operating agency personnel.

It is extremely important to establish the right atmosphere during various stages of customer surveys. If the survey findings are handled so as to focus on negatives and on attributing blame, program manager reactions will be defensive, and the survey information may not be used. Therefore, to the extent possible, a constructive atmosphere should be maintained—one that encourages constructive changes and gives credit to successful programs and program improvements without causing the government or individual agencies to be continually on the defensive.

It is critical that the program manager from the program being evaluated be given the opportunity to review and comment on the survey findings before they are presented to higher level officials (or, of course, the press). The program manager should provide reasons for any problems identified in the survey findings and indicate actions he or she plans to take to correct such problems—before the findings are transmitted further. This step can allay the concern and fear program managers will feel if the findings are promulgated without their initial review.

Costs of Surveys

Telephone Surveys

Costs for telephone surveys contracted to professional survey firms are likely to be approximately $15 to $20 per interview. The annual out-of-pocket outlay for contracted telephone surveys, thus, is likely to range from approximately $9,000 to $12,000 for a sample of 600 households. For repetitive surveys, particularly some of the shorter questionnaires presented in this report, the costs could be as low as $10 per interview.

These figures cover pretesting, final questionnaire preparation and printing, interviewing, editing, card punching, and basic summary tabulations. Not included are such tasks as developing the initial set of topics for the questionnaire, the time of central staff or operating agency personnel, any special effort to develop the list of the population from which the sample is drawn, or any in-depth analysis of survey results. Local government personnel will need to work for many days to determine questionnaire topics and wording. Computer software is widely available for processing questionnaire data, but some special modifications may be needed for each individual survey application.

Small local governments can reduce their costs by using smaller samples and by seeking volunteer help from local professional or volunteer organizations or from local colleges and universities for such activities as telephone interviewing. A problem here is the undependability of free help and the need to train new volunteers each time the survey is administered.

Mail Surveys

Mail surveys such as those used for user surveys probably can be conducted under for $5 per person surveyed. Clerical help will be needed to undertake the various mailings, to keep track of responses, and for data entry.

Quarterly Surveys

Do quarterly samples, in which one-fourth of the annual sample is surveyed each quarter, cost more than completing the whole sample at once? Throughout this report, quarterly samples (at season-end) have been recommended rather than a one-time annual survey. For example, a public agency can request four seasonal samples of 125 each, rather than one year-end sample of 500. Survey firms probably can achieve some economies of scale and reduce interviewer training cost if they survey everyone at one time. However, if the local government lets one contract at the beginning of the year covering all four quarterly samples, this is likely to be attractive to many survey firms. The total annual cost for four quarterly segments probably will be within 10 percent of the cost for one annual sample.

The very considerable advantage to public officials of timely, seasonal feedback greatly outweighs the small added cost. The findings from quarterly samples can be reported each quarter both as quarterly findings and as cumulative results for the year to date. The latest findings also can be compared to the same quarter in previous years and can be compared to quarterly and/or year-to-date targets that are set at the beginning of the year by agency managers.

Customer Survey Accuracy

The validity of specific survey questions is addressed in the various chapters on individual services. This section discusses validity issues relevant to surveys as a whole.

Sources of survey inaccuracy that public agencies need to guard against include the following:

- Problems in obtaining a sample that is a reasonable cross section of the population of customers
- Problems in obtaining interviews with those included in the sample
- Problems in wording of questions
- Respondents' lack of knowledge
- Poor interviewing techniques
- Respondents' memory lapses or lack of honesty
- Clerical, coding, or tabulation errors in processing the interview results.

Obtaining a Representative Interview Sample

Numerous issues are involved in obtaining a representative sample, some highly technical. Four are briefly discussed here: (1) selecting the source from which the sample is to be drawn, (2) selecting statistically sound samples from the population to be sampled, (3) determining who in a particular household should be interviewed, and (4) checking, though crudely, how well the sample represents various demographic characteristics of the whole customer population.

Selecting the Source from Which the Sample Is to Be Drawn. For *user* samples, the list will be drawn from the records of customers who are the subject of the follow-up. For *household* surveys, however, many options exist, including: local tax rolls, lists of water service customers, voter lists, vehicle registration lists, telephone directories, directories of addresses. The choice will depend on such factors as the mode of interviewing, availability of current lists, the coverage of each, and other special considerations. The government needs to avoid omitting major population segments such as poor people, renters, persons living in mobile homes, and persons with unlisted telephone numbers.

As indicated earlier, with *telephone* interviewing random digit dialing is a good approach since most persons have telephones and this method will reach even unlisted numbers. For *mail* administration, some form of up-to-date listing of addresses is needed. The public agency, however, will need to determine which population segments are not covered in the listing and assess whether special supplementary interviewing is needed to reach these segments.

Selecting Statistically Sound ("Random") Samples from the Population to Be Sampled. When 100 percent coverage of customers is not feasible, the agency will need to survey a sample of customers. It is vital that the sample be drawn in a statistically sound way. The basic principle is that each customer in the category from which a sample is to be drawn should have an equal chance of being drawn (at least an *approximately* equal chance; perfection in sampling is seldom possible). Agencies may need expert help to do this sampling if there seem to be too many complications in drawing the desired sample.

Determining Who Should Be Interviewed in a Particular Household (in Household Surveys). To keep costs down, only one adult should be interviewed per household. Questionnaires, such as that in Appendix 1, ask respondents to answer only for themselves concerning most questions. For some issues, however, they are asked to respond for all members of the family; examples are crime victimization and reasons for nonuse of libraries.

On some issues, survey professionals believe it best to interview the adult who spends the most time at home and thus is likely to be more knowledgeable than other members of the household about such activities as family use of recreation or library facilities. About such questions as family income, a working adult is likely to be most knowledgeable. On other issues, such as perception of library accessibility, it seems preferable to obtain responses from a cross section of household members.

Survey firms often choose to interview adults so that the total sample represents a proper proportion of each sex and age category relative to the entire population. The omission of children as respondents is a concern, particularly when measuring the effectiveness of recreation and library services, but children probably would not be able to answer many questions on other services.

Checking Demographic Characteristics. A somewhat crude procedure can be used to check the representativeness of samples in terms of a few demographic characteristics. This procedure involves determining the extent to which the sample seems to have characteristics similar to those of the large population it is supposed to represent. A check should be made after the findings have been obtained on characteristics of the sample such as age, race or ethnic group, geographical and income distribution.

Significant deviations in the sample might be partly compensated for by weighing the responses of the various population groups so that weights are increased for under-represented groups, thus yielding a community average that is more nearly representative. At the very least, the sensitivity of jurisdiction-wide totals to possible undersamplings of some groups should be identified.

As census information on the whole population becomes dated, this comparison will be less useful, unless such bodies as the local planning agency update estimates of population size and of the various characteristics noted above.

Obtaining Interviews

At least three problems can arise as survey staff members try to reach the targeted sample. First, persons to be interviewed may not be at home when the interviewer calls. Second, individuals may refuse to be interviewed or may not return mailed questionnaires. Third, people may terminate interviews before they are completed.

Not-at-Homes. The problem with telephone interviews is that those who are often not home (at least when interviewers call) may have experiences and viewpoints on government services that are quite different from those of people who are more often at home.

When telephone interviews are used, a reasonable number of call-backs should be undertaken, at least three, because of the relatively small added costs. The calls should be made at various times of the day and on various days of the week.

If interviewee age and sex quotas are being used (so that the resulting sample will be roughly representative of the community age and sex mix), the callers can attempt to schedule interviews with the desired household member.

Refusal Rates. Refusal rates are sensitive to the survey procedures used. Earlier, we presented suggestions for reducing refusals on mail surveys. For telephone (and at-home) interviewing, refusal rates also are affected by the quality of the interviewers. Interviewing by professional organizations with previous experience in survey work should keep refusal rates reasonably low, well below 20 percent.

In recent years, telephone refusal rates have been climbing, especially as many more commercial organizations have begun to use telephone surveys and phone soliciting. However, people appear considerably more willing to respond to a survey by a local government. For this reason, interviewers should identify themselves at the start of their calls as interviewers for the specific public agency.

Persons asked to complete questionnaires at a public facility before they leave the facility (in order to capture the quality of their experiences) may be in a hurry or otherwise not motivated to complete the questionnaire. The agency personnel administering the questionnaire at the facility should be trained to encourage completion. A questionnaire that takes only a few minutes to complete at the site is usually needed to obtain a good response rate.

Early Terminations. The willingness of a cross section of citizens to complete the interview once it has started is a matter of concern, particularly when the questionnaire is as long as the questionnaire in Appendix 1, which requires about thirty minutes. However, completion rates have been high even with this length of interview. (In some instances, the chief problem may be how to end the interview tactfully, especially interviews with elderly persons who may enjoy talking to the interviewer.)

Wording of Questions

Questionnaires should be screened and pretested for obvious bias and for clarity.

A useful procedure for pretests is to ask respondents a question such as, "Why did you give the rating you did?" The responses may indicate that respondents are interpreting questions differently from the way that was intended.

Respondents' Knowledge

Can survey respondents be expected to be knowledgeable about the topics on which information is requested? An important ground rule to use in developing questions to obtain effectiveness measurement data is to ask individuals only about events within their own personal experience or the experience of other members of their household, in a sense, the service characteristics about which they are "expert." The performance measurement questions should not include technical questions or expressions of opinions requiring knowledge that the respondents normally cannot be expected to have.

Some operating agency personnel express concern that citizens may not be qualified to answer particular questions, for example, a question about the condition of roads in the respondent's neighborhood. However, the measure for which the question is used is intended to reflect the "comfort" aspect of streets as perceived by users, and not the technical condition of the road. As long as individuals are asked about effects on themselves and their families rather than technical issues, such questions seem to be legitimate candidates for surveys.

Interview Quality

Adequate training and supervision of interviewers are important elements in conducting a quality survey. Major problems can develop if a local government decides to do the interviewing itself with inexperienced interviewers. Regardless of who manages the interviewing, it is important to maintain interviewing quality. This can be done by having a supervisor listen in periodically on a sample of each interviewer's interviews, at least to hear the interviewer's end of the conversation (especially practical when telephone interviewing is done at a central location) and by verifying a percentage of the interviews conducted by each interviewer (perhaps 10 percent) to assure that interviews actually were undertaken and were of reasonable quality. The supervisor recontacts the respondent to verify that the interview took place and to verify some of the answers recorded by the interviewer. This is a common and appropriate practice used by survey organizations.

Respondents' Memory and Honesty

Some survey questions ask for factual information, for example, the frequency of certain events, such as use of transit or library facilities, or crime victimization. The recall period suggested in this report is three months, assuming that a survey is repeated quarterly. If the survey work is done less frequently, say annually, the agency probably will want a long recall period, say twelve months. This period is somewhat arbitrary and could be reduced. For other survey questions, in which the rating is primarily about current conditions, the memory problem is of less concern.

There is little conclusive information on memory, especially as related to the specific topics that are the subject of these questionnaires.[4]

Respondent ratings can be influenced by the timing of the interview. Both the season of the year and current events can affect responses. For example, recent announcements of a crime wave are likely to affect respondents' feeling of security.

Many public services are affected by seasonal weather conditions. This is one reason that surveying part of the annual sample each quarter is recommended, perhaps shortly after the end of each season so that respondents' "seasonal" experiences can be readily recalled. (If a survey is undertaken only annually, it should occur at about the same time each year to increase the comparability of findings from one year to the next.)

The issue of honesty of responses is not a major concern. The topics included on the questionnaires illustrated in this volume generally are not "threatening" to respondents or their self-image, except possibly the questions asking for income and age. Even in these instances, if respondents are asked only for broad, approximate ranges, most of them are willing to answer. A small proportion of the respondents may not take the interview seriously, but if the interviewers are well trained, this situation should be minimized and the findings, and trends over time, are not likely to be distorted significantly.

Clerical and Tabulation Errors

The unit responsible for processing returned questionnaires must be trained and motivated to do an accurate job of transferring the findings to the computer. And the computer must be properly programmed. Entries should be double-checked before tabulations are made.

Summary of Issues to Be Considered in Survey Design

A list of survey issues is presented below, to alert local governments to key issues that need to be resolved when designing surveys.

Questionnaire Issues
- How long a memory can the respondent be expected to have in recalling the various types of events? (The recall and seasonality issues)
- Should individuals be asked to respond only for themselves or should they also answer for their whole household?
- What is the maximum appropriate interview length for this subject matter?
- How valid are respondents' answers to questions about reasons for their non-use of services?
- What rating categories should be used for various types of questions?

Sample Selection and Design Issues
- How frequently should these surveys be undertaken?
- Should interviewing be conducted by telephone, by in-person interviews, by mail, by self-administration at a public facility where the respondent has just used the service, or by combinations of these techniques?
- How can the most representative sample be obtained? To what extent is there a need for callbacks of, or remailings to, those not responding on the initial attempt to contact? What list of the population should be used from which the sample will be drawn?
- How can the validity of the survey data be checked?

Implementation Issues
- How accurate and precise must the results be? How should information regarding the precision of the findings be presented to government officials?
- How should the large amounts of data coming from the surveys be handled? What specific report formats will be most useful and understandable?
- Who should be responsible for the various parts of the survey effort?
- To what extent will public release of the survey results cause major problems for local officials, and how should the release be handled?
- Will citizens be oversurveyed?

Uses for Customer Surveys

Chapter 16 discusses the uses for information on service effectiveness regardless of source. The following paragraphs discuss the uses of data that come from customer surveys.

City officials in St. Petersburg, Florida, many years ago gave the following examples of uses they had made of the information obtained from a questionnaire very similar to the one in Appendix 1.

- The police department used the victimization data to improve its understanding of the relationship between reported and unreported crimes. The data were also used to determine where emphasis should be placed in crime prevention programs.
- The city manager and council used the results when considering water, sewer, and sanitation rate changes.
- The transit department used the results for designing and scheduling new routes.
- The city manager and council used the survey findings to determine citizen reaction when establishing a program to assess sidewalk improvement.
- Responses to a question about the frequency of rat sightings in various neighborhoods helped to determine which locations would receive emphasis in the rat control program.
- Responses led to special attention for parks rated low on cleanliness.

Local governments will find it tempting to add items to questionnaires that ask for a variety of other information on respondents' attitudes and opinions. It is reasonable for a government to include a few special questions each year. These could, for example, seek citizen assessments of specific projects or programs. For example, the city of Nashville included a question in its questionnaire (one similar to that in Appendix 1) to obtain feedback on the size of the government radio station's listening audience and the reasons respondents did not listen to the station. A variety of other information on specific government programs also might be sought. For example, Nashville also included a question that asked for information on the willingness of citizens to allow fire fighters into their homes to check for fire hazards. The purpose of this question was to pretest the probable success of such a program.

Questions asking for citizens' opinions of current issues are particularly susceptible to bias in their wording. This problem can be illustrated by an example. A question worded "Are you in favor of your government's providing more of service 'x'?" would probably receive a much higher percentage of "yes" responses than one worded "Are you in favor of your government's providing more of service 'x' with the cost paid for by increasing property taxes?" Neither wording is likely to solicit very informed responses. The respondents would be able to give informed responses only if they were provided estimates of the amount of tax increase and what benefits they would probably gain from the added level of service.

If such opinions are sought, special care should be taken to determine that the questions are unbiased, clear, and that they request information about which citizens are likely to be knowledgeable.

Finally, it should be remembered that customer survey findings provide information for only a part, perhaps one-third, of all effectiveness measures. In general, customer survey findings alone should not be used to direct government programs and policies. Information is needed on other measures (such as those based on government records or on systematic observation by trained observers), on program costs, and on other program and political information.

1 See, for example, Fink and Kosecoff, *How to Conduct Surveys: A Step-by-Step Guide;* van Houten and Hatry, *How to Conduct a Citizen Survey;* Miller and Miller, *Citizen Surveys.*

2 For example, if 20 percent of the sample gives a particular rating on a specific question, the agency has 90 percent confidence that the percentage for the total population actually falls between 13 percent and 27 percent. If two population groups each with sample sizes of 100 reported 20 percent and 10 percent respectively, there would be less than a 10 percent probability that a difference as large as that observed was the luck of the draw rather than a real difference. Tables are available that show the tradeoffs of precision versus sample size so that each government can judge for itself what minimum sample sizes are appropriate.

3 The discussion here has been considerably simplified. See bibliography for texts on survey sampling.

4 See the discussion in Chapter 6 of "victimization" questions. The U.S. Department of Justice uses a six-month recall period when asking respondents about past victimization incidents. To some extent, there may be offsetting sources of errors as the recall period is lengthened. On one hand, events are forgotten, but on the other, respondents appear to include in their responses events from prior periods. The latter practice is sometimes referred to as "telescoping."

Chapter 14

Surveying the Business Community

Business establishments located within a jurisdiction are major clients for many services provided by the local government. Many of the effectiveness measures and measurement procedures discussed in the chapters on individual government services also concern the economic or business life of the community. For example, businesses have a direct interest in fire and police protection, cleanliness and condition of the streets, parking and traffic control, and water and sewer services—in their locations. Thus, an important source of customer feedback should be the businesses in the community.

Procedures similar to those used for the surveys discussed in Chapter 13 can be used to obtain information from a sample of business managers on their perceptions of the quality of individual services. The survey also can be used to obtain certain factual data that may be unavailable in existing government records, such as unreported crime victimization.

This chapter offers some suggestions for procedures for surveying the business community. Appendix 2 presents an illustrative questionnaire. The questionnaire focuses on questions likely to be of concern to a large number of businesses. Few local governments have surveyed businesses to obtain feedback on service performance. (Sioux City, Iowa, is one city that has surveyed its business community about local government services.) A local government planning a survey of businesses should thoroughly review the questionnaire and carefully pretest it.

The questionnaire in Appendix 2 contains one or more questions on each of the following services:

- Local transportation services, including public transit
- Crime control
- Health and sanitation inspections
- Fire control

- Sanitation
- Water supply
- Wastewater removal and storm drainage, including sewer services
- City handling of complaints and requests for services and information
- Consumer affairs.

The questions in the survey questionnaire are intended to elicit data for the measures of service effectiveness identified in the previous chapters. Boldface numbers on the sample questionnaire relate particular questions to particular measures. To limit the size of the questionnaire (and thus keep down costs and make it more practical), the questionnaire does not cover all service characteristics. The questionnaire in Appendix 2 requires approximately 20 to 30 minutes to complete.

Questions relating to services not provided by a particular local government can of course be deleted. Some government services not covered in this questionnaire might be included, such as zoning and land development decisions, licensing, regulation of advertising signs, building codes, local "blue laws," and so forth.

Other questions that might be added (or substituted) include questions on: water quality (of particular interest to restaurants and laundries), landscaping, police crime prevention activities, fire prevention activities, zoning and code enforcement, and various local economic development attraction (such as tourism attraction and business assistance).

Two services, recreation and library services, are included in the household survey (see Appendix 1), but are not represented in the illustrative questionnaire for businesses because these two services are likely to be of less direct concern to the business community.

Suggestions for Conducting the Survey

Who Should Be Included? From What Part of the Business Population Should the Sample Be Drawn?

There are a number of options. One is to include all kinds of businesses. The Standard Industrial Classification (SIC) code of the U.S. Department of Commerce provides a useful starting point for the classifications of businesses from which choices might be made, but the local government will need to be sure to include categories meaningful to the commerce and industry in the jurisdiction. Rather than attempting to survey even a sample of all types of businesses, the local government might find the survey more manageable if it used such alternatives as the following:

- Only "for profit" establishments
- All profit-making firms except those considered to provide professional services (such as doctors, lawyers, consultants, accountants)
- Only profit-making establishments in certain industries, such as those that sell retail goods or provide services directly to the public.

The following issues need to be considered in the selection:

- For some businesses located in a building with a number of business establishments or in a shopping center, some services, such as solid waste collection, are provided collectively to the building or center. The interviewer, therefore, may need to ask some questions of the main occupant only, and other questions of all businesses.

- Some of the businesses selected may receive such services as solid waste collection or security protection from private firms not under contract to the government. Other businesses may provide their own services. A business probably should be asked to rate only those services under the responsibility of the government.

- Some businesses, such as chain stores, have more than one location. Should stores under the same ownership be treated as separate firms—and possibly interviewed at more than one location—or should they be treated as one firm?

- The person who should be interviewed, ideally, is the person who is familiar with all the services delivered, such as an owner, manager, or assistant manager.

How Many Businesses Should Be Surveyed?

The answer here will depend mainly on the type and number of business subgroups on which separate measurement information is wanted, the precision needed in the findings, and, of course, resource constraints.

At one extreme, no stratification may be needed, and the business community can be considered as a whole. A sample of perhaps only 100 interviews will be sufficient to provide a reasonable representation of the total population of businesses.

Another alternative is to group the responses by major locations in the city. This method would help to identify differences in perceived service levels by geographical area. If this is done, 100 interviews from each area is likely to be sufficient.

A third alternative is to group responses by type of firm (such as retail, wholesale, or service). This classification can be as specific as "eating and drinking places," "cleaning businesses," "food stores," "apparel stores," and so forth. As the number of subgroups increases, however, the total sample size also should be increased to provide perhaps 50 to 100 interviews from each category.

A local government should limit its survey to only a few categories of businesses or to three to five geographic areas of the city with at most 100 interviews from each.

How Should the Sample Be Selected?

A number of sources can provide a listing of businesses from which a random sample can be drawn, for example:

- *Local government lists of business establishments.* Local governments keep such lists for licensing, taxing, or occupancy and property inspection purposes. Tax lists include profit-making firms and are generally reasonably up-to-date. Because requirements for inspection vary (for example, some businesses are inspected once a year, others every two years), inspection lists may be somewhat outdated. Moreover, some businesses that have been granted a license may no longer be operating in the city.

- *Classified section of the local telephone directory.* Most local businesses are listed here, but there are two problems with using the directory. First, multiple listings for the same firm are common. For example, a single appliance store could be listed under "appliances," "refrigerators," "washers," "dryers," "freezers," "air conditioners," "service and repair," and so on. A random sample drawn without accounting for multiple listings will give those businesses so listed a greater chance of being selected. A second problem with the telephone directory is that it often includes establishments located outside the jurisdiction. However, most of these probably could be screened out before interviewing.

- *Directories of businesses.* The relative currency and comprehensiveness of these lists should be considered.

- *Member lists of local and area merchant associations (or the local chamber of commerce).* These associations chiefly represent local retail establishments and may be the least complete source.

Local governments should evaluate each available list or directory for the following characteristics: its coverage of businesses; its currentness; the completeness of its information for each business (address, telephone number, and name of manager); and the ease with which information it offers can be acquired and used.

Once a list has been settled on, the businesses should be selected in a statistically random way. As noted above, the local government might want to set certain criteria for those businesses to be included before the selection process begins. For example, the sample could be restricted to certain types of businesses, and to those in business in certain locations for at least twelve months. If possible, the criteria should be examined for each business drawn for the sample in advance of any interviewing, and replacements selected only when necessary to replace inappropriate ones.

How Should the Survey Be Conducted and Who Should Conduct It?
Three basic techniques exist: in-person interviews, telephone surveys, and mail surveys (plus combinations thereof). If the resources for in-person interviewing—usually the most expensive and time-consuming technique—are available, this method is generally preferred because its results are likely to be the most thoughtful and complete. In addition, such interviews can be good public relations for the local government; they indicate that it is interested in its business. Rock Island, Illinois, found good public relations to be a major product of its annual in-person interviews with samples of businesses (undertaken as part of a regional "Business Connection" effort). If personal interviewing is used, an appointment should be arranged for the interview. The caller also can determine in advance of the interview whether the business establishment meets such requirements as length of time at the location or class of business to be included in the sample.

With a questionnaire such as the one in Appendix 2 (20 to 30 minutes in length), telephone interviewing should also be feasible. It is less expensive and less time-consuming than the in-person interview because no travel time is involved.

Appointments may still be necessary, as it is difficult to retain the businessperson's attention for a long telephone interview without advance notice and commitment. With either telephone or in-person interviewing, interruptions may occur, making it necessary to postpone completing the interview. Three to five contacts with a business are likely to be required to arrange for and complete the survey. A letter explaining in advance the purpose and use of the information to be gathered can help gain business managers' cooperation both in initially agreeing to and in completing the interviews.

The mail survey is the least expensive and most feasible, but it is also the least reliable. A large percentage of those contacted may not respond. Persons who respond may well have opinions that are not representative of the entire business community. The respondents may also be less likely to answer honestly if they feel their written responses could "float around city hall." Moreover, someone other than the desired respondents (owner, manager, or assistant manager) may complete the survey. These factors could have a marked effect on the findings. If the response rate is low (that is, if less than half of those who are mailed surveys complete and return them), the representativeness of the survey statistics will be questionable.

The percentage of businesspersons responding can be increased if special efforts are made to send out follow-up mailings or make telephone calls as reminders and to offer a telephone interview. Governments should consider making this survey a joint government-business venture. Local business associations, such as the chamber of commerce, can be consulted and asked to help with such tasks as selecting survey topics, pretesting candidate questions, selecting or preparing the list from which the sample is drawn, and, especially important, requesting businesses to participate in the survey, thereby helping to obtain high response rates with fewer contacts.

Interviewing, if used, can be conducted by professional survey personnel or, to reduce costs, by government personnel, volunteers, or persons from business associations who have been trained by, and are supervised by, professional survey personnel.

How Frequently Should Businesses Be Surveyed?
Businesses should be surveyed at least annually. However, to make the information more useful to program managers, an agency should consider split-

ting the annual sample into four quarterly samples (surveying one-fourth of the sample each quarter). The additional samples will provide program managers with more frequent, timely feedback and identify seasonal variations.

Need for Confidentiality of Individual Responses
All businesses contacted should be assured that at no time will any response be identified with a particular business.

Survey Cost

Costs will depend chiefly on the sample size, the method of interviewing, and the amount of analysis of the data collected. If extensive effort is not required to prepare the list from which the sample is drawn, a 20- to 30-minute, in-person survey of 300 business establishments using a local contractor and a questionnaire similar to that shown in Appendix 2 should cost approximately $6,000 to $10,000. Costs for a telephone survey would be 25 to 50 percent less. Cash outlays for the business survey will be reduced if, as suggested above, some of the work is done by current government employees or by volunteers. If government employees or volunteers are used for sample selection and interviewing, professional survey guidance still should be obtained to prepare the questionnaire (at least for the initial survey), to develop the specific procedures for selection of persons to be interviewed, and to train interviewers.

The above estimates do not include costs for detailed development of the questionnaire or for analysis of the results. Basic tabulations of the results are included.

Survey Accuracy

Will the responses to the business survey actually represent the experiences and perceptions of the population of business establishments in the community on various aspects of the quality of government services? It is extremely difficult to prove that the findings are valid, but certain steps can be taken to increase the likelihood that the findings accurately represent the experiences and views of the business community. Some of these steps are described in Chapter 13 on customer surveys; they apply equally to surveys of citizens or of business people.

As indicated earlier, it is highly desirable when undertaking a business survey to enlist the aid of local business associations to achieve maximum cooperation of the respondents. A high response rate will reduce the chance of bias stemming from an inability to interview some businesses in the sample. It is also very important that the survey procedure provide for anonymity of responses in order to encourage frank and honest answers. In the end, however, each local government that undertakes a survey will need to utilize the approaches outlined above and in Chapter 13 to make sure its own survey efforts are as sound as possible.

Analysis of Findings

Chapter 16 contains a number of suggestions for analyzing survey and other performance data. Here are some considerations for analyzing the data obtained from surveys of businesses.

First, calculate the percentage of respondents that gave each category of response to each question (for example, the percentage of respondents that responded "about right," "not enough lighting," and "too much lighting" to the question "How adequate is the amount of public street lighting at night in your business area?" (See Question 8 in Appendix 2.) Use these percentages as the primary indicators of performance on these questions.

Second, break out the responses to each question being used as a performance indicator by such characteristics as the following:

- Major geographical area of the community
- Type of business
- Size of business (perhaps grouped in three categories: small, medium, and large). Size can be based either on the number of employees or on past sales. The information on these characteristics can be obtained from the questionnaire. (See, for example, Questions 51 and 53 in Appendix 2.)

Third, compile the responses to open-ended questions (such as Question 50 in Appendix 2) and the reasons respondents give for giving "poor" ratings to individual services. Provide these compilations anonymously to the agencies responsible for the particular services. Also, summarize the responses to each such open-ended question to identify issues raised by a significant number of respondents.

Chapter 15

Measuring Local Government Efficiency: A Preliminary Examination

Measuring the effectiveness and quality of local government services has been discussed in the preceding chapters. But it is also important for governments to measure their efficiency in using resources to produce these levels of public services. Ideally, each government, and each of its agencies, should measure regularly the following: To what degree does the government produce as effective a service as possible from its resources? Or alternatively, to what degree does it produce the product as inexpensively as it could? Regular measurement of various aspects of efficiency should give a perspective on the current level of efficiency and how it is changing over time for individual government services. In this chapter a framework is provided to help governments answer these questions and the vital, but often neglected, relationship between effectiveness and efficiency is discussed.

Some governments have been conducting limited efficiency measurement for years, generally by relating the amount of work accomplished to the number of employee-hours or dollars expended.

The first part of this chapter presents a classification of the types of efficiency measures that local governments might use and identifies some of the principal problems. The second part presents a list of efficiency measures that local governments may wish to consider.

Classifying Efficiency Measures

Five types of efficiency measures are described and illustrated below:

1. Output-input ratio measures, using work load data as the unit of output
2. Output-input ratio measures, using effectiveness data as the unit of output

3. Equipment and personnel utilization rates
4. Combinations of the preceding types of measures
5. Measures of relative change: "productivity indices."

The ratios in (1) and (2) presented here generally will be expressed as the "amount of output per unit of input," but the ratios can be inverted and used in the form "cost per unit of output." In general, these forms are equivalent. Each government can decide which form it prefers. (The term "productivity" traditionally has been used for measures in the form "amount of output per unit of input." The term "efficiency" has, in typical government usage, been used for measures in the form "cost per unit of output," that is, amount of input divided by the amount of output.)

These five types of measures are complementary. As with effectiveness measurement, seldom do single measures of efficiency adequately portray efficiency for any major service area. Thus, more than one efficiency measure for any given government service should be considered in order to obtain an overall perspective on efficiency. Also, as with effectiveness measurement, in-depth analysis generally will be needed to determine why the efficiency level is as it is and what is responsible for any improvement or deterioration.

In examining efficiency in government, it is often forgotten that efficiency implies a certain level and quality of service. If the quality of service is not at least maintained, an increase in output-input ratios is not really an efficiency improvement. Thus, to obtain a complete picture of government performance, both effectiveness and efficiency measures must be examined. Efficiency may seem to be improving (or worsening), while in reality the service quality may be deteriorating (or improving). For example, an increase in tons of refuse collected per dollar could result from accelerated worker effort—but at the expense of more litter scattering or missed collections. Improved output-input ratios that are achieved at the expense of the quality of the service are not improved efficiency.

Type 1: Output-input ratio measures, using work load accomplished as the measure of output.

Most local governments are familiar with this kind of measure, though even today there is surprisingly little regular measurement being undertaken. For most government activities, one or more physical work load units can be identified as the outputs. Examples of such outputs include tons of refuse collected, miles of street repaired, acres of park grass mowed, number of park trees trimmed, number of complaints or requests handled, and number of government vehicles serviced. These outputs can be related to the amount of resources used in producing them. Normally dollars or employee-hours are used as the input units. The measure can thus be expressed as a ratio such as "the number of tons collected per dollar or per employee-hour."

The amount of work performed, such as tons of refuse collected, is not by itself a measure of efficiency. Also, the work load *facing* a government (but not yet accomplished), even if divided by expenditures, is not an efficiency measure. Measures such as pupil-teacher ratios and ratios of the number of cases per caseworker reflect chiefly the work load facing employees; they indicate nothing about output and thus are not measures of efficiency.

A variation of the output-input ratio measure, sometimes used in local governments, is "work standards." In this variation, the "number of work units produced per employee-hour" is compared with the expected number of hours to complete that amount of work. The resulting ratio indicates the extent to which the employees exceeded or were under the standard. This variation is applicable to those activities for which work standards can be developed, generally the more repetitive activities, such as repetitive maintenance activities. In effect the government estimates the amount of time a specific work activity "should" take (the "standard") and compares actual performance against the standard.

"Costs per capita" for individual services while interesting are not efficiency measures, since the population size is seldom, if ever, the output of a service. This form of measure may be appropriate when a product is provided directly to persons or households, as with waste collection and water supply. It seems less useful, and probably misleading for efficiency measurement purposes, to count all the population in the jurisdiction as being served when a significant part of the population may not actually use the particular service (as is likely to be the case with recreation or transit services).

In some instances, "dollars expended per capita" has been used as a ratio to *maximize*, not minimize; in these instances "dollars expended" is used as a proxy for *output*. These measures have been used in this way for such services as education and libraries. The use of dollars expended as an output measure begs the question as to what output was actually achieved. It is recommended that dollars not be used as a proxy for output.

In undertaking and using output-input ratios, public agencies should consider the quality of the output. Improvement in the ratio of work accomplished per unit of input is not an improvement in efficiency if the level of service has deteriorated. When providing comparisons of this type of measure over time or among various work groups, and no statement is made to the contrary, the user of the data should be able to assume that the quality of the output has not been reduced. This means that a government should provide for explicit assessment of that quality and report those findings along with the output-input ratios. Alternatively, one may utilize the second type of efficiency measure.

Type 2: Output-input ratio measures, using effectiveness data as the measure of output.

Agencies should consider the real product of public services and not merely rely on some physical output that happens to be easily measured. For example, should an inadequately patched pothole, or an arrest that was subsequently dropped because of inadequate police evidence, or a citizen request that was not satisfactorily resolved, be credited in counting output? No, it should not. In the case of the defective pothole repair, the repair should not be included in the output until it is done properly, and the extra expense of the repatching should be included in the costs. Thus, this second type of efficiency measure considers explicitly the quality of service as part of the measure.

This kind of efficiency measure is seldom used in local government today, probably because of the shortage of effectiveness data and a lack of familiarity with this type of measure. As meaningful effectiveness data become available for government services, measures of this type should come into more general use.

Many of the effectiveness measures identified throughout this volume are candidates for the output portion of this efficiency measure. Some illustrations are as follows:

- To measure the efficiency of police in solving crimes, it is tempting to use the measure "number of arrests per dollar or per police-officer-hour" as the key measure of efficiency. But arrests can be of poor quality, and the possibility of encouraging perverse effects, such as harassment of citizens, is sufficiently great that another measure reflecting the quality of arrests seems preferable. A preferable efficiency measure is "number of arrests *that pass the preliminary hearing* per dollar (or per police-officer-hour)." (See Chapter 6 for a discussion of the procedures for measuring the number of arrests that pass the preliminary hearing.)

- For human resource treatment programs such as employment and training programs, physical and mental health treatment, vocational rehabilitation, offender rehabilitation, and social services such as family counseling, the meaningful output unit should be something like "number of clients *improved* per unit of resource." The typical current form, number of clients *served* per unit of resources," says nothing about the results of the service provided, and its use as an efficiency measure is questionable.

- Another measure under this classification is "estimated number of households, citizens, or clients *satisfied* with the service (or with a particular aspect of the service) per dollar or per employee-hour." This form of efficiency measure will be particularly important to those who believe that customer satisfaction is a major product of local government services. The output count is "number of persons served" *multiplied by* the percentage of customers satisfied with the service. This information can be obtained with the use of systematic customer surveys discussed in other chapters. The percentages obtained from the sample surveys can be projected to the appropriate total population to provide estimates of the total number of customers who are satisfied.

This type of measure is subject to the problems that affect all effectiveness measures. One of these problems is the virtual impossibility of obtaining some highly desirable measures of effectiveness, such as the assessment of the success of "prevention" activities (prevention of crimes, fires, traffic accidents, or illnesses). The ideal efficiency measure, "number of events (crimes, fires, traffic accidents, or illnesses) prevented per dollar or per employee-hour," is rarely measurable. (An effort to estimate these, however, might be made periodically in special studies.) In effectiveness measurement, the approach generally used is to measure the number of incidents *not* prevented—that is, the number of crimes, fires, traffic accidents, or illnesses that do occur. These are useful and appropriate as measures of effectiveness, but constructing a ratio with these outputs related to dollars or employee-hours does not make sense. For example, the "number of crimes per dollar" and the "number of traffic accidents per dollar" are not meaningful efficiency ratios. If both the numerator (for example, the number of crimes) and the denominator (for example, the number of dollars) are reduced by 10 percent, the ratio will remain the same, implying that no improvement has occurred; in fact, there has been obvious improvement, because both crimes and costs are lower.

Effectiveness measures expressed as percentages, such as the percentage of clients satisfied with a particular service characteristic, cannot be used directly for these ratios. Such percentages should instead be converted to numbers of households or numbers of events, which can be used in the ratios.

Finally, a special type of effectiveness-to-input ratio is the benefit-cost (or cost-benefit) ratio. Here the output units (the benefits) are converted to monetary units that are presumed to represent the monetary value of the benefits. These dollars are then divided by the costs of achieving the benefits (or the costs can be subtracted from the benefits) to give the benefit-cost ratios (or net benefits). These can be considered measures of efficiency. The attribution of dollar values to the various products of government services is complex and can involve very shaky assumptions, as, for example, in attributing dollar value to the time saved by a new road. The principal use for these benefit-cost computations probably will be in special studies (if reasonable dollar value attributions can be made of the benefits) rather than in regular monitoring by a government.

Type 3: Equipment and personnel utilization rates.

This common type of efficiency measure reflects the amount of specific resources of the local government (equipment-hours or employee-hours) that are utilized (or not utilized) for potentially "productive" activities. This type of measure does *not* directly assess the amount of output obtained from these resources and thus should be considered only as a "proxy" indicator. Yet, versions of it can be useful for some government services. The most prevalent form of the measure is the ratio of the amount of the resource actually used to the amount potentially available.

In general, the more downtime a piece of government equipment has, or the larger proportion of time that a government employee is not utilized for operational duties, the less efficiently those resources are being used.

In most cases it is impossible, as well as undesirable, to achieve 100 percent utilization of equipment or personnel. But for the most part, it is desirable to increase the percentage of time that they are utilized up to some practical limit.

Although "total available hours" is the unit often used in the denominator of the ratio, utilization and availability rates may not be equivalent. A piece of equipment or an employee may be available for work but not be used. In practice, governments often collect data on obvious downtime, such as time that a vehicle is in the shop being repaired. These statistics will not, however, capture the amount of time that the vehicle is available for use but unused because of lack of work or other scheduling problems. Preferably, this type of measure would focus on utilization, but as a practical matter it may be more feasible to measure availability.

Utilization and availability rates can be reported in a number of ways. Some of the most common are as follows:

- Percentage of available hours that each type of equipment (or employee) was utilized (or not utilized) for productive operation
- Average amount of utilization (or nonutilization or downtime) per piece of equipment (or employee)
- Average percentage or average number of pieces of equipment (or employees) utilized (or not utilized).

These rates also may be expressed in a form that emphasizes preselected thresholds rather than averages:

- Number of instances in which nonutilization of a piece of equipment (or employee) exceeded x hours
- Percentage of total hours that y or more pieces of equipment (or employees) were not utilized.

Here x and y are preselected threshold values.

This type of efficiency measure is somewhat complicated by the problem of backup equipment or personnel. The effect on government services of the breakdown of a piece of equipment, or the unavailability of personnel, will vary with the extent to which backup equipment, or personnel, is available. Similarly, if equipment breaks down at the end of a shift and is not scheduled for use in the next shift, its unavailability is of less consequence than if it breaks down during hours when it is needed. The

same goes for an employee who is sick during slack work periods.

Note that measures of delays in serving citizens have not been included under the term "efficiency measures." Promptness is considered a quality of the service to citizens and is thus included in the classification as a measure of effectiveness.

Two special variations of utilization rates are as follows:

- In water supply, the "percentage of water that does not generate revenue or is otherwise not used 'productively'"
- In public transit, the load factors, such as the ratio of actual passenger-miles to the total available capacity (seat-miles).

In the first case, resources are used to treat and distribute the water; water loss due to such circumstances as leaks does not provide a service. In the second case, seats for potential passengers are transported from one point to another at some cost; if those seats are not filled, no service is delivered by those seats.

Type 4: Combinations of the preceding types of measures.

Normally, more than one output measure is relevant to the efficiency of a local government service. Each such relevant measure should be calculated and presented separately. It is tempting, however, to try to combine measures into a more comprehensive measure. An example of such a combined measure is shown in Exhibit 15-1.[1] Such measures usually are difficult to understand, and they tend to contain hidden value judgments about the relative importance of each factor in the index. If a combined measure is used, each component measure should also be presented, as in Exhibit 15-1, to provide full information to users.

Type 5: Measures of relative change: "productivity indices."

These indices are used to measure percentage changes as related to a preselected base period. They measure relative efficiency rather than absolute efficiency. A productivity index can be constructed for any of the previous types of measures. A base year (or base period of perhaps two or three years) can be used for any measure. The base period is given the value of 100. For example, if tons collected per employee-hour were 200 in the base year, and 225 in a subsequent year, the productivity index for the subsequent year would be $225/200 \times 100 = 112.5$—indicating 12.5 percent higher productivity. Indices can be calculated for each such efficiency measure. Line 10 in Exhibit 15-1 provides an example. By weighting different indices (such as by the relative amount of total employee-hours for each service in the base year), different government activities can be combined to form an overall index.

For many years the U.S. Bureau of Labor Statistics has used such indices for tracking productivity of federal government, as well as private industry, activities.

Problems in Collecting Input Data

At first glance, it may seem that measuring the amounts of inputs is easy. Unfortunately, in actual practice many complications arise. Some of the chief issues follow.

Cost Accounting and Allocation
The figures representing the input resources—generally dollars or employee-hours—ideally should represent all the resources required to produce the outputs that are measured and only those. For solid waste collection, for example, estimates should include all the dollars or employee-hours involved in collection activities, but exclude costs for disposal. The total costs of any activity of which the efficiency is being measured should include employee-benefit costs (including full pension costs); costs of clerks,

secretaries, and supervisors; costs of procuring and maintaining equipment; and costs of obtaining and maintaining necessary facilities. When estimating the efficiency for subfunctions (such as solid waste collection for residential customers as distinct from collection for commercial customers), the problem of allocating costs or employee-hours becomes more difficult. Unfortunately, local government accounting systems in most jurisdictions do not automatically provide costs in the needed categories.

A further complication in the measurement of costs and employee-hours is the problem of shared costs. For example, solid waste collection and disposal activities may share some of the same supervisors and some of the same facilities. Similarly, a single police officer may undertake crime prevention, criminal apprehension, and perhaps traffic-control activities. Procedures are needed for allocating these joint costs if it is deemed desirable to examine separately the efficiency of these individual activities. The allocation rules probably will have to be arbitrary.

Capital and Investment Costs
Another difficult issue in cost measurement is how to handle capital and other investment costs. If investment costs are charged only to the year in which the costs are obligated or in which expenditures occur, the efficiency estimate for those years would be too low and for subsequent years, too high. Investment costs should probably be spread over the years

---

Exhibit 15-1

Illustrative Efficiency Measurement Presentation (Solid Waste Collection)

	1990	1991	Changes
Data			
1. Tons of solid waste collected	90,000	100,000	+10,000
2. Average litter cleanliness rating[1]	2.9	2.6	−0.3
3. Percentage of survey population expressing satisfaction with collection[1]	85%	80%	−5%
4. Cost (unadjusted)	$1,200,000	$1,500,000	+$300,000
5. Cost (1990 dollars)	$1,200,000	$1,300,000	+$100,000
Efficiency Measures[2]			
6. Tons per dollar (unadjusted)	75 tons per $ thousand	67 tons per $ thousand	−11%
7. Tons per dollar (1990 dollars)	75 tons per $ thousand	77 tons per $ thousand	+3%
8. Combined measure: $\frac{(1)\times(2)\times(3)}{(4)}$ (unadjusted dollars)	0.185	0.139	−25%
9. Combined measure: $\frac{(1)\times(2)\times(3)}{(5)}$ (1990 dollars)	0.185	0.160	−14%
10. Productivity index for Measure 9 (1990 base year)	100	86	−14%

[1]For such procedures, see Chapter 2. The rating in line 2 is based on a scale of 1 to 4, with 4 the cleanest.
[2]The figures in line 7 indicate some improvement in efficiency, but those in line 6 suggest that cost increases such as wages have more than exceeded the efficiency gains. Efficiency, as indicated by the combined measures used, has gone down

because of decreases in the street cleanliness ratings and decreased citizen satisfaction. Like most such complex measures, they are somewhat arbitrary and difficult to interpret. Measures such as these must be studied carefully before being accepted for use.

for which the investment is used, but the best method for doing this remains a matter for debate. Possible approaches are to use the appropriate annual debt service charges (if the funds are raised by borrowing) or to use amortization procedures. Another approach is to estimate what it would cost to lease the piece of equipment or rent the facility and then use that figure as the cost for the year. If the municipality leases the equipment or rents the facility, those costs can be used. In some cases a local government may be using revolving funds; for example, a central garage may charge each agency for vehicle maintenance in such a way as to cover all the costs of the garage, including equipment and even facilities. If the local government does not already use one of these procedures, a procedure will be needed to estimate a fair share of the costs for each activity.

The common practice is to exclude capital costs from the measures and to consider only operating costs in the calculations. This means, however, that the efficiency measures will not be useful for comparisons between capital-intensive and labor-intensive practices. For example, output per *operating* cost dollar may have increased, but when the capital investment that led to reduced operating cost is considered, efficiency in terms of total expenditures may actually be found to have decreased.

Comparing Costs over Time

Another problem occurs when cost comparisons are made over time. Changes may occur in price levels, in accounting procedures, or in definitions of the costs. Such changes may require data adjustments. Cost data for different years can be adjusted for changes in price to indicate how "real" efficiency is changing in terms of quantity of physical resources used. Price indices should be applied to convert the dollar costs for each year to a base year.

The question arises as to whether the government should use one overall deflator (an index of prices of all government items) or different deflators that permit the reflection of different mixes of inputs for each service area. The latter is preferable, but it is more arduous. Because local governments probably are interested in both "real" changes and changes in output per actual dollar, unadjusted for price-level changes, it is recommended that both be calculated and presented. (See lines 6-9 of Exhibit 15-1 for an illustration of the use of such price indices.)

Employee-Hours or Dollars

Both "output per employee-hour" and "output per dollar" (with dollars adjusted for price changes) are desirable for measuring efficiency. The employee-hour measure produces major insights into the principal government input—personnel commonly called "labor productivity." Dollar cost represents, at least roughly, all inputs and, thus, in effect permits simultaneous consideration of the efficiency of use of all resources, not just personnel.

Miscellaneous Issues

Current Efficiency versus Future Performance

When a local government undertakes to measure efficiency, there is a danger of encouraging excessive concern with current performance at the expense of future performance. If too much emphasis is put on current efficiency, expenditures aimed at improving future performance may be neglected. (This danger, of course, also exists for local governments that are not measuring performance at all.) One way to alleviate this problem, as discussed earlier, is to avoid charging total investment and development costs to the current year's budget but to spread these costs over future years as well.

Interpreting Efficiency Data

Many factors can affect the values calculated for efficiency measures, even though the work force itself has not altered its pace or procedures. Substantial increases or decreases in the incoming work load can by themselves significantly affect efficiency values. The type of service provided by the government may change. In addition, differing external characteristics of neighborhoods (such as the terrain or resident population) can make it difficult to compare various facilities or different units of workers in different areas.

These qualifications do not mean that examining efficiency is not useful, but rather that conclusions should not be jumped at or be based on only the efficiency data without careful consideration of likely causes. As with effectiveness data, it is highly desirable to classify the work load in terms of its "difficulty." Displaying measurement results by categories of difficulty permits analysts to consider differences in mixes of work load difficulty when interpreting changes in efficiency measures. For example, data on measures involving solutions of crimes, such as "number of arrests that pass preliminary hearing per police-officer-hour," should be grouped to distinguish arrests relating to crimes with little evidence at the scene of the crime from those with considerable evidence.

Efficiency measurements that cover a whole year can be compared with data from other years without concern for seasons. For shorter time periods, consideration of seasonal effects on efficiency will be necessary. Service managers might set different efficiency targets (against which to compare actual efficiency) for each season. Alternatively, after gaining experience, a local government may choose to make statistical, seasonal adjustments to measured values so that efficiency comparisons can be made among time periods within a year.

Avoiding Excessive Efficiency Measurement

The number of activities and subactivities in local government that can be measured for efficiency seems endless. Some local governments that engaged in very detailed efficiency measurement efforts found they were unable to survive their own tests of cost-effectiveness. Moreover, efforts requiring highly detailed time-keeping can cause considerable annoyance to the personnel involved. Excessive data collection leads to knowing more and more about less and less, and it should be avoided.

Elements Affecting Usefulness of the Measurements

Individual local governments should assess the desirability of using both efficiency and effectiveness measures by considering such criteria as the following:

- Do the measures collectively cover all important aspects of the service activity? If not, improvements or deterioration in those aspects that are being measured should be kept in perspective. Users of efficiency measurement data should consider the unmeasured aspects and should not, for example, reward or penalize government personnel solely on aspects that can be quantified.

- To what extent can the government affect the measured values? Particularly with measures that use effectiveness estimates for output calculations (Type 2 measures), a government will not have complete control over the measured values. If a government has little or no control, the measure probably will not be useful to it.

- Is the measure understandable to users? The combination measures (Type 4) are particularly likely to pose a comprehension problem, but other types of measures can as well.

- Are the costs and personnel requirements to collect the data reasonable? For Type 2 measures, unless the government has ongoing effectiveness-measurement procedures (for example, regular customer survey procedures), it may not be practical to collect such measurements solely for efficiency measurement. It may be tempting,

especially for Type 1 measures, to measure activities in increasing detail. If extensive daily activity reports are required, the costs of data processing can quickly become excessive.

- Is there provision for analyzing the findings from the measurement process? The government should provide for the examination of changes in measured values. The following possibilities, among others, should be considered: The change may have occurred primarily because of an increase (or decrease) in work load without an accompanying increase or (decrease) in personnel or dollars; or the apparent improvement may have been achieved at the expense of a reduced level or quality of service.

Illustrative Measures of Efficiency

In this section, a number of illustrative measures of efficiency of Types 1–3 are identified for the municipal services discussed in this report: solid waste collection and disposal, parks and recreation, library services, crime control, fire protection, local transportation services, water supply, and handling of complaints and requests for services and information.

The measures shown here are intended to provoke discussion and more in-depth examination and testing by individual local governments and their agencies. Some governments already are collecting data regularly on some of these efficiency measures, and many other governments are collecting data that can be readily adapted for calculating some of these measures. However, most of the measures that relate amount of input to units of effectiveness (Type 2) are unfamiliar to most government managers.

Governments seeking to employ measures requiring effectiveness data will need to use the appropriate data collection procedures such as described in other chapters of this volume. As indicated in the section on data collection problems earlier in this chapter, calculating values for the relevant amounts of dollars or employee-hours poses some problems. Therefore, some effort by individual governments may be required before some of these measures will be fully operational.

The measures are listed by service area and are classified by type. Ratio measures are expressed in the form "output divided by input," but the inverse, "input divided by output," is equivalent. In most cases, the input units can be either dollars or employee-hours. They have been expressed here in terms of one or the other somewhat arbitrarily. Measures of utilization (Type 3) can be expressed either in terms of degree of utilization or nonutilization.

All the measures illustrated for any single service area can be used together; they are complementary, not substitutes for each other. Together with effectiveness measures, measures such as these should provide a reasonably full perspective on the performance of those government services.

Solid Waste Collection—Measures of Efficiency

Type 1: Output in units of work load ÷ input.

1-1 Tons collected per dollar.
1-2 Number of curb-miles of streets cleaned per dollar.
1-3 Number of large items hauled away (such as abandoned autos, refrigerators) per dollar.
1-4 Number of residential (or commercial) customers served per dollar.

Type 2: Output in units of "effectiveness" ÷ input.

2-1 Estimated number of total households and commercial customers satisfied with their collection services (as estimated from responses to a customer survey and survey of businesses) per dollar.

Type 3: Utilization measures.

3-1 Average percentage of vehicles out of commission at any one time (during working hours).
3-2 Percentage of crew-shifts with shortage of personnel.

Solid Waste Disposal—Measures of Efficiency

Type 1: Output in units of work load ÷ input

1-1 Number of tons disposed per dollar.
1-2 Number of tons disposed per acre (or per cubic yard of fill used). (Note: Here an input measure other than dollars or employee-hours, that is, acreage, is used. A major scarce resource, in this case land, can be used as the input unit.)

Type 2: Output in units of "effectiveness" ÷ input.

2-1 Estimated number of site-days of environmental-hazard-free disposal per dollar.

Type 3: Utilization measures.

3-1 Percentage of working hours that major equipment is available.
3-2 Number of days that same-day cover was not achieved because of equipment failure or shortage of personnel.

Parks and Recreation—Measures of Efficiency

Type 1: Output in units of work load ÷ input.

1-1 Acres (or square feet of facility) maintained (mowed, cleaned, and so forth) per dollar, for various types of facilities. This can be split into more detailed work activities to provide such measures as "acres of grass mowed per employee-hour," "number of trees trimmed per employee-hour," "tons of litter removed per employee-hour," and "pieces of playground equipment repaired per dollar." Comparisons between facilities should allow for differences in terrain, use levels, and other characteristics that lead to different maintenance requirements at different locations.
1-2 Number of hours of operation per dollar, for individual programs.

Type 2: Output in units of "effectiveness" ÷ input.

2-1 Attendance- or visit-days per dollar, perhaps for individual programs or facilities.
2-2 Estimated number of *different* households using recreation services (at least once a year) per dollar, perhaps for individual facilities. (These estimates could be based on the participation rates obtained from a household survey; see Chapter 4.)
2-3 Estimated number of households satisfied with recreation services (as estimated by data from a household or user survey) per dollar.

Type 3: Utilization measures.

3-1 Major equipment in-commission rates (perhaps calculated as the total number of equipment-days in commission divided by the total potential number of equipment-days).
3-2 Percentage of time facilities are closed for maintenance (percentages should be calculated for individual facilities such as swimming pools and tennis courts, as well as overall).

Library Services—Measures of Efficiency

Type 1: Output in units of work load ÷ input.

1-1 Number of items circulated (books, records, and other items) per dollar (see Chapter 5).
1-2 Number of items cataloged per employee-hour.
1-3 Number of items shelved per employee-hour.
1-4 Number of hours of operation per dollar.

Type 2: Output in units of "effectiveness" ÷ input.

2-1 Number of individual uses of library (including attendance counts plus telephone requests for information) per dollar.
2-2 Estimated number of different households (or persons) using library services at least once (as estimated from a household survey) per dollar.
2-3 Estimated number of households satisfied with library services (as estimated from a household or user survey) per dollar.

Type 3: Utilization measures.

3-1 Percentage of computer terminals available during library service hours.

3-2 Bookmobile out-of-commission rates.

Crime Control—Measures of Efficiency

Type 1: Output in units of work load ÷ input.

1-1 Number of service calls responded to per police-officer-hour, by type of call.

1-2 Number of investigations conducted per police-officer-hour, by type of case.

1-3 Number of arrests per police-officer-hour (but see Measure 2-1 below).

Type 2: Output in units of "effectiveness" ÷ input.

2-1 Number of felony arrests that pass preliminary hearing per police-officer-hour, overall and by type of category. (Ideally, Measure 1-3 should be replaced by this measure to provide assurance that arrests were sound; see discussion in Chapter 6.)

2-2 Estimated number of households reporting a reasonable feeling of security in walking in their neighborhoods at night (as estimated from household survey findings) per dollar.

2-3 Estimated number of nonvictimized households and commercial establishments per dollar. (The household survey can be used to provide estimates of the number of crime incidents not reported; see Chapter 6.)

Type 3: Utilization measures.

3-1 Percentage of total potentially available police-officer-time that is spent on "productive" activities (productive time would exclude such time as waiting for car repair, waiting in court, and so forth).

3-2 Average percentage of police officers available for "productive" activities.

Fire Protection—Measures of Efficiency

Type 1: Output in units of work load ÷ input.

1-1 Number of fire calls responded to per dollar. (But note the problem that more fires in the community will "improve" the results on this measure.)

1-2 Number of fire prevention inspections per dollar, perhaps categorized by residential or commercial.

Type 2: Output in units of "effectiveness" ÷ input.

2-1 Number of fires fought for which less than a target amount of spread occurred per suppression dollar spent. (Target amount of spread would be defined relative to the size of the fire on arrival and possibly other relevant variables, such as occupancy type; see Chapter 7 for a discussion of these procedures.)

2-2 Number of households and business establishments "protected" per dollar, with "protected" defined as those establishments without a fire during the period.

Type 3: Utilization measures.

3-1 Percentage of downtime of major fire equipment.

3-2 Percentage of time fire crews are understaffed.

Local Transportation Services—Measures of Efficiency

Street Maintenance

Type 1: Output in units of work load ÷ input.

1-1 Number of miles (or lane-miles) of street maintained per dollar.

1-2 Number of repairs made (or number of square yards of repairs made) per employee-hour. (Individual street and maintenance activities might be broken out by, for example, "repairs with cold patch," "repairs with asphalt concrete," and "curb and gutter repair.")

1-3 Number of square yards of street surface constructed per dollar.

Type 2: Output in units of "effectiveness" ÷ input.

2-1 Number of lane-miles of street maintained in rideability-condition x or better per dollar. (See Chapter 8 on local transportation for a discussion of procedures for assessing rideability.)

2-2 Number of lane-miles of street improved to rideability-condition x per dollar.

2-3 Number of repairs made satisfactorily (for example, "patches lasting at least x months after repair") per dollar.

Type 3: Utilization measures.

3-1 Proportion of time that crews are "nonproductive" (for such reasons as being in transit or waiting for materials).

Traffic

Type 1: Output in units of work load ÷ input.

1-1 Number of signs installed per employee-hour.

1-2 Number of signals installed per employee-hour.

1-3 Number of feet of street markings laid per dollar.

1-4 Number of signs or signals repaired per employee-hour.

Type 2: Output in units of "effectiveness" ÷ input.

2-1 Number of signs or signals maintained in acceptable operating condition per dollar.

2-2 Number of intersections without an accident per dollar (with intersections grouped by amount of traffic).

Type 3: Utilization measures.

3-1 Percentage of traffic signal time that signals were known to be defective.

3-2 Average amount of downtime of traffic signals from time signals were reported defective.

3-3 Average time to restore to service defective traffic signs.

Public Transit—Measures of Efficiency

Type 1: Output in units of work load ÷ input.

1-1 Number of vehicle-miles per dollar.

1-2 Number of transit vehicle-hours of operation per dollar.

Type 2: Output in units of "effectiveness" ÷ input.

2-1 Number of passenger-trips per dollar.

2-2 Number of passenger-miles per dollar.

2-3 Estimated number of "satisfied" users (as estimated from household or user survey) per dollar.

Type 3: Utilization measures.

3-1 Average percentage of time transit vehicles are available as a percentage of potentially available hours, by type of vehicle.

3-2 Percentage of scheduled arrival times that are late or missed because of unavailable personnel or equipment.

3-3 Load factor: Ratio of actual passenger-miles to capacity, with capacity perhaps defined by seat-miles.

Water Supply—Measures of Efficiency

Type 1: Output in units of work load ÷ input.

1-1 Number of gallons distributed per dollar.

1-2 Number of gallons treated per dollar.

1-3 Number of customers served per dollar (perhaps broken out by residential and commercial customers).

1-4 Number of repairs completed per employee-hour, by type and size of repair.

1-5 Number of meters read/inspected/repaired per employee-hour.

1-6 Number of water quality tests per dollar.

Type 2: Output in units of "effectiveness" ÷ input.

2-1 Estimated number of customers indicating satisfaction with their water (as estimated from the user survey) per dollar.

2-2 A weighted amount of "pollutants" removed per dollar. (The amount of improvement between the quality of the incoming, untreated water and the quality of the water supplied to consumers is a vital indicator of water supply effectiveness. A satisfactory efficiency measure covering this element has not been identified.)

Type 3: Utilization measures.

3-1 Average percentage of downtime for major equipment as a percentage of total, potentially useful, equipment hours, by category of equipment.

3-2 Percentage of water distributed that generates revenue or is otherwise used productively (such as for government uses, including fire fighting) as distinguished from water lost to leakage or other problems.

Handling of Citizen Complaints and Requests for Services and Information—Measures of Efficiency

Type 1: Output in units of work load ÷ input.

1-1 Number of complaints and requests for services and information handled per employee-hour or per dollar. (Note: It may not be feasible to distinguish the time or dollar costs for complaints from those for services and information.)

Type 2: Output in units of "effectiveness" ÷ input.

2-1 Number of complaints and requests for services and information resolved satisfactorily (as estimated from customer surveys or from examination of government records—see the data collection procedures discussed in Chapter 11). Because of difficulties in distinguishing costs for each activity, it may not be feasible to distinguish complaints from requests for services and information.

Type 3: Utilization measures.

None identified.

---

1 More complex approaches—more appropriate to in-depth analysis than to regular performance status monitoring—are possible. For example, statistical, multiple-regression analysis can be used to relate past output magnitudes to magnitudes of resources. The amount of resources actually used in a subsequent time period can then be inserted into the regression equation to estimate the effectiveness levels *expected to be achieved* with those resources. These can then be compared against actual outputs as an estimate of efficiency.

Chapter 16

Using Effectiveness Measurement Information

T his chapter discusses specific uses for effectiveness measurement data, suggests procedures for analyzing the data, and suggests ways of reporting such data to facilitate their use.

Uses for Effectiveness Data

This section presents ten potential uses for effectiveness measurement information:

- Accountability—to review progress and trends of government services
- Resource allocation
- Budget formulation and justification
- Program evaluation and analysis
- Employee motivation
- Performance contracting
- Quality control checks on efficiency measurements
- Management control
- Improvement of communication between citizens and local government officials
- *Above all*, improvement of services to customers.

Accountability—to Review Progress and Trends of Government Services

If data collection procedures such as those described in this report are undertaken quarterly, or at least annually, performance can be reviewed and compared from period to period, to identify problems, progress, and, after several periods of data collection, time trends. Progress and time trends can indicate to government officials whether a service is adequate.

Resource Allocation

By identifying problem areas, effectiveness measurement information can provide guidance to management concerning allocation of resources. Breaking out the measurement data by neighborhood residential areas and other important client-group characteristics will provide information on the *specific* geographic areas and client groups with major problems or needs. Breakouts that distinguish service quality for individual facilities, organizational units, and other service characteristics, can guide program managers to areas needing improvement. In addition, measures that yield information on specific service quality characteristics (as distinguished from the overall ratings for service areas) can provide operating agency management with information on specific problems. For example, the city of St. Petersburg used information on the percentage of respondents reporting rat sightings by geographic area to help guide its rodent-control program. Savannah, Georgia, has used effectiveness measurement information to help quantify the liveability of the city's 29 geographic planning areas in order to design service programs to correct unacceptable conditions. Savannah's procedures attempt to distinguish high-need areas of the community and allocate resources in accordance with need.[1]

New York City has used its frequent ratings of street cleanliness to help assign cleaning crews. A related issue is equality in the distribution of services.

Effectiveness data adds an important ingredient to reviews of equality of distribution of services, if the performance data are broken out by client groups.

The use of effectiveness measurement information to help with the allocation of resources can be a significant move away from squeaky-wheel decision making.

Budget Formulation and Justification

The budget process is clearly an important element in a government's allocation of resources. Budget information should include information on service effectiveness. After effectiveness measurement procedures have been tested and found to yield reliable data, effectiveness information can be required in budget preparation and justification. This information can help managers make initial budget decisions and can help government officials justify expenditures to the council and to the public. Effectiveness information should be of considerable importance in making rational budget choices.

Program Evaluation and Analysis

Local governments periodically undertake in-depth studies of important program issues. An essential requirement for these studies is detailed information on program effectiveness. This information will be more easily assembled if service-area effectiveness measurement data are collected regularly. Even when special data are needed for particular studies, measures of effectiveness and data collection procedures such as those discussed in this report are likely to be useful for these studies.

For example, if an agency wants to experiment with a new program procedure, it can apply that procedure to a sample of clients, or to particular geographic areas of the community. The analysts can then compare service effectiveness data from the agency's regular effectiveness measurement process on these particular clients, or areas, against the measurement data for clients, or areas, for which the old program procedures continue to be used. The analysts need only alter the effectiveness measurement procedures to indicate into which of the two groups the client, or area, was placed. The data can then be tabulated for each of the two groups to compare the relative service quality levels of the new and old program procedures (a *comparison-group* analysis).

Similarly, analysts can examine the regularly collected measurement data to assess the extent to which a particular action, project, or procedure has affected service effectiveness over time (a *time-series* analysis).

An example of an evaluation is the District of Columbia's use of the street cleanliness-rating and citizen survey procedures (see Chapter 2) to evaluate a special clean-up campaign, "Operation Clean-Sweep." This intensive, one-time clean-up campaign removed accumulated litter and wastes from public and private property. Several hundred regular and supplemental cleaning personnel combed the city, cleaning all public streets and alleys one area at a time. Residents were encouraged to tackle their own properties and to set out refuse for collection.

The city evaluated the procedure to determine its potential to bring about short-term and lasting improvements in neighborhood cleanliness. The three bases for evaluation were:

- Changes in cleanliness ratings of streets and alleys. Visual inspections of virtually every street and alley were made the week before and the week after the special collection in each area; results were expressed in terms of average cleanliness ratings and the percentage of blocks with ratings of 2.5 or worse, grouped for each sanitation district (see Chapter 2 for a description of this procedure).

- Changes in citizen perceptions of cleanliness. Results of a citizen survey taken four months after "Clean-Sweep" were compared with those of a citizen survey taken four months previous to the operation.

- Program costs.

Exhibit 16-1 illustrates the effectiveness information that was obtained.

A trend toward auditing government services and programs by performance or results has been growing.[2] The legislative body or the chief executive can sponsor such auditing. Auditing program results is, in effect, program evaluation, the principal distinction being the evaluators' independence from the agency responsible for the program. Such auditing depends on the existence of adequate measurements of program effectiveness and quality.

Employee Motivation

Effectiveness information makes establishment of performance targets or incentive systems for both management and nonmanagement employees considerably more practical and meaningful. The development of performance incentives in the public sector in the past has been greatly handicapped by the lack of meaningful measures of the effectiveness and quality of services. Local governments attempting to focus on objective measures of performance have often had to rely on measures of input, process, or work load. Unfortunately, sole reliance on such measures can encourage government employees to overemphasize "quantity" aspects of their job, with resulting deterioration in the overall quality of government services.

Some local governments link annual employee compensation to performance. Designing procedures for tying earnings to performance involves complex issues that need careful handling—if employees are to be offered incentives to provide better service or to improve efficiency without lowering the quality of service. Objective measurements of quality are badly needed.

Local governments using some version of "management by objectives" should also find measures similar to those discussed in this report useful for inclusion in their lists of objectives, to ensure that service quality is explicitly addressed.

Even if performance is not formally tied to employee benefits, it can be beneficial to provide employees with feedback about the outcomes of their efforts. For example, findings from customer surveys can help make government employees more sensitive to citizens' perceptions of the services provided and encourage them to be more responsive to citizens' needs.

| Exhibit 16-1 |

Illustration of Use of Effectiveness Measurement Procedures for Program Evaluation: D.C. Operation Clean-Sweep

A. Trained observer cleanliness ratings

Service Area	Percentage of streets with litter ratings of 2.5 or worse	
	Before	*After*
1	3	1
2	19	5
3	21	12
4	20	7
5	20	15
6	46	47
7	40	6
8	0	0
9	4	4
TOTAL	19	11

B. Citizen survey results

Question	Percentage of responses	
	4 months before Clean-sweep (101 respondents)	4 months after Clean-sweep (110 respondents)
What do you think of the cleanliness of the street on which you live?		
a. Clean	14	13
b. Mostly clean	45	50
c. Fairly dirty	27	24
d. Very dirty	14	13
e. No opinion	0	0
Percentage satisfied (a + b)	59 ± 8	63 ± 7
Percentage dissatisfied (c + d)	41 ± 8	37 ± 7
Have you noticed any change in the cleanliness of your streets in the last 3 or 4 months?		
a. Very much cleaner		10
b. Somewhat cleaner		28
c. Somewhat dirty	not	3
d. Very much dirtier	applicable	2
e. No change noticed		52
f. Don't know/no opinion		5

Source: Blair and Schwartz, *How Clean Is Our City?*

Performance Contracting

Governments that contract for public services, such as solid waste collection, can use effectiveness measures to control the quality of the contractor's performance. Minimum quality levels can be included in the contract. Financial incentives for attainment of high quality levels can be included in the contract if reliable measurements exist.

Quality Control Checks on Efficiency Measurements

Governments attempting to assess efficiency and productivity need to consider the quality as well as the quantity of the work performed. Increases in work accomplished per dollar or per employee-hour do not in themselves guarantee real net improvement in performance. Reductions in cost per unit of work accomplished that are made at the expense of quality of the service should not be considered improvements in efficiency or productivity. Measures similar to those identified here are useful for quality checks. At the very least, effectiveness data should be presented along with the unit-cost data to give public officials a perspective on the relationship between effectiveness and efficiency. This issue is discussed at greater length in Chapter 15.

Management Control

In some cases, the measurement procedures also can be used to help managers operate their programs. The determining factors for this use are the frequency of data collection and timeliness of feedback to managers. When data are collected weekly, monthly, and even quarterly, managers may be able to use the information to reallocate their resources. For example, frequent collection of street cleanliness ratings such as those undertaken in New York City can permit allocation of crews to increase frequency of coverage in areas of greatest need. Some data, such as crime and arrest clearance rates, are already reported frequently, and can affect resource allocations from month to month.

Improvement of Communication between Citizens and Local Government Officials

Elected officials want information obtained directly from the customers of municipal services. Unstructured approaches are not likely to yield information representative of the views of the full population. Data collection procedures such as customer surveys, trained observer ratings, and business surveys can yield more representative information than can other common sources of citizen feedback, such as citizen complaint data, personal observations by managers, or periodic contacts between officials and selected parts of the population.

Also, the availability of effectiveness information can enhance communication in the other direction—from agency officials to elected officials and citizens. The measures presented in this report focus on service characteristics of direct concern and interest to the citizens of a given jurisdiction. These measures are likely to be more important to citizens than the typical municipal statistics such as level-of-activity (work load) measurements.

Improvement of Services to Customers

Ultimately, the predominant rationale for regularly measuring performance is to improve services to the public and so provide greater value for the dollars spent on services. Effectiveness data should be used to: identify where service delivery problems exist, identify whether past procedures and actions have improved conditions and thus warrant continuation or expansion, and encourage public employees (both management and nonmanagement employees) to find ways to *improve program performance*. This is the bottom line for effectiveness measurement.

Analysis of the Data

This section describes some basic, straightforward analyses that most agencies should undertake and then suggests some additional in-depth types of analyses.

Break Out Effectiveness Data

Break out the effectiveness measurement data so that each service manager has data pertaining to his or her own area of responsibility. The data should be broken out further by key geographic and work load characteristics to permit the manager and staff to identify more specifically where problems exist (in what areas of the community and among which categories of customers). Aggregate measurements are not sufficient. Like the man who drowned in a lake where the average depth was two feet, the manager looking at aggregate information can miss information on the *distribution* of the problem. The individual service chapters of this report suggest such breakouts.

A highly useful but less common breakout is *level of work load difficulty*. Most (if not all) services include work that varies considerably in difficulty. For example, some roads will have much heavier traffic, more truck traffic, or poorer soil conditions than other roads. The street maintenance agency will have considerably more difficulty keeping these roads in rideable condition. Similarly, police are more likely to solve certain types of crimes and crimes in which evidence has been left at the crime scene. Some categories of complaints will be much more difficult to resolve than others.

A basic approach to differentiating work load difficulty is for the agency to develop categories of difficulty and to define each category thoroughly. Each unit of work load (each street, each reported crime, each client, and so forth) should be categorized and coded as to its category. If outcomes of the service are identified for each such unit of work load, the performance data can be tabulated and reported for each category of difficulty. For example, the agency can then identify the percentage of roads in poor condition for each group of roads, the percentage of crimes solved (cleared) that fell into each category of difficulty, or the percentage of complaints satisfactorily resolved for each category of complaint.

The resulting information should be helpful to managers in identifying trends in their ability to deal with each category of work load. Perhaps even more important, the data will provide users of the performance data with a much better, and fairer, perspective of the agency's ability to produce favorable results. The agency will be able to identify differences in aggregate results that occurred because of differences in the mix of incoming work. Lower aggregate performance values, for example, can occur because the manager had more difficult work than in previous time periods, or as compared to otherwise similar work groups.

Track Change

Undertake such "simple" and straightforward analyses (requiring relatively small amounts of analytical time) as calculations of the percentage of change from one time period to another. After data covering periods of more than two years are available, the time series for individual measures can be analyzed for longer-term trends. Use time-trend lines to provide projections against which measurements taken after program changes have been made can be compared, to indicate whether improvements occurred because of those program changes.

Cross-Tabulate Results

Cross-tabulations can provide further insights into what has happened. For example, customer survey ratings of neighborhood street cleanliness or street rideability might be compared to more "objective" trained observer measures for these same characteristics. This comparison would help to identify whether lower satisfaction levels were due to a degradation in physical conditions or to an increase in citizens' expectations or to some other factor. The latter possibilities would be indicated if citizen satisfaction decreased while the trained observer ratings stayed at about the same level or improved. If "alienation" questions have been included in the customer survey, cross-tabulations might show whether a problem indicated by the citizen responses stemmed largely from citizen alienation with government. Another example: if persons in only one geographic area rate a service as poor, special neighborhood needs rather than service deficiencies might be indicated.

Identify External Factors

Because many factors outside government control can affect individual service ratings, ask operating agency personnel to identify major external events that occurred during the relevant period and other likely explanations for changes observed in service effectiveness. For example, unusually bad weather during the year is likely to affect significantly ratings of such measures as street rideability, street cleanliness, and storm drainage. Of course, this practice could open the door to all sorts of "excuses," but if analysts examine such explanations objectively, the additional information should be useful in interpreting performance.

Identify Neighborhood Factors

Statistically relate the values of measures in particular areas of the community with factors peculiar to such areas. For example, such conditions as age of buildings, level of education, level of income, and stability of families might be found by statistical analysis to be highly correlated with fire-rate differences among neighborhoods. This analysis also can provide a basis for a program to set different performance targets for different neighborhoods. For example, areas with older, more dilapidated buildings would be expected to have more fires than others. If these basic underlying conditions change, targets should also be adjusted.

Reporting Effectiveness Measurement Data

How measurement data are reported can have a major impact on whether and how they are used. The information should be provided frequently and in a timely way. It should be presented in a meaningful, concise, and interesting fashion. Unclear or overly long reports, especially those heavily dependent on statistics, should be avoided.

Collect and Report Information Frequently

Collect and report information on performance indicators *frequently*, at least quarterly. Program personnel need timely information. Frequent collection also will provide information on seasonal considerations, and it will enable program personnel to obtain feed-

back quickly on the results of new actions they have taken to improve services. Quarterly, or more frequent, collection is already done in many local governments for many indicators whose measurements are obtained from agency records (such as numbers of traffic accidents, reported crimes, crime clearances, incidence of fires). Public agencies using indicators based on customer surveys or trained observer procedures can divide the annual samples into four segments and then collect and report the data quarterly.

Report Meaningful Comparisons

Include in reports comparisons of interest (rather than merely presenting jurisdiction totals), such as changes from one year to the next, differences between areas of the community, findings for various clientele groups (different age, sex, income, race or ethnic groupings and work-load difficulty categories), and projected performance versus performance achieved. Exhibits 16-2 and 16-3 present two summary formats that highlight comparisons among geographic neighborhoods within the community. Each format also compares the current year's findings with those of the previous year.

With customer surveys, summarizing the voluminous data generated is a special problem. The format shown in Exhibit 16-4 provides a useful, concise summary of the results. For each major question on the survey, this "multi-cross tabulation" format provides a one-page summary of the findings for each of the number of demographic and geographic breakouts of the data. The compact format eliminates the need to pore through pages of printout and allows quick identification of the significant problem areas and instances of unusually high performance. (Survey results usually are presented on many individual sheets, each of which provides one question tallied for one demographic breakout. The format shown in Exhibit 16-4 can be generated manually by having clerical personnel transfer information from individual computer sheets to the illustrated format. An alternative is to use a computer program to generate the form directly from the data. Many survey firms have such a program available.)

After a customer survey has been repeated, comparisons of results over time will be of considerable importance and interest. A summary format that facilitates comparisons of the current year's findings with those of previous years can be readily prepared.

Prepare Executive Summaries

Ask program personnel to review the findings and summarize the highlights in a written "executive summary" for upper management and perhaps for the local legislative body. An oral version of the major findings is also desirable for presentation to some officials.

Exhibit 16-2

Format for Presentation of Selected Effectiveness Measurement Data: Recreation Services

Measure of effectiveness	Region (Current year)									All regions	
	I	II	III	IV	V	VI	VII	VIII	IX	Current year	Previous year
1. Percentage of persons who used government facilities fewer than 5 times during the year.	15	25	25	70	10	60	5	70	80	40	50
2. Percentage of persons who used government facilities fewer than 5 times during the year and whose reasons for nonuse were at least partly capable of being affected by government action.	7	20	10	40	2	40	4	50	60	25	30
3. Percentage of persons *not* within 15 minutes' driving time of a park.	6	8	10	8	7	21	3	16	22	11	14
4. Total number of severe injuries.	4	0	2	3	1	3	1	4	7	25	32
5. Percentage of persons rating overall recreation opportunities as either "fair" or "poor."	10	7	5	18	14	30	5	12	25	12	12

Note: Space could be provided on the form for listing highlights and important problem areas, and steps planned or already taken to alleviate the problem.

Exhibit 16-3

Format for Presentation of Selected Effectiveness Measurement Data: Street Cleanliness Services

Measure of effectiveness	Last year		Current year		Improvement		Comments
	Inner city	Remainder of city	Inner city	Remainder of city	Inner city	Remainder of city	
Street cleanliness: Percentage of streets rated 2.5 or worse. (4.0 is very dirty; 1.0 is very clean).	47%	11%	21%	14%	Yes	?	Definite improvement in inner city sample; change in rest of city was small.
Street cleanliness: Average street litter rating.	2.8	1.6	2.3	1.8	Yes	No	Confirmation that inner city has improved and that rest of city got slightly dirtier.
Alley cleanliness: Percentage of alleys rated 2.5 or worse.	54%	14%	34%	21%	Yes	No	Rest of city dirtier, apparently because special collection items are normally placed in alleys awaiting collection.
Citizen opinions of street cleanliness: Percentage responding "fairly clean" or "very clean."	31%	68%	47%	64%	Yes	?	With cleanliness ratings, tends to confirm cleanliness improvements in inner city and slight worsening elsewhere.
Number of complaints of dirty streets.	57	16	114	46	No	No	More complaints; possibly inner-city residents increasingly feel that if they complain, something will happen.
Offensive odors: Percentage of citizens who noticed widespread odors.	22%	4%	19%	3%	?	?	Little change.
Noise: Percentage of citizens complaining of being bothered by noise.	11%	12%	11%	12%	No	No	Most complaints of noise from refuse collection packer operation. No change.

Report Exceptions

Report to managers using the principle of "management by exception." Define systematically what constitutes an "exception." For example, the agency might select upper and lower "control" limits for the magnitude of each measure, for the magnitude of differences between population groups, and for the magnitude of changes for a given group from one time period to the next.

Each of the findings for the various population-group breakouts could be compared to the government-wide results. Differences exceeding, for example, 20 percent (or for measures expressed as percentages, perhaps 10 percentage points) would then be highlighted. Similarly, after the measurement data have been collected for more than one year, the government might select certain limits for differences from the previous year's results. Any measure found to exceed these limits in the current year would be reported to management. Such "out-of-control" findings might also be highlighted by flagging them on the reports.

For findings derived from samples, such as customer survey data, statistical significance also should be considered; deviations that are likely to result from the "luck of the draw" should be so identified. It is not recommended, however, that *statistical* significance be used as the principal criterion for identifying findings of concern. With relatively large samples, a difference of three percentage points or less might be statistically significant, but such small differences may be of little practical concern for program and policy decisions. Therefore, "practical" significance should be the primary criterion, with statistical significance used to identify the likelihood that chance caused unusual differences or changes.

Because the findings of customer surveys are likely to be politically sensitive, upper-level management probably should receive a complete set of these findings. Staff members should flag those results that indicate unusual problems or unusually good performance (as illustrated in Exhibit 16-4 by the circled entries).

Report Progress against Target Values

After enough data has been accumulated to permit realistic assessments of what achievements are possible, ask service managers to develop target values for each measure (with input from their staffs).

Exhibit 16-4

Format for Summarizing Data for Each Survey Question (Hypothetical Data)

Question 2: About how often have you ridden on inter-city buses in the past 12 months?

	Daily	Less than daily but at least once a week	Less than once a week but at least once a month	Less than once a month	Not at all	Don't know	Total responding
Number responding	36	49	50	63	429	0	625
Percentage of total responding	5	8	8	10	68	1	100
Respondent class				Percentage of total respondents in class			
(Percentage by responses)							
Sex and race White male	4	7	7	10	71	1	265
White female	5	8	8	11	68	0	284
Nonwhite male	19	11	11	6	53	0	36
Nonwhite female	10	7	10	8	65	0	40
Age: 18–34	5	11	13	13	58	0	272
35–49	3	8	6	8	75	0	125
50–64	8	3	3	5	80	1	105
65 and over	7	4	6	9	74	0	123
Family income: under $3,000	9	13	12	11	55	0	150
$3,000–4,999	9	10	15	11	55	0	117
$5,000–7,999	5	11	4	10	70	0	100
$8,000–9,999	3	2	7	10	78	0	69
$10,000–15,000	3	6	2	11	78	0	104
over $15,000	1	1	3	7	88	0	85
Region: 1. Central	4	13	12	11	60	0	150
2. Northeast	4	12	13	11	59	1	174
3. Northwest	9	3	6	8	74	0	76
4. Southeast	5	4	3	11	77	0	113
5. Southwest	4	5	5	15	71	0	112

Note: The linked circles illustrate how key findings might be highlighted.

Actual performance can subsequently be compared to the target in performance reports. Exhibit 16-5 illustrates such a format. A local government can either use the community-wide average performance level for each measure as the target for performance or use the rating for the cleaner areas of the community as targets for the other areas.

Targets can be based on past performance, adjusted for new conditions expected for the coming year (including the resources expected to be available for doing the work). Targets for particular geographic areas, work units, or client groups also can be based on past community-wide averages, or on the performance levels achieved in the past for the better (or best) performing areas, units, or client groups. For example, next year's targets for each region for Measure 5 in Exhibit 16-2 might be based on the values achieved in the current year for the particular region (ranging from 5 to 30 percent), on the overall community-wide average (12 percent), or on the higher performing region (25-30 percent). The managers for the regions will, of course, need to decide on the targets based on the local situation.

The determination of targets can be difficult and complex, particularly for effectiveness measures such as those presented in this report. There are few national standards or comparative data for most of them, although in a few instances, comparative data such as numbers of reported crimes and fires and crime clearance rates are available. Despite their many problems, these national data can be used to provide some crude targets. For example, a jurisdiction might use the average clearance rates for specific categories of crime in local governments with similar demographic characteristics as "target" values for itself.

The use of targets should be deferred until the agency gains confidence in the performance measurement values, or until sufficient analysis has been made of the particular service area. Then the agency will have confidence that the targets are reasonable.

Include Commentary by the Program Manager
Along with the "reporting" of effectiveness measurement findings, include explanatory information from the program personnel regarding the meaning of the findings and what should be done, or has already been done, in response to them.

Exhibit 16-5

Format for Reporting Actual versus Targeted Performance: Solid Waste Collection

Measure of effectiveness	Actual value previous year	Target current year		Quarterly performance			
				1st	2nd	3rd	4th
Percentage of blocks whose appearance is rated unsatisfactory ("fairly dirty" or "very dirty"—2.5 or worse on visual rating scale)	18%	13%	Target	16%	14%	12%	10%
			Actual				
Average block cleanliness rating	2.2	1.8	Target	2.1	1.9	1.7	1.6
			Actual				
Number of fires involving uncollected solid waste	17	12	Target	3	4	3	2
			Actual				
Percentage of households reporting having seen one or more rats during the period of a year	15%	8%	Target	Citizen survey undertaken once, in third quarter		8%	
			Actual				
Percentage of households reporting one or more missed collections during a year	17%	12%	Target	Citizen survey undertaken once, in third quarter		12%	
			Actual				
Percentage of households rating overall neighborhood cleanliness as usually "fairly dirty" or "very dirty"	23%	18%	Target	Citizen survey undertaken once, in third quarter		18%	
			Actual				

Notes: (a) A government may also want to display the cumulative results at the end of each quarter. (b) Space for agency comments on its performance on each measurement would also be desirable. (c) Quarterly targets should be set to reflect seasonal variations. (d) Ideally, estimates of the amount of statistical uncertainty should be provided when appropriate, as with citizen survey data.

The local government and agency management should make it a policy that the *manager responsible for the service covered by a performance report will be the first person to review the performance data* (after a review by technical specialists to check the quality of the tabulations). The service manager, and that manager's staff, should have the first opportunity to review the data and to prepare a highlights report with commentary on the findings, including any explanations and steps planned to make improvements.

Reports, especially those going outside the agency, should contain the following:

- Clear *definitions* for each performance indicator whose meaning is not likely to be fully clear to report readers

- Identification of any significant *changes* in the definition of any of the performance indicators from previous reporting periods, including the way the data have been collected or calculated

- If samples have been used, such as in customer surveys, identification of the applicable statistical confidence ranges and response rates and any other information about the survey likely to be relevant to readers' understanding of the findings.

Hold "How Are We Doing?" Sessions

An excellent way for agency managers to use performance measurement reports is to make each report the basis for a "How Are We Doing?" session. Shortly after receiving the regular (for example, quarterly) performance report, and after the program manager and manager's staff have had an opportunity to review the report, the manager can hold a staff meeting to:

- Examine the latest period's results
- Identify areas of good performance, commend the persons responsible, and discuss whether the actions leading to the good performance are transferable elsewhere
- Identify problems indicated by the report
- Discuss reasons for those problems
- Suggest ways these problems can be alleviated
- Begin development of an action plan to bring about improvements
- Review aspects of performance previously found to be a problem, and for which corrective steps were taken in a previous reporting period, in order to assess the extent to which the steps have worked and what else needs to be done.

To be most useful for such meetings, the performance reports should clearly identify the outcomes and quality of the programs for which the work group is responsible. If the reports commingle the results of more than one manager (at the same level), the managers and their staff will have trouble accepting responsibility for the combined results.

Limitations of Performance Measurement

Procedures such as those described in this report should provide much-improved information on service effectiveness in producing intended service outcomes and quality. Inevitably, however, some important aspects of service effectiveness will be neglected.

Furthermore, these procedures do not, and are not intended to, provide information on why the results are the way they are, or *what should be done* to improve future results. Some of the procedures, however, will give clues. For example, surveys of customers can ask respondents to give their perspectives on what they did not like about a service and how it might be improved. Also, if the findings on performance indicators are broken out by client group, level of work difficulty, or service unit, this will help the agency identify where problems exist.

Like profit-and-loss statements of private firms, and like scorecards kept by a manager of a professional sports team, performance measurements for public agencies should provide reasonably accurate information on results but not on why the results are as they are. More in-depth analysis by agency personnel will be needed to determine the reasons and to provide specific recommendations for improvement.

If performance measurement information is not used by managers and their staffs to help them to improve services to their customers, the local government (or individual agency) should determine why not and attempt to overcome the obstacles. If after sufficient trial, measurement data are still not being used, the measurement effort should be discontinued.

---

1 See city of Savannah, Georgia's "Responsive Public Services Program." Savannah has obtained current performance levels for each of its 29 geographic planning areas for most of its performance indicators. Savannah places each area into one of three priority groups (first, second, and third). To generate priority rankings it originally used the statistical concept of standard deviation from the city-wide average. It has since switched to a simpler procedure. For each performance indicator, the analysts divide the difference between the highest and lowest values of its 29 areas by three, to determine the dividing points between priorities.

2 A chief element in the initiation of this trend was the issuance by the U.S. General Accounting Office of *Standards for Audit of Governmental Organizations, Programs, Activities, and Functions.* See also the Canadian Comprehensive Auditing Foundation's *Effectiveness Reporting and Auditing in the Public Sector* and ICMA's *Performance Auditing for Local Government.* More recently, the Government Accounting Standards Board has issued its series of reports encouraging public agency reporting of service accomplishments data; see, for example, Government Accounting Service Board, *Service Efforts and Accomplishments Reporting: Its Time Has Come—An Overview.*

Chapter 17

Some Implementation Suggestions

This chapter provides suggestions for implementing effectiveness measurement procedures and describes specific steps to follow.[1]

Guidelines

1. *Involve the operating agencies in the development, implementation, and use of the measurement procedures.*

Operating agency employees not only have the most interest in the measurement findings, but they also can do the most about the findings if they require action. Local governments are urged to involve agency staff members at all stages of the work, from the initial identification of the measures and the development of data collection procedures to the review of the findings. This practice will greatly increase the likelihood that the procedures will work and that the information will be used.

Three problems may limit involvement of agency personnel:

- Operating agencies' interest in customer-provided data is mixed. Some organizations, such as park and recreation agencies, have tended to be quite interested in obtaining customer feedback on their services. Others, however, have tended to be considerably more skeptical about the value of procedures calling for citizen ratings of their service.

- Central staff members are sometimes impatient. They may not want to take the often considerable amount of time necessary to work with agency personnel.

- Agency staff time for analysis is limited or nonexistent. Few local government agencies have staff analysts. Where analysts are present, the pressure of daily activities often prevents them from spending much time analyzing performance data. Agency managers can obtain many useful insights from even a brief examination of the measurement findings. However, to gain a fuller perspective on the data, it is desirable to use trained analysts. (Some types of analyses are presented in Chapter 16.) The lack of analytical staff members is less a problem when central staff analysts are available to help agencies.

2. *Use effectiveness measurement in a positive, constructive manner; make effectiveness measurement as rewarding and unthreatening as possible to government managers.*

This is a tall order, since measurement implies evaluation and accountability, which are inherently threatening to those being evaluated. The cooperative approach to selection of measures and development of procedures suggested above will help alleviate the concern of operating staff. In addition, local governments are urged to use the effectiveness measurement data not only to identify problem areas but also to provide appropriate commendations or rewards to agencies and personnel when the measurements point out major improvements or maintenance of prior levels of service in the face of adverse external factors. When problems are identified, it is important to focus not on attributing blame but rather on identifying constructive improvements.

It is vitally important that the service manager be the first government official to see the performance measurement reports relating to the manager's responsibility. This will give the manager the opportunity to comment on the findings, provide explanations, and identify actions planned (or in process) to correct the problems indicated by the findings. The local government, as a policy, should include this review by the program manager in the performance measurement system to reduce its threatening aspects. Moreover, explanatory material provided by the service manager will give other staff a more informed perspective on the reported results data.

3. *Provide specific incentives to government managers to participate constructively in performance-monitoring activities.*

It is not clear how to do this but incentives are needed. Disincentives currently predominate in most governments' systems of reward; for example, budget and staff size are important status symbols, but improvements in performance can lead to reduced budgets and staff. Potentially appropriate and practical rewards include the following:

- Favorable performance ratings
- Formal commendations and public service awards
- Reduction of selected management controls for those demonstrating high effectiveness and efficiency
- Monetary rewards such as merit increases or bonuses.

The best single incentive for government management employees may be the *use* of the measurement information by top government management and the legislative body.

4. *Provide central staff technical assistance to help operating agencies develop and use measurement procedures.*

Central staff personnel should provide technical assistance to operating agencies in establishing goals and objectives, in developing measures, and in implementing data collection activities. The central staff probably also should assist agency personnel in analyzing measurement findings and helping the agencies use the information.

5. *Maximize the usefulness and application of the data produced by measurement procedures.*

The promise of usefulness is, of course, the justification for the effort and expense in implementing effectiveness measurement procedures. Some ways to increase the utility of the effectiveness data are suggested in Chapter 16. Failure of operating agency personnel to use the measurement information for improving their performance has been a major weakness in measurement efforts to date.

As the exhibits in Chapter 16 illustrate, the measurement findings should be summarized concisely and clearly. Each agency should be asked to identify key problem areas indicated by the findings, to comment on areas in which significant progress has been made, and to recommend any follow-up actions that seem desirable. When agency recommendations are made, they should be reviewed carefully and feedback should be provided to the agency.

Local governments should encourage individual managers to hold "How Are We Doing?" sessions for their staff after each performance report is received. As Chapter 16 indicates, the periodic performance reports give the manager an opportunity to review with employees the unit's recent performance to stimulate their ideas for improving performance.

After the measurement data have been gathered for several periods, the government should consider asking agency managers to set targets for the values of individual measures for forthcoming reporting periods. At the end of each period and at the end of the year, the outcomes would be compared to the targets as a review of performance.

The seriousness with which program managers treat performance measurement will be greatly affected by the degree to which they perceive that agency and central management (and the legislative body) take it seriously.

6. *Work out a balance between client-oriented outcome measures and activity measures (for example, work-load counts).*

Designers of any system of effectiveness measurement will inevitably encounter a tug-of-war between measures oriented to citizen impact and those over which operating managers have more direct influence, especially those measures of units of work load accomplished. Citizens, upper-level management, and the legislative body will tend to be more interested in client-oriented measures. Operating managers will be more interested in accepting responsibility for the activity measures. In solid waste collection, for example, program managers usually will be interested in and accept responsibility for measures of the amount of waste collected, but they may be less interested in measurements of the resulting cleanliness of the neighborhood (which are at least partly affected by the behavior of the residents).

Both types of measures are useful, but the measures of activity, such as work load accomplished, should not be mistaken for measures of the effectiveness of government services. The problem is that including activity measures under the label of measures of effectiveness may divert attention from real measures of outcome. When activity measures are included with effectiveness measures in performance reports, they should be labeled as activity measures and not as measures of effectiveness.

7. *If measurement resources are scarce, exclude, at least initially, government "support" services such as personnel, finance, purchasing, data processing, building maintenance, and motor vehicle repair.*

Measuring the effectiveness of services that directly affect the public should be of higher priority than support services, and handling these public services is likely to be enough work for any local government entering the measurement field. But many of the principles and approaches discussed in this report apply to support services as well, and support services can be added to the measurement effort in later stages. For example, obtaining feedback from the "clients" of each support service (that is, other government agencies receiving the service) on various aspects of the quality of the service (such as timeliness, correctness, and courteousness) will provide relevant indicators of the quality of these services. Trained observer rating procedures can provide relevant indicators of the quality of services such as custodial and building maintenance.

8. *Institutionalize measurement activities.*

Difficulties in maintaining the measurement effort are likely to arise in part because some important data collection procedures, such as the use of trained observers and customer surveys, require special resources and their use is not familiar to local government managers. Special data collection procedures are the first items to be dropped in a short-term budget crunch, particularly if no cost savings or effectiveness improvements attributable to the measurement system are being documented. Reinstitution, moreover, is likely to be difficult.

   To help institutionalize measurement activities, two steps are recommended: (1) effectiveness measurement should be incorporated into the formal, annual, budget-planning process (by including the requirement for effectiveness information in the agency budget instructions) and (2) an explicit effort should be made to "sell" the process to program managers, as discussed below. With these two steps, effectiveness measurement procedures will have a firmer basis for continuation and will not be so vulnerable to personnel turnover and to candidates for public office making an issue of "overhead" costs.

   In effect, collection of effectiveness measurement information should be established as a routine procedure, in much the same way as the collection of expenditure data is. To ensure that effectiveness measurement is truly established, it probably will be necessary to make effectiveness information an integral part of the information regularly provided to the chief executive's office and the legislative body.

It is also important to standardize and document measurement procedures and to make sure that enough staff members know how to conduct measurements so that the loss of one or two key persons will not halt the measurement effort in an agency.

9. *Work to sell the process to program managers.*

Agencies must work to sell performance measurement to their managers (and staff), to alleviate their concerns and encourage effective use of performance data. Some ways to sell it are as follows:[2]

- Include a module on performance measurement and its use for improving operations in basic management and staff training programs. This material should emphasize the potential *usefulness* of performance information (See Chapter 16) in helping managers and staff oversee and improve the quality of services for which they are responsible.

- Point out to managers that it is better that they discover any shortcomings in their programs before others do.

- Have managers provide a written summary to accompany each performance report. It should identify the report's highlights, identify problem areas, present the manager's explanation for problems, and identify actions that are being taken or proposed to correct the problems. Giving program managers the opportunity to explain unfavorable performance data increases their feeling of control.

- Emphasize that upper-level management *expects* that every program will have some areas that need improvement. Any performance report not identifying some problem areas will be suspect.

- Point out that quality-driven performance monitoring is becoming the standard in the private sector, and public managers should be no less dedicated to quality than their private sector counterparts.

10. *If measurement data are used to develop employee incentives, provide for comprehensive discussion in advance of the measures and measurement procedures.*

Thus far the local governments undertaking effectiveness measurement have used the effectiveness information primarily for purposes that do not directly affect nonmanagement employees. But management decisions on programs and policies based on effectiveness measurement information will eventually affect employees in those programs. If effectiveness information is used in the development of specific employee incentives—be they monetary rewards or elements in productivity bargaining—individual employees and their labor organizations will become vitally concerned. They can be expected to raise major objections to such uses unless the local government carefully discusses with them in advance the measurements and incentives, to head off problems before they develop.

11. Provide regular measurement and reporting, at least quarterly, for most performance indicators.

As discussed in Chapter 16, regular reporting will provide more timely and useful information that program managers can use to operate their programs. This measurement and reporting includes indicators based on the findings from customer surveys and trained observer ratings. Break up annual samples into quarterly samples to provide more timely and useful feedback to program personnel and to reflect seasonal variations. This step generally is not done by local government agencies, but it should be if the measurements are to be fully useful.

12. Provide strong organizational support.

A System for Monitoring Effectiveness

The following steps might be used for implementing procedures to monitor effectiveness:

1. Establish a working group for each participating service or program. The group should consist of a central staff member, the service manager and selected members of the manager's staff, and a person experienced in measurement techniques. The group should be responsible for coordinating the effort, identifying desired measures, developing measurement procedures, and following through on implementation of the appropriate effectiveness measurement procedures.

2. Identify service objectives and an associated set of measures appropriate to each service area. The measures identified in this report can be used as a starting point.

3. Review existing data and data collection procedures for those that might be easily incorporated into the measurement effort. Consider new procedures, such as use of trained observers and customer surveys, for those measures that are not obtainable from existing data.

4. Pilot test the set of effectiveness measures and data collection procedures. (If the test is successful, the findings can be used as a baseline for comparing data collected in the future.)

5. Develop and implement the selected procedures, including necessary design of forms, selection of survey and sampling methods, training of personnel (such as trained observers), and pretesting of new procedures for clarity, feasibility, and reliability. The procedures should be checked by "experts" to assure their validity.

6. Develop a plan to use the data collected. This plan should include establishment of procedures for review, analysis, and presentation of findings. Establish links with continuing decision-making processes such as the preparation of the operating and capital budget, any management-by-objectives or other kind of performance assessment process (especially those for managers), and any formal program evaluation or program analysis efforts.

7. Provide the measurement findings regularly (for example quarterly) to management.

8. Prepare information on the costs of the measurement efforts including data collection and analysis.

9. Collect data on the measures for at least two to three years. Conduct annual reviews of the procedures after each of these years to determine significant problems and make necessary modifications

10. At the end of the three-year period, review the utility of the individual measures and the set as a whole. Revise those procedures with significant deficiencies; drop procedures that have little use. Move toward institutionalization of the procedures that have proved their value so that collection will proceed without special go-ahead decisions each year.

---

1 Chapter 13 of this report provides some implementation suggestions specifically relevant to customer surveys. For more extensive discussions of the implementation of performance measurement procedures, see ICMA's "Strategies for Implementing Performance Measurement" and "Monitoring the Quality of Local Government Services."

2 A number of these ideas have been adapted from Munich and Quilin, "Program Agency Perspectives."

An Illustrative Questionnaire for a Multiservice Household Survey

Many of the questions are preceded by a boldface code. These codes relate to the specific effectiveness measures cited in earlier chapters. Throughout, "Metro" is the term used for the government. Cities and counties should, of course, substitute the name of their own government. The coding is as follows: P&R = parks and recreation; L = library; P = police (crime control); F = fire protection; GT = general transportation (other than public transit); PT = public transit; SWC = solid waste collection; SWD = solid waste disposal; WS = water supply; CC = handling of citizen complaints; SI = handling of requests for services or information. For example, GT-14 at Question 3 indicates that this particular question is used to obtain information for Measure 14 in the general transportation chapter. This questionnaire calls for a 3-month respondent recall period. Throughout this report, quarterly samples are suggested, rather than one large annual survey—in order to provide managers with seasonal and more timely information.

Customer Survey

Hello, my name is . . . . I would like to speak to the youngest male (oldest female) 18 years of age or over who happens to be at home. (TO QUALIFIED RESPONDENT) The Metropolitan Government has asked us to conduct an independent survey of citizens to help Metro improve its services.

(TIME INTERVIEW BEGAN: _____)

1. How long have you lived in Metro?
(DO NOT READ RESPONSES)

   ( ) Less than 3 months (TERMINATE)
   ( ) 3 to 12 months
   ( ) 1 to 5 years
   ( ) More than 5 years
   ( ) Don't know

2. Have you driven an automobile in Metro in the past 3 months?
(DO NOT READ RESPONSES)

   ( ) Yes, I have driven
   ( ) No, don't drive } (GO TO NO. 7)
   ( ) Don't know

(NUMBERS 3–6 DRIVERS ONLY)
GT-14

3. When you drive into downtown Metro in the daytime to shop or for personal business, would you say finding a satisfactory parking space is hardly ever a problem, sometimes a problem, usually a problem, or don't you ever try to park downtown?

   ( ) Hardly ever a problem
   ( ) Sometimes a problem
   ( ) Usually a problem
   ( ) Don't park downtown
   ( ) Don't know or don't remember

GT-16

4. While driving in Metro during the last 3 months, how often have you found pavement markings, such as the center lines, hard to see? Would you say this occurred rarely or never, once in a while, fairly often, or very often?

   ( ) Rarely or never
   ( ) Once in a while
   ( ) Fairly often
   ( ) Very often
   ( ) Don't know

GT-16

5. Do you think Metro traffic signs, that is, its directional signs, stop signs, one-way signs, and so forth (but not including street name signs) are usually easy to see and understand quickly, sometimes hard to see or understand quickly, or often hard to see or understand quickly?

   ( ) Usually easy to see and understand quickly (GO TO NO. 6)
   ( ) Sometimes hard to see or understand quickly
   ( ) Often hard to see or understand quickly } (ASK NO. 5a)
   ( ) Don't know (GO TO NO. 6)

GT-16

5a. What is the problem with the signs? (DO NOT READ RESPONSES—Check the response that comes closest to what respondent says.)

   ( ) Blocked from view
   ( ) Too small
   ( ) Not at the same place on each intersection
   ( ) Missing where they are needed
   ( ) Hard to understand
   ( ) Changed too often
   ( ) Too many signs in same place
   ( ) Other _____

6. In your personal experience during the past 3 months, would you say that enforcement of parking laws in Metro is generally too strict? Not strict enough? About right? Inconsistent?

( ) Too strict
( ) Not strict enough
( ) About right
( ) Inconsistent
( ) Don't know

(ASK ALL FROM HERE ON)
GT-16
7. Do you think street name signs on streets and roads in Metro are usually easy to see and understand quickly, sometimes hard to see or understand quickly, or often hard to see or understand quickly?

( ) Usually easy to see and understand quickly
( ) Sometimes hard to see or understand quickly
( ) Often hard to see or understand quickly
( ) Don't know

GT-19
8. During the last 3 months, have you ever been bothered by traffic noise or construction noise in this neighborhood? (IF YES, ASK:) On the average, were you bothered by this noise almost daily, at least once a week, or only once in a while?

( ) No, never (GO TO NO. 9)
( ) Yes, almost daily
( ) Yes, at least once a week } (ASK NO. 8a)
( ) Yes, only once in a while
( ) Don't know (GO TO NO. 9)

GT-19
8a. What seems to cause the most noise?
(DO NOT READ RESPONSES)

( ) No specific thing
( ) General traffic
( ) Motorcycles
( ) Trucks
( ) Construction
( ) Other _____

GT-13
9. How would you rate the condition of street and road surfaces in your neighborhood? Are they in good condition all over, mostly good but a few bad spots here and there, or are there many bad spots?

( ) Good condition all over
( ) Mostly good but a few bad spots here and there
( ) Many bad spots
( ) Don't know

GT-22
10. Would you say the amount of street lighting at night in this neighborhood is about right, too low (need more lighting), too bright (more lighting than necessary), or no lighting is needed?

( ) About right
( ) Too low
( ) Too bright
( ) No lighting is needed
( ) Don't know

GT-21
11. Would you say there are enough sidewalks in this neighborhood?

( ) Yes, enough
( ) No (too few)
( ) None exist and none needed
( ) Don't know

GT-20
12. Are the sidewalks in this neighborhood generally in good condition?
(DO NOT READ RESPONSES)

( ) Yes
( ) No
( ) No sidewalks in this neighborhood
( ) Don't know

PT-19
13. Now I have a few questions about *Metro bus service*. About how often have you ridden on Metro buses in the past 3 months? Would you say daily or almost daily; not daily, but at least once a week; occasionally, less than once a week; or not at all?

( ) Daily or almost daily
( ) Not daily, but at least once a week   } (GO TO NO. 15)
( ) Occasionally, less than once a week
( ) Not at all   } (ASK NO. 14)
( ) Don't know

PT-19
14. Has anyone else in your household ridden on Metro buses in the past 3 months?

( ) Yes
( ) No   } (GO TO NO. 17)
( ) Don't know

15. For most of the trips *you* make by bus, would you say the frequency of *your* bus service is excellent, good, fair, or poor? How about the reliability of *your* bus service; that is, buses running on schedule? How about. . . .?
(ASK FOR 15c–15h, REPEATING RATINGS WHEN NECESSARY.)

	Excellent	Good	Fair	Poor	Don't know
PT-7 15a. Frequency of your bus service......	( )	( )	( )	( )	( )

PT-7

15b. Reliability of your bus service— buses running on schedule .... ( ) ( ) ( ) ( ) ( )

PT-2

15c. Ability to get where you want to go in a reasonable length of time......... ( ) ( ) ( ) ( ) ( )

PT-7

15d. Ability to get schedule and routing information .... ( ) ( ) ( ) ( ) ( )

PT-10

15e. Helpfulness and courtesy of bus drivers............... ( ) ( ) ( ) ( ) ( )

PT-7

15f. Ability to get where you want to go without transferring ... ( ) ( ) ( ) ( ) ( )

PT-7

15g. Closeness of bus stop to your home................. ( ) ( ) ( ) ( ) ( )

PT-10

15h. Waiting conditions at bus stops you use................... ( ) ( ) ( ) ( ) ( )

16. Were the Metro buses on which you have ridden in the past 3 months ever *uncomfortably hot or cold*? (IF YES, ASK:) Would you say this occurred very often, fairly often, or only once in a while? How about . . .? (REPEAT FOR 16b–16f)

	No, never	Very often	Fairly often	Once in a while	Don't know

PT-10

16a. Uncomfortably hot or cold .... ( ) ( ) ( ) ( ) ( )

PT-10

16b. Dirty or smelly .. ( ) ( ) ( ) ( ) ( )

PT-10

16c. Driven in a reckless or rough way .... ( ) ( ) ( ) ( ) ( )

16d. Crowded .... ( ) ( ) ( ) ( ) ( )

16e. Equipped with uncomfortable seats... ( ) ( ) ( ) ( ) ( )

16f. Noisy .... ( ) ( ) ( ) ( ) ( )
(GO TO NO. 20)

17. Do you regularly travel more than ¼ mile to work? (IF YES, ASK:) About how far?
(DO NOT READ RESPONSES)

( ) No (GO TO NO. 19)

( ) ¼ to 1 mile
( ) More than 1 but less than 5 miles
( ) More than 5 but less than 10 miles   } (ASK NO. 18)
( ) Over 10 miles
(NOTE: Include people who don't work regularly or who work at home in Response 1)

PT-3, 8, and 11

18. Different people have different reasons for *not traveling to work by bus*. Please tell me what are the two or three most important reasons why you do NOT travel to work by Metro bus more often?

( ) _____
( ) _____
( ) _____

18a. Which of these is the most important reason? (DO NOT READ RESPONSES—Check the response that comes closest to what respondent says.)

( ) Service not frequent enough
( ) Bus stop not close enough
( ) Takes too long
( ) Fares are too high
( ) Poor waiting conditions at bus stops
( ) Don't know schedules and routes
( ) Don't like people who use buses
( ) Other _____
(GO TO NO. 20)

PT-3, 8, and 11

(ASK ONLY IF RESPONSE WAS "NO" TO NO. 17)
19. Different people have different reasons for not riding Metro buses. Please tell me what are the two or three most important reasons why you do not ride Metro buses more often?

( ) _____
( ) _____
( ) _____

19a. Which of these is the most important reason? (DO NOT READ RESPONSES—Check the response that comes closest to what the respondent says.)

( ) Service not frequent enough
( ) Bus stop not close enough
( ) Takes too long
( ) Fares are too high
( ) Poor waiting conditions at bus stops
( ) Don't know schedules and routes
( ) Don't like people who use buses
( ) Other _____

(ASK ALL)
PT-21

20. In general, would you rate the Metro bus service *available* to you and members of your household as excellent, good, fair, or poor?

( ) Excellent
( ) Good
( ) Fair
( ) Poor
( ) Don't know

L-1 and 2

21. In the following questions on libraries, please consider only Metro libraries and exclude university libraries. How would you evaluate Metro public library services? Would you rate them excellent, good, fair, or poor?

( ) Excellent
( ) Good
( ) Fair
( ) Poor
( ) Don't know

L-4

22. Do you or any other member of this household have a library card for a Metro Public Library? (DO NOT READ RESPONSES)

( ) Yes, have card
( ) No, don't have card
( ) Don't know

L-3

23. Other than for group meetings, about how often during the past 3 months have you or members of your household (including children) used the Metro Public Library, including the Main Library, its branches, bookmobile, or telephone reference service? Would you say . . .?

( ) At least once a week
( ) At least once every month   } (ASK NO. 24)
( ) At least once in the last 3 months
( ) Not at all
( ) Don't know; don't remember   } (GO TO NO. 25)

23a. Which one do you use most often? (Name and Location)
( ) _____

24. How would you rate this library on the following characteristics? Would you rate the hours of operation as excellent, good, fair, or poor? How about the availability of reading materials you wanted? How about . . .?
(ASK FOR 24c–24g, REPEATING RATINGS WHEN NECESSARY.)

	Excellent	Good	Fair	Poor	Don't know
L-18 24a. Hours of operation	( )	( )	( )	( )	( )
L-7b 24b. Availability of reading materials you wanted	( )	( )	( )	( )	( )
L-13 24c. Comfort and cleanliness	( )	( )	( )	( )	( )
L-15 24d. Convenience to your home	( )	( )	( )	( )	( )
L-10 24e. Helpfulness and courtesy of library personnel	( )	( )	( )	( )	( )
L-9 24f. Ease in finding and checking out library materials	( )	( )	( )	( )	( )
L-15 24g. Ease of parking	( )	( )	( )	( )	( )

(GO TO NO. 26)

L-3

25. I am going to read a list of reasons *some* people have given for *not* using Metro libraries more often. Please tell me which, if any, generally are *true* for you or members of this household? Let's start with "Library does *not* have books I want." Is this statement generally *true* or generally *not true* for you or members of this household? How about "Too busy to go to the library"? True or not true? How about. . . .? (ASK FOR 25c– 25l, REPEATING RATINGS WHEN NECESSARY.)

	True	Not true	Don't know
25a. Library does not have books or other items I want	( )	( )	( )
25b. Too busy to go to library	( )	( )	( )
25c. Not interested in library	( )	( )	( )
25d. Buy my own books and magazines	( )	( )	( )
25e. Health problems prevent my using the library	( )	( )	( )
25f. Not familiar with Metro's library services	( )	( )	( )
L-19 25g. Library not open night hours	( )	( )	( )
L-16 25h. Library hard to get to/no transportation	( )	( )	( )
L-14 25i. Library too noisy/too crowded	( )	( )	( )
25j. Poor staff service at library	( )	( )	( )
25k. Lack of adequate parking at library	( )	( )	( )
25l. Use libraries other than Metro's	( )	( )	( )

25x. What would you say is the *most important* reason that you or members of your household do not use the Metro library system more often than you do? (DO NOT READ RESPONSES—Check the response that comes closest to what respondent says.)

( ) Library does not have books or other items I want
( ) Too busy to go to library
( ) Not interested in library
( ) Buy my own books and magazines
( ) Health problems prevent my using the library
( ) Don't know about the library
( ) Library not open night hours
( ) Library hard to get to/no transportation
( ) Other _____

26. During the past 3 months have you or anyone in your household listened to the Metro Library FM radio station? (IF YES, ASK:) How many times a week would you say your household listens?

( ) 1 or 2 times
( ) 3 or 4 times
( ) More than 4 times
( ) No, never listens
( ) Don't know

P&R-1

27. Now, I would like to know how your household would rate the park and recreation opportunities in your immediate area. Would you rate them excellent, good, fair, or poor?

( ) Excellent
( ) Good
( ) Fair
( ) Poor
( ) Don't know

P-14

28. Turning now to police protection and public safety— How safe would you feel walking alone in this neighborhood at night? Would you feel very safe, reasonably safe, somewhat unsafe, or very unsafe?

( ) Very safe
( ) Reasonably safe
( ) Somewhat unsafe
( ) Very unsafe
( ) Don't know

P-14

29. Are there some parts of Metro where you would like to go at night but do not because you would not feel safe? (DO NOT READ RESPONSES)

( ) Yes, some parts (ASK NO. 29a)

( ) No
( ) Don't know } (GO TO NO. 30)

29a. Which parts of Metro are these?
( ) _____

30. In the past 3 months, have you had any direct contact with the Metro police for *any* reason, such as calling for assistance, reporting a crime, or being stopped by police? (IF YES, ASK:) How many *total contacts* did you have with the Metro police?

( ) Yes, one contact

( ) Yes, two contacts
( ) Yes, three contacts
( ) Yes, four or more contacts
( ) No, no contacts
( ) Don't remember
Comments _____

P-2, P-3

31.* During the past 3 months in Metro, did anyone steal or use any vehicles belonging to you or to members of this household without permission? Do not include vehicles borrowed by other members of the household. (DO NOT READ RESPONSES)

( ) Yes, did steal or use (ASK 31a and 31b)
( ) No
( ) Don't know } (GO TO NO. 32)

P-2, P-3

31a. How many times did this occur?
(DO NOT READ RESPONSES)

( ) One
( ) Two
( ) Three
( ) Four or more
( ) Don't know

P-2, P-3

31b. Were all incidents reported to the Metro police? (IF NO, ASK:) How many were *not* reported? (DO NOT READ RESPONSES)

( ) Yes (GO TO NO. 32)
( ) No, one not reported
( ) No, two not reported
( ) No, three not reported } (ASK NO. 31c)
( ) No, four or more not reported
( ) Don't know (GO TO NO. 32)

P-2, P-3

31c. What was the *main reason* for *not* notifying the police? (DO NOT READ RESPONSES—Check the response that comes closest to what respondent says.)

( ) Didn't want to go to court
( ) Didn't think it was important enough
( ) Didn't think it would do any good
( ) Didn't want to get involved
( ) Didn't want to get anybody in trouble
( ) Afraid of retaliation
( ) Afraid my insurance would go up or be cancelled
( ) Other (specify) _____
( ) Don't know, don't remember

*The following "shorthand" version might be substituted for Questions 31–36: "Were you a victim of any crime(s) in the past 3 months?" IF YES, "What crime(s)?" "How often?" "Were all incidents reported to the police?" IF NOT, "How many were not reported?" "What was the main reason for your not notifying the police?" Using this version of the questions would, however, require the interviewer or coder to subsequently categorize the information as Questions 31–36 do, if data on major categories of crime are desired.

P-2, P-3

32. In the past 3 months, did anyone break in or was there strong evidence someone tried to break into your home or garage? (DO NOT READ RESPONSES)

( ) Yes, broke in ⎫
( ) Yes, tried to break in ⎬ (ASK 32a and 32b)
( ) No, neither ⎫
( ) Don't know ⎬ (GO TO NO. 33)

P-2, P-3

32a. How many times did this occur? (Break-ins *or* attempted break-ins) (DO NOT READ RESPONSES)

( ) One
( ) Two
( ) Three
( ) Four or more
( ) Don't know

P-2, P-3

32b. Were all incidents reported to Metro police? (IF NO, ASK:) How many were not reported? (DO NOT READ RESPONSES)

( ) Yes, all reported (GO TO NO. 33)
( ) No, one not reported ⎫
( ) No, two not reported ⎪
( ) No, three not reported ⎬ (ASK NO. 32c)
( ) No, four or more not reported ⎭
( ) Don't know (GO TO NO. 33)

P-2, P-3

32c. (IF ANY NOT REPORTED, ASK:) What was the *main reason* for *not* notifying the police? (DO NOT READ RESPONSES—Check the response that comes closest to what respondent says.)

( ) Didn't want to go to court
( ) Didn't think it was important enough
( ) Didn't think it would do any good
( ) Didn't want to get involved
( ) Didn't want to get anybody in trouble
( ) Afraid of retaliation
( ) Afraid my insurance would go up or be cancelled
( ) Other (specify) _____
( ) Don't know; don't remember

P-2, P-3

33. To rob means to take something from a person by force, fear, or by the threat of force. Did anyone rob or try to rob you or a member of your household in the past 3 months in Metro? (DO NOT READ RESPONSES)

( ) Yes (ASK 33a and 33b)
( ) No ⎫
( ) Don't know ⎬ (GO TO NO. 34)

P-2, P-3

33a. (IF YES, ASK:) How many times did this occur? (DO NOT READ RESPONSES)

( ) One
( ) Two
( ) Three
( ) Four or more
( ) Don't know

P-2, P-3

33b. Were all incidents reported to the Metro police? (IF NO, ASK:) How many were *not* reported? (DO NOT READ RESPONSES)

( ) Yes (GO TO NO. 34)
( ) No, one not reported ⎫
( ) No, two not reported ⎪
( ) No, three not reported ⎬ (ASK NO. 33c)
( ) No, four or more not reported ⎭
( ) Don't know (GO TO NO. 34)

P-2, P-3

33c. (IF ANY NOT REPORTED, ASK:) What was the *main reason* for *not* notifying the police? (DO NOT READ RESPONSES—Check the response that comes the closest to what respondent says.)

( ) Didn't want to go to court
( ) Didn't think it was important enough
( ) Didn't think it would do any good
( ) Didn't want to get involved
( ) Didn't want to get anybody in trouble
( ) Afraid of retaliation
( ) Afraid my insurance would go up or be cancelled
( ) Other (specify) _____
( ) Don't know; don't remember

P-2, P-3

34. Considering serious physical attacks to include such things as beatings, knifings, shootings, rapings, and so forth, in the last 3 months, were you or any members of your household seriously attacked in Metro? (DO NOT READ RESPONSES)

( ) Yes (ASK 34a and 34b)
( ) No ⎫
( ) Don't know ⎬ (GO TO NO. 35)

P-2, P-3

34a. (IF YES, ASK:) How many times did this occur? (DO NOT READ RESPONSES)

( ) One
( ) Two
( ) Three
( ) Four or more
( ) Don't know

P-2, P-3

34b. Were all incidents reported to the Metro police? (IF NO, ASK:) How many were *not* reported? (DO NOT READ RESPONSES)

( ) Yes (GO TO NO. 35)

( ) No, one not reported
( ) No, two not reported
( ) No, three not reported $\Big\}$ (ASK NO. 34c)
( ) No, four or more not reported
( ) Don't know (GO TO NO. 35)

P-2, P-3
34c. (IF ANY NOT REPORTED, ASK:) What was the *main reason* for *not* notifying the police? (DO NOT READ RESPONSES—Check the response that comes closest to what the respondent says.)

( ) Didn't want to go to court
( ) Didn't think it was important enough
( ) Didn't think it would do any good
( ) Didn't want to get involved
( ) Didn't want to get anybody in trouble
( ) Afraid of retaliation
( ) Afraid my insurance would go up or be cancelled
( ) Other (specify) _____
( ) Don't know, don't remember

P-2, P-3
35. In the last 3 months, has anyone vandalized, that is, intentionally damaged, your home, car, or other property or that of members of your household in Metro? (DO NOT READ RESPONSES)

( ) Yes (ASK 35a and 35b)
( ) No $\Big\}$ (GO TO NO. 36)
( ) Don't know

P-2, P-3
35a. (IF YES, ASK:) How many times did this occur? (DO NOT READ RESPONSES)

( ) One
( ) Two
( ) Three
( ) Four or more
( ) Don't know

P-2, P-3
35b. Were all incidents reported to the Metro police? (IF NO, ASK:) How many were *not* reported? (DO NOT READ RESPONSES)

( ) Yes (GO TO NO. 36)
( ) No, one not reported
( ) No, two not reported
( ) No, three not reported $\Big\}$ (ASK NO. 35c)
( ) No, four or more not reported
( ) Don't know (GO TO NO. 36)

P-2, P-3
35c. (IF NOT ANY REPORTED, ASK:) What was the *main reason* for *not* notifying the police? (DO NOT READ RESPONSES—Check the response that comes closest to what the respondent says.)

( ) Didn't want to go to court.
( ) Didn't think it was important enough

( ) Didn't think it would do any good
( ) Didn't want to get involved
( ) Didn't want to get anybody in trouble
( ) Afraid of retaliation
( ) Afraid my insurance would go up or be cancelled
( ) Other (specify) _____
( ) Don't know, don't remember

P-2, P-3
36. In the last 3 months, has anyone committed any other crimes against you or any member of your household in Metro, such as stealing a bicycle, or something from your car like hubcaps or packages, or something from your yard, or given you a bad check? (DO NOT READ RESPONSES)

( ) Yes (ASK 36a–36c)
( ) No $\Big\}$ (GO TO NO. 37)
( ) Don't know

P-2, P-3
36a. (IF YES, ASK:) What were these crimes?
( ) _____

P-2, P-3
36b. What was the total number of crimes committed? (DO NOT READ RESPONSES)

( ) One
( ) Two
( ) Three
( ) Four
( ) Five
( ) Six
( ) Seven
( ) Eight
( ) More than nine (specify) _____

P-2, P-3
36c. Were all incidents reported to the Metro police? (IF NOT, ASK:) How many were *not* reported? (DO NOT READ RESPONSES)

( ) Yes (GO TO NO. 37)
( ) No, one not reported
( ) No, two not reported
( ) No, three not reported $\Big\}$ (ASK NO. 36d)
( ) No, four or more not reported
( ) Don't know (GO TO NO. 37)

P-2, P-3
36d. (IF ANY NOT REPORTED, ASK:) What was the *main reason* for *not* notifying the police? (DO NOT READ RESPONSES—Check the response that comes closest to what the respondent says.)

( ) Didn't want to go to court
( ) Didn't think it was important enough
( ) Didn't think it would do any good
( ) Didn't want to get anybody in trouble
( ) Afraid of retaliation
( ) Afraid my insurance would go up or be cancelled
( ) Other (specify) _____
( ) Don't know, don't remember

P-2, P-3

36x. *Coder* inserts total number of times household was victimized (that is, the sum of reported and unreported incidents for all police questions 31–36)—if not done by computer.

( ) No crimes
( ) One crime
( ) Two crimes
( ) Three crimes
( ) Four crimes
( ) Five crimes
( ) Six crimes
( ) Seven crimes
( ) Eight crimes
( ) Nine or more crimes

P-2, P-3

36y. *Coder* inserts total number of *unreported* incidents (zero if all are reported)—if not done by computer.

( ) No unreported crimes (all reported)
( ) One unreported crime
( ) Two unreported crimes
( ) Three unreported crimes
( ) Four unreported crimes
( ) Five unreported crimes
( ) Six unreported crimes
( ) Seven unreported crimes
( ) Eight unreported crimes
( ) Nine or more unreported crimes

37. Did you receive any traffic tickets for a *moving violation* in Metro during the past 3 months? (DO NOT READ RESPONSES)

( ) Yes
( ) No
( ) Not a driver
( ) Don't know

37a. In your personal experience, would you say the enforcement of traffic laws against *moving vehicles* in Metro is generally too strict, generally not strict enough, about what it should be, or inconsistent?

( ) Generally too strict
( ) Generally not strict enough
( ) About right
( ) Inconsistent
( ) Don't know

P-15

38. In your personal experience, do you think the Metro police are generally fair in their handling of people? (DO NOT READ RESPONSES)

( ) Yes
( ) No
( ) Don't know

P-16

39. In your personal experience, do you think the Metro police are generally courteous in their dealings with people? (DO NOT READ RESPONSES)

( ) Yes
( ) No
( ) Don't know

40. Do you think the amount of police patrolling in your neighborhood is too much, about right, or not enough?

( ) Too much
( ) About right
( ) Not enough
( ) Don't know

P-21

41. On the whole, would you say the service provided to you and your household by the Metro police over the past 3 months was excellent, good, fair, or poor?

( ) Excellent
( ) Good
( ) Fair
( ) Poor
( ) Don't know

42. Did you personally appear in a court proceeding in Metro in the past 3 months as a witness, complainant, juror, or for any other reason other than as a spectator?

( ) Yes (ASK NO. 42a)
( ) No ⎫
( ) Don't know ⎬ (GO TO NO. 43)

42a. (IF YES) Based on your personal experience, would you rate the performance of the court system as very satisfactory, moderately satisfactory, or not satisfactory at all?

( ) Very satisfactory ⎫
( ) Moderately satisfactory ⎬ (GO TO NO. 43)
( ) Not satisfactory (ASK NO. 42b)
( ) Don't know (GO TO NO. 43)

42b. What was the major problem? (DO NOT READ RESPONSES—Check the response that comes closest to what respondent says.)

( ) Inconvenient
( ) Lack of fairness
( ) Amount of time required
( ) Not courteous
( ) Other _____
( ) Don't know

F-6

43. Turning to the area of fire protection—Were there any fires in your home in the past 12 months? (IF YES, ASK:) How many were there?

( ) Yes, one ⎫
( ) Yes, two ⎪
( ) Yes, three ⎬ (ASK NO. 43a)
( ) Yes, more than three ⎪
( ) Yes, don't know how many ⎭

( ) No
( ) Don't know, don't remember } (GO TO NO. 44)

F-6

43a. Was it (were all) reported to the Metro fire department or some other government agency? (DO NOT READ RESPONSES)

( ) Yes, fire was reported (GO TO NO. 45)
( ) Not reported (ASK NO. 43b)
( ) Don't know if reported (GO TO NO. 44)

F-6

43b. (IF NOT REPORTED, ASK:) What was the main reason for not reporting it (them)? (DO NOT READ RESPONSES—Check the response that comes closest to what respondent says.)

( ) Too small, didn't think it was important enough
( ) Already out or almost out when fire first noticed
( ) Handled by own fire defense (fire extinguisher, sprinkler system, hoses, etc.)
( ) Didn't think it would do any good
( ) Didn't want to get anybody in trouble
( ) Afraid my (our) insurance would go up or be cancelled
( ) Other _____
( ) Don't know, don't remember

44. Have you or anyone in your household called the fire department for assistance of any kind or have you had any other firsthand contact with the fire department during the past 12 months (for example, watched a fire being fought or a fire prevention inspection at work)? (DO NOT READ RESPONSES)

( ) No, no contact (GO TO NO. 46)
( ) Yes, called for assistance
( ) Yes, other firsthand contact—watched a fire being fought
( ) Yes, other firsthand contact—watched a fire inspection
( ) Yes, other firsthand contact—attended or heard fire department presentation (talk, lecture) } (ASK NO. 45)
( ) Yes, other firsthand contact—questioned in fire investigation
( ) Yes, other firsthand contact—all other
( ) Don't know (GO TO NO. 46)

(ASK ONLY IF RESPONDENT HAS HAD CONTACT WITH THE FIRE DEPARTMENT)
F-23

45. How would you rate the overall service provided by the Metro fire department? Would you rate it as excellent, good, fair, or poor?

( ) Excellent
( ) Good

( ) Fair
( ) Poor
( ) Don't know

46. Would you allow a fireman to inspect your home or apartment to help you check for fire hazards? (DO NOT READ RESPONSES)

( ) Yes
( ) Probably yes
( ) Probably no
( ) No
( ) Don't know

SWC-2

47. Turning now to neighborhood cleanliness—Would you say your neighborhood is usually very clean, fairly clean, fairly dirty, or very dirty?

( ) Very clean
( ) Fairly clean
( ) Fairly dirty
( ) Very dirty
( ) Don't know

(ASK NUMBERS 48a–48d ONLY OF PEOPLE WHO LIVE IN SINGLE-FAMILY HOMES OR DUPLEXES)
SWC-12

48a. In the past 3 months, did the collectors ever miss picking up your trash and garbage on the scheduled pick-up days? (IF YES, ASK:) How many times would you say this occurred? (DO NOT READ RESPONSES)

( ) No, never missed
( ) Yes, 1 or 2 times
( ) Yes, 3 or 4 times
( ) Yes, 5 or 6 times
( ) Yes, _____ times
( ) Don't know, don't remember

SWC-13

48b. In the past 3 months, did the collectors ever spill or scatter trash or garbage? (IF YES, ASK:) How many times would you say this occurred? (DO NOT READ RESPONSES)

( ) No, never spilled
( ) Yes, 1 or 2 times
( ) Yes, 3 or 4 times
( ) Yes, 5 or 6 times
( ) Yes, _____ times
( ) Don't know, don't remember

SWC-14

48c. In the past 3 months, did the sanitation collectors ever damage your property when picking up trash and garbage? (IF YES, ASK:) What type of damage was it?

( ) No damage (GO TO NO. 49)
( ) Yes, _____
(IF DAMAGE TO TRASH OR GARBAGE CONTAINER, ASK NO. 48d)
( ) Don't know (GO TO NO. 49)

48d. Do you have a plastic or metal container?
( ) Plastic
( ) Metal
( ) Other _____
( ) Don't know

SWC-4
49. During the past 3 months, have collectors ever made so much noise that it bothered you? (IF YES, ASK:) How many times did this occur and what type of noise was it? (DO NOT READ RESPONSES)

( ) No, never
( ) Yes, 1 or 2 times; type _____
( ) Yes, 3 or 4 times; type _____
( ) Yes, 4 or 5 times; type _____
( ) Yes, ____ times; type _____
( ) Don't know, don't remember

SWC-3
50. During the past 3 months, have you noticed widespread odors from uncollected garbage? (IF YES, ASK:) How often have you noticed odors? (DO NOT READ RESPONSES)

( ) No, never
( ) Yes, 1 or 2 times
( ) Yes, 3 or 4 times
( ) Yes, 5 or 6 times
( ) Yes, ____ times
( ) Don't know, don't remember

51. During the past 3 months, have you had any problems with getting your tree limbs or brush picked up?

( ) Yes
( ) No
( ) Don't know

SWC-9a
52. During the past 3 months, did you or members of your household see any rats on your block? (IF YES, ASK:) About how many times were rats seen? (DO NOT READ RESPONSES)

( ) No, never
( ) Yes, 1 or 2 times
( ) Yes, 3 or 4 times
( ) Yes, 5 or 6 times
( ) Yes, ____ times
( ) Don't know, don't remember

53. About how often over the past 3 months have you been seriously inconvenienced by standing water in the streets of your neighborhood after a rainstorm? Would you say after almost every rain, only after every heavy rain, only after some heavy rain, never?

( ) After *almost every* rain
( ) Only after *every heavy* rain
( ) Only after *some heavy* rains
( ) Never
( ) Don't know

54. About how often over the past 3 months have you been seriously inconvenienced by standing water on this property after a rainstorm? Would you say after almost every rain, only after every heavy rain, only after some heavy rains, or never?

( ) After *almost every* rain
( ) Only after *every heavy* rain
( ) Only after *some heavy* rains
( ) Never
( ) Don't know

WS-4
55. Turning now to your drinking water—Do you consider the *taste*, *odor*, *appearance*, and *temperature* of your drinking water to be satisfactory or unsatisfactory?

( ) Satisfactory (GO TO NO. 56)
( ) Unsatisfactory (ASK 55a AND 55b)
( ) Don't know (GO TO NO. 56)

WS-4
55a. What is the most important problem you have had with your water? (DO NOT READ RESPONSES—Check reasons that come closest to those given by respondent.)

( ) Chlorine taste or odor
( ) Sediment in water/water looks cloudy
( ) Water looks rusty
( ) Fluoride in water
( ) Bad taste
( ) Temperature
( ) Taste/odor (Other—specify) _____
( ) Appearance (Other—specify) _____

WS-4
55b. How often have you had this problem with your water in the last 3 months? Would you say it has always or usually been a problem, has been a problem a large number of times, a few times, or in one or two isolated cases?

( ) Always or usually a problem
( ) A large number of times
( ) A few times
( ) One or two isolated cases

WS-8
56. During the past 3 months, have there been any occasions when the *rate of flow* or *pressure* of your water caused you problems?

( ) Yes (ASK NO. 56a)
( ) No   } (GO TO NO. 57)
( ) Don't know

WS-8
56a. What was the problem you had? (DO NOT READ RESPONSES)

( ) Water shut off or reduced because of work on water lines or streets
( ) Always too low
( ) Pressure drops when washer or dishwasher in use

( ) Can't get good spray from shower/hose
( ) Other (specify) _____
( ) Don't know

WS-8

57. How many times over the past year were you without water for more than one hour? (DO NOT READ RESPONSES)

( ) None
( ) Once
( ) Two or three times
( ) Four or more times
( ) Don't know

CC-11

58. I would like to ask you a few questions about contacts you may have had with Metro. During the past 3 months, did you ever contact any Metro employee to seek service or information or to complain about something like poor Metro services or a rude employee, or for *any* reason?

( ) Yes (ASK NO. 58a)
( ) No
( ) Don't know, don't remember } (GO TO NO. 62)

CC-8, 9, and 10

58a. How many different problems or situations did you *complain* about to Metro officials during that period?

( ) None
( ) One
( ) Two
( ) Three
( ) Four
( ) Five
( ) Six
( ) More than six
( ) Don't know

59. Please describe the 3 complaints or requests that were most *important* or *significant* to you over that period, starting with the most *important* one. (RECORD EACH ITEM ON A SEPARATE LINE BELOW)

( ) A. _____
_____
( ) B. _____
_____
( ) C. _____

59a. Which department or official did you contact *initially* regarding _____ (READ ITEM A ABOVE)? (DO NOT READ RESPONSES)

( ) Mayor's Office/City Hall
( ) Councilmember
( ) Police
( ) Sanitation
( ) Streets/Public Works (excluding Sanitation)
( ) Water and Sewers
( ) Health

( ) Welfare/Social Services
( ) Other (specify) _____
( ) Don't remember

59b. Were you ever told that Metro had no authority to deal with this matter, or that it was out of Metro's jurisdiction? For instance, because it was a private matter or a state responsibility? (DO NOT READ RESPONSES)

( ) Yes
( ) No
( ) Don't remember
( ) No response

CC-2 and 5, SI-2 and 5

59c. Were you generally satisfied with Metro's response? (IF DISSATISFIED, ASK:) What was the *main* thing or things you were dissatisfied with? (DO NOT READ RESPONSES— Check responses closest to what respondent says.)

( ) Response not yet completed
( ) Satisfied
( ) Dissatisfied, never responded or corrected condition, or otherwise never provided the requested service or information
( ) Dissatisfied, poor quality or incorrect response was provided
( ) Dissatisfied, took too long to complete response, had to keep pressuring them to get results, etc.
( ) Dissatisfied, too much run-around, red tape, etc.
( ) Dissatisfied, personnel were discourteous, negative, etc.
( ) Dissatisfied, other (specify) _____
_____

( ) Don't know

(IF MORE THAN ONE ITEM WAS REPORTED UNDER 59, GO TO 60a–60c; OTHERWISE, GO TO NO. 62)

CC-2 and 5, SI-2 and 5

60a. Which department or official did you contact *initially* regarding _____? (READ ITEM B ABOVE IN QUESTION 59) (DO NOT READ RESPONSES)

( ) Mayor's Office/City Hall
( ) Councilmember
( ) Police
( ) Sanitation
( ) Streets/Public Works (excluding Sanitation)
( ) Water and Sewers
( ) Health
( ) Welfare/Social Services
( ) Other (specify) _____
( ) Don't remember

60b. Were you told that Metro had no authority to deal with this matter, or that it was out of Metro's jurisdiction? For instance, because it was a private matter or a state responsibility? (DO NOT READ RESPONSES)

( ) Yes
( ) No

( ) Don't remember
( ) No response

CC-2 and 5, SI-2 and 5

60c. Were you generally satisfied or dissatisfied with Metro's response? (IF DISSATISFIED, ASK:) What was the *main* thing you were dissatisfied with? (DO NOT READ RESPONSES)

( ) Response not yet completed
( ) Satisfied
( ) Dissatisfied, never responded or corrected condition, or otherwise never provided the requested service or information
( ) Dissatisfied, poor quality or incorrect response was provided
( ) Dissatisfied, took too long to complete request, had to keep pressuring them to get results, etc.
( ) Dissatisfied, too much run-around, red tape, etc.
( ) Dissatisfied, personnel were discourteous, negative, etc.
( ) Dissatisfied, other (specify) _____
_____
( ) Don't know

(IF THREE ITEMS WERE REPORTED UNDER NO. 59, ASK 61a–61c; OTHERWISE, GO TO NO. 62)

61a. Which department or official did you contact *initially* regarding _____(READ ITEM C ABOVE IN QUESTION 59)? (DO NOT READ RESPONSES)

( ) Mayor's Office/City Hall
( ) Councilmember
( ) Police
( ) Sanitation
( ) Streets/Public Works (excluding Sanitation)
( ) Water and Sewers
( ) Health
( ) Welfare/Social Services
( ) Other (specify) _____
( ) Don't remember

61b. Were you ever told that Metro had no authority to deal with this matter, or that it was out of Metro's jurisdiction? For instance, because it was a private matter or a state responsibility?

( ) Yes
( ) No
( ) Don't remember

CC-2 and 5, SI-2 and 5

61c. Were you generally satisfied or dissatisfied with Metro's response? (IF DISSATISFIED, ASK:) What was the *main* thing or things you were dissatisfied with?

( ) Response not yet completed
( ) Satisfied
( ) Dissatisfied, never responded or corrected condition, or otherwise never provided the requested service or information

( ) Dissatisfied, poor quality or incorrect response was provided
( ) Dissatisfied, took too long to complete response, had to keep pressuring them to get results, etc.
( ) Dissatisfied, too much run-around, red tape, etc.
( ) Dissatisfied, personnel were discourteous, negative, etc.
( ) Dissatisfied, other (specify) _____
_____
( ) Don't know

CC-7, 8, 10, and 11

62. Thinking back over the past 3 months, were there any *complaints* that you would have liked to have made to Metro officials but didn't?

( ) Yes (ASK 62a and 62b)
( ) No
( ) Don't know   } (GO TO NO. 63)
( ) No response

62a. About how many unreported complaints did you have over that period? _____

62b. Please describe briefly the nature of those unreported complaints. (LIST UP TO TWO ONLY)

( ) #1 _____
_____
( ) #2 _____
_____

CC-6 and 7

62c. What was the *main* reason or reasons you did *not* make the complaint(s)? (DO NOT READ RESPONSES)

( ) Didn't think it would do any good
( ) Expected or had previously experienced delays, run-around, red tape, etc.
( ) Problem not important enough to complain about
( ) No time, or just never got around to it
( ) Thought officials already knew about the problem or that someone else would report it
( ) Contacted wrong department
( ) Didn't know how or where to complain
( ) Could not get through to appropriate Metro official
( ) Other (specify) _____
( ) Don't know

SI-6

63. Thinking back over the past 3 months, were there any times you wanted to request services or information from the Metro government and didn't? (IF YES, ASK:) What was the *main* reason or reasons you didn't? (DO NOT READ RESPONSES)

( ) No
( ) Yes, didn't think it would do any good
( ) Yes, unable to file request (no phone, unable to get to City Hall, etc.)
( ) Yes, filing procedures too complex or too demanding
( ) Yes, didn't know how or where to file a request

( ) Yes, expected or had previously experienced run-around, delays, red tape, etc.
( ) Yes, didn't want to bother anyone
( ) Yes, other (specify) _____
( ) Don't know

64. Do you feel you could have a say about the way the Metro government is running things if you wanted to?

( ) Yes
( ) No
( ) Don't know

65. In general, how good a job do you feel Metro government is doing in meeting your needs and the needs of your family—excellent, adequate, somewhat inadequate, or very inadequate?

( ) Excellent
( ) Adequate
( ) Somewhat inadequate
( ) Very inadequate
( ) Don't know

66. Finally, a few questions about you and your family. What are the ages of all the members of this household, including children?
Respondent's age _____ Ages of all other members of household _____

Respondent's Age
( ) 18–24
( ) 25–34
( ) 35–49
( ) 50–64
( ) 65 and over

67. Family Size. (NOTE TO INTERVIEWER: CHECK FAMILY SIZE BASED ON RESPONSES TO NO. 66)

( ) 1
( ) 2
( ) 3
( ) 4
( ) 5
( ) 6
( ) 7 or more
( ) Won't say

68. How many motor vehicles do you and members of this household own?

( ) One
( ) Two
( ) Three or more
( ) None
( ) Don't know

69. What is the last grade or class *you completed* in school? (DO NOT READ RESPONSES)

( ) Grade 8 or less
( ) High school, incomplete
( ) High school, complete
( ) Technical, trade, or business school beyond high school
( ) College, incomplete
( ) College, complete
( ) Refused to say

70. Which type of home do you live in?

( ) Single-family
( ) Duplex
( ) Multifamily, less than 4 units
( ) Multifamily, 4 or more units
( ) Residential hotel, rooming or boarding house
( ) Mobile home
( ) Other (specify) _____

71. Of which race or ethnic group do you consider yourself?

( ) Black
( ) Hispanic
( ) Non-Hispanic white
( ) Asian
( ) Other _____

72. Please give me the *letter* that comes closest to your *total* household income last year?

( ) A—Under $10,000
( ) B—$10,000–$19,999
( ) C—$20,000–$29,999
( ) D—$30,000–$39,999
( ) E—$40,000 and over
( ) Don't know
( ) Refused to say

(NOTE TO INTERVIEWER: THIS COMPLETES THE QUESTIONS TO BE ASKED. THANK THE RESPONDENT. THEN ANSWER THE FOLLOWING QUESTION BASED ON YOUR OWN BEST JUDGMENT.)

73. What was the respondent's sex?

( ) Male
( ) Female

An Illustrative Questionnaire for a Survey of Businesses

The questionnaire shown here is for telephone (or in-person) interviewing. It would need to be revised somewhat for mail administration. If the local government provides for four quarterly samples rather than one annual sample, the time period asked about in this questionnaire should be changed from 12 months to 3 months. The questions obtain data for specific measures of effectiveness as described in earlier chapters. Many of the questions are preceded by a boldface code. The code refers to the chapter topic—GT = general transportation; P = police (crime control); SWC = solid waste collection; WS = water supply; CC = handling citizen complaints; and SI = handling requests for service and information—and the measure number. For example, GT-13 at Question 4 indicates that this question is used to obtain information for Measure 13 in the general transportation chapter.

Survey of Businesses

NOTE: THIS SECTION IS TO BE COMPLETED BY THE INTERVIEWER BEFORE QUESTIONING THE RESPONDENT

ADDRESS: _____ DATA OF SURVEY: _____

A. Check type of business:

Retail
_____ Food or grocery store
_____ Eating and drinking
_____ General merchandise
_____ Apparel
_____ Automotive
_____ Furniture and appliances
_____ Drug and proprietary
_____ Liquor
_____ Other retail (specify) _____
Manufacturing (specify type) _____

Service
_____ Cleaning establishment
_____ Auto repair or service
_____ Beauty or barber shop
_____ Hotel or motel
_____ General home or business service
_____ Other (specify) _____
Real Estate
_____ Apartment
_____ Other real estate
Wholesale

_____
All other (specify) _____

B. Service District (or other location code): _____

Hello, my name is . . . . . . I work for the . . . . . . and I would like to speak to: _____ (name of person with whom the interview has been scheduled). The government of . . . . . . has asked us to conduct an independent survey of businesses to help it improve its services. Please be assured that all information will be kept strictly confidential. No names of persons or businesses will be identified.

The first question I'd like to ask is . . . . . .

Demographic Information
(IF NOT ESTABLISHED IN ADVANCE OF INTERVIEW, ASK:)

1. What is your position in this business establishment?

_____ Owner or partner
_____ Manager
_____ Assistant manager
_____ Other (specify) _____

1a. How long have you held this position?

_____ Under 1 year (How many months? _____)
_____ Over 1 year

2. How long has this business been in existence at this location?

_____ Less than 1 year*
_____ 1–3 years
_____ 4–10 years
_____ 11–20 years
_____ over 20 years

Now I'd like to ask you a few questions about your *local transportation services*.

3. Over the past 12 months, how would you rate the ability of the city public transit system to bring customers and employees to your business?

*To obtain opinions from persons with substantial experience with government services, the government might decide that it wants to interview only persons who have held the position for at least 1 year and businesses that have been at one location for at least 1 year.

(a) Customers?   (b) Employees?
    ____ Excellent   ____ Excellent
    ____ Good   ____ Good
    ____ Fair   ____ Fair
    ____ Poor (Why?)   ____ Poor (Why?)
    _____   _____

GT-13

4. How would you rate the condition of the street in front of your business?

    ____ Satisfactory (does not need improvement)
    ____ Fair (needs minor improvement)
    ____ Unsatisfactory (needs major improvement)

(ASK ONLY IF THERE IS A SIDEWALK)
GT-21

5. How would you rate the condition of the sidewalk in front of your business?

    ____ Satisfactory (does not need improvement)
    ____ Fair (needs minor improvement)
    ____ Unsatisfactory (needs major improvement)

6. How often in the past 12 months has your business or have customers been inconvenienced by streets or sidewalks blocked by construction, delivery trucks, or refuse collection vehicles in the vicinity of your business?

    ____ Never (GO TO NO. 7)
    ____ Very often
    ____ Fairly often
    ____ Once in a while

6a. How was your business inconvenienced?

    ____ Parking blocked
    ____ Traffic tied up
    ____ Sidewalk blocked
    ____ Other (specify) _____

7. During the past 12 months, were you, your customers, or employees ever bothered by traffic or construction noises occurring outside your business?

    ____ No, never (GO TO NO. 8)
    ____ Once in a while
    ____ Frequently

7a. What was the most annoying source of the noise?

    ____ General vehicular traffic
    ____ Buses
    ____ Trucks
    ____ Motorcycles
    ____ Construction
    ____ Emergency police, fire, or ambulance sounds
    ____ Other (specify) _____

8. How adequate is the amount of public street lighting at night in your business area?

    ____ About right
    ____ Not enough lighting
    ____ Too much lighting; too bright
    ____ Business not open at night

GT-14

9. How satisfactory is the availability of parking (public and private) for your customers and employees?

    ____ Completely satisfactory (they can almost always find a place nearby at no cost or reasonable cost)
    ____ Usually satisfactory (they are often unable to park nearby)
    ____ Extremely unsatisfactory (they are almost never able to park nearby)
    ____ Not applicable

10. How would you rate parking law enforcement along your block?

    ____ About right (police use good judgment)
    ____ Too strict
    ____ Too lax (police allow too much illegal parking)

Now I would like to ask you a few questions about security and your local *police services*.

11. How safe do you feel while working in your business during the day?
    ____ Very safe
    ____ Reasonably safe
    ____ Somewhat unsafe
    ____ Very unsafe

P-14

12. How safe do you feel while working in your business at night?

    ____ Very safe
    ____ Reasonably safe
    ____ Somewhat unsafe
    ____ Very unsafe
    ____ Do not work at night at this location

13a. Do you employ or use any means of private security?

    ____ Yes
    ____ No (GO TO NO. 14)

13b. What type of private security do you use? (CHECK ALL THAT APPLY)

    ____ Burglar alarm system
    ____ Watchdog
    ____ Private security force or guards
    ____ Other (specify) _____

P-2 and 3

14. In the past 12 months did anyone break into your business or attempt to illegally enter your business?

_____ Yes
_____ No (GO TO NO. 15)

14a. How many times did this occur in the past 12 months?

_____ One
_____ Two
_____ Three
_____ Four
_____ Five
_____ Six
_____ Seven or more times

14b. Were all of these incidents reported to the police?

_____ Yes (GO TO NO. 15)
_____ No

14c. How many were not reported?

_____ One
_____ Two
_____ Three
_____ Four
_____ Five
_____ Six
_____ Seven or more

14d. What were the major reasons for not reporting them?

_____ Did not think it was important enough
_____ Did not think it would do any good
_____ Did not want to get involved or spend my time with the police and the courts
_____ Did not want to get the person who did it in trouble
_____ Afraid of adverse publicity in the media
_____ Afraid of retaliation or that I would get in trouble
_____ Other (specify) _____

P-2 and 3

15. To rob means to take something from a person or business by force, fear, or threat of force. In the past 12 months, so far as you know, did anyone rob or attempt to rob you, your employees, or your customers on your premises (including your parking lot)?

_____ Yes
_____ No (GO TO NO. 16)

15a. How many times did this occur in the past 12 months?

_____ One
_____ Two
_____ Three
_____ Four
_____ Five
_____ Six
_____ Seven or more times

15b. Were all of these incidents reported to the police?

_____ Yes (GO TO NO. 16)
_____ No

15c. How many were not reported?

_____ One
_____ Two
_____ Three
_____ Four
_____ Five
_____ Six
_____ Seven or more

15d. What were the major reasons for not reporting them?

_____ Did not think it was important enough
_____ Did not think it would do any good
_____ Did not want to get involved or spend my time with the police and the courts
_____ Did not want to get the person who did it in trouble
_____ Afraid of adverse publicity in the media
_____ Afraid of retaliation or that I would get in trouble
_____ Other (specify) _____

P-2 and 3

16. In the last 12 months, has anyone vandalized, that is intentionally damaged, your facility, business vehicles, or other business property?

_____ Yes
_____ No (GO TO NO. 17)

16a. How many times did this occur in the past 12 months?

_____ One
_____ Two
_____ Three
_____ Four
_____ Five
_____ Six
_____ Seven or more times

16b. Were all of these incidents reported to the police?

_____ Yes (GO TO NO. 17)
_____ No

16c. How many were not reported?

_____ One
_____ Two
_____ Three
_____ Four
_____ Five
_____ Six
_____ Seven or more

16d. What were the major reasons for not reporting them?

_____ Did not think it was important enough

_____ Did not think it would do any good
_____ Did not want to get involved or spend my time with
        the police and the courts
_____ Did not want to get the person who did it in trouble
_____ Afraid of adverse publicity in the media
_____ Afraid of retaliation or that I would get in trouble
_____ Other (specify) _____

P-2 and 3

17. During the last 12 months, do you know of any incidents of shoplifting from your establishment?

_____ Yes
_____ No (GO TO NO. 18)

17a. How many times did this occur in the past 12 months?

_____ One
_____ Two
_____ Three
_____ Four
_____ Five
_____ Six
_____ Seven or more times

17b. Were all of these incidents reported to the police?

_____ Yes (GO TO NO. 18)
_____ No

17c. How many were not reported?

_____ One
_____ Two
_____ Three
_____ Four
_____ Five
_____ Six
_____ Seven or more

17d. What were the major reasons for not reporting them?

_____ Did not think it was important enough
_____ Did not think it would do any good
_____ Did not want to get involved or spend my time with
        the police and the courts
_____ Did not want to get the person who did it in trouble
_____ Afraid of adverse publicity in the media
_____ Afraid of retaliation or that I would get in trouble
_____ Other (specify) _____

P-2 and 3

18. During the past 12 months, was your business the victim of any other crimes, such as fraud, embezzlement, employee pilferage, theft of items outside the store, arson, or any other crime?

_____ Yes
_____ No (GO TO NO. 19)

18a. What were the major types of crimes that occurred?

1) _____

2) _____
3) _____

18b. How many incidents of each type of crime occurred in the past year?

1) _____ One   2) _____ One   3) _____ One
   _____ Two   _____ Two   _____ Two
   _____ Three   _____ Three   _____ Three
   _____ Four   _____ Four   _____ Four
   _____ Five   _____ Five   _____ Five
   _____ Six   _____ Six   _____ Six
   _____ Seven or   _____ Seven or   _____ Seven or
         more   more   more

18c. How many of each type of crime were not reported?

1) _____ One   2) _____ One   3) _____ One
   _____ Two   _____ Two   _____ Two
   _____ Three   _____ Three   _____ Three
   _____ Four   _____ Four   _____ Four
   _____ Five   _____ Five   _____ Five
   _____ Six   _____ Six   _____ Six
   _____ Seven or   _____ Seven or   _____ Seven or
         more   more   more

P-2 and 3

18d. What were the major reasons for not reporting them?

_____ Did not think it was important enough
_____ Did not think it would do any good
_____ Did not want to get involved or spend my time with
        police and the courts
_____ Did not want to get the person who did it in trouble
_____ Afraid of adverse publicity in the media
_____ Afraid of retaliation or that I would get in trouble
_____ Other (specify) _____

19. During the past 12 months have you or your employees had any direct contact with police for any reason other than the above relating to your business, such as calling for assistance or being questioned by police?

_____ No (GO TO NO. 20)
_____ Yes

19a. How many contacts occurred?

_____ One
_____ Two
_____ Three
_____ Four
_____ Five
_____ Six
_____ Seven or more

19b. What were the main purposes?

1) _____
2) _____
3) _____

P-13

20. Over the past 12 months how would you rate the speed of the (name of city) police in responding to calls?

_____ Excellent
_____ Good
_____ Fair
_____ Poor (Why?) _____

P-16

21. How would you rate the courtesy of the police toward yourself and other persons in your establishment during the past 12 months?

_____ Excellent
_____ Good
_____ Fair
_____ Poor (Why?) _____

P-15

22. How would you rate the fairness of the police in dealing with your business during the past 12 months?

_____ Excellent
_____ Good
_____ Fair
_____ Poor (Why?) _____

P-21

23. Overall, how would you rate the police protection for your business?

_____ Excellent
_____ Good
_____ Fair
_____ Poor (Why?) _____

Now, I'd like to ask you some questions concerning _fire protection services_.

24. During the past 12 months, was your facility inspected by the fire department?

_____ No (GO TO NO. 25)
_____ Yes

24a. How would you rate the adequacy of the inspection?

_____ Adequate
_____ Inadequate or underinspected (specify) _____
_____ Too extensive or too petty or particular

24b. How would you rate the courtesy of the fire inspectors?

_____ Excellent
_____ Good
_____ Fair
_____ Poor (Why?) _____

24c. Overall, do you feel that the inspections helped improve the fire safety of your establishment?

_____ Yes, quite a bit
_____ Yes, slightly
_____ No apparent help

25. How many times in the last 12 months was the fire department called to put out a fire or for emergency service?

_____ None (GO TO NO. 26)
_____ One
_____ Two
_____ Three
_____ Four or more

25a. How would you rate the speed of the fire department in responding to the call(s) for service?

_____ Excellent
_____ Good
_____ Fair
_____ Poor (Why?) _____

25b. How would you rate the effectiveness of the fire department in extinguishing the fire(s)?

_____ Excellent
_____ Good
_____ Fair
_____ Poor (Why?) _____

SWC-2

26. Turning now to the cleanliness of the neighborhood and street where your business is located—Would you say that the streets in this neighborhood are usually:

_____ Very clean?
_____ Fairly clean?
_____ Fairly dirty?
_____ Very dirty?

27. Is there a publicly maintained alley beside or behind your business?

_____ No (GO TO NO. 28)
_____ Yes

SWC-2

27a. How would you rate the cleanliness of the alley in the past 12 months? Would you say it has usually been:

_____ Very clean?
_____ Fairly clean?
_____ Fairly dirty?
_____ Very dirty?

SWC-9

28. During the past 12 months, did you or your employees see any rats outside of your establishment?

_____ No (GO TO NO. 29)
_____ Yes

SWC-9

28a. How many times during the past 12 months were rats seen?

_____ Once or twice
_____ Three or four times
_____ Five or six times
_____ More than six times

(NOTE: THE FOLLOWING SECTION ASSUMES THAT THE LOCAL GOVERNMENT EITHER OPERATES, MONITORS, OR REGULATES COMMERCIAL REFUSE COLLECTION. IF NOT, QUESTIONS 29–33 MAY BE SKIPPED.)

SWC-12

29. In the past 12 months did the refuse collectors ever miss picking up your trash and/or garbage on scheduled pick-up days? (IF YES, ASK:) How many times did this occur?

_____ No
_____ Yes, 1 to 5 times
_____ Yes, 6 to 10 times
_____ Yes, more than 10 times

SWC-13

30. In the past 12 months, did the collectors ever spill or scatter trash or garbage in the area of your business? (IF YES, ASK:) How many times did this occur?

_____ No
_____ Yes, 1 to 5 times
_____ Yes, 6 to 10 times
_____ Yes, more than 10 times

SWC-14

31. In the past 12 months did the sanitation collectors ever damage your property when picking up trash and garbage? (IF YES, ASK:) What type of damage?

_____ No
_____ Yes (specify) _____

SWC-4

32. During the past 12 months, have refuse collectors—when collecting either your refuse or someone else's—ever made so much noise that it bothered you, your employees, or your customers? (IF YES, ASK:) How many times did this noise occur?

_____ No
_____ Yes, at least once a week
_____ Yes, at least once a month
_____ Yes, once every few months
_____ Yes, only once or twice

SWC-3

33. During the past 12 months, have you ever noticed odors from uncollected garbage? (IF YES, ASK:) How many times in the past 12 months have you noticed such odors?

_____ No
_____ Yes, one or two times

_____ Yes, three or four times
_____ Yes, five or six times
_____ Yes, more than six times

34. In the past 12 months, how many times has your establishment been inspected for cleanliness, health, or general sanitation?

_____ None (GO TO NO. 36)
_____ One
_____ Two
_____ Three or more times

35a. How would you rate the adequacy of the inspection?

_____ Adequate
_____ Underinspected or inadequate
_____ Overinspected or too particular

35b.&c. How would you rate the courtesy and fairness of the inspectors?

b) _Courtesy_   c) _Fairness_
_____ Excellent   _____ Excellent
_____ Good   _____ Good
_____ Fair   _____ Fair
_____ Poor (explain) _____   _____ Poor (explain) _____
_____   _____

Now, I'd like to ask you some questions about your _storm drainage and water services._

36. About how often over the past 12 months have you, your employees, or your customers been seriously inconvenienced by standing water or flooding in the immediate vicinity of your establishment after a rainstorm?

_____ Never
_____ Only after _some heavy_ rains
_____ Only after _every heavy_ rain
_____ After _almost every_ rain

WS-8

37. During the past 12 months, have there been any occasions when the rate of flow or pressure of your water caused inconvenience in your operations? Or do you not use the water for any commercial or business purposes?

_____ Yes
_____ No (GO TO NO. 38)
_____ Don't know (GO TO NO. 38)
_____ Not applicable—Don't use water for any commercial or business purposes (GO TO NO. 38)

WS-8

37a. What was the problem you had? (DO NOT READ THE RESPONSES)

_____ Water shut off or reduced because of work on water lines or streets
_____ Always too low

____ Pressure drops when water-using machines (dishwasher, etc.) are in use

____ Other (specify) _____

37b. On about how many working days did this occur in the past 12 months?

____ 1 or 2 days
____ 3–10 days
____ 11–20 days
____ More than 20 days (specify) _____

38. During the past 12 months, have you had any occasions of sewer stoppage, backup, or overflow? (IF YES, ASK:) About how often have these stoppages occurred during the past 12 months?

____ No
____ Yes, about one or two times a year
____ Yes, more than two times a year/at most once a month
____ Yes, more than once a month/at most once a week
____ Yes, more than once a week

39. Overall, how would you rate your sewer facilities and sewer service?

____ Excellent
____ Good
____ Fair
____ Poor (explain) _____

Now that we are nearing the end of our survey, I'd like to ask you a few questions about *complaints*, *requests for service and information*, and *consumer affairs*.

CC-11
40. In the past 12 months, have you ever called a city office to complain about something like poor city services or a rude city official, or for any other reason?

____ No (GO TO NO. 41)
____ Yes

CC-8, 9, and 10
40a. How many different problems or complaints did you contact the city about in the past 12 months?

____ One
____ Two
____ Three to five
____ More than five

40b. Please describe briefly the nature of your complaints, starting with the one you feel was most important.

1) _____
2) _____
3) _____

41. Which departments or officials did you contact initially regarding these complaints?

____ Mayor's Office/City Hall
____ Councilmember
____ Police
____ Sanitation
____ Streets/Public Works (excluding Sanitation)
____ Water and Sewers
____ Health
____ Licenses & Inspections/Building Codes
____ Other (specify) _____

CC-2 and 5
41a. Were you generally satisfied with the city's response to your complaints? (IF DISSATISFIED, ASK:) What were the major reasons for your dissatisfaction? (DO NOT READ RESPONSES—CHECK RESPONSES CLOSEST TO RESPONDENT'S ANSWER.)

____ Response not yet completed
____ Satisfied
____ Dissatisfied, never responded or corrected condition
____ Dissatisfied, poor quality or incorrect response was provided
____ Dissatisfied, took too long to complete response, had to keep pressuring them to get results, red tape, etc.
____ Dissatisfied, personnel were discourteous, negative, etc.
____ Dissatisfied, other (specify) _____

42. During the past 12 months, have you ever contacted the city to seek service or information, such as having your water turned on, obtaining a building permit, etc.?

____ No (GO TO NO. 43)
____ Yes
____ Don't know/don't remember

42a. How many different service or information requests did you contact the city for during the past 12 months?

____ 1–5
____ 6–10
____ 11–20
____ More than 20

SI-2 and 5
42b. Were you generally satisfied with the city's response to your request? (IF DISSATISFIED, ASK:) What was the major reason for your dissatisfaction? (DO NOT READ RESPONSES—CHECK RESPONSE(S) CLOSEST TO RESPONDENT'S ANSWER.)

____ Response not yet completed
____ Satisfied
____ Dissatisfied, never responded or corrected condition
____ Dissatisfied, poor quality or incorrect response was provided
____ Dissatisfied, took too long to complete response, had to keep pressuring them to get results, red tape, etc.
____ Dissatisfied, personnel were discourteous, negative, etc.
____ Dissatisfied, other (specify) _____

CC-7, 8, 10, and 11

43. Over the past 12 months have there been any complaints or requests for service or information related to your business that you would have liked to have made to city officials but didn't?

_____ No (GO TO NO. 44)
_____ Yes

43a. Please describe briefly the nature of these items.

_____

_____

CC-6 and 7 and SI-6

43b. Why didn't you communicate these to city officials?

_____ Didn't think it would do any good
_____ Unable to file request (could not get to City Hall, etc.)
_____ Filing procedures too complex or demanding
_____ Didn't know how or where to file complaint or request
_____ Expected—or had previously experienced—run-around, delay, red tape, etc.
_____ Item not important enough to contact city about
_____ No time, or just never got around to it
_____ Didn't want to bother anyone
_____ Thought someone else would contact city about it
_____ Other (specify) _____

44. During the past 12 months, have you had any strong reason to suspect that pressure was put on your business or any of its employees by any city employee for financial or nonfinancial payments (not regular legal fees, charges, or taxes)? If so, which agency? (CHECK ALL THAT APPLY)*

_____ Never (GO TO NO. 45)
_____ Building inspector
_____ Assessors
_____ Tax collectors
_____ Police
_____ Fire
_____ Sanitation
_____ Refuse to say
_____ Other (specify) _____

44a. How many times did this occur?

_____ One
_____ Two
_____ Three
_____ Four or more

44b. Please describe the circumstances. _____

_____

_____

*It seems desirable to attempt to cover government employees' "honesty" in their dealings with businesses. Question 44 is an attempt to cover this very difficult issue. Preliminary interviews with businesses confirmed that this is a very sensitive area of questioning. If this version seems too "direct," a jurisdiction may prefer to change the wording or delete the question entirely.

CC-2 and 5, SI-2 and 5

45. Overall, how satisfied have you been with the outcomes of your contacts with the city government over the past 12 months?

_____ Very satisfied
_____ Fairly satisfied
_____ Somewhat dissatisfied
_____ Extremely dissatisfied

CC-5 and SI-5

46. Overall, how would you rate the courtesy of city officials in the course of your contacts with city government over the past 12 months?

_____ Very courteous
_____ Fairly courteous
_____ Somewhat courteous
_____ Very discourteous

(IF NO LOCAL CONSUMER AFFAIRS OFFICE EXISTS, EXCLUDE QUESTIONS 47 and 48.)

47. During the past 12 months, has the Office of Consumer Affairs contacted you or another employee for any reason relating to your business?

_____ No (GO TO NO. 49)
_____ Yes

47a. Please describe briefly the circumstances of those dealings.

_____

_____

47b. Did you experience any problems in the course of your dealings with the Office of Consumer Affairs in the past 12 months? (IF YES, ASK:) Which of the following were problems for you?

_____ No
_____ Too much run-around or red tape involved
_____ Never resolved the problems or matters involved
_____ Unfair, biased against business and/or toward the consumer's position
_____ Unnecessarily hurt business, increased costs, etc.
_____ Personnel were discourteous
_____ Too "political" in their actions
_____ Procedures are too time-consuming
_____ Other (specify) _____

48. Overall, are you satisfied with the usefulness, courtesy, and effectiveness of the Office of Consumer Affairs, as you have experienced it or perceived it?

_____ Definitely yes
_____ Generally yes
_____ Generally no (explain) _____
_____ Definitely no (explain) _____

49. In general, how good a job do you feel government is doing in meeting the needs of your business?

_____ Excellent
_____ Good
_____ Fair
_____ Poor

50. Is there any other comment or problem that you would like to make about the services provided to you by your local government?

_____
_____

_____

51. Excluding yourself, approximately how many full-time and how many part-time employees did this facility have on the average during the past 12 months?

1) *Full-time*	2) *Part-time*
_____ None	_____ None
_____ 1–10	_____ 1–10
_____ 11–30	_____ 11–30
_____ 31–50	_____ 31–50
_____ More than 50	_____ More than 50

52. What are your regular business hours?

	From	*To*
Monday	_____	_____
Tuesday	_____	_____
Wednesday	_____	_____
Thursday	_____	_____
Friday	_____	_____
Saturday	_____	_____
Sunday	_____	_____

53. What were the approximate gross sales (of merchandise or services) at this establishment for the previous 12 months?

_____ None	_____ $100,000–499,999
_____ Under $25,000	_____ $500,000–999,999
_____ $25,000–99,999	_____ $1 million and above

Interviewer: _____ Date: _____
Time interview ended: _____
Area #: _____ Census tract #: _____

Trained Observer Rating Procedures for Solid Waste Disposal Sites

The trained observer rating procedure consists of two parts: (1) an external inspection of the entrance and selected perimeter points around the disposal or incineration area (to obtain ratings on appearance, odors, and noise) and (2) an internal inspection of the landfill or incineration area (to obtain ratings on the presence of airborne emissions such as smoke, dust, and ash; the presence of insects and rodents; and the presence of other health and safety hazards).

The following sections discuss these procedures. The scales used for each characteristic to be rated are shown in Exhibit 3-4. Exhibit 3A-1 in this appendix presents an example of an inspection form with ratings noted.

Measurements for the External Inspection

External inspection should focus on perimeter points around the disposal site that represent points of maximum citizen contact with the site—in other words, points adjacent to or visible from transportation corridors or residential or commercial areas. Inspections should cover the appearance, odor, and noise at those points as they are affected by the disposal operations, whether landfill or incinerator.

Selection of the Perimeter Points
The perimeter points should be distributed around the site. These points should be kept far enough apart that the lines connecting them to the current fill area or to the incinerator do not form angles of less than 45 degrees, which means a total of eight perimeter points at most. (This limitation is aimed at holding down the number of observations required per inspection, while still assuring that problems noticeable to passing citizens will be discovered.) If one assumes that the site entrance always will be used as one perimeter point, there will be at most seven other perimeter points. In practice, most disposal sites are located so as to avoid citizen exposure to much

of the perimeter. For example, the sites are located beside a bay, gorge, or some other physical feature that prevents exposure to citizens. Thus, the required number of perimeter points may be much lower than eight, often only three or four.

The perimeter points can be selected roughly from aerial photographs, which greatly aid the identification of symmetrically distributed points around the perimeter. The points then can be defined precisely by reference to prominent landmarks that are likely to remain in place for the foreseeable future (for example, a point on the highway shoulder that lines up with a billboard or street light). Because the perimeter points represent areas of maximum citizen contact or exposure to actual disposal operations, their locations may have to be changed when the current disposal activity is moved.

Cleanliness of Areas Near Site
The cleanliness of the perimeter point and its immediate area can be rated on a scale of 1 (clean, no litter) to 4 (extremely littered), using photographs and written descriptions similar to those for street and alley cleanliness ratings (see Chapter 2 and Exhibit 2-2 in particular). The perimeter point area to be rated for cleanliness may be defined as the open ground in a circle of, for example, a ten-yard radius from the selected perimeter point. Or the area might be some segment between a road and a fence surrounding the site. However, the area associated with a point should be readily located and small enough to be visible in its entirety from the point where the observer will be standing.

Appearance of the Site from Areas Nearby
The effects of blowing smoke, dust, and ash on site appearance are not dealt with here, because they will be covered in the internal inspection rating of smoke, dust, and ash conditions.

"Substantial general traffic" in an area, a term used in Exhibit 3-4 to define level 3 in the rating, means that the observer can see at least one car for every lane of traffic but not necessarily one car in each lane of traffic at all times.

Odors

The detection of disposal site odors can be extremely sensitive to wind speed and direction. Thus, observers should take a few minutes to allow gusts of wind to blow in their direction from the site. This procedure is especially important if previous inspections or other information suggest that odors are likely to be a problem.

Noise

Most of the noises associated with site operation will not be sufficiently near, loud, or shrill to be strongly offensive; thus, a rating of 4 generally will not be needed. However, noise from vehicles entering and leaving the site may be a problem if sanitation trucks constitute the only traffic on the road. If there is uncertainty as to whether the rating should be 3 or 4, or if there are numerous complaints about noise, it may be desirable to check the noise level beside a nearby house or other structure. This check can be made either subjectively (with the human ear) or objectively (with a decibel meter). However, the procedure will not work so well if there are other major sources of noise in the area.

Measurements for Internal Inspections

Previous guidelines have concerned measurements made outside the disposal site at points of public exposure. This section deals with measurements made within the disposal site area. For nonincinerator sites, the measurements should be made at the point of current disposal operations, at points of past or future disposal operations, and at points where citizens bringing refuse can be expected to come into contact with disposal operations. For incinerator sites, inspections probably should examine the following areas:

- Central receiving area (known as tipping area in incinerator operations)

- Citizen tipping area, where only private citizens may dump waste for processing

- Special areas for receiving and processing hazardous or other special wastes; sorting and transferring areas where wastes can be separated by hand or transferred from processing or storage to vehicles; land disposal areas for processed residues or unprocessed special wastes.

Smoke, Dust, and Ash

Inspections for smoke, dust, and ash should be made in the current fill area for land disposal sites and in the tipping area and around the incinerator for incineration disposal sites. The principal finding will be the presence or absence of smoke, dust, ash, or particulates in the air.

Further refinement of the term "visible smoke" used in defining level 4 in the scale can be achieved by making use of the Ringlemann scale, a procedure for relating the "blackness"

of smoke. This rating generally is related to the degree of health hazard posed by the smoke and the degree to which smoke affects the appearance of surrounding areas. The Ringlemann scale consists of a series of reference grids of black lines on white; these correspond to ratings running from 1 to 4, which may be used to assess the darkness of a stack plume. The scale is described in U.S. Bureau of Mines circular 7718, dated March 1955, and has been reproduced in a number of other sources dealing with monitoring of stack emissions. Also, public health tests conducted on the Ringlemann procedure have established that consistent evaluations are possible by trained observers properly positioned with respect to stack, sun, and wind direction.

Ratings 3 and 4 distinguish between "intermittent" and "continuous" blowing of smoke, dust, or ash. "Intermittent blowing" means that only a very small amount of airborne material is involved, even when substantial gusts of wind occur. "Continuous blowing" of smoke, dust, or ash means that trained observers standing in the area where the material is being blown have to shield their eyes and nose from the material.

Incinerators may have smoke and ash problems of short duration when the start-up process begins, or when the waste input stream is not properly mixed. Cities that find ratings of 4 at incinerator sites will want to consider these possible explanations and examine the actual duration of the problems. Also, ratings made at the start of the operating day should be noted as such.

Pests

Flies or mosquitoes are the insects most often present at disposal sites. Rats will probably be visible only at night; evidence will consist of rat droppings, burrows, or tracks. Disposal sites often are inspected by county and state health officials for pest control, and it may be possible to obtain ratings from these officials, who are likely to be well trained in what to look for and where to look.

Health Hazards

Health hazards consist of accumulations of exposed toxic wastes or wastes capable of harboring or supporting rats or insects. For the current and other general fill areas, this rating usually will be determined by the presence or absence of food wastes because toxic wastes probably will not be accepted at the sites, and large items are easy to cover. Measurement can generally be made only after hours, when the daily final cover of earth has been applied to the refuse. In looking for food wastes, the most common items are likely to be fruit wastes such as orange, lemon, or banana peels and contaminated, greasy food wrappers.

In determining whether wastes are scattered or widespread, as required by the rating definitions for levels 3 and 3.5, the suggested procedure is to determine whether all or almost all of the individual waste items can be recognized by a visual scan. If wastes are so cluttered that they must be pulled apart to be counted, or if the observer must be right on top of the wastes to count them, then the waste in that area is con-

Exhibit 3A-1 **Sample Inspection and Evaluation Form for Solid Waste Disposal Sites**

Site inspected _____

Location _____

Perimeter point locations and directions for observation

(Rate cleanliness of each perimeter point in terms of litter within ten feet of where you stand)

(1) City limits sign near US 20 overpass on Santac Highway. When making observations of site, look toward site, keeping current fill area in the middle of your field of vision.

(2) At the WWWW billboard on US 20 opposite landfill site. When making observations of site, look toward site, keeping street lamp pole to the right of your field of vision.

(3) At the Joe's Restaurant billboard sign on US 20 opposite landfill site. When making observations of site, look toward site, keeping XYZ billboard to the right of your field of vision.

(4) Southeast corner of landfill. When making observations of site, look due northwest.

Weather conditions during inspection

(a) Current fill area inspection
   Time/date
   Temperature _____
   Wind speed and direction _____
   Humidity _____
   Precipitation _____

(b) Other internal inspection
   Time/date _____
   Temperature _____
   Wind speed and direction _____
   Humidity _____
   Precipitation _____

(c) External inspection
   Time/date _____
   Temperature _____
   Wind speed and direction _____
   Humidity _____
   Precipitation _____

Phone number for weather _____

Inspectors: _____
_____
_____

External Inspection

Characteristic	Entrance	Perimeter point no. 1	Perimeter point no. 2	Perimeter point no. 3	Perimeter point no. 4	Definition of rating
Cleanliness of areas near site	2	1	1	1	4	Assign ratings of 1, 2, 3, or 4, according to photographs used in the citywide street cleanliness ratings.
Appearance of site from areas nearby	1	4	2	2	2	1—No unattractive features in the foreground of the observer's field of vision. 2—Only unattractive features in view are raw earth or trucks. 3—Sanitation equipment other than trucks in view. 4—Uncovered refuse, paper blowing, or dust blowing toward point can be seen.
Odors	1	1	1	1	1	1—No odor detectable. 2—Odor detected that could be from site but cannot confirm, or it is indistinguishable from other odors in area. 3—Odor detected and confirmed as principally coming from site, but not offensive enough to cause an individual to seek to avoid it. 4—Odor detected, confirmed as principally coming from site, and is offensive enough to cause an individual to seek to avoid it.

(continued on next page)

Exhibit 3A-1 (continued)

External Inspection (continued)

Characteristic	Entrance	Perimeter point no. 1	Perimeter point no. 2	Perimeter point no. 3	Perimeter point no. 4	Definition of rating
Noise	1	1	1	1	1	1—No noise detectable. 2—Noise detected that could be from site but cannot confirm, or it is indistinguishable from other noises in area. 3—Noise detected, confirmed as principally coming from site, but is not offensive enough to cause an individual to seek to avoid it. 4—Noise detected, confirmed as principally coming from site, and is offensive enough to cause an individual to seek to avoid it.

Internal Inspection

Characteristic	Current fill area	Other general fill area	Definition of rating
Smoke, dust and ash	1	1	1—No blowing dust, no burning. 2—No blowing dust, no visible smoke escapes area of burning operation. 3—Considerable blowing dust *or* some visible smoke from burning does escape area of burning operations. 4—Visible smoke is escaping continuously or almost continuously from area of burning operations.
Pests	1	2	1—No evidence of rats or insects. 2—Evidence of insects but no evidence of rats. 3—Evidence of rats but no rats seen. 4—Rats seen.
Health hazards	2	3	1—No uncovered wastes. 2—A few scattered wastes but no food wastes, no hazardous or toxic wastes, no dead animals, and no bulky goods providing potential shelter for pests. 3—A few scattered items including some food wastes *or* some toxic or hazardous wastes *or* some dead animals *or* some bulky goods providing potential shelter for pests. 3.5—Widespread uncovered wastes but no piles of waste, and most of the ground is still visible. 4—Large areas of ground covered with wastes *or* some wastes in piles.
Other hazards	1	1	1—Restricted area not open to citizens. 2—Unrestricted area with no hazards. 3—Unrestricted area with some hazards but none likely to lead to serious injury. 4—Unrestricted area with some hazards capable of leading to serious injury.

sidered widespread and should be rated at least 3.5.

If separate areas are maintained for bulky goods, hazardous and toxic wastes, or demolition waste, these areas can be given a rating of 2 only if all wastes are covered.

Sewage solids handled at the landfill can present a health hazard if citizens come into contact with them or if drainage from them is not controlled. The latter problem can be dealt with as part of the general measurement of landfill impacts on water quality (see Measures 1–3 in Chapter 3).

Other Hazards

This rating should be made only if citizens are allowed access to the site to dispose of their trash, or if the site is not completely fenced off or otherwise controlled to keep citizens, particularly children, from the area. Certain parts of the disposal site may be closed off to the public, while others, such as a tipping area for private citizens, may be open; in that case, ratings would be made only in the latter areas.

Timing and Weather Conditions

Each inspection of landfill sites—or incineration sites with subsequent landfilling of the residue—normally will have to be performed in two parts. The evaluation of the current fill area can be done only *after* working hours, when wastes will be covered, if they ever are, and when rats are most likely to be visible. The evaluations at perimeter points can be done only during working hours, when odors and noises from operations may be detectable. The inspection of any internal areas where disposal operations are not currently being performed can be done at any time.

Temperature and humidity vary primarily by the season. If inspections are performed only quarterly or less frequently, they probably should be timed so that the temperature is at or above the seasonal average for that city. Probably the easiest way to be sure of measuring the most troublesome periods is to select the inspection day for a particular quarter from the two-week period that is historically the hottest for that quarter. If inspections are made only once a year, they should be made in the summer, when site problems are most noticeable.

Wind speed should be considered when inspections are infrequent (less often than once a month). Problems with blowing paper are aggravated as wind speeds increase, while odor problems are most noticeable at very low wind speeds, in the presence of temperature inversions. Wind speeds over 25 mph are likely to exaggerate blowing paper problems while obscuring odor problems; wind speeds under 4 mph are likely to conceal blowing paper problems. Inspectors should record the approximate wind speed. Any sizable shifts in the distribution of wind speeds during inspections from one year to the next should be considered when comparing the two years' ratings.

Precipitation should be noted because it can have an effect on site operations. For example, precipitation can make the ground difficult to drive on. Such effects result in the use of areas other than the designated current fill area and thus reduce the effectiveness of cover operations in covering all refuse. This, in turn, can affect the health hazard rating.

The inspection day should be selected randomly from all days the site is open during the rating period, except for the restrictions noted above for infrequent inspections. If inspections are done less often than once every two weeks and if, on the selected day, the wind speed is too high or two low during midday, inspection should be delayed until the appropriate conditions are met. This delay should involve no more than a day or two at the most.

An Illustrative Questionnaire for a Household Park and Recreation Survey

This questionnaire was adapted from one used for telephone interviewing; with modification it could be used for mail or in-person surveys.

Park and Recreation Survey

Hello, my name is _____.
I work for the _____Parks and Recreation Department. We would like your opinion of the park and recreational centers in your neighborhood.

(IF THE RESPONDENT IS TOO BUSY TO TALK NOW, SAY:)
I'll call back later. What time is convenient for you?

_____.

(IF RESPONDENT AGREES TO INTERVIEW, THEN CONTINUE)

1. Are you 18 years or older?   Yes ____ No ____

2. Are you a member of this household?   Yes ____ No ____

(IF RESPONDENT IS UNDER 18 YEARS, OR NOT A MEMBER OF THE HOUSEHOLD, SAY:)
Is the mother or father of the household at home?
Yes ____ No ____

(IF NEITHER IS AT HOME, SAY:)
Is some other adult at home?   Yes ____ No ____

(IF THE ADULT CANNOT BE REACHED, ASK WHAT TIME AN ADULT WILL BE HOME. IF THERE IS NO ADULT, CONCLUDE THE INTERVIEW.)

3. How would you rate the park and recreation opportunities in your neighborhood?

Excellent ____   Fair   ____   No opinion ____
Good   ____   Poor   ____   Don't know ____

(IF THE OPINION IS "POOR," ASK:)
Would you tell me why you say that?

_____
_____
_____

4. Has anyone in your household used these facilities (NAME EACH FACILITY) during the past 3 months?*

a. Park _____   Yes ____ No ____ Don't know ____
b. Center _____   Yes ____ No ____ Don't know ____
c. Pool _____   Yes ____ No ____ Don't know ____

5. Has anyone in the household used any other public park or recreation facility during the past 3 months?

Yes ____ No ____ Don't know ____

(IF YES, ASK:)
Which ones were they?

(ENTER EACH GOVERNMENT-OPERATED FACILITY USED. DO NOT ENTER NON-GOVERNMENT FACILITIES.)

d. _____
e. _____
f. _____
g. _____

(IF NO ONE IN HOUSEHOLD USED ANY GOVERNMENT FACILITY (QUESTION 4 AND QUESTION 5), GO TO QUESTION 7.)

6. How do you and the other members of your household rate each facility used on each of the following characteristics?

(ASK ONLY ABOUT THOSE FACILITIES WITH HOUSEHOLD ATTENDANCE DURING THE PAST 3 MONTHS. WRITE IN THE NAME OF EACH FACILITY AS SHOWN IN QUESTIONS 4 AND 5.)

*These are the pre-selected facilities about which the agency wants specific information. Large local governments may want to select facilities in the area of the residence of the respondents—say, based on the first 3 digits of the telephone number (a phone survey) or the ZIP code (a mail survey).

Facility name: _____

Characteristic	Excellent	Good	Fair	Poor	Don't know
a) Hours of operation..........	____	____	____	____	____
b) Accessibility	____	____	____	____	____
c) Attractiveness.....	____	____	____	____	____
d) Cleanliness	____	____	____	____	____
e) Condition of equipment	____	____	____	____	____
f) Helpfulness and attitude of staff...............	____	____	____	____	____
g) Variety of activities	____	____	____	____	____
h) Amount of space.............	____	____	____	____	____
i) Safety.............	____	____	____	____	____
j) Overall rating......	____	____	____	____	____

Facility name: _____

Characteristic	Excellent	Good	Fair	Poor	Don't know
a) Hours of operation..........	____	____	____	____	____
b) Accessibility	____	____	____	____	____
c) Attractiveness.....	____	____	____	____	____
d) Cleanliness	____	____	____	____	____
e) Condition of equipment	____	____	____	____	____
f) Helpfulness and attitude of staff...............	____	____	____	____	____
g) Variety of activities	____	____	____	____	____
h) Amount of space.............	____	____	____	____	____
i) Safety.............	____	____	____	____	____
j) Overall rating......	____	____	____	____	____

Facility name: _____

Characteristic	Excellent	Good	Fair	Poor	Don't know
a) Hours of operation..........	____	____	____	____	____
b) Accessibility	____	____	____	____	____
c) Attractiveness.....	____	____	____	____	____

	Excellent	Good	Fair	Poor	Don't know
d) Cleanliness	____	____	____	____	____
e) Condition of equipment	____	____	____	____	____
f) Helpfulness and attitude of staff...............	____	____	____	____	____
g) Variety of activities	____	____	____	____	____
h) Amount of space.............	____	____	____	____	____
i) Safety.............	____	____	____	____	____
j) Overall rating......	____	____	____	____	____

Facility name: _____

Characteristic	Excellent	Good	Fair	Poor	Don't know
a) Hours of operation..........	____	____	____	____	____
b) Accessibility	____	____	____	____	____
c) Attractiveness.....	____	____	____	____	____
d) Cleanliness	____	____	____	____	____
e) Condition of equipment	____	____	____	____	____
f) Helpfulness and attitude of staff...............	____	____	____	____	____
g) Variety of activities	____	____	____	____	____
h) Amount of space.............	____	____	____	____	____
i) Safety.............	____	____	____	____	____
j) Overall rating......	____	____	____	____	____

7. Would you tell me why during the last 3 months your household has not used _____?

(ASK ONLY ABOUT THE FACILITIES WITH NO HOUSEHOLD USE DURING THE PAST 3 MONTHS AS LISTED IN QUESTION 4.)

Names of facilities	Reasons
a. _____	_____
b. _____	_____
c. _____	_____

8. Let me read a list of possible reasons, in case we have overlooked some. For (Facility a), . . .

(READ REASONS. INDICATE RESPONSE BY CHECK MARK IN BOX.)

Reasons	Facilities		
	a. _____	b. _____	c. _____
a. Don't know about facility or its programs			
b. Not open the right times			
c. Too far away			
d. It's too crowded			
e. It's not attractive			
f. Costs too much to go there			
g. Too dangerous there			
h. Do not like other users			
i. Do not like staff			
j. Personal health			
k. Activities not interesting (IF CHECKED, ASK WHAT *WOULD* BE INTERESTING)			
l. Too busy			
m. Other (SPECIFY)			

Now I have some general questions to complete the questionnaire.

9. Does the household have a family vehicle like a car or truck?

Yes _____ No _____ Don't know _____ Won't say _____

10. What was the last grade or class the head of the household completed in school?

_____ Grade 8 or less
_____ High school, incomplete
_____ High school, completed
_____ Technical, trade, or business
_____ College, university, incomplete
_____ College, university, graduated

11. Do you own or do you rent the place you live in?

_____ Own
_____ Rent
_____ Don't know

12. How many years have you lived in the neighborhood?

_____

13. How many adults are in the household? _____

14. How many children (18 or younger) are in the household?

15. Would you describe your household as White, Black, Hispanic, Asiatic, or Other?

_____ White
_____ Black
_____ Hispanic
_____ Asiatic
_____ Other

16. Approximately what was the household income for the past 12 months?

_____ Less than $25,000
_____ $25,000–$50,000
_____ More than $50,000
_____ Don't know/won't say

17. Do you have any suggestions for the _____ Parks and Recreation Department to improve its services to you or others in the community? _____
_____
_____

Thank you very much for your time and cooperation.

An Illustrative Questionnaire for an On-Site Park and Recreation Survey

> *This questionnaire was adapted from one used by several agencies to interview their park and recreation users.*

On-Site Park and Recreation Survey

We need your help in evaluating and improving our programs. Please take a few minutes before you leave to complete this questionnaire. Your responses will be very helpful to us in improving our services.

Facility Name _____ Date _____

Read each question. Choose and circle the number that best applies to you.

1. About how often have you come here during the past 3 months?

   (1) This is my first visit
   (2) Almost daily
   (3) At least once a week
   (4) At least once a month
   (5) Less than once a month

2. How long do you generally stay at this facility?

   (1) Less than 1 hour
   (2) 1 hour or more but less than 4 hours
   (3) 4 hours or more

3–15. How would you rate the following?

	Excellent	Good	Fair	Poor	Not applicable
3. Hours of operation.........	1	2	3	4	5
4. Cleanliness	1	2	3	4	5
5. Condition of equipment	1	2	3	4	5
6. Availability of equipment	1	2	3	4	5

	Excellent	Good	Fair	Poor	Not applicable
7. Amount of space (lack of crowding)........	1	2	3	4	5
8. Safety conditions (including feeling of security).......	1	2	3	4	5
9. Physical attractiveness	1	2	3	4	5
10. Variety of programs	1	2	3	4	5
11. Helpfulness and attitude of staff...	1	2	3	4	5
12. Parking area	1	2	3	4	5
13. Restrooms	1	2	3	4	5
14. Convenience to your home.......	1	2	3	4	5
15. Amount of supervision.......	1	2	3	4	5

16. If you rated any of the above items "fair" or "poor," please indicate why. _____
_____
_____

17. Is there anything else you particularly like about this facility? _____
_____
_____

18. Is there anything else you particularly dislike about this facility? _____
_____
_____

19. How would you rate this facility overall?

    (1)   Excellent
    (2)   Good
    (3)   Fair
    (4)   Poor

20. How long have you lived in _____?

    (1)   Less than 1 year
    (2)   1–5 years
    (3)   More than 5 years
    (4)   Not a resident

21. What is your age?

    (1)   Younger than 6
    (2)   6–13
    (3)   14–19
    (4)   20–34
    (5)   35–64
    (6)   Over 65

22. What is your sex?

    (1)   Male
    (2)   Female

23. What is your race or ethnic group?

    (1)   White
    (2)   Black/Afro-American
    (3)   Hispanic
    (4)   Asiatic
    (5)   Other

24. What was your household's approximate income for the past 12 months?

    (1)   Less than $25,000
    (2) $25,000–$50,000
    (3)   Over $50,000
    (4)   Don't know/prefer not to say

25. Do you have any suggestions for improving this facility/ program? _____

_____

_____

Thank you very much for your help. Please return this questionnaire to the person who gave it to you, or put it in the ballot box.

Trained Observer Rating Procedures for Park and Recreation Facilities

Chapter 4 discusses the use of trained observers to collect information on park and recreation effectiveness attributes. This appendix presents procedures for collecting and tabulating such data. It builds on the discussion in Chapter 4, which should be used in conjunction with this appendix.

The procedures described here were developed for use in rating 17 Massachusetts cities and towns in the early 1980s. They have subsequently been used by a number of other local governments. Further details can be found in "Guidelines for Trained Observer Ratings of Parks and Beaches" (Washington, D.C.: The Urban Institute, October 1983) and *Raters' Manual for Capital Plant Assessment*, second edition, prepared for the Office of the City Manager (Charlottesville, Virginia) by TriData Corporation (Arlington, Virginia, 1986).

Items Rated

The following aspects of park and playground maintenance are rated under this procedure:

- Landscaping
- Playgrounds and playing fields or courts
- Restrooms
- Other facilities
- Overall cleanliness.

Each aspect is subdivided into several basic maintenance elements, and each element is rated using the rating (problem) categories shown in Exhibit 6A-1. Governments may wish to supplement or split the above elements and aspects to highlight additional features of special interest, for instance, water fountains, golf greens, or recreation centers.

When rating a given element, the raters check for the presence of specific types of problems. A sample form for recording and summarizing the ratings is included at the end of this appendix (Exhibit 6A-6). The rating form provides space for noting and rating any other types of problems encountered. Broken glass—a pervasive problem in many parks—is included as a separate potential problem for most elements.

Rating Scales

The ratings are made in two phases. First, the rater assesses the presence and extent of each type of problem, using a simple three-level scale: (1) no problems, (2) limited problems, or (3) widespread (or major) problems. If any problem also constitutes a safety hazard, the fact is noted.

The second phase of the rating process involves combining the problem-by-problem ratings into overall assessments of the jurisdiction's park and recreation facilities, including overall ratings of specific "elements" and "aspects" of park maintenance.

Ratings of Problems

A *limited problem* is defined as a problem that involves one-third or less of the element rated. A *widespread (or major) problem* is defined as a problem that is quite extensive in scope or frequency with respect to the element being rated (i.e., involving *over one-third* of a given type of facility). The following examples illustrate the differences between limited and widespread (or major) problems:

Landscaping
Limited problem: Untrimmed grass in one or two small areas
Widespread problem: No evidence of trimming; numerous instances of untrimmed grass

Playgrounds
Limited problem: One broken (unusable) swing out of five
Widespread problem: Many broken swings (e.g., three out of five)

Rest Rooms
Limited problem: One broken or unusable toilet in a rest room with four toilets
Widespread problem: All toilets inoperable in one of the rest rooms, or at least one toilet inoperable in *each* rest room

Other Facilities

Limited problem: One or two broken benches or overturned picnic tables (out of nine in the park); paths exhibit a few holes or ruts

Widespread problem: Numerous broken benches or over-turned tables (more than one-third of them). Broken benches or tables that pose serious safety problems should be flagged as hazards (see below). Extensive rutting or potholing of paths.

A dash (—) should be entered on the rating form (see Exhibit 6A-2 for an example of a completed form) if a given type of facility *does not exist* or if a given type of condition *does not apply*. For instance, if a park has no unpaved paths, a dash should be entered as the rating for "Dirt/gravel paths rutted, overgrown, muddy, blocked, etc." A dash should be entered after "Other" if no other problems are present.

A *hazard* is defined as a problem that is potentially dan-

Exhibit 6A-1   **Summary of Problems Examined in Rating Parks and Playgrounds**

Aspect	Element	Problem
Landscaping—care and general appearance	Grass and lawns	1. Grass unmowed, unkempt 2. Weeds present in grass, along fences, walls, etc. 3. Grass not trimmed 4. Grass not properly edged 5. Grass brown, unhealthy, worn 6. Broken glass hazard 7. Other
	Shrubs, trees, and plantings	1. Trimming needed 2. Weeds present in planted areas 3. Dead trees, shrubs, or foliage 4. Broken glass hazard 5. Other
Playgrounds and playing fields	Playing areas	1. Equipment broken, cracked, or loose 2. Equipment defaced 3. Equipment in need of repainting or refinishing 4. Area infested with weeds 5. Broken glass hazard 6. Other
	Playing fields and courts	1. Basketball/tennis court lines or surface in poor condition 2. Equipment broken or damaged 3. Base paths, rutted, muddy 4. Base paths, skinned areas poorly defined 5. Playing fields infested with weeds 6. Broken glass hazard 7. Other
Rest rooms	Odors	1. Objectionable odors
	Cleanliness	1. Toilets/basins/mirrors, etc., dirty or stained 2. Walls dirty or stained 3. Floor dirty, stained, littered, or wet 4. Broken glass hazard 5. Other
	Maintenance	1. Lack of toilet paper, towels, etc. 2. Broken/leaking/inoperable fixtures 3. Facilities in need of repainting (due to graffiti, etc.) 4. Other
Other facilities	Paths, walks, and parking areas	1. Dirt/gravel paths rutted, overgrown, muddy, blocked, etc. 2. Paved walks have holes, ruts, water, defects, etc. 3. Parking area pavement bumpy (rated 2.5 or more) 4. Broken glass hazard 5. Other
	Park benches, picnic tables	1. Tables broken, overturned, or damaged 2. Table surfaces dirty, greasy, littered, etc. 3. Benches broken, overturned, or damaged 4. Benches in need of painting or refinishing 5. Broken glass hazard 6. Other
	Structures and related facilities (includes buildings, bleachers, pools, signs, lights, fences, retaining walls, etc.)	1. Structures dirty or stained 2. Structures damaged or broken, parts missing 3. Structures in need of repainting (due to graffiti, etc.) 4. Lights/electrical services broken or hazardous 5. Broken glass hazard 6. Other
Overall cleanliness	Litter	1. Litter rating of 2.5 or more

gerous to health or safety (for example, a loose slide or swing set, or a sharp point in a play area). Because of their importance, each hazard is counted separately: two dangerous swings are two hazards. Broken glass is such a common hazard that separate lines are provided on the rating form for noting its presence in connection with each element rated.

Any problem considered a hazard must also be noted as either a "limited" or "widespread" problem. For example, if one bench in a park is broken and shows protruding, jagged edges, it would be recorded both as a "limited" problem *and* as a "hazard." If more than one-third of the benches in the park are broken but only one is dangerous, the situation should be recorded

Exhibit 6A-2   **Example of a Completed Page from a Park Rating Form**

Aspect	Element	Step 1: Identification of problem — Potential problem	Notes and comments on problems found	Step 2: Rating of each problem	Step 3: Element totals	Step 4: Aspect totals
Rest rooms	Odors	Objectionable odors	—	NP		
	Cleanliness	Toilets, basins, mirrors, etc. dirty or stained	Rust stains - 2 of 4 basins	Wide	NP 3 Lim. 1 Wide. 1 Haz. 0	
		Walls dirty or stained	Mud, dirt on one wall	Lim		
		Floors dirty, stained, littered, or wet	Recently cleaned	NP		NP 4 Lim. 3 Wide. 1 Haz. 0
		Broken glass hazard	—	NP		
		Other	—	—		
	Maintenance	Lack of toilet paper, towels, etc.	—	NP	NP 1 Lim. 2 Wide. 0 Haz. 0	
		Broken/leaking/inoperable fixtures	Leaking faucets - 1 of 4	Lim		
		Facilities in need of repainting (due to grafitti, etc.)	Small amounts of graffiti	Lim		
		Other	—	—		
Other facilities	Paths, walks, parking areas	Dirt/gravel paths rutted, overgrown, muddy, blocked, etc.	No unpaved paths	—	NP 1 Lim. 1 Wide. 1 Haz. 1	
		Paved walks with holes, ruts, water, defects, etc.	Over half cracked - 2"hole near shelter	Wide/1 Haz		
		Parking area pavement rated 2.5 or worse	Overall pavement rating: 2 * *Limited area (10%) rated 2.5	Lim		
		Broken glass hazard	—	NP		NP 6 Lim. 5 Wide. 3 Haz. 6
		Other	—	—		
	Park benches and picnic tables	Tables broken, overturned, or damaged	—	NP	NP 3 Lim. 2 Wide. 0 Haz. 2	
		Table surfaces dirty, littered, greasy, etc.	—	NP		
		Benches broken, overturned, or damaged	3 broken (of 10); 2 of them hazardous	Lim; 2 Haz		
		Benches in need of painting or refinishing	Two need painting	Lim		
		Broken glass hazard	—	NP		
		Other		—		
	Structures and other facilities	Structures dirty or stained	Heavy graffiti on shelter	Wide	NP 0 Lim. 3 Wide. 3 Haz. 3	
		Structures damaged or broken, parts missing	Missing bricks in N. wall of shelter	Lim		
		Facilities in need of repainting (due to graffiti, etc.)	Shelter needs painting	Wide		
		Lights/electrical services broken or hazardous	Exposed wiring-base of NE light pole	Lim; 1 Haz		
		Broken glass hazard	On shelter floor-left of bleachers	Lim; 2 Haz		
		Other	Fence posts loose, leaning	Wide		

Key:
"—"—No such facility/not applicable   NP —No problem   Lim. —Limited   Wide. —Widespread   Haz. —Hazard

as a "widespread" problem with one "hazard." Similarly, if a small amount of broken glass is found on a basketball court, it should be noted as a "limited" problem *and* a "hazard." If the broken glass is found in an inaccessible location under the bleachers, it should be rated a "limited" problem but *not* counted as a "hazard."

The overall rating for each "element" or "aspect" of a given facility's maintenance is obtained by combining the ratings for the relevant potential problems. There are several ways to do this. Exhibit 6A-2 illustrates one approach, in which the agency tallies the number of limited and widespread problems and the number of hazards for each element, each aspect, and—ultimately—the entire park. The number of "no problem" ratings should also be tallied, to allow one to compute the percentage of the *potential* maintenance issues investigated that exhibited limited, widespread, or no problems.

The Rating Process

The members of the trained observer team should walk through the facility being rated, covering all major paths and facilities and entering any structures and rest rooms present. As they go, the raters should note in the "Comments" section of the rating form the nature of the problems found. (See Exhibit 6A-2 for examples.)

The following steps should be used to rate the various "aspects" of park maintenance:

1. For each maintenance "element" to be assessed, the rater should first consider whether any of the relevant "problems" indicated on the form (or any *other* problems) are present. The rater should briefly describe the nature of each problem and hazard identified in the spaces provided on the form. (See Step 1 on the form, Exhibit 6A-6.)

2. If a problem is present, the rater should judge whether it constitutes a limited or widespread problem and whether it is a hazard, based on the foregoing definitions. (See Step 2 on the form.)

3. Next, an overall rating of the "element" should be prepared, based on the extent and intensity of *all* the problems found. (See Step 3 on the form.) The combined rating can be simply a tally of the number of limited problems, widespread problems, hazards, and "no problem" ratings recorded for potential problems associated with the given element. Non-applicable elements (denoted by a dash) are not counted.

Exhibit 6A-3   Park Litter/Cleanliness Rating Scale

Ratings of park cleanliness are based on a scale of 1 (very clean) to 4 (very dirty). The ratings are described in writing below and can be referenced to the photographs shown in Chapter 2 for rating street litter. The rater can extrapolate the linear incidence of litter shown in the street cleanliness photographs to an areawide measure for use in parks by comparing the photographs with the incidence of litter along several imaginary lines through the park. Special attention should be paid to areas around trash receptacles. However, the rating should summarize litter conditions throughout the park.

Condition	Description
1	*Park completely clean or almost completely clean.*
2	*Park largely clean:* A few pieces of litter observable, but only in the form of isolated discarded items. For a generally clean park (Condition 1), a single accumulation of uncontained trash with a volume less than or equal to the volume of a grocery bag should be rated Condition 2.
3	*Lightly scattered litter* along all or most of the paths or grass areas, or one heavy pile of litter. For a generally clean park (Condition 1), a single accumulation of litter larger than a Condition 2 accumulation but smaller in size than a standard-size (30-gallon) garbage can should be rated Condition 3.
4	*Heavily littered park:* Litter accumulation in piles or around trash receptacles, or heavy litter distributed over all or nearly all of the park. For a generally clean park (Condition 1 or 2), a single accumulation of litter with a volume greater than that of a standard 30-gallon garbage can/should be rated Condition 4.

Ratings of 1.5, 2.5, and 3.5 can also be used, as discussed in Chapter 2.

Note: Grass clippings and leaves are not considered litter and are not counted in any rating. Cut brush not piled up for pick-up and strewn so as to make the park unsightly is counted as litter. Glass is rated separately; it should not be included in the litter rating.

The rater should enter the overall litter rating in the space provided on the rating form. If conditions rated 2.5 or worse exist, assess their extent (frequency) and note in the column headed "Step 2" whether they constitute a widespread or limited problem.

Exhibit 6A-4   Rating Scale for Parking Area Pavements

A rating of parking area smoothness is to be made by combining a visual inspection with, if necessary, a "seat-of-the-pants" assessment made by driving over the lot. The following scale should be used in conjunction with the photographic standards reproduced in Chapter 8.

Condition	Description
1	*Smooth* rideability (i.e., appears to be and feels smooth) a. No noticeable defects b. One or two minor defects: Small bump, crack, or hole. Can have many small cracks, as long as there is no noticeable effect on rideability.
2	*Slightly bumpy* rideability a. Several minor defects or minor potholes, but none appears or feels severe b. A single large bump or many minor bumps
3	*Very bumpy* rideability: Much of the area is broken up, but no single hazard is apparent
4	*Potential safety hazard* or *severe jolt* present: One or more large potholes or other major defects

Ratings of 1.5, 2.5, or 3.5 can also be used.

Note: A large pothole is defined as a hole 3½" deep and at least 12" in diameter. A major defect is defined as an abrupt change of pavement surface level greater than 3½". A minor defect is defined as being less than 3½" deep or less than 12" in diameter.

The rater should enter the overall parking area rating in the space provided on the rating form. If conditions rated 2.5 or worse exist, assess their extent; then note whether they constitute a widespread or limited problem in the column headed "Step 2." All hazardous areas (Condition 4) should be noted (separately) as hazards under "Step 2" so that they can be tallied.

Exhibit 6A-5 Sample Format for Reporting Trained Observer Ratings of Parks

(By Individual Park, by Area, and Citywide)

Columns under **Number of items (potential problems) examined that received the given rating** are grouped by category (Rest rooms, Other facilities, Playgrounds/playfields, Landscaping, Cleanliness), each with sub-columns NP (no problems), L (limited problems), W (widespread problems), H (hazards). Columns under **Number of items with:** are NP, L, W.

Park name and ward	RR NP	RR L	RR W	RR H	OF NP	OF L	OF W	OF H	PG NP	PG L	PG W	PG H	LS NP	LS L	LS W	LS H	CL NP	CL L	CL W	CL H	No problems (NP)	Limited problems (L)	Widespread problems (W)	Total items rated*	Percentage with problems	Total no. with hazards (H)
Greenbrier-Greenleaf Terr.																										
Greenbrier	6	—	—	—	6	—	—	—	—	—	—	—	7	—	—	—	1	—	—	—	14	—	—	14	—	—
Greenleaf	—	2	—	—	11	1	1	—	7	—	1	—	5	4	—	1	1	—	—	—	30	7	1	38	21%	1
Jackson	—	—	—	—	9	—	—	—	—	—	—	—	9	—	—	—	1	—	—	—	19	—	1	20	5	—
Lee	—	—	—	—	9	2	—	1	—	—	—	—	9	1	—	—	—	1	—	—	18	4	—	22	18	1
McGuffey	—	—	—	—	13	—	—	—	8	1	—	—	8	2	—	—	—	1	—	—	29	4	—	33	12	—
Star Hill	—	—	—	—	—	—	—	—	5	—	—	—	9	1	1	2	1	—	—	—	15	1	1	17	12	2
Washington	4	4	—	—	7	5	—	1	3	6	—	1	3	5	1	2	—	—	1	—	17	20	2	39	56	4
AREA TOTAL	10	6	—	—	55	8	1	2	23	7	1	1	50	13	2	5	4	2	1	—	142	36	5	183	22%	8
Belmont-Locust																										
Baily	—	—	—	—	—	1	—	—	—	—	—	—	6	2	—	—	1	—	—	—	7	3	—	10	30%	—
Belmont	—	—	—	—	13	1	—	1	10	1	—	1	9	1	—	—	1	—	—	—	33	3	—	36	8	2
Mail	—	—	—	—	3	2	1	1	—	—	—	—	8	2	—	—	1	—	—	—	12	4	1	17	29	1
McIntire	4	6	—	—	6	7	2	2	9	2	—	—	6	4	—	2	1	—	—	—	26	19	2	47	45	4
Meade	—	—	—	—	13	1	—	—	10	2	—	—	9	1	—	1	1	—	—	—	33	4	—	37	11	1
Northeast	—	—	—	—	7	1	—	—	8	—	—	—	8	1	—	1	1	—	—	—	24	2	—	26	8	1
Pen	5	4	—	1	9	5	—	2	7	5	—	1	7	3	—	—	1	—	—	—	29	17	—	46	37	4
Quarry	8	—	—	—	14	—	—	—	11	—	—	—	10	—	—	—	1	—	—	—	44	—	—	44	—	—
Rives	—	—	—	—	6	1	—	1	6	4	1	—	7	2	—	—	1	—	—	—	20	7	1	28	29	1
Rothwell	—	—	—	—	6	—	—	—	—	—	—	—	9	1	—	—	1	—	—	—	16	1	—	17	6	—
AREA TOTAL	17	10	—	1	77	19	3	7	61	14	1	2	79	17	—	4	10	—	—	—	244	60	4	308	21%	14
Fifeville-Fry's Spring																										
Azalea	3	5	2	2	11	3	—	—	9	2	—	—	8	1	—	—	1	—	—	—	32	11	2	45	29%	2
Fifeville	1	1	—	—	3	—	—	—	8	1	—	—	7	1	—	—	1	—	—	—	20	3	—	23	13	—
Forest Hills	—	—	—	—	8	4	—	3	10	2	—	1	6	6	—	3	1	—	—	—	24	12	—	36	33	7
Jordan	—	—	—	—	11	—	—	—	9	—	—	—	8	2	—	1	1	—	—	—	29	2	—	31	6	1
Tonsier	—	—	—	—	8	2	3	2	7	1	3	2	8	—	1	1	—	—	1	—	24	3	8	35	31	5
AREA TOTAL	4	6	2	2	41	9	3	5	43	6	3	3	37	10	1	5	4	—	1	—	129	31	10	170	24%	15
Golf Courses																										
McIntire	7	2	1	—	9	2	1	—	4	—	—	—	7	3	—	1	1	—	—	—	28	7	2	37	24%	1
Pen Park	6	2	—	—	12	2	—	—	—	—	—	—	6	4	—	1	1	—	—	—	25	8	—	33	24	1
CITY TOTAL	44	26	3	3	194	40	8	14	131	27	5	6	179	47	3	16	20	2	2	—	568	142	21	731	22%	39
PERCENTAGE OF ITEMS	60%	36%	4%		80%	17%	3%		80%	17%	3%		78%	21%	1%		83%	8%	8%		78%	19%	3%		100%	

*Each hazard is also listed as a limited or widespread problem, so total items rated includes no problems, limited problems, and widespread problems only.

Source: Schaenman, Greiner, Camozzo, Stambaugh, Peacock, and Lockard, "What Is the Condition of Charlottesville's Capital Plant?", p. 83.

4. A summary rating should be prepared for each "aspect" of park maintenance by combining the results for the relevant "elements," using the same process employed in Step 3.

5. Finally, the agency can calculate the number of elements and aspects that have one or more widespread (or major) problems, and the number with one or more hazards. This can be done for each facility, and then the agency can tabulate the number of facilities with one or more major problems and with one or more hazards.

Exhibit 6A-6   **Rating Form for Parks and Recreation Facilities**

Name of park/facility:_____

Location (Streets): _____ Neighborhood area: _____

Type of park: _____

Date: _____ Weather: _____ Name: _____ Time of day: _____

Aspect	Element	Step 1: Identification of problem		Step 2: Rating of each problem	Step 3: Element totals	Step 4: Aspect totals
		Potential problem	Notes and comments on problems found			
Land-scaping	Grass and lawns	Grass unmowed, unkempt				
		Weeds present in grass, fences				
		Grass not trimmed				
		Grass not properly edged			NP ___ Lim. ___ Wide. ___ Haz. ___	
		Grass brown, unhealthy, worn				NP ___ Lim. ___ Wide. ___ Haz. ___
		Broken glass hazard				
		Other				
	Shrubs, trees, plantings	Require trimming				
		Weeds present in planted areas				
		Dead shrubs, trees, foliage			NP ___ Lim. ___ Wide. ___ Haz. ___	
		Broken glass hazard				
		Other				
Cleanli-ness	Litter	Litter rating of 2.5 or worse	Overall litter rating: _____			
Play-grounds and play-ing fields	Play areas	Equipment broken, cracked, or loose			NP ___ Lim. ___ Wide. ___ Haz. ___	
		Equipment defaced				
		Equipment in need of repainting or refinishing				
		Area infested with weeds				
		Broken glass hazard				NP ___ Lim. ___ Wide. ___ Haz. ___
		Other				
	Playing fields and courts	Basketball/tennis court lines or surface in poor condition				
		Equipment broken or damaged			NP ___ Lim. ___ Wide. ___ Haz. ___	
		Base paths rutted, muddy				
		Base paths, skinned areas poorly defined				
		Playing fields infested with weeds				
		Broken glass hazard				
		Other				

The raters may complete the first two steps in the field and reserve Steps 3-5 for when they are analyzing and tallying the data.

It is often easiest to walk around the entire facility to get an overall picture of its condition before beginning Step 2. The team can then go back to reexamine any particular features that cannot be rated on the basis of the initial quick pass.

In most cases, the "problems" listed in Exhibit 6A-1 (and on the rating form, 6A-6) are self-explanatory. Rating the problem consists of identifying the presence and extent of the indicated condition. However, for two potential problems—litter

Exhibit 6A-6 continued

Aspect	Element	Step 1: Identification of problem		Step 2: Rating of each problem	Step 3: Element totals	Step 4: Aspect totals
		Potential problem	Notes and comments on problems found			
Rest rooms	Odors	Objectionable odors				
	Cleanliness	Toilets, basins, mirrors, etc. dirty or stained			NP ___ Lim. ___ Wide. ___ Haz. ___	
		Walls dirty or stained				
		Floors dirty, stained, littered, or wet				NP ___ Lim. ___ Wide. ___ Haz. ___
		Broken glass hazard				
		Other				
	Maintenance	Lack of toilet paper, towels, etc.			NP ___ Lim. ___ Wide. ___ Haz. ___	
		Broken/leaking/inoperable fixtures				
		Facilities in need of repainting (due to grafitti, etc.)				
		Other				
Other facilities	Paths, walks, parking areas	Dirt/gravel paths rutted, overgrown, muddy, blocked, etc.			NP ___ Lim. ___ Wide. ___ Haz. ___	
		Paved walks with holes, ruts, water, defects, etc.				
		Parking area pavement rated 2.5 or worse	Overall pavement rating: _____			
		Broken glass hazard				NP ___ Lim. ___ Wide. ___ Haz. ___
		Other				
	Park benches and picnic tables	Tables broken, overturned, or damaged			NP ___ Lim. ___ Wide. ___ Haz.	
		Table surfaces dirty, littered, greasy, etc.				
		Benches broken, overturned, or damaged				
		Benches in need of painting or refinishing				
		Broken glass hazard				
		Other				
	Structures and other facilities	Structures dirty or stained			NP ___ Lim. ___ Wide. ___ Haz. ___	
		Structures damaged or broken, parts missing				
		Facilities in need of repainting (due to graffiti, etc.)				
		Lights/electrical services broken or hazardous				
		Broken glass hazard				
		Other				

Key:
"—"—No such facility/not applicable   NP —No problem   Lim. —Limited   Wide. —Widespread   Haz. —Hazard

and parking area pavements—the procedures are slightly different. In these cases, the trained observer rates the overall condition of the facility using scales analogous to those for rating street cleanliness and road rideability (see Chapters 2 and 8). A *widespread problem* is then recorded if a litter or cleanliness rating of 2.5 or higher is found to apply to *over one-third of the entire facility*. A *limited problem* is defined as the presence of conditions rated 2.5 or worse in only a few small areas (less than one-third of the facility). Exhibits 6A-3 and 6A-4 describe the rules and scales used to rate park litter and parking area pavements.

The litter and parking area ratings make use of photographs to illustrate and anchor the scales. While Exhibits 6A-3 and 6A-4 describe how to make park ratings using photographs developed for making street cleanliness and pavement ratings (for instance, using the photographs reproduced in Chapters 2 and 8), a local government may want to develop its own photographic standards designed specifically for park ratings. Procedures for preparing such pictures are described in Chapters 2 and 8.

Photographic rating scales can also be used to help rate other park maintenance problems. Again, the procedures described in Chapters 2 and 8 can be used. Photographic standards can be useful for indicating the differences between the "no problem" and "limited problem" ratings and for illustrating various types of hazards. They are also helpful for training the observers. On the other hand, the "widespread" versus "limited" distinction often depends on conditions over a large area, conditions that are difficult to capture adequately in a photograph.

Tabulating the Results

The trained observer team needs to summarize its results for each park and facility rated after completing its field assessments. An illustrative format for reporting these ratings is shown in Exhibit 6A-5.

Three types of measures are usually of interest—the individual problem ratings (the column headed "Step 2" on the rating form), the "element" ratings (the "Step 3" column), and the overall "aspect" ratings (the column headed "Step 4"). Several composite ratings for the entire park, for the neighborhood or maintenance district, and for the jurisdiction as a whole can be developed from these data.

Hazardous conditions should be rated and reported separately because they pose an immediate danger to health or safety.

Average ratings could be calculated based on, for example, assigning values of 0, 1, and 2 respectively to ratings of "no problem," "limited problem," and "widespread problem." But because of the ordinal nature of the scales employed, the use of average ratings is not strictly correct and may distort the results. Although averages constitute a popular way to summarize numerical ratings, it is more appropriate, and probably more informative, to use percentages. Percentages also have the advantage of being able to highlight the incidence of even a few serious (e.g., widespread or hazardous) problems that might otherwise be lost in an "average" rating.

An Illustrative Questionnaire for a Library User Survey

Library Survey

Dear Library User:

To help improve library service, we are surveying a sample of users. Please read each question, then choose and circle the number to the left of the response that best applies to you. It is NOT necessary to put your name on the survey form. The answers you provide will be kept strictly confidential. IF THIS IS YOUR FIRST VISIT TO A _____ LIBRARY, PLEASE RETURN THE QUESTIONNAIRE TO THE ATTENDANT.

1. Which _____ library facilities have you used during the past 3 months? (Please circle all that apply.)

   1. Main
   2. _____
   3. _____
   4. _____
   5. _____

2. Do you or any other persons in your household have a _____ library card?

   1. Yes
   2. No

3. What activity brought you to the library today? (Please circle one.)

   1. Leisure-time material (reading/viewing/listening)
   2. School assignment
   3. Job-related reading or research
   4. Personal business/investment reading or research
   5. Attend a meeting
   6. Other (please specify) _____

4. Did you come to (please circle one):

   1. Use materials in the library?
   2. Check out materials?
   3. Both use *and* check out materials?
   4. Other (please specify) _____

5. About how often would you say that you have used *this* particular library during the past 3 months? (Please circle one.)

   1. Almost daily
   2. At least 12 times or more
   3. At least 3 times
   4. At least once
   5. This is my first visit to this library. (If so, skip to Question 18.)

6. About how long do you usually stay each time you visit the library?

   1. Less than 15 minutes
   2. 15–30 minutes
   3. 30–60 minutes
   4. More than 60 minutes
      (Please estimate how long.) _____

How would you rate this library in the following areas? (Please circle your answer.)

	Excel-lent	Good	Fair	Poor	Don't know
7. Hours of operation.........	1	2	3	4	5
8. Days of operation.........	1	2	3	4	5
9. Availability of material you want	1	2	3	4	5
10. Comfort and cleanliness.......	1	2	3	4	5
11. Convenience to your home	1	2	3	4	5
12. Helpfulness and courtesy of library staff.......	1	2	3	4	5

13. Ease in finding
    materials......... 1   2   3   4   5
14. Ease in checking
    out materials..... 1   2   3   4   5
15. Ease of parking... 1   2   3   4   5
16. Reference help... 1   2   3   4   5
17. Overall service... 1   2   3   4   5

If you chose "excellent" or "poor" for any of your answers, please tell us why: _____
_____
_____

18. About how far do you live from this library?

    1. Less than 5 blocks (less than ½ mile)
    2. 5–10 blocks (½–1 mile)
    3. 10–20 blocks (1–2 miles)
    4. More than 20 blocks (over 2 miles)

19. What street intersection is nearest to your home?

    _____

20. How did you get to this library today?

    1. Car
    2. Bike
    3. Walked
    4. Bus or train
    5. Taxi
    6. Motorcycle

21. Is there anything you particularly like about this library?
    _____
    _____

22. Is there anything you particularly dislike about this library?
    _____
    _____

23. What additions or changes would you like to see made in this library?
    _____
    _____

24. How long have you lived in _____?

    1. Less than 3 months
    2. 3 to 12 months
    3. 1 to 5 years
    4. More than 5 years
    5. Not a resident

25. Are you presently:

    1. Student?
    2. Employed?
    3. Housewife?
    4. Retired?
    5. Other (please specify) _____

26. What is your age?

    1. Under 13
    2. 13–17
    3. 18–34
    4. 35–49
    5. 50–64
    6. 65 and over

27. What is your sex?

    1. Male
    2. Female

28. What is your race or ethnic group?

    1. White
    2. Black/Afro-American
    3. Hispanic
    4. Asiatic
    5. Other

Thank you!
Please place completed form in ballot box.

An Illustrative Questionnaire for a Water Service User Survey

A local government choosing to undertake a water service user survey should review the questions for applicability and test the final questionnaire for clarity and understandability prior to full-scale implementation. Demographic questions should be included, such as length of residence in the community, type of housing unit, and income group. While this questionnaire has been designed for telephone administration, it can be readily adapted for mailing.

Water Service User Survey

Hello, my name is _____. The (*name of city or county*) Water Department is surveying persons who have called the department to request service or to report a complaint over the past year. The department plans to use the survey results to help improve its services. Your answers will not be identified by name, so the answers you give will be completely confidential.

1. Our records show that you called about (*enter nature of service request or complaint*) on (*enter date of call*). Do you remember calling about service or a complaint at about that time?

    (1) Yes _____ (GO TO QUESTION 1b)
    (2) No _____   } (GO TO QUESTION 1a)
    (3) Don't know _____

1a. Is there anyone else in the household who might know about that call?

    (1) Yes _____ (ASK TO SPEAK TO THAT PERSON; THEN BEGIN AGAIN WITH "HELLO, . . .")
    (2) No _____ (STOP INTERVIEW)

1b. Was the reason for the call as I have stated?

    (1) Yes _____
    (2) No _____ (ENTER CORRECTION) _____
    (3) Don't know (STOP INTERVIEW)

1c. How many departments of the (city/county) did you have to call before someone was willing to check out your complaint?

    (1) One _____
    (2) Two _____
    (3) Three or more _____

    (4) No one agreed to check out complaint _____
    (5) Other (Specify) _____
    (6) Don't know _____

IF CALL *WAS NOT* ABOUT A BILLING COMPLAINT, GO TO QUESTION 2.
IF CALL *WAS* ABOUT A BILLING COMPLAINT, GO TO QUESTION 10.

2. How urgent did you consider your request to be? That is, did you feel that same-day service was required? Or, rather, that prompt service was required but not necessarily same-day service? Or that your request was not urgent?

    (1) Same-day service required _____
    (2) Prompt service required but same-day service not required _____
    (3) Not urgent _____

3. Was the service you requested provided to your satisfaction? Were you completely satisfied, satisfied, dissatisfied, or completely dissatisfied?

    (1) Completely satisfied _ } (GO TO QUESTION 8)
    (2) Satisfied _
    (3) Dissatisfied _ } (GO TO QUESTION 4)
    (4) Completely dissatisfied _

4. What was unsatisfactory?

    (1) Service refused or no service provided _____ (GO TO QUESTION 5)
    (2) Wrong service provided on first service call _____   }
    (3) Faulty or ineffective service provided on first service call _____ } (GO TO QUESTION 7)
    (4) Other (Specify) _____

5. What was the reason you were given for their not providing the service?

(1) City/county lacked authority or jurisdiction over problem ____
(2) City/county lacked resources or technical capability ____
(3) Denied that service was justified by stated facts ____
(4) Denied that facts of case were validly stated ____
(5) Promised service but never fulfilled promise ____
(6) Did not promise or refuse to give service but never followed up ____
(7) Refused service with no reason given ____
(8) Other (Specify) _____
(9) Don't know ____

6. Were you satisfied that the explanation given was reasonable?

(1) Yes, the explanation seemed reasonable ____
(2) No, the explanation seemed unreasonable ____

STOP THE INTERVIEW.

7. Did the water department provide the correct service in a later visit?

(1) Yes ____ (GO TO QUESTION 7a)
(2) No ____ ⎫
(3) Don't know ____ ⎬ (GO TO QUESTION 8)

7a. How many service calls did the water department make?

(1) Two ____
(2) Three ____
(3) Four or more ____
(4) Other (Specify) _____
(5) Don't know ____

8. What condition did the service personnel leave the work area in? Was it cleaner than before they arrived, as clean as when they arrived, somewhat messy, or very messy, or did they perform all their work off your property?

(1) Cleaner than it was before they got here ____
(2) Kept it as clean as they found it ____
(3) Somewhat messy ____
(4) Very messy ____
(5) Did all work off my property ____

9. Was service provided conveniently for you, as far as scheduling was concerned? Was it convenient, inconvenient, or extremely inconvenient, or were they able to do all work without you present?

(1) Convenient ____   ⎫
(2) Inconvenient ____   ⎬ (GO TO
(3) Extremely inconvenient ____ ⎬ QUESTION 11)
(4) Did all work without me present ____ ⎭

10. What was done about your complaint?

(1) Claimed bill correct after checking it ____
(2) Promised to check it but never followed up ____
(3) Refused to check billing complaint ____
(4) Acknowledged bill was too high and corrected it ____
(5) Acknowledged bill was too high but refused to correct it ____
(6) Acknowledged bill was too high and promised to correct it but never followed up ____
(7) Claimed bill was too low after checking it ____
(8) Other (Specify) _____
(9) Don't know ____

11. How satisfied were you with the promptness of the service personnel? Were you very satisfied, satisfied, dissatisfied, or very dissatisfied?

(1) Very satisfied ____
(2) Satisfied ____
(3) Dissatisfied ____
(4) Very dissatisfied ____

12. Were the personnel you dealt with courteous?

(1) Yes ____
(2) No ____

13. How satisfied were you overall with the efforts on your behalf? Were you very satisfied, satisfied, dissatisfied, or very dissatisfied?

(1) Very satisfied ____
(2) Satisfied ____
(3) Dissatisfied ____
(4) Very dissatisfied ____

14. How satisfied were you with the resolution of your request? Were you very satisfied, satisfied, dissatisfied, or very dissatisfied?

(1) Very satisfied ____
(2) Satisfied ____
(3) Dissatisfied ____
(4) Very dissatisfied ____

An Illustrative Questionnaire for a Survey of Citizens Who Register Complaints or Request Services or Information

Symbols in boldface refer to effectiveness measures in Chapter 11. Those coded "C," on citizen complaints, are found in Exhibit 11-2; those coded "R," on requests for services and information, are found in Exhibit 11-5.

The term "request" is used in this questionnaire to refer to a request for service or a request for information.

Demographic questions on age, race, sex, and income— similar to those used in a general citizen survey—should be asked after Question 12 so that responses can be cross-tabulated by population subgroups.

Survey of Citizens Registering Complaints or Requesting Services or Information

INTERVIEWER: BEFORE PLACING CALL, FILL IN THE FOLLOWING DATA AND THE BLANKS IN QUESTION 1, USING INFORMATION FROM THE COMPLAINT OR REQUEST RECORD.

C3, C4, R3, R4

Check whether: _____ Complaint _____ Request for service

Name of citizen: _____

Telephone number: _____

Address:_____

Response time: _____ days. Neighborhood: _____

Time interview began: _____

Good afternoon. May I speak to _____?
My name is _____ and I am calling for (name of city or county). You recently contacted us for (help) (service) (information). We would like to know how you feel about the way your call was handled so that we may better serve *all* residents of _____.
The information you give us will be strictly confidential.

1. Our records show that you contacted the (city or county) about

_____

_____

(ENTER NATURE OF REQUEST OR COMPLAINT) on _____ (ENTER DATE). Do you remember calling about a request or a complaint at that time?

_____ Yes ⎫
_____ No ⎬ (TERMINATE INTERVIEW)
_____ Don't know ⎭

1a. Was the reason for your contact as I stated? (IF "NO," ASK:) What was it?

_____ Yes
_____ No (ENTER CORRECTION) _____
_____ Don't know (TERMINATE INTERVIEW)

C6, R6

2. Overall, how easy would you say it was to report your (complaint) (request) to the proper officials?

_____ Very easy ⎫
_____ Fairly easy ⎬ (GO TO QUESTION 3)
_____ Somewhat difficult⎫ (GO TO QUESTION 2a)
_____ Very difficult ⎭
_____ Don't know (GO TO QUESTION 3)

C6, R6

2a. What were the main difficulties you experienced? (INTERVIEWER: DO NOT READ RESPONSES. MARK *ALL* RELEVANT RESPONSES.)

_____ Didn't know how or where to file complaint/request
_____ Could not get to the complaint or request office (too far away, not open, no transportation, disabled, no telephone, etc.)
_____ Could not get through to the complaint or request office (line busy, put on hold, appropriate person never in)
_____ Procedures too complex or demanding, too much red tape
_____ Too many referrals, got a runaround
_____ No one willing or able to take down the complaint or request
_____ Took too long
_____ Other (specify) _____

3. How many times did you have to contact us regarding this same matter?

_____ Once
_____ Twice
_____ Three times
_____ Four times
_____ Five or more times
_____ Don't remember

3a. Which department or departments did you contact or deal with regarding this matter? (INTERVIEWER: IF NECESSARY, DETERMINE FIRST AND LAST DEPARTMENTS CONTACTED.)

First department: _____
Last department (if different from above): _____
Others: _____
Don't know _____

C2-4, R2-4

4. How urgent do you regard your (complaint) (request)?
_____ Very urgent—same- or next-day service required
_____ Moderately urgent—response needed within 10 days
_____ Not urgent—response not needed within 10 days
_____ Don't know

I would like to ask you a few questions now about the *final response* you received from (the city or county) with regard to your (complaint) (request).

5. As far as you can tell, has (the city or county) done all it is going to do with regard to your (request) (complaint)?

_____ Yes
_____ No   } (GO TO QUESTION 5d)
_____ Don't know

C2, R2

5a. How satisfied were you with the final outcome or resolution of your (complaint) (request)? Were you:

_____ Very satisfied   }
_____ Satisfied   } (GO TO QUESTION 5d)
_____ Somewhat dissatisfied }
_____ Very dissatisfied   } (GO TO QUESTION 5b)
_____ Don't know (GO TO QUESTION 5d)

C2, R2

5b. What was unsatisfactory about the outcome? (INTERVIEWER: DO NOT READ RESPONSES. MARK *ALL* RELEVANT RESPONSES.)

_____ Never finally responded, refused to respond, could not respond (GO TO QUESTION 5c)
_____ Referred me to another office or organization
_____ Response incomplete or never completed
_____ Response was erroneous
_____ Response was of poor quality or ineffective (problem not corrected)
_____ Other (specify) _____

} (GO TO QUESTION 5d)

C1, C2, R1, R2

5c. What reason was given for not doing anything about your (complaint) (request)? (INTERVIEWER: DO NOT READ RESPONSES. MARK CLOSEST REASON.)

_____ Lacked authority or jurisdiction over matter
_____ Lacked resources or technical capability
_____ Denied facts of case were validly stated
_____ Denied any response was justified by facts
_____ Promised service but never fulfilled promise
_____ Refused service, no reason given
_____ Never responded at all, one way or the other
_____ Other (specify) _____
_____ Don't know

C2, R2

5d. Were you satisfied with (the city's or county's) explanation of its response?

_____ Yes, satisfied
_____ Partly satisfied
_____ No, not satisfied
_____ Explanation needed but not provided
_____ Explanation not needed or relevant
_____ Don't know

6. Were you contacted by someone from _____ (STATE *LAST* DEPARTMENT DEALT WITH, FROM QUESTION 3a) about your (complaint) (request)?

_____ Yes
_____ No
_____ Don't know or remember

Now I would like to ask about the way you were *treated* during your contacts with (city or county) personnel in regard to this matter.

C5a, R5a

7. Do you feel that your (complaint) (request) was handled fast enough?

_____ Yes
_____ No
_____ Don't know or remember

C5b, R5b, C6, R6

8. Were you inconvenienced by red tape or a runaround?

_____ Yes
_____ No
_____ Don't know or remember

C5d, R5c

9. Were the persons you dealt with fair in their treatment of you?

_____ Yes
_____ No
_____ Don't remember

C5c, R5d

10. Were you treated courteously?

_____ Yes
_____ No
_____ Don't remember

C5c, R5d

11. Were you satisfied with the efforts made by (city or county) personnel on your behalf?

_____ Yes
_____ No
_____ Don't know or remember

12. Do you have any general comments on the way (the city or county) handles citizen complaints and requests for services or information? _____
_____
_____

Thank you for your cooperation.
Date of interview: _____
Time interview ended: _____

Examples of Guidelines for Trained Observer Ratings

Definitions

Abandoned automobile: A motor vehicle that is left unattended on public or private property, without current tags, and apparently totally inoperable—it may be on blocks, or have four flat tires, missing wheels, broken windows, and the like.

Alley: A roadway intended to provide access to the rear or side areas of lots or buildings in urban districts and not intended for through vehicular traffic. For the purpose of this survey, the edges of buildings and fences will be used to indicate alley boundaries. When no buildings or fences are present, utility poles will be considered to represent the boundaries, and when no utility poles are present, the alley boundaries will be considered to be five feet on each side of the edges of the alley's surface.

Block face: The area bounded by the property line and the street center line and the cross streets at each end of the block. Alleys shall be deemed to be on the block face if they may be entered from the block face or if they run parallel to the block face within the square block formed by the block face and three other streets.

Bulk items: Large discarded objects such as stoves, refrigerators, sofas, other furniture, crates, tires, piles of lumber, or other items that do not bend easily or are other-wise too large to fit into a standard-size garbage can. Brush, rock, gravel, and abandoned automobiles are not considered bulk items.

Dirt and gravel: Loose rock, sand dirt, heavy dust, or other such materials on a paved street that can be aesthetically displeasing and possibly unsafe.

Litter: An untidy array of small discarded objects such as scattered newspapers, wrappers or other scraps of paper, beverage or food containers, and the like. Materials in containers or in neat piles, apparently placed for refuse collection, are not considered litter. Grass clippings, limbs, leaves in bags, brush, or parts of trees piled for collection are not considered litter. Any piles of wood or lumber, other than those mentioned above, will be counted as litter.

Pothole: A roughly circular depression in a street where surface pavement has been worn or washed away to create a hole with steep sides all around.

Rideability: The smoothness (or conversely, the roughness) of the main surfaced portion of a street (not including the shoulder).

Road defects: An irregularity in street surface other than a pothole (including utility cuts, cracks, and manhole covers or other built-in equipment not flush with the street surface).

Note: This appendix is an adaptation of the manual prepared by Martha Groomes, Richard Caster, David Cushman, and John Logan of the finance office, Nashville-Davidson County Metropolitan Government, 1974. These guidelines cover both street cleanliness and various street transportation-related conditions. Although they are old, these guidelines remain appropriate.

Sidewalk: A hard-surface walkway between the curbstone edge or the lateral lines of a roadway and the adjacent property lines. Curbstones are not included in the sidewalk area.

Signs: Markers designed to provide information and maintained by the city. Ratings are suggested for three categories of signs:

1. Stop signs;
2. Other traffic control signs, including curve, intersection, and yield warnings; and signs indicating speed limits, pedestrian crossings, school zones, and school bus stops; and
3. Street name signs.

Note that parking signs and signs giving directions to specific places were not included in the procedure.

Street: There are two types of streets, those with curbstones and those without. Streets are delineated as follows: for streets with curbstones, from the center of the road to the curbstone, inclusive; for streets without curbstones, the area within the public right-of-way, which includes shoulders and ditches and is generally marked by utility poles. All fences and buildings are assumed to be on private property.

Vegetation (street): A growth of weeds or underbrush along a street. Only areas with a thick growth higher than two feet are reported as "weeds" by the trained observer.

Vegetation (yard): A growth of weeds or underbrush in the yard of a home or other building along a block face. Only areas with a thick growth more than two feet high are reported as "weeds—private property."

Street Litter Grades

Ratings for street litter are based on a scale of 1 (very clean) to 4 (very dirty) with the ratings defined by a set of photographs and further described in writing. Inspections are made by an observer in an automobile. For streets with curbstones, street litter will be rated from the center of the street to the edge of the curbstones but not beyond it (that is, sidewalk litter is not counted). For streets with no curbstones, litter will be rated from the center of the street to the edge of the public right-of-way, usually indicated by utility poles; in all cases, fences and buildings will be considered to stand on private property.

Condition	Description (to supplement photographs)
1	Street completely clean or almost completely clean (two pieces of litter are permitted).
2	Street largely clean; a few pieces of litter observable, but only in the form of isolated discarded items. On a generally clean block face (number 1), a single accumulation of uncontained trash

with a volume less than or equal to the volume of a large grocery bag that has not been set out for collection shall be rated as 2.

3	Lightly scattered litter along all or most of the street, or one heavy pile of litter, but no accumulations of litter large enough to indicate dumping. On a generally clean block face (number 1), a single accumulation of litter that is larger than a number 2 accumulation but smaller than a 30-gallon garbage can (and not set out for collection) shall be rated a number 3.
4	Heavily littered street; litter accumulation in piles; or heavy litter distributed down all or nearly all the block face. On a generally clean block face (number 1 or 2), a single accumulation of litter with a volume greater than that of a 30- gallon garbage can (and not set out for collection) shall be rated a 4.
Note:	Live vegetation and dirt are counted separately. Cut brush not piled for pickup and strewn so as to make the street unsightly is counted as street litter. Grass clippings are not considered litter and are not counted in any rating. Bulk items are not considered as litter in these ratings, but the number of bulk items that exist in the street is to be noted in the appropriate column.

Alley Litter Grades

Ratings for alley litter are based on a scale of 1 (very clean) to 4 (very dirty) with the points defined by a set of photographs and further described in writing. Inspection is made by an observer from an automobile. The alley parallel to the block face should be rated if possible. If no alley runs parallel to the block face, the alley intersecting the block face is to be rated. If bulk items are present in the alley, the number of such items shall be included in the proper column and will not be counted as litter.

Condition	Description (to supplement photographs)
1	Alley is completely clean or almost completely clean (two pieces of litter are acceptable).
2	Alley largely clean, a few pieces of litter observable, but only in the form of isolated discarded items. On a generally clean alley (number 1), a single accumulation of uncontained trash with a volume less than or equal to the volume of a large grocery bag that has not been set out for collection shall be rated as 2.
3	Lightly scattered litter along all or most of the al-

ley; or one heavy pile; but no large accumulations of litter such as might indicate dumping. On a generally clean alley (number 1), a single accumulation of litter that is larger than a number 2 accumulation but smaller than a 30-gallon garbage can (and not set out for collection) shall be rated a number 3.

4   Heavily littered alley; litter accumulation in piles; or heavy litter distributed down all or nearly all the alley. On a generally clean alley (number 1 or 2), a single accumulation of uncontained litter with a volume greater than that of a 30-gallon garbage can not set out for collection shall be rated a 4.

Note: Bulk items are not considered litter in these ratings, but the number of bulk items that exist in the alley is to be noted in the appropriate column.

Yard Litter Grades

Ratings for yard litter are based on a scale of 1 (very clean) to 4 (very dirty) with the points defined by a set of photographs and further described in writing. Inspections are made by an observer from an automobile. Yard litter is rated only for front yards, which are bounded by the edge of the street and the front of the house or other buildings on that yard.

Condition   *Description (to supplement photographs)*

1   Yards completely clean or almost completely clean (two pieces of litter in a yard on the block face are acceptable).

2   Yards generally clean, but some isolated pieces of litter visible in less than one-half of the yards on the block face. On a generally clean block face (number 1), a single uncontained accumulation of litter with a volume less than or equal to the volume of a large grocery bag shall be rated as 2.

3   Yards in the area are generally littered. (Some litter in one-half or more of the yards on the block face.) On a generally clean block face (number 1 or 2), a single uncontained accumulation of litter larger than a number 2 accumulation but smaller than or equal to the volume of a 30-gallon garbage can shall be rated a 3.

4   Yards in the area are heavily littered; litter in almost every yard on the block face. On a generally clean block face (number 1), a single uncontained accumulation of litter with a volume

greater than that of a 30-gallon garbage can shall be rated a 4.

Note: Bulk items are not considered as litter in these ratings, but the number of bulk items present in the yards on the block face is to be noted in the appropriate column.

Street Rideability Grades

Ratings of streets for smoothness of ride are made by visual inspection from an automobile.

Condition   *Description*

1   Probably smooth rideability (that is, appears to be smooth).
   a. No noticeable defects.
   b. One or two minor defects (small bump, crack, or hole).
   c. Many small cracks apparent but no noticeable effect on rideability.

2   Slightly bumpy rideability (bumps appear in photos).
   a. Several minor defects or minor potholes, but none appears severe.
   b. A large single bump or many minor bumps.

3   Considerably bumpy rideability. Much of the street is broken up, but no single hazard is apparent.

4   Potential safety hazard (or severe jolt) present (one or more large potholes or other major defects).

Note: A large pothole is defined here as a hole 3½ inches deep and at least 12 inches across. A major defect is defined as an abrupt change of street surface level greater than 3½ inches. A minor defect is defined as less than 3½ inches deep or less than about 12 inches in diameter.

Sidewalk Condition Grades

The "walkability" of sidewalks—the degree of walking comfort and safety for pedestrians—is rated visually from an automobile. Ratings shall indicate the worst portion of the sidewalk and shall not include nonstructural defects, such as heavy litter or limbs on the sidewalk. Grates, water meters, driveway indentations, and other intentional sidewalk interruptions will not cause downgrading if level with sidewalk and in good condition. Pebble and brick surfaces are also acceptable if in good condition.

Condition	Description
1	No visual signs of walking discomfort. Some hairline cracks may be present, but surface still presents a smooth appearance with no perturbations likely to cause pedestrians to stumble.

2   Some visual signs of minor walking discomfort but not hazardous.
   a. Sidewalk is basically good but has a severe side-to-side slope or other minor deterioration that could cause walking discomfort.
   b. Sidewalk has some breaks or unevenness less than 1½ inches high or deep, or holes deeper but too narrow to catch even a child's foot.

3   One or more potential hazards or many signs of severe walking discomfort. A hazard is an abrupt rise or depression measuring more than 1½ inches above or below the sidewalk surface.

Stop-Sign Condition Grades

Visual ratings of readability and appearance of stop signs are made from an automobile. These are very strict conditions for a stop sign, which is designed by shape, color, lettering, and reflectivity to be recognizable even when badly tilted, partially defaced, or obscured. But it simplifies the rating system if the same degrees of tilt are used for all signs.

Condition	Description

1   Conveniently visible.
   a. Sign head and support in good condition (tilted, twisted, or bent less than 5°); and
   b. Sign not defaced in any manner; and
   c. Sign continuously unobscured for the last 200 feet.

2   Visible but somewhat inconvenient to see.
   a. Sign head or support slightly tilted; sign twisted, bent (between 5° and 30°) but readable; or
   b. Sign partially obscured or intermittently obscured within the last 200 feet of approach; or
   c. Sign defaced but still readable.

3   Missing, ambiguous, difficult to see, or not visible.
   a. Sign broken off pole or otherwise missing, or major part defaced and difficult to read;

   b. Sign tilted, twisted, or bent more than 30°; or
   c. Sign totally obscured by a tree, bush, brush, pole, another sign, or other object so that it cannot be seen from the observer's position for the last 200 feet of approach.

Note: Intermittent observation of a stop sign can be ignored in the rating if there is a "stop ahead" sign present and in good condition. That is, the stop sign could be rated a 1 even though intermittently obscured under such circumstances.

Street-Name Sign Grades (Applicable to All Regulatory Signs except Stop Signs)

A visual rating of readability and appearance of all regulatory signs other than stop signs can be made from an automobile.

Condition	Description

1   Conveniently visible.
   a. Sign head and support in good condition (tilted, twisted, or bent less than 5°); and
   b. Sign not defaced in any manner; and
   c. Sign continuously unobscured for the last 50 feet.

2   Visible but somewhat inconvenient to read or find, or unpleasant to see.
   a. Sign head or support slightly tilted, twisted, or bent (between 5° and 30°), but visible even though inconvenient or unpleasant to see; or
   b. Sign partially obscured, or intermittently obscured within the last 50 feet; or
   c. Sign defaced but still readable.

3   Missing, ambiguous, difficult to see or read.
   a. No sign on any corner of the intersection; or
   b. Sign broken off pole; or
   c. Sign tilted, twisted, or bent more than 30°; or
   d. Sign ambiguous, misleading, or incorrect (sign twisted 45° to 90°, or with wrong street name—a sign twisted 90° may appear normal at first glance); or
   e. Sign totally obscured by a tree, bush, brush, pole, another sign, or other objects so that it cannot be read from the car continuously within the last 50 feet of approach; or
   f. Printing on sign not legible.

Instructions for Coding Driver's Form (See Exhibit 10A-1)

Column	Instructions
Date	Month and day of the inspection. Use four digits; for example, June 6 is written as 0606.
Inspector	Code for inspector. Use single digit to identify each inspector.
Hour of day	Use the whole hour or a code for the hour.
Unique identifier	The identifier can consist of the last two digits of the census tract and the three-digit number for the block face being inspected.
Census tract	Modified census tract number.
Street name and address	Address range and street name for block face being inspected. This should be preselected and entered before starting inspections.

Type	Street type: 1 - Freeway 2 - Expressway 3 - Proposed scenic road 4 - Major street or road 5 - Secondary street or road 6 - Minor street or road
Rideability	Rating for street rideability. This rating must consist of one digit followed by a decimal and another digit.
Stop sign	Rating for stop signs. This rating must consist of one digit followed by a decimal and another digit.
Other traffic signs	Rating for other traffic control signs. This rating must consist of one digit followed by a decimal and another digit.
Street name sign	Rating for street name signs. This rating must consist of one digit followed by a decimal and another digit.

Exhibit 10A-1   Driver's Inspection Form

Date	Inspector	Hour of day	Unique identifier	Census tract	Street name and range of address	Type	Rideability	Signs			Visibility blocked	Alley litter	Card no.	Comments
								Stop	Other traffic	Street-name				

Visibility blocked   Enter code 9 if visibility is blocked at the end of the block face; otherwise, leave blank.

Alley litter   Rating for litter observed in alley. If no alley, leave blank.

Card number   Enter card number 1.

Instructions for Coding Rider's Inspection Form (See Exhibit 10A-2)

Column   *Instructions*

Date   Month and day of the inspection. Use four digits; for example, June 6 is written as 0606.

Inspector   Code for inspector. Use single digit to identify each inspector.

Hour of day   Use the whole hour or a code for the hour.

Unique identifier   The identifier can consist of the last two digits of the census tract and the three-digit number for the block face being inspected.

Census tract   Modified census tract number.

Street name and address   Enter the address range and street name for block face being inspected.

Road litter   Rating for road litter. This rating must consist of one digit followed by a decimal and another digit.

Bulk   Code for bulk items present.
1 - One bulk item
2 - Two bulk items
3 - Three bulk items
9 - More than three bulk items

Weeds   Enter code 9 if there is heavy vegetation on street or roadway; otherwise, leave blank.

Dirt   Enter code 9 if there is heavy dirt or gravel on street or roadway; otherwise, leave blank.

Abandoned auto   Enter code if there is an abandoned automobile on street or roadway; otherwise, leave blank.

Exhibit 10A-2   Rider's Inspection Form

Date	Inspector	Hour of day	Unique identi-fier	Census tract	Street name and address	Road litter	Bulk	Weeds	Dirt	Abandoned auto	Blocked lane	Yard litter	Bulk	Weeds	Abandoned auto	Side-walks	Type	Alley litter	Card no.	Comments

1 - One abandoned auto
2 - Two abandoned autos
3 - Three abandoned autos
9 - More than three abandoned autos

Blocked lane   Enter code 9 if the lane of traffic is blocked; otherwise, leave blank.

Yard litter   Rating for yard litter. This rating must consist of one digit followed by a decimal and another digit.

Bulk   Enter code if a bulk item is present in any yard; otherwise, leave blank.
1 - One bulk item
2 - Two bulk items
3 - Three bulk items
9 - More than three bulk items

Weeds   Enter code 9 if heavy vegetation is observed in the yards on the block face; otherwise, leave blank.

Abandoned auto   Enter code 9 if there is an abandoned automobile in the yards on the block face; otherwise, leave blank.

Sidewalks   Rating for sidewalk walkability. This rating must consist of one digit followed by a decimal and another digit. If no sidewalk, leave blank.

Type   Enter code for type of sidewalk surface. If no sidewalk, leave blank.
1 - Concrete
2 - Pebble
3 - Asphalt
4 - Brick
5 - Mixed
9 - Other

Alley litter   Enter rating for alley litter. The rating must consist of one digit followed by a decimal and another digit. If no alley, leave blank.

Card no.   Enter card number 2.

This appendix identifies a number of elements a government should consider in its contractual arrangements for a survey.

Finding firms to bid may be a problem in some localities. Check with other local governments, city and county planning agencies, local universities, and professional associations in the survey field, especially those with codes of ethics and professional-level meetings and publications. Sources include the American Association of Public Opinion Research, the American Marketing Association, and the Market Research Association. Some of these issue geographically classified directories. Check the local classified telephone directory, both for regional offices of nationally recognized firms and for local firms. A survey professional, perhaps from a nearby university, might help in this screening process.

Each of the following elements should be considered for inclusion in a request for proposal so that contractors can bid on an appropriate and reasonably common basis. These same elements also should be considered for inclusion in the final contractual agreement.

Even if the local government decides to administer the customer survey itself, it will need to consider explicitly most of these elements before undertaking the survey. The local government should, however, employ a professional expert to help, at least with its first customer survey.

Elements of guidelines, as discussed below, include:

1. The minimum number of interviews to be completed
2. The sampling method
3. The role of the contractor in the development of the questionnaire
4. Specification of how the questionnaire will be administered
5. Pretesting of the questionnaire
6. Verification of a certain percentage of the interviews
7. Confidentiality of responses
8. Special coding to be done by the contractor
9. Comparison of sample versus total population characteristics
10. Products to be provided to the government
11. The time schedule for the work
12. The survey firm's credentials
13. Cost quotations

Chapter 13 (Surveying Customers) provides additional discussion of some of these issues.

1. *Minimum number of interviews to be completed.* The number is determined by considerations such as cost, the degree of precision sought, and the number of different clientele groupings within the jurisdiction for which the government seeks data (area of residence, age group, sex, race, income group, and so forth). Arguably, a minimum of about 100 interviews should be sought for each clientele group. Thus, if a city wants information on each of six neighborhood groups, it should seek about 600 interviews.

   The degree of precision needed is a complex question, the resolution of which is beyond the scope of this report. Nevertheless, important judgments on precision are implied in the selection of sample size. The precision obtainable from population subgroup samples of 100 or even fewer can, for most uses of these data, probably provide information that is sufficiently precise—at least as accurate as much other information currently available to local officials.

   Where funds permit, larger samples are desirable. (Note that the Gallup and Harris polls use samples of approximately 1,600 adults, often categorized by age group, sex, race, education levels, or whatever, to represent the complete adult population of the United States.)

2. *Sampling method.* The principal concern is to obtain interviews that are at least roughly representative of the population. The contractor should fully specify the sampling method to be used; indeed, any professional firm should be willing to describe fully the methods it uses for its sampling process. Some issues require governmental consideration:

a. An important question is what will be done about those households targeted for interviews whose members are not at home. For at-home and telephone interviews, the minimum number of call-backs and the time allotted for them should be specified. More call-backs entail higher cost but yield greater confidence in the way the sample was drawn. A large number of call-backs—even up to six or more—is more practical for telephone interviewing than for at-home interviewing.

b. The bidding firm should also make explicit the approximate distribution of interviews by day of the week and hour of the day. This is particularly important when, as will usually be the case, the person answering is the person to be interviewed. The only methods exempt from this problem are relatively expensive ones that use specific, preselected individuals (or preselected age or sex) and that require considerable effort to find these individuals at home.

    Moreover, instead of concentrating the interviewing on weekdays and normal working hours, interviewers should schedule some calling for weekends and early evenings. This practice should produce a more representative sample because it avoids interviewing an excessive proportion of persons who are normally at home during the day.

c. Both parties to the survey—the consultant firm and its client government—should decide the kind of listing from which the sample will be randomly drawn. The survey firm probably should draw the sample, but the government should approve the list from which it will be drawn. The government will want to assure that the listing is reasonably current and covers the majority of the population.

    Special problems may arise, for example, in covering mobile homes or new housing developments not included in the available listings. Another problem might arise from using listings such as tax assessors' block books, which include only specific street addresses; some procedure must then be used that allows for adequate representation of multiple dwelling units, such as apartment houses, at any one address.

d. Another decision is who should be interviewed once a dwelling unit has been selected for the sample. In general, because of cost constraints, only one adult will be interviewed per household. (This will somewhat undercount adults from households with more than one adult, but this problem can be partly compensated for if responses are weighted according to the number of adults in each household.)

    Also, the age group to be included in the interviews should be decided. For the information sought in several of the questionnaires illustrated in these reports, it is probably most appropriate to interview only persons 18 years old or older, but for some services, such as recreation and libraries, it would be desirable to obtain information from juveniles as well. Juveniles could be included in surveys of users of specific government facilities but probably should be excluded from household surveys.

    A related decision is which adult should be interviewed at a household. For some questions in the survey, an adult who takes care of the home may be the most informed person, while for others, the "working" head of the household may be best. Adequate representation of various age groups and both sexes is desirable to obtain a cross section of adult viewpoints.

3. *Role of the contractor in the development of the questionnaire.* The local government rather than the contractor should undertake the major effort in developing the questionnaire, perhaps using as a starting point questionnaires such as those included in this report. Nevertheless, the contractor, after pretesting results, should work out the final wording of the questions. Also, the survey firm will normally want to put the questionnaire into its own format to provide for its style of editing, coding, and keypunching. The contractor and government should agree on the final wording of questions.

    In essence, the government is responsible for content and the contractor for technique. However, *to maintain comparability across repeat surveys, the local government should require that new contractors use questionnaires used for previous administrations with only minor alterations* (unless, of course, a major problem with the past questionnaires arises).

4. *Specification of how the questionnaire will be administered.* Either an at-home visit or a telephone call, or a combination, is appropriate for a lengthy interview (up to 30 minutes in length). Longer questionnaires may be feasible in these cases. Mail surveys are not likely to be appropriate for such lengths. Jurisdictions having a significant proportion of families without telephones will likely need to supplement mail surveys with at-home interviews.

    In a telephone survey, care should be taken to cover families with unlisted telephone numbers; a random-digit dialing approach can be employed to select respondents from the complete population of households with telephones.

    Jurisdictions with large proportions of ethnic and language groups may also need to ensure that interviewers will be able to communicate with such groups. This will require translation of the questionnaire and, for telephone and in-person interviews, interviewers that are bilingual.

5. *Pretesting of the questionnaire.* A pretest of the questionnaire is essential to check on the adequacy of the

wording, and a minimum amount of pretesting should be specified. Ten interviews are probably sufficient, if no significant problems show up.

Even if the questionnaire is taken intact from other jurisdictions, pretesting should still be undertaken in the jurisdiction in which the questionnaire is to be used to detect any local language problems or situational differences. Any questions modified for use, or new ones added, should be tested before use.

6. *Verification of a certain percentage of the interviews.* The survey organization should provide for verification of at least a small proportion of the interviews. Verification is a process in which someone other than the original interviewer, perhaps the field supervisor, calls back a household to check responses to a few carefully chosen questions. This process should give assurance that the interviews have been accomplished correctly. Verification rates of perhaps ten percent for each interviewer are probably adequate. An early review of completed interviews will help spot any particularly careless or inaccurate interviewers.

7. *Confidentiality of responses.* Adequate provision must be made to ensure the anonymity of individual respondents. Interviewers should be required to assure interviewees of the confidentiality of their responses at the beginning of each interview. All reputable survey firms—or the government, if it undertakes the interviewing itself—will protect the names and identifying characteristics of all respondents.

The government will probably want a copy of the tape containing the basic information received from the individual questionnaire. The nature of the survey, however, does not require the government to have information that would permit identifying specific individuals interviewed.[1] No names should be included on the tape, and location of residence should identify the individual only down to a geographic area of the city or neighborhood service area, perhaps a census tract. For household surveys, names and addresses should probably be destroyed after verification has been completed.

The effort to protect the confidentiality of the respondents should not be confused with the question of the releasability of the survey data. Because one purpose of the survey is to increase accountability, grouped survey data, regardless of the findings, should be made public. An exception should be made only if some circumstance arises that clearly invalidates the survey.

8. *Special coding to be done by the contractor.* The responses to some questions may require special coding after the interview has been completed. Generally, the government will have established code categories before the interviewing. (This will be particularly true for repeat surveys.) In some instances, however, this coding may be deferred, or some interpretation may be required that

the interviewer cannot do "on the spot."

For example, it may be necessary to translate resident addresses into a special area-of-residence code. The survey organizations should be clearly notified in advance of such special coding requirements. For the purposes of the surveys discussed here, coding of open-ended questions should be kept to a minimum; coding can require significant added effort and cost.

9. *Comparison of sample versus total population characteristics.* Proper sampling is intended to provide survey responses that are representative of the whole population. One approach to determining whether those responding are reasonably representative is comparison of the available demographic characteristics of respondents against known values for these characteristics for the whole population from which the sample is drawn.

For all modes of interviewing, at the end of the survey, characteristics obtained for the sample from the questionnaires, such as age group, sex, race, and income class, should be compared against the latest available figures for the whole population from which the sample was drawn (generally, all persons 18 or older). The results of this comparison should appear in the final report to the government to provide information on the degree of representativeness of the sample.

Note that the usefulness of census data for comparisons declines with age. In fact, late in the period between censuses, the sample drawn may be more up-to-date than the census data, especially in areas of rapid growth.

10. *Products to be provided to the government.* Survey firms will normally be asked to provide some or all of the following:

a. A tape containing the individual responses to the questionnaire information. Even though the government may have the survey firm make the main tabulations, government analysts may later want to undertake special cross-tabulations or further examination of the data. In addition, the questionnaires themselves should be accessible to the government (although not with names and addresses of respondents attached to individual responses) so that responses, such as those to open-ended questions, are available.

b. A report describing in detail the methodology used, a guide to the use of data on the tape, any comparisons made of the sample with total population characteristics, and information on the precision of the findings, including the response rates obtained (such as refusals).

c. A copy (or its equivalent) of the questionnaire, showing overall jurisdiction percentages and sample sizes.

d. Specified tabulations of survey results. Although a government with its own computer capability may prefer to undertake these tabulations itself, most governments are likely to find it convenient to have the contractor do at least some tabulations. The government can request either (1) a complete set of cross-tabulations of each demographic characteristic against each of the other questions or (2) a selected set of tabulations.

Findings should be expressed as percentages of particular client groups that gave each response to each question. To facilitate judging the precision of the findings, the sample size for each client group should also be displayed.

Exhibit 16-4 in Chapter 16 presents a recommended summary format for each question. As the exhibit illustrates, a *multi-crosstab* format is highly recommended. Responses to a question are shown on pages that each contain several cross-tabulated respondent characteristics. This kind of display makes analysis much easier and considerably reduces the number of pages users have to read.

e. (Optional) A detailed analysis identifying the highlights of the findings prior to government review. Many governments may choose to perform this step themselves. When the survey results are publicly released, all basic tabulations—not only the highlights—should be made available to the interested public, perhaps through displays in public libraries.

11. *Time schedule for the work.* Completion dates should be specified but may be related to the time the government itself takes to give final approval of the questionnaire wording after the pretest. Illustrative time requirements for surveys are: two weeks for pretest and modifications, three weeks for conducting up to perhaps 600 interviews, and three weeks for providing the final tabulations—a total of approximately two months. This schedule assumes that both the proposed questionnaire and selected population sample will need little revision and that detailed analysis of findings is not included. If the contractor is undertaking repeat surveys with few, if any, changes, results can be expected within about one month from the start of interviewing.

12. *Survey firm's credentials.* Background information on the firm should be examined before the contract is awarded. If a bidder has not previously worked for the local government, previous clients of the bidder should be consulted regarding the firm's performance, including the specific nature of the survey work performed; the timeliness, thoroughness, and quality of the product; and the apparent success with interviewees. Qualifications of the specific members of the firm who will be involved with the survey, especially the field coordinator, should be ex-

amined carefully. Firms with experience will usually have a stable group of regular interviewers.

13. *Cost quotations.* Costs will depend on the decisions made on the questions discussed above. The contractor's degree of responsibility should be established with regard to drawing the sample, wording the questionnaire, coding open-ended questions, keypunching, tabulating, and analyzing results. The local government might request cost estimates based on a small number of alternative arrangements, such as various numbers of interviews, different sampling methods, or different outputs.

For the type and length of survey described in this report, costs can probably be kept within the range of $15 to $20 (in 1991 prices) per interview for telephone interviewing. Probably, the costs will fall at the lower end of this range for repeat surveys. At-home interviewing is likely to add at least an additional $10 per interview. Mail surveys should be considerably cheaper, probably closer to $5 per returned questionnaire.

These costs include pretesting, final questionnaire preparation and printing, interviewing, editing, coding, cardpunching, and tabulations. These estimates assume that no extensive effort is required to develop the questionnaire or to develop the list of households from which the sample is to be drawn.[2]

Exhibit 11A-1 contains a short checklist of key elements that should be included in a contract for a customer survey.

Exhibit 11A-1   Elements That Should Be Included in a Contract for a Customer Survey

The following elements should be specified in contracts for surveys:

- The size of samples
- Survey administration details, such as whether the mails, telephone, or both are to be used; the number of mailings or number of follow-up telephone calls; and the time between mailings and telephone follow-ups
- The role of the contractor in development of the questionnaire
- The role of the contractor in pretesting the questionnaire (the agency may want to do some of its own pretesting, but the contractor should also do some)
- Maintenance of confidentiality of responses
- Special coding to be done by the contractor (e.g., transforming geographical data into a smaller number of areas)
- Specification as to how tabulations are to be handled, such as whether "no answer" and "don't know" responses should be included in the denominators for the percentages that are calculated
- Products to be provided to the government and in what formats. Products should include, at a minimum: multiple cross-tabulation tables for each question, frequency counts for each question, and a fully legible printout of the input data for each returned questionnaire
- The time schedule for the work
- Cost

1 Freedom-of-information laws, including "sunshine" laws, do not make identities of survey respondents public information.

2 For further discussion of survey costs, see Chapter 13 of this report, and Weiss and Hatry, *An Introduction to Sample Surveys*.

Solid Waste Collection (Chapter 2)

Blair, Louis H., and Alfred I. Schwartz. *How Clean Is Our City?* Washington, D.C.: The Urban Institute, 1972.

Fleming, Rodney R., ed., *Street Cleaning Practice.* Chicago: American Public Works Association, 1978, pp. 110-121.

Fukuhara, Rackham S., "Improving Effectiveness: Responsive Public Services," in Richard D. Bingham and Claire L. Felbinger, *Evaluation in Practice: A Methodological Approach.* New York: Longman, 1989, pp. 302-327.

Fund for the City of New York, "Project Scorecard: Purpose, Function, Method, and Structure." 1975.

ICMA, "Landfill Management," Management Information Service Report. Washington, D.C.: October, 1990.

The Mayor's Management Report. New York: Citybooks, September 17, 1990.

Ruben, Marc A., *Service Efforts and Accomplishments Reporting: Solid Waste Collection and Disposal Service.* Stamford, Connecticut: Government Accounting Standards Board, 1991.

Savannah, Georgia, Community Housing and Economic Development Department, "Responsive Public Services Program: 1988." October 1988.

Sullivan, Richard H., "Measurement of Relative Amounts of Litter," *Journal of Resource Management and Technology,* Vol. 14, No. 1, October 1985, pp. 91-93.

Solid Waste Disposal (Chapter 3)

Blair, Louis H., and Alfred I. Schwartz, *How Clean Is Our City?* Washington, D.C.: The Urban Institute, 1972.

Commonwealth of Virginia, Department of Waste Management, Solid Waste Management Regulations, VR 672-20-10. December, 1988.

Cristofano, Sam M., and William S. Foster, eds., *Management of Local Public Works.* Washington, D.C.: ICMA, 1986.

State of Maryland, Department of the Environment, Solid Waste Management, Regulation of Water Supply, Sewage Disposal, and Solid Waste, Title 26, Subtitle 04, Chapter 7, Annotated Code of Maryland. (1988).

U.S. Environmental Protection Agency, Office of Waste Programs Enforcement, *RCRA Inspection Manual.* March 1988.

———, Solid Waste Disposal Facility Criteria, *Federal Register* (1988) (to be codified in 40 CFR 257, 258).

———, Emission Guidelines and Standards of Performance for New Stationary Sources: Municipal Waste Combustors, *Federal Register,* 54, 243 (1989).

———, *The Solid Waste Dilemma: An Agenda for Action.* February 1989.

———, *Decision-Makers' Guide to Solid Waste Management.* November 1989.

Park and Recreation Services (Chapter 4)

Alexandria, Virginia, "What Is the Condition of Our Capital Plant?" TriData Corporation and the Alexandria Office of Management and Budget, October 1982.

Bannon, Joseph J., *Current Issues in Leisure Services.* Washington, D.C.: ICMA, 1987.

Butler, George, "Summer Playground Attendance Formula," *Recreation,* April 1961.

Chatfield, Don, Charles B. Deans, Jr., and Diana Barnes Freshwater, "Computerizing Parks and Recreation," *Parks and Recreation,* June 1990, pp. 54-59.

Dean, Denis J., *Public Assessment Survey System, Technical Assistance Manual,* Department of Conservation and Recreation, Commonwealth of Virginia, 1989.

———, *Public Assessment Survey System, User's Guide to the PASS Computer Program.* Department of Conservation and Recreation, Commonwealth of Virginia, 1989.

Dean, Denis J., Douglas Wellman, and Bob Charles, "PASSing the Computer Test," *Parks and Recreation,* June 1990, pp. 46-53.

Fund for the City of New York, "Development of Scorecard Monitoring System for the Department of Parks and Recreation." February 1978.

Hatry, Harry P., and Diana R. Dunn, *Measuring the Effectiveness of Local Government Services: Recreation.* Washington, D.C.: The Urban Institute, 1971.

Hendon, William S., *Evaluating Urban Parks and Recreation*. New York: Praeger, 1981.

Jendrek, Margaret P., "Outdoor Recreation Needs Assessments: The Importance of Drawing Two Samples from the Community," *Journal of Leisure Research*, 1988, Vol. 20, pp. 154-161.

Kozlowski, James C., "Are You Familiar with the Public Playground Safety Guidelines?" *Parks and Recreation*, September 1987, pp. 16-22.

Nashville-Davidson County Metropolitan Government, Board of Parks and Recreation, "Summary Report of Citizen Surveys of Metro Park and Recreation Opportunities in Nashville-Davidson County." May 1974.

The Urban Institute, "Guidelines for Trained Observer Ratings of Parks and Beaches." Washington, D.C.: October 1983.

U.S. Consumer Product Safety Commission, *A Handbook for Public Playground Safety*, Vol. I, *General Guidelines for New and Existing Playgrounds*, and Vol. II, *Technical Guidelines for Equipment and Surfacing*. Washington, D.C.: 1981(?).

U.S. Department of the Interior, Bureau of Outdoor Recreation, *How Effective Are Your Community Recreation Services?* Washington, D.C.: U.S. Government Printing Office, April 1973.

———, *How to Conduct a Recreation Effectiveness Telephone Survey*. Washington, D.C.: U.S. Government Printing Office, 1974.

Wallach, Frances, "Playground Safety Update," *Parks and Recreation*, August 1990, pp. 46-50.

Westover, Theresa N., "Urban Parks as Social Settings: Visitors' Perceptions of Anti-Social Behavior and Crowding," *Trends*, Vol. 25, No. 3, 1988.

Library Services (Chapter 5)

Childers, Thomas, and Nancy A. Van House, "Dimensions of Public Library Effectiveness," *Library and Information Science Research* (11), 1989, pp. 273-301.

D'Elia, George, "Materials Availability Fill Rates: Additional Data Addressing the Question of the Usefulness of the Measures," *Public Libraries*, Vol. 27, No. 1, Spring 1988, pp. 15-23.

DeProspo, Ernest R., et al., *Performance Measures for Public Libraries*. Chicago: American Library Association, 1973.

———, *A Data Gathering and Instructional Manual for Performance Measures in Public Libraries*. Chicago: Oberon Press, 1976.

Hernon, Peter, *Statistics for Library Decision Making: A Handbook*. Norwood, New Jersey: Ablex Publishing Corporation, 1989.

Lancaster, F.W., *The Measurement and Evaluation of Library Services*. Washington, D.C.: Information Resources Press, 1977.

———, *If You Want to Evaluate Your Library....* Chicago: University of Illinois Graduate School of Library and Information Science, 1988.

McClure, Charles, et al., *Planning and Role Setting for Public Libraries*. Chicago: American Library Association, 1987.

McDonald, Lynn, and Holly Willett, "Interviewing Young Children," in Jane Robbins et al., *Evaluation Strategies and Techniques for Public Library Children's Services: A Sourcebook*. Madison: University of Wisconsin School of Library and Information Studies, 1990, pp. 115-130.

Newhouse, Joseph P., and Arthur J. Alexander, *An Economic Analysis of Public Library Services*. Santa Monica, California: RAND Corporation, 1972.

Van House, Nancy A., "Public Library Effectiveness: Theory, Measures and Determinants," *Library and Information Science Research*, October 1986, pp. 261-283.

———, "In Defense of Fill Rates," *Public Libraries*, Vol. 27, No. 1, Spring 1988, pp. 25-27.

Van House, Nancy A., et al., *Output Measures for Public Libraries*, 2nd edition. Chicago: American Library Association, 1987.

Zweizig, Douglas, and Brenda Dervin, "Public Library Use, Users, Uses: Advances in Knowledge of the Characteristics and Needs of the Adult Clientele of American Public Libraries," *Advances in Librarianship*, #7. New York: Academic Press, 1977, pp. 231-255.

Crime Control (Chapter 6)

Barnett, C.C., and R.A. Bowers, "Community Policing—The New Model for the Way Police Do Their Job," *Public Management*, July 1990.

Bertram, Deborah K., and Alexander Vargo, "Response Time Analysis Study: Preliminary Findings on Robbery in Kansas City," *The Police Chief*, May 1976.

Brown, Lee P., "Community Policing: A Practical Guide for Police Officials," in *Perspectives on Policing*, No. 12. Washington, D.C.: U.S. Department of Justice, Office of Justice Programs, National Institute of Justice, September 1989.

Drebin, Allan, and Marguerite Brannon, "Measuring Service Efforts and Accomplishments of Police Departments." Northwestern University, J.L. Kellogg Graduate School of Management, prepared for the Governmental Accounting Standards Board, Washington, D.C., 1989.

Forst, Brian, et al., "Arrest Convictability as a Measure of Police Performance." Washington, D.C.: U.S. Department of Justice, National Institute of Justice, July 1982.

ICMA, "Community-Oriented Policing," Management Information Service Report. Washington, D.C.: September 1989.

Kelling, George L., "What Works—Research and the Police," National Institute of Justice Crime File Study Guide, NCJ-104564. Washington, D.C.: U.S. Department of Justice, 1988.

Mastrofski, Stephen D., and Robert C. Wadman, "Personnel and Agency Performance Measurement," in *Local Government Police Management*, edited by William A. Geller. Washington, D.C.: ICMA, 1990.

"Police Department Survey," citizen survey prepared by the Port St. Lucie, Florida, Police Department, 1990. Available from Florida Innovation Group, Tampa, Florida.

Schnelle, John F., et al., "Evaluation of the Quality of Police Arrests by District Attorney Ratings," *The Police Chief*, January 1977.

Tuchfarber, Alfred J., and William R. Klecka, *Random Digit Dialing: Lowering the Cost of Victimization Surveys*. Washington, D.C.: Police Foundation, December 1976.

U.S. Department of Justice, *San Jose Methods Test of Known Crime Victims*. National Institute of Law Enforcement, Criminal Justice Division, June 1972.

———, *The National Crime Survey—Working Papers*, Volume I, NCJ-75374, December 1981; Volume II, NCJ-90307, October 1984.

———, "The Nation's Two Crime Measures," undated brochure. 1983.

———, *Uniform Crime Reporting Handbook*. Washington, D.C.: 1984.

———, *Report to the Nation on Crime and Justice*, 2nd edition, NCJ-105506, March 1988.

———, *Crime in the United States: Uniform Reports 1989*. Federal Bureau of Investigation, August 1990.

———, "Redesign of the National Crime Survey," NCJ-111457, February 1989.

———, "Criminal Victimization 1988," *Bureau of Justice Statistics Bulletin*, October 1989.

———, *Criminal Victimization in the United States, 1973-88 Trends,* Office of Justice Programs, Bureau of Justice Statistics, NCJ-129392, July 1991.

Fire Protection (Chapter 7)

Coleman, Ronny J., and John A. Granito, eds., *Managing Fire Services*. Washington, D.C.: ICMA, 1988.

Hall, John R., Jr., *U.S. Arson Trends and Patterns*. Quincy, Massachusetts: National Fire Protection Association, Fire Analysis and Research Division, annual.

———, *U.S. Experience with Smoke Detectors*. Quincy, Massachusetts: National Fire Protection Association, Fire Analysis and Research Division, annual.

———, *U.S. Experience with Sprinklers*. Quincy, Massachusetts: National Fire Protection Association, Fire Analysis and Research Division, annual.

———, *U.S. Fire Death Patterns by State*. Quincy, Massachusetts: National Fire Protection Association, Fire Analysis and Research Division, annual.

———, *U.S. Fire Department Profile*. Quincy, Massachusetts: National Fire Protection Association, Fire Analysis and Research Division, annual.

———, *The U.S. Fire Problem Overview Report*. Quincy, Massachusetts: National Fire Protection Association, Fire Analysis and Research Division, annual.

———, "Use of Fire Loss Information," in *Fire Protection Handbook*, 17th edition. Quincy, Massachusetts: National Fire Protection Association, 1991.

Hall, John R., Jr., Margo Koss, Alfred H. Schainblatt, Michael J. Karter, Jr., and Thomas C. McNerney, *Fire Code Inspections and Fire Prevention—What Methods Lead to Success?* Boston: National Fire Protection Association, 1979.

Karter, Michael J., Jr., and Paul R. LeBlanc, "U.S. Fire Fighter Injuries," *Fire Command*, November, annual.

Karter, Michael J., Jr., and Alison L. Miller, *Patterns of Fire Casualties in Home Fires by Age and Sex*. Quincy, Massachusetts: National Fire Protection Association, Fire Analysis and Research Division, annual.

National Fire Protection Association, *Fire Safety Educator's Handbook*, edited by Robert C. Adams. Quincy, Massachusetts: 1983.

———, "Evaluation Instruments," *Learn Not to Burn Curriculum*. Quincy, Massachusetts: 1987.

Parry, Robert, Jr., Florence Sharp, Jannet Vreeland, Wanda Wallace, "Service Efforts and Accomplishment—Measurement of Fire Department Activity." Prepared for Governmental Accounting Standards Board, January 1989.

Schaenman, Philip S., John R. Hall, Jr., Alfred H. Schainblatt, Joseph Swartz, and Michael Karter, *Procedures for Improving the Measurement of Local Fire Protection Effectiveness* (Boston: The Urban Institute and National Fire Protection Association, 1977), and three supplementary technical reports: "Supplemental Field Incident Report—Forms and Associated Notes," "Measuring the Effectiveness of Fire Inspections," and "Fire Rates vs. Community Characteristics" (Washington, D.C.: The Urban Institute, 1976).

Schaenman, Philip S., and Joseph Swartz, *Measuring Fire Protection Productivity in Local Government*. Boston: National Fire Protection Association, 1974.

Schaenman, Philip S., et al., "Proving Public Fire Education Works," TriData Corporation, 1990.

U.S. Fire Administration, *Fire in the United States, 1983-1988*. Washington, D.C.: 1990.

Washburn, Arthur E., Paul R. LeBlanc, and Rita F. Fahy, "U.S. Fire Fighter Fatalities," *Fire Command*, June, annual.

General Transportation Services (Chapter 8)

Hyman, William, and Joan Allen, "Road Maintenance Performance Indicators." Washington, D.C.: The Urban Institute and Governmental Accounting Standards Board, January 1989.

Ostrom, Elinor, "Multi-Modal Approaches to Measurement of Government Productivity," Workshop on Political Theory and Policy Analysis. Bloomington: Indiana University, 1975.

Second North American Conference on Managing Pavements: Proceedings, Volume 3. Toronto: Ontario Ministry of Transportation, 1967.

State of Florida Maintenance Office, Roadway Maintenance and Operations Section, "Instructions: Data Collection for Maintenance Rating Program," Topic No. 850-065-002-b. Tallahassee, Florida: July 1990.

Walker, William P., "Speed and Travel Time Measurement in Urban Areas," *Traffic Speed and Volume Measurements*, Highway Research Bulletin 156. Washington, D.C.: 1956.

Williams, Jon, and Abdurahman Mohammed, "Arterial Travel Time Survey." Washington, D.C.: Metropolitan Washington Council of Governments, 1990.

Public Mass Transit (Chapter 9)

Greiner, John M., John R. Hall, Harry P. Hatry, and Philip S. Schaenman, *Monitoring the Effectiveness of State Transportation Services*. Washington, D.C.: U.S. Government Printing Office and The Urban Institute, 1977.

Wallace, Wanda, "Service Efforts and Accomplishments: Measurement of Mass Transit." Prepared under a grant from the Governmental Accounting Standards Board. Texas A&M University, January 1989.

Water Supply (Chapter 10)

American Public Health Association, *Standard Methods for the Examination of Water and Wastewater*, 17th edition. Washington, D.C.: 1989.

American Water Works Association, "Public Notification: A Working Explanation of the Public Notification Regulation Rule." Safe Drinking Water Act Series. Denver: 1990.

Burnaby, Priscilla, and S. Herhold, "Performance Measures for Drinking Water, Waste Water Treatment and Storm Drainage." 1990.

De Zuane, John, *Handbook of Drinking Water Quality: Standards and Controls*. New York: Van Nostrand Reinhold, 1990.

Pontius, Frederick, "Complying with the New Drinking Water Quality Regulations," *American Water Works Association Journal*, February 1990, pp. 32-52.

Pontius, Frederick, ed., *Water Quality and Treatment: A Handbook of Community Water Supplies*, 4th edition. New York: McGraw-Hill (for American Water Works Association), 1990.

Handling Citizen Complaints and Requests (Chapter 11)

Charlottesville, Virginia, "Measurements of Effectiveness for Processing of Citizen Complaints." Memo to the city manager. 1973.

Chauncey Bell and Associates, Inc., *'You Wouldn't Believe What We Had to Go Through . . .': A Guide for Assessing Relationships with Citizens, for Government Managers and Elected Officials*, NTIS No. PB-287 515. Washington, D.C.: National Technical Information Service, U.S. Department of Commerce, May 1978.

"Choosing a Complaint Tracking System," *Government Microcomputer Newsletter*, Vol. 7, No. 2, March/April 1990, pp. 7, 8.

Cotton, Ryan D., "Request for Service Systems." Management Information Service Report. Washington, D.C.: ICMA, May 1989.

Coulter, Philip B., *Political Voice: Citizen Demand for Urban Public Services*. Tuscaloosa: University of Alabama Press, 1988.

"Customer Complaints—A Powerful Evaluation Tool," *Service Evaluation*, Vol. 1, No. 1, August 1981, pp. 1-5.

Dallas, Texas, "Performance Audit of City of Dallas Action Center." Office of the City Auditor, September 26, 1979.

Danet, Brenda, "Toward a Method to Evaluate the Ombudsman Role," *Administration and Society*, Vol. 10, No. 3, November 1978, pp. 335-370.

Eau Claire, Wisconsin, "Citizen Response System Manual." January 1, 1990.

"Exploring Citizen Complaint Programs," *Government Microcomputer Newsletter*, Vol. 6, No. 2, March/April 1989, p. 7.

Gelhorn, Walter, *When Americans Complain*. Cambridge, Massachusetts: Harvard University Press, 1966.

Hein, Clarence J., and David R. Gaebler, "Citizen Assistance Offices in Cities 100,000 and Over in Population." Urban Data Service Reports, Vol. 13, No. 1. Washington, D.C.: ICMA, January 1981.

Herman, Robert D., and Nicholas C. Peroff, "Measuring City Agency Responsiveness: The Citizen-Surrogate Method." Urban Data Service Reports, Vol. 13, No. 5. Washington, D.C.: ICMA, May 1981.

"Information and Services: Available by Touch," *Government Microcomputer Newsletter*, Vol. 7, No. 4, July/August 1990, pp. 7, 8.

Jones, Brian D., *Service Delivery in the City: Citizen Demand and Bureaucratic Rules*. New York: Longman, 1980.

Myers, Ben, and Tony Iannacone, "Service Requests Managed by Municipal Computer," *Pennsylvanian*, November 1987, pp. 8ff.

New York, New York, "Citizen Feedback: An Analysis of Complaint Handling in New York City." Office of the Mayor, April 1971.

Percy, Stephen L, and Eric J. Scott, *Demand Processing and Performance in Public Service Agencies*. Tuscaloosa: University of Alabama Press, 1985.

Rehfuss, John, "Contracting Out and Accountability in State and Local Governments—The Importance of Contract Monitoring," *State and Local Government Review*, Vol. 22, No. 1, Winter 1991, pp. 44-48.

Saratoga, California, "Achieving Excellence in Customer Service." Field assessment report prepared by the Center for Excellence in Local Government. Palo Alto, California: July 1988.

Seattle-King County, Washington, "First Annual Report to the King County Council, the Seattle City Council, and the Office of Economic Opportunity." Office of the Ombudsman, August 1972.

Sharp, Elaine B., *Citizen Demand-Making in the Urban Context*. Tuscaloosa: University of Alabama Press, 1986.

Sunnyvale, California, "City Services Effectiveness Measurement Procedures: Citizens' Complaints." Memo to the city manager, December 19, 1973.

Tibbles, Lance, and John H. Hollands, *Buffalo Citizen's Administrative Service: An Ombudsman Demonstration Project*. Berkeley: Institute of Governmental Studies, University of California, 1970.

Trained Observer Rating Procedures (Chapter 12)

Schaenman, Philip, John Greiner, Elyse Camozzo, Hollis Stambaugh, Linda Peacock, and Teresa Lockard, "What Is the Condition of Charlottesville's Capital Plant?" Final Report for the City of Charlottesville, Virginia. Arlington, Virginia: TriData Corporation, 1986.

TriData Corporation, *Raters' Manual for Capital Plant Assessment*, second edition, prepared for the Office of the City Manager, Charlottesville, Virginia. Arlington, Virginia: 1986.

Surveying Customers (Chapter 13)

Babbie, Earl R., *Survey Research Methods*. Belmont, California: Wadsworth Publishing Company, 1973.

Blair, Louis H., and Alfred I. Schwartz. *How Clean Is Our City?* Washington, D.C.: The Urban Institute, 1972.

Fink, Arlene, and Jacqueline Kosecoff, *How to Conduct Surveys: A Step-by-Step Guide*. Beverly Hills, California: Sage Publications, 1985.

Groves, Robert M., Paul P. Biemer, Lars E. Lyberg, James T. Massey, William L. Nicholls, II, and Joseph Waksberg, eds., *Telephone Survey Methodology*. New York: John Wiley & Sons, 1988.

Lavrakas, Paul J., *Telephone Survey Methods: Sampling, Selection, and Supervision*. Newbury Park, California: Sage Publications, 1990.

Lockhart, Daniel C., ed., "Making Effective Use of Mailed Questionnaires," in *New Directions for Program Evaluation*, No. 21. San Francisco: Jossey-Bass, March 1984.

Miller, Thomas I, and Michelle A. Miller, *Citizen Surveys: How to Do Them, How to Use Them, What They Mean*. Washington, D.C.: ICMA, 1991.

Sudman, Seymour, and Norman M. Bradburn, *Asking Questions: A Practical Guide to Questionnaire Design*. San Francisco: Jossey-Bass, 1987.

van Houten, Therese, and Harry P. Hatry, *How to Conduct a Citizen Survey*. Chicago: American Planning Association, November 1987.

Weiss, Carol H., and Harry P. Hatry, *An Introduction to Sample Surveys for Government Managers*. Washington, D.C.: The Urban Institute, 1971.

Using Effectiveness Measurement Information (Chapter 16)

Blair, Louis H., and Alfred I. Schwartz. *How Clean Is Our City?* Washington, D.C.: The Urban Institute, 1972.

Canadian Comprehensive Auditing Foundation, *Effectiveness Reporting and Auditing in the Public Sector.* 1987.

Carter, Reginald K., *The Accountable Agency.* Beverly Hills, California: Sage Publications, 1983.

Comptroller General of the United States, *Government Auditing Standards: Standards for Audit of Governmental Organizations, Programs, Activities, and Functions.* Washington, D.C., revised 1988.

Epstein, Paul D., *Using Performance Measurement in Local Government.* New York: Van Nostrand Reinhold, 1984.

Government Accounting Service Board, *Service Efforts and Accomplishments Reporting: Its Time Has Come—An Overview.* Norwalk, Connecticut: 1990.

ICMA, "Performance Auditing for Local Government." Management Information Service Report. Washington, D.C.: January 1989.

The Mayor's Management Report. New York: Citybooks, annual.

Savannah, Georgia, Community Housing and Economic Development Department, "Responsive Public Services Program: 1988." October 1988.

Some Implementation Suggestions (Chapter 17)

ICMA, "Strategies for Implementing Performance Measurement," Management Information Service Report. Washington, D.C.: November 1986.

———, "Monitoring the Quality of Local Government Services," Management Information Service Report. Washington, D.C.: February 1987.

Munich, Lee W., Jr., and Daniel Quilin, "Program Agency Perspectives." Presentation to the Mid-American Intergovernmental Audit Forum, Kansas City, Missouri, May 14, 1991.